A History
of the
URANTIA PAPERS

BOOKS BY LARRY MULLINS

Jesus: God & Man

Personality

The Apostles

The Search for Joshua

Living the Teachings

Reincarnation and the Urantia Papers

The Step Beyond

Get Real

Immature People with Power - How to Handle Them

60 Minutes that will Change Your Life

Goal Setting for Women Only

Penumbra

People Media

The Seven Lost Secrets of Retail Advertising

A History of the URANTIA PAPERS

BY LARRY MULLINS
with DR. MEREDITH J. SPRUNGER

PENUMBRA PRESS
BOULDER, CO

A HISTORY OF THE URANTIA PAPERS

FIRST PRINTING
AUGUST 21, 2000
2,000 COPIES

Editing and Production Team:

Joan Batson Mullins
Michelle Mullins
Dr. Ángel F. Sánchez-Escobar
Donald Shea Green
Eric Cosh
James "JJ" Johnson
David Kantor
Victor McGonegal
Merritt Horn
Jeanne Horn
Dr. Jill Strunk
Norm Du Val
Rosey Lieske
David Biggs
Andre Radatus

© COPYRIGHT 2000
LARRY MULLINS, BOULDER CO
ALL RIGHTS RESERVED

PENUMBRA PRESS, INC.
P.O. BOX 11248, BOULDER, CO 80301

Library of Congress Cataloging-in-Publication Data

Mullins, Larry
    A history of the Urantia Papers/Larry Mullins with Dr. Meredith Sprunger
    p. cm.
    Includes bibligraphical information, illustrations, photographs and index.
    ISBN NUMBER 0-9677263-1-X
    1. Urantia Papers I. Mullins, Larry II. Title

Library of Congress Number 00-091235

iv

To the
EARLY URANTIANS
who faithfully performed the clerical duties
associated with the publication of the original
1955 text of *The Urantia Book.*

FORMATTING OF QUOTES:

Quotes from the Urantia Papers are set in **bold-face, standard** *(not italic)* type. Reference pages and paragraphs of these notes refer to, and were derived from, the original text of the 1955 printing of *The Urantia Book*, unless otherwise stated.

SOURCE MATERIALS:

Key source materials used as references in this history may be found and down-loaded. A summary list of these documents will be found in Appendix A.

The main website access is through **http://urantiabook.org** (English) and through **http://librourantia.org** (Spanish).

Access to source material documents will be found at:
http://urantiabook.org/mullinshistory

Contents

PREFACE —Page xi
by Dr. Ángel F. Sánchez-Escobar

INTRODUCTION — Page 2

Are there Spiritual Beings of higher intelligence in the vast universe? Do they take any notice of us? Presuming there are such intelligences and they do care about us, would they ever try to communicate with us and attempt to assist us? In other words, is the concept of *revelation* a valid premise? What would — or what could — higher, more mature celestial intelligences safely reveal to us?

CHAPTER ONE — Page 14

"If this is not an authentic picture of reality, it is the way it ought to be!"

Dr. Meredith Sprunger first saw *The Urantia Book* in 1955, when he was 40 years of age. He was not impressed. However, in 1956, while on an automobile trip to a church conference board meeting, a conversation with a companion set into motion a series of events that would cause him to reconsider *The Urantia Book,* events that would eventually reconfigure his life.

CHAPTER TWO — Page 26

Chicago and Dr. William S. Sadler

On May 7, 1958, the stage was set for a remarkable meeting. Dr. Meredith Justin Sprunger sought out Dr. William S. Sadler in hopes of learning more about the origin of the Urantia Papers. Dr. Sprunger wanted to know how the Urantia Papers came to be written, and who had authored them. What Dr. Sprunger learned in that Chicago meeting so intrigued him that he began a lifelong search to better understand the origin and meaning of the Urantia Papers.

A HISTORY OF THE URANTIA PAPERS

CHAPTER THREE — Page 42

"Something has happened to my husband"

One summer between 1906 and 1911, there was a remarkable encounter involving two couples. One of the couples was Dr. William Sadler and his wife, Doctor Lena Sadler; the identity of the other couple is not known. The event would completely alter the lives of all four individuals, and have implications that are still not fully grasped nearly a century later.

CHAPTER FOUR — Page 64

"There is one peculiar case I have not yet been able to solve"

Dr. Sadler: "With one or two exceptions, all the psychic phenomena which I have investigated have turned out to be either conscious or unconscious frauds. Some were deliberate frauds — others were those peculiar cases in which the performer was a victim of the deceptions of his own subconscious mind." Another member of the group spoke up. "What were the exceptions? Doctor, if you have found cases which you have been unable to solve, this would be interesting. Tell us more about them."

CHAPTER FIVE — Page 86

"We were introduced to many new, and to us, somewhat strange concepts"

Dr. Sadler: "We never realized how much our religious thinking had expanded until the Papers began to arrive. As the revelation progressed we came to more fully appreciate how much we had been prepared for the vast alteration of our religious beliefs by these preliminary contacts extending over a period of twenty years of pre-education."

CHAPTER SIX — Page 112

"The majority of your Forum shock me with their lack of enthusiasm"

The purported message said in part: "Your group of Seventy may seem to show more interest because you are selected and because you are under more or less discipline. But the majority of your Forum shock me with their lack of enthusiasm. . . I admonish you to be ever alert to the importance of the extraordinary trust that has been placed in your hands."

CONTENTS

CHAPTER SEVEN — *Page 134*

"It was not portrayed to be error-free"

Carolyn Kendall: "The multiple processes of transcribing from handwritten manuscript to typewritten pages; the retyping of these pages two to five times; and from typewritten to typeset form, presented opportunities for errors to creep into the papers which were not caught by even two professional proofreadings. By publication day, Christy and Marian had already collected a list of errors noticed by sharp-eyed Forum members. The midwayers did not volunteer the location of errors, just that there were errors in the published text."

CHAPTER EIGHT — *Page 164*

"You are now on your own"

Shortly after the publication of *The Urantia Book,* a final message from the Revelators was received: *"You are now on your own."* After nearly fifty years, the connection between the mortals of our planet and the unseen Revelators was severed and went dead. "They didn't even say goodbye," remarked Dr. Sadler.

CHAPTER NINE — *Page 186*

"In my opinion there can be only one edition of The Urantia Book, the first"

Trustee Emeritus James C. Mills believed there was only one editorial change in *The Urantia Book,* and that it had been changed back. When confronted with evidence to the contrary, he wrote to Ken and Betty Glasziou in the letter dated March 5, 1991: "It looks like we need to carefully proofread the present printing against the first printing. In my opinion, there can be only one edition of The Urantia Book, the first."

CHAPTER TEN — *Page 232*

"The baptism of joys and sorrows"

Dr. Sprunger has noted: "Most of us now realize that the Fifth Epochal Revelation has been launched on the troubled and turbulent seas of evolutionary struggle."

A HISTORY OF THE URANTIA PAPERS

EPILOGUE — Page 274

The purpose of this epilogue is twofold. First, to review some of the most important information and some conclusions the team reached about the history of the Urantia Papers. Second, to consider examples of the effects of proprietary and entitlement attitudes toward the Urantia Papers.

APPENDIXES — Page 309

A. Key Documents and References — 310

Affadavit of Dr. Meredith Justin Sprunger — *316 - 320*

B. Reproductions of Historic Correspondence — 321

1- 3:	The Sadler-Adams correspondence	322 - 328
4:	The Scott M. Forsythe letter to JJ Johnson	329
5:	Letter from Vern Bennom Grimsley to the author	330
6:	Richard Keeler resignation from FOG	331 - 332
7:	Letter from Trustee Emeritus James Mills to Ken and Betty Glasziou	333 - 334

C. The Garden of Ediacara Breakthrough — 336

D. Changes in the Text of Urantia Foundation Printings of The Urantia Book: *Merritt Horn's Investigations and Conclusions* — 347

E. The International Copyright Status of *The Urantia Book* — 392

F. Key Pages from Urantia Foundation Declaration of Trust — 395

INDEX TO TEXT — 405

Preface

by Dr. Ángel F. Sánchez-Escobar

A NOMALIES IN THE "OFFICIAL" interpretation of the origins of the Urantia Papers along with a much needed restructuring of events within a sound historical inquiry prompted Larry Mullins to write *A History of the Urantia Papers*.

Conventional wisdom tells us that a narrative is a recorded account of how specific events followed each other in the temporal flow of things. And this has been done by Urantians without too much disagreement. However, more than a laundry list of a series of milestones, history is ideally an interpretation of linkages. To be truly understood and meaningful, events must be examined within the context of numerous connections and the holistic patterns they collectively create. Among Urantians, there has been considerable disagreement about the *meaning* of the various remarkable episodes that have driven the movement. Indeed, this second level of historic endeavor, the discovery and interpretation of meaningful patterns, had not been significantly achieved until the publication of *A History of the Urantia Papers*.

The historic inquiry cannot simply leap from the discovery of documentary evidence to analysis. There are rules that govern historical narrative, all of which have been followed by Larry Mullins. Initially, the historian must seek evidence, and historical evidence is not solely restricted to recorded text. Of course, primary sources are clearly better than secondary sources. Corroborative sources are also valuable. In his narrative, Larry Mullins, after identifying the problem of biased existing narratives, follows very carefully this empirical stage by providing and corroborating textual evidence, at the same time disregarding weak secondary sources. Mullins proceeds to the second stage of the historical inquiry, the interpretative one, by relying on this textual evidence and introducing more logical, significant connections between the events. Although challengeable as any other narrative, these connections are plausible enough to lead the Urantian community to agree that, in light of this documented evidence, this interpretation makes sense.

Many members of the Urantian community on both sides of the Atlantic have so far suffered the consequences of an "official," biased interpretation of the events leading to the materialization, authorship, and controlled dissemination of the Papers, and find them unacceptable. It is my experience, being a Spanish reader of the Papers acquainted with this issue, that due to the lack of a sound narrative, many members of the Spanish-Urantian community are being deceived by a misleading, undocumented interpretation of the origins of the Papers. Mullins' dissemination and translation into different languages of his competing, well-founded version of the facts will, of course, not be welcomed by the "establishment" with its vested interest in its "rightness," but it will open the eyes of many readers around the world.

Ángel F. Sánchez-Escobar, Ph.D. (Vanderbilt University)

Seville, Spain

"There exists in all personality associations of the cosmic mind a quality which might be denominated the 'reality response.' It is this universal cosmic endowment of will creatures which saves them from becoming helpless victims of the implied a priori assumptions of science, philosophy, and religion. This reality sensitivity of the cosmic mind responds to certain phases of reality just as energy-material responds to gravity. It would be still more correct to say that these supermaterial realities so respond to the mind of the cosmos."

THE URANTIA BOOK
pages 191-192

"Out of intense complexities, intense simplicities emerge."
WINSTON CHURCHILL

Introduction

Introduction 3

ARE THERE SPIRITUAL BEINGS OF higher intelligence in the vast universe? Do they take any notice of us? Presuming there are such intelligences and they do care about us, would they ever try to communicate with us and attempt to assist us? In other words, is the concept of *revelation* a valid premise? What would — or what could — higher, more mature intelligences of greater spiritual development safely reveal to us?

If you have pondered the plausibility of such things, the story of the Urantia Papers will interest you. *("Urantia" is the name given in the Papers to identify the planet Earth.)* The story of the Urantia Papers spans a period from approximately 1906 to 1955, culminating in the publication of *The Urantia Book*. Although there are over a half-million copies of *The Urantia Book* in print, an appropriately documented and complete presentation of the story behind them has never before been presented. Yet, this virtually unknown epic is perhaps the most remarkable of the turbulent twentieth century.

The first and most common question about *The Urantia Book* is: "Who wrote this?" Sometimes even a casual reader, with no intention of studying the material, is stimulated to curiosity. The over one million words of the Urantia Papers are nothing less than an unprecedented attempt to establish an immense integration of three bodies of knowledge: *[1]. Scientific fact; [2]. Spiritual realities; and [3]. Philosophical truth.*

Traditionally, the three great disciplines have been restricted to logic-tight compartments and dealt with separately. Each of these disciplines — science, religion, and philosophy — contains essential, but inadequate, information about *who we are, where we came from,* and *where we are going.* The Urantia Papers drew upon the highest human knowledge available up to the time of their writing to propose extraordinary new relationships between the key disciplines. The Papers suggest fresh possibilities and augment their ideas with original revelatory information. The result is an uplifting vision for humankind that is without parallel or precedent in literature.

The Urantia Papers claim to be an epochal revelation; yet they take the unique revelatory position of disclaiming infallibility.[1] The Papers are unquestionably profoundly religious, yet they do not attempt to establish a new religion. Rather, they seek to philosophically integrate evolutionary scientific knowledge with spiritual truth. Although some of the scientific content of the Urantia Papers is dated, if the most modern scientific data were to be substituted it its place, the broad philosophical synthesis would still work. The Papers are essentially an exposition and expansion of the life and teachings of Jesus of Nazareth placed in a splendid cosmological context — on a scale that has never before been attempted on this planet. Perhaps the suspicions of any thinking person will be aroused by such sweeping claims. However, an honest mind will also discover that there are far too many substantial and original concepts in the Urantia Papers for them to be brushed off as an esoteric fabrication.

I have spent more than thirty years studying the Urantia Papers. I have had dozens of discussions with many people who had personal knowledge about the events that culminated in the materialization of the Papers. As a result, I am utterly convinced

---

1. Although the claim of Revelation is made, the Papers disclaim infallibility: "The Urantia Papers . . . of which this is one, constitute the most recent presentation of truth to the mortals of Urantia. These papers differ from all previous revelations, for they are not the work of a single universe personality but a composite presentation by many beings. But no revelation short of the attainment of the Universal Father can ever be complete. All other celestial ministrations are no more than partial, transient, and practically adapted to local conditions in time and space. While such admissions as this may possibly detract from the immediate force and authority of all revelations, the time has arrived on Urantia when it is advisable to make such frank statements, even at the risk of weakening the future influence and authority of this, the most recent of the revelations of truth to the mortal races of Urantia." [1008 – par. 2]

that, circa 1906 - 1955, non-material beings of super-human intelligence and maturity interfaced regularly with a group of (eventually) six mortals for the purpose of providing a religious revelation of epochal significance.

The people involved were neither psychics nor dilettantes. On the contrary, the key figure, Dr. William S. Sadler, was a nationally prominent psychiatrist and the author of 42 books. Dr. Sadler had a well-deserved reputation as a debunker of psychic phenomena. In his book, *The Mind at Mischief,* he refers to those who engage in such esoteric phenomena as generally: *"Fraudulent mediums and self-deceived psychics."* The story of his struggle against honest recognition of what took place before his eyes — and the validation of what he had trained all his life as a scientist to debunk, is a fascinating subplot to the history of the Urantia Papers.

However, Dr. Sadler and the other five central protagonists in these events are all gone now. Aside from the Papers themselves, the six key players left only fragments of information about how the Urantia Papers came to be. There is not, nor has there ever been, an authority on the Urantia Papers — neither on their origin nor their remarkable contents. How the Papers were materialized into the English language is not fully known. Although no human author has ever been associated with the Urantia Papers, there was a seventh individual who is critically important to this discussion. He has been called the *"sleeping subject,"* or the *"contact personality."* All accounts indicated he was an ordinary person who was somehow involved with the materialization of the Urantia Papers. We know only that he was not a so-called medium, and although the entire text of the Urantia Papers was originally in written form, we can reasonably declare that he was not the author — nor did he "channel" or "automatic-write" the text of the Urantia Papers. The Urantia Papers tell us that a part of God indwells each normal and morally conscious mortal, and this Divine Fragment somehow participated in the materialization, but the mind of the human *sleeping subject* was not used. Dr. Sadler emphatically and repeatedly stated that no known psychic phenomena were associated with the materialization of the

A HISTORY OF THE URANTIA PAPERS

Urantia Papers. The *sleeping subject* has never been, and will probably never be, identified.

Surely, the original intent of the unseen Revelators was not to create mysteries, but rather establish a framework that would allow the Urantia Papers to stand on their own. It was apparently deemed desirable by the Revelators that readers would base their evaluation of the Urantia Papers purely upon their content, and not upon some supposed "miraculous" source. Therefore, neither the identity of the "sleeping subject" nor what little the team of six knew about the materialization of the Papers were to be disclosed. However, human nature being what it is, there has gradually developed much speculation about the identity of the subject and the method and circumstances by which the Urantia Papers came to be.[1]

For these reasons, conjecture has unfortunately filled the void. Due to the nature of the material in the Urantia Papers, they attract a great variety of individuals. Some are allured by the apocrypha surrounding the origin of the Urantia Papers more than by the spiritual message of the Papers themselves. Likewise, critics of the Urantia Papers have generally focused upon erroneous accounts of the origin of the Papers and the alleged foibles of the people involved in the Urantia Movement, and have not seriously considered the content of the Revelation. Serious scholars have been repelled by the bizarre speculations of a few Urantian pretenders — as well as by commentaries by critics of the Papers — many of whom claim to have special status and to have exclusive possession of "inside" information.

However, in recent years a valid body of known historical background facts about the Papers has gradually emerged. If we could stand back, so to speak, and view all the information

---

1.   The identity of the sleeping subject continues to fascinate readers. A book published in 1999 by John M. Bunker and Karen L. Pressler sought to prove Edgar Cayce was the subject. (*Edgar Cayce and The Urantia Book,* 1996). The Cayce family denies this, and Dr. Sprunger and other Urantian scholars remained unpersuaded as well. My own judgment compels me to refute this idea. Cayce died in 1945, which was very probably ten years before the final messages were received. Also, the Cayce writings, with their emphasis on reincarnation and psychic phenomena, are far afield from the Urantia Papers.

Introduction 7

available in one sweeping glance, we would likely be confused. Yet, if we cautiously and discriminatively begin to follow the chronological thread of verifiable data, we can trace a consistent, documented, and continuous path. The sources are scattered and varied, but the emerging body of information is consistent within itself — plausible, and generally satisfying.

I have hoped that an accurate, documented history of the Urantia Papers would eventually be formulated, but this has not happened. So, I have decided to make the effort. This account will not be encumbered by any "official" sanction or approval. At the outset, it is important to understand that this is a history of the Urantia *Papers*, not a history of what has been called the Urantia *Movement*. We will discuss the readership and the personalities involved only to the degree they are related to the history of the Urantia Papers.

I would not attempt the writing of this history without the help of Dr. Meredith Justin Sprunger. He is an ordained minister with an educational background in philosophy and theology, a social scientist with a doctorate in psychology, and has had a distinguished career as a college professor and administrator. He has also had an extensive writing career, and is currently the editor of *The Spiritual Fellowship Journal*. Dr. Sprunger was acquainted with three of the six individuals who made up the team (known as the *Contact Commission)* that interfaced with the celestial Revelators. When I met Dr. Sprunger in the mid-seventies, I had many questions about the origin of the Urantia Papers. Information was extremely difficult to come by in those days. I knew that he had written several papers on the origin, content and the significance of the Urantia Papers, and had authored the only "official" material that was published by Urantia Foundation (the publishers of *The Urantia Book*) on the origin of the Revelation. I was certain that Dr. Sprunger knew more than he was allowed to present in his official pamphlets. To my surprise, I found him to be open and candid about what he knew. Unlike any individual in the "inner circles," his explanations were clear and refreshing. He supplied me (as he has many seekers) with his own writings about the Papers, and also prudently disclosed many interesting things Dr. Sadler had told him. My curiosity was soon dispelled, and I followed Dr. Sprunger's advice and continued to evaluate the Urantia Papers on the basis of their content. Over the years I have become completely convinced that the Urantia Papers are exactly what they purport themselves to be: a Revelation of epochal significance.

However, I was convinced that many questions about the origin remained unanswered, and several "forbidden" doors had never been opened to candid investigation. As stated, I had hoped eventually some Urantian old-timer would fearlessly open those doors and begin an authentic historical investigation. Then it dawned on me one day that I had become an "old-timer" myself. I had been handed a first edition of *The Urantia Book* by Clyde Bedell, who was one of the first Urantians, and a charter member of a group called the *Forum*. I had watched Clyde pore over an immense table covered with files of 3 x 5 cards, as he prepared his original *Concordex of The Urantia Book*. I worked for Clyde for three years, and discussed the Urantia Papers and his experiences in the Forum numerous times. In the seventies I had several conversations with one of the surviving Contact Commissioners, and served for eight years as a General Councilor in what was then called the Urantia Brotherhood.

Fortunately, my wife Joan (who had originally suggested this project) has a remarkable knowledge of the Papers. I have always depended upon Joan's insights and integrity when developing Urantia undertakings. Even so, we came to realize that we needed help, and that an adequate history of the Urantia Papers could only be achieved with group wisdom and collaboration. A team effort by several Urantians would be necessary. I first sought out our friend Dr. Sprunger. Gradually we added several seasoned Urantians who have an exceptional knowledge of the Urantia Papers, and a great deal of experience in the Urantia Movement.

The following pages will delve deeply into the origin of the Revelation. Dr. Sprunger's early investigations have produced a great deal of information. His knowledge is the product of years of research and hours of discussion with those associated with the origin of the Papers. During the period of his inquiry, Dr. Sprunger had continued to serve pastorates in the United Church of Christ. His career as a faculty member of the Indiana Institute of Technology also went forward. In addition to serving as head of the Department of Psychology, he also chaired the division of Liberal Arts and served as President. In his own investigations, he has been careful to maintain academic objectivity and to exercise critical evaluation of both the Urantia Papers and the Urantia Movement. He cross-validated the essential elements of the episodes we are about to relate with people who had first-hand experience with the events associated with the origin of the Urantia Papers.

The story of the Urantia Papers also required the assembling of a mosaic of older documents and correspondence, more recently available documents, and testimony from a great number of sources. Not all sources I used were friendly to this inquiry. Yet, some individuals who have strong agendas to prove the Urantia Papers to be a fraud have sometimes provided vital links and illuminated dark corners. At other times, individuals who have sought to explain or rationalize errors or obscure the facts have provided information that could not have otherwise been obtained. Whatever the source, I drew upon evidence that was plausible, verifiable and consistent with other credible elements of the puzzle. The reader can develop personal conclusions from the resulting assemblage.

I pledge to the reader that I have been candid in these pages. In the spirit of a sincere quest for truth, with the guidance and suggestions of Joan, Dr. Sprunger and several esteemed Urantians, I have related everything I have personally learned from various sources, and have documented those sources. When in doubt, I admitted it. If I needed to speculate, or draw a general conclusion, I have disclosed this to the reader. If an editing team member strongly disagreed with a conclusion, I have drawn out and presented his or her views in addition to my own. The essential testimonies of the protagonists who *were there*, and who played roles in this extraordinary drama have been documented. Otherwise, in the case of verbal information that I have personally acquired from various Urantian veterans, I used only things I have heard from at least *two or more sources independently, and that were generally harmonious with other data.* On this basis, I believe the basic historical facts have been fairly, reasonably and clearly established. Even when not varnished, embellished or speculated upon, these facts form clear patterns and weave an intriguing and fairly complete tapestry.

Histories are inescapably adversarial and painful processes. The people who undertook this task of developing a good, sound history are aware that the final product is a compelling argument that could help shape the destiny of the Urantia Papers. The stakes are high, because what is ultimately at issue are the various philosophies and agendas of those who seek to control the Urantia Revelation. It will come as no surprise then, that the *interpretations* of the events relating to the Urantia Papers are destined to be fiercely contested. Sometimes the facts about the Urantia Papers are at issue, but more often the *meaning* of the facts will be the center of historical controversy. Our effort to develop a good history was very carefully orchestrated, but we are aware that it will not contain the final words. Our team discovered many unexpected things along the way that need a great deal more research. What we will attempt to achieve here are three cardinal goals: *[1]. To establish a reasonable foundation of documented facts, [2]. To open as many heretofore "forbidden" doors as possible for further investigation, and [3]. To lay down threads for future Urantians to pick up, follow, and develop. In short, we are attempting a beginning.*

ACKNOWLEDGEMENTS

First of all, thank you to the Urantians upon whose shoulders I needed to stand to write this history. I thank first the original **Urantians** who produced the 1955 printing, and next, my thanks to **Meredith Sprunger,** for all of his years of leadership, wisdom and insight. Thanks to **Joan Batson Mullins**, my partner and unfailing inspiration, whose remarkable knowledge of the Papers, fairness and integrity always lift Urantian projects to another level. Thank you, Joan, for making the last several years for me the happiest of my life. To young Urantian **Michelle Mullins**, for her help with the charts and graphs, for deciphering the worn and fading documents of the early Urantians, and for her faith in her dad. To **Kathleen Mullins**, whose dauntless search for truth changes lives, one of which has been my own. To **Eric Cosh**, a Urantian who has faithfully, over the years, given lavishly of his time, talent and effort in behalf of the Revelation. To **James "JJ" Johnson**, a steadfastly committed Urantian who went far beyond the "second" mile to help in this project. JJ's remarkable observation and unsurpasssed knowledge of the Urantia Papers has helped make this effort much more than it would have been without him. To **Dr. Ángel Sánchez-Escobar** of Seville, Spain, for his forbearance, insight and valiant service to Spanish-speaking Urantians, and his support, assistance and Spanish translation of our history. To **Jeanney Horn,** whose exceptional editing skills greatly lifted and improved the final product. To **Merritt Horn**, whose remarkable insights and uncompromising scholarship brought to full disclosure the loss of an inviolate printed version of the original text, and helped this history beyond measure. To **David Kantor**, whose energetic commitment to the Urantia Revelation and intense integrity and courage are a benchmark for this day and generation of Urantians. To **Andre Radatus**, who brings balance, forebearance and reasonable fairness to any Urantian project he undertakes. To **Rosey Lieske,** for her years of support and encouragement, and for her exemplary interface with Spanish speaking countries and her grasp of meta-values that is unexcelled in the movement. To **Norm Du Val,** a passionate, devoted Urantian who is always willing to assist in absolutely anything to help the Revelation. To **David Biggs**, one of those great Urantians who have toiled tirelessly for years in behalf of the Revelation with little recognition or acknowlegement. To **Dr. Jill Strunk,** a devoted Urantian who has been of immeasurable help as a skilled editor and advisor over the years. To **Victor McGonegal**, who has been a lifelong friend, who got his book about the same time I did from Clyde Bedell, and who has long provided servant-leadership to the large, independent Urantia group in Washington D.C. To **Kristen Maaherra** and **Eric Schaveland**, whose insights, advice and documentation over the years have widened my perspective and understanding immeasurably, and for their courage in standing steadfast on the principle of a free Revelation. To **Donald Shea Green**, friend, supporter and faithful anchor of our Living the Teachings Group. To

Mary Doubek, who inspires and serves her sisters and who lifts the hearts of her students. To the young Kruger men, **Micah, Damon, and Aaron,** who strive to *live the teachings* with us and who will one day go forth to help turn the world upside down. To **Angie, Jesse and Haley Thurston** of our youth's study group who remind me every week what this Revelation is all about — and to **Claire** and **Chuck Thurston** for supporting the group so energetically. To **Tom Choquette** for his encouragement and many kind assists, his deep insights into the real meaning and mission of the Urantia Papers, and for his remarkable outreach to youth. To **Behzad Sarmast** and **Marielle Tavares** for their understanding friendship and beautiful fellowship. "Behz," as we know him, is one of those extraordinary Urantians who fearlessly research and seek the truth — and who skillfully write and generously present their findings to make them accessible to others. To **Clyde Bedell,** who gave me my first Urantia Book and told me, just before his death, *"There are dozens of unseen helpers all around us who are itching to help us if we would only start doing something."* To **Berkeley Elliott,** who first taught me about servant-leadership and who introduced me to my first Urantian "family" in Oklahoma City. Of course, thank you to those unseen and unheard helpers whom I hope one day to meet. **To the entire fellowship of believers of all faiths** who strive to serve humankind and to actualize integrity, benevolence and excellence. **To** *all* **those Urantians whose work I have referenced**, without whom we would have virtually no record at all. **To those who agree with my conclusions, and to those who dispute them and will help clarify issues by reasonable debate,** and especially **to those who will create vastly improved histories in the future**, thank you my brothers and sisters.

I have made a sincere effort to disclose the truth fairly, to the best of my ability, as it appeared to me. In striving to do this, I may have unavoidably offended some people. If so, in the words of Shakespeare: *"As you from crimes would pardoned be, let your indulgence set me free."*

LARRY MULLINS
BOULDER, COLORADO

*D*R. MEREDITH JUSTIN SPRUNGER IS A successful academician grounded in hard reality. As a theologian and philosopher, he has seen many so-called "revelations" come and go. Perhaps a reader may wonder:

What was it about *The Urantia Book* that set him upon a quest, many years ago, to discover who wrote it — and who was financing its distribution?

Dr. Sprunger first saw *The Urantia Book* in 1955, when he was 40 years of age. He was not impressed. However in 1956, while on an automobile trip to a church conference board meeting, a conversation with a companion set into motion a series of events that would cause him to reconsider *The Urantia Book* and would eventually completely reconfigure his life . . .

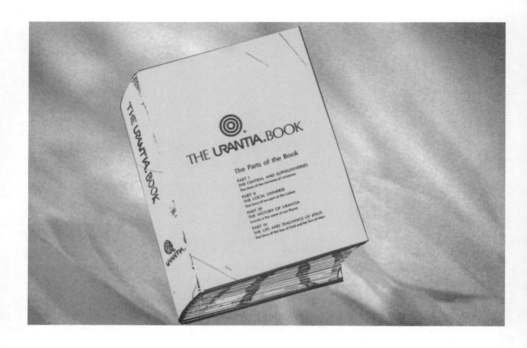

Chapter One

"If this is not an Authentic Picture of Reality, it is the Way it Ought to Be!"

IN DECEMBER OF 1955, REVEREND Edward Brueseke, Pastor of the Zion United Church of Christ of South Bend, Indiana, handed Dr. Meredith Sprunger a copy of the newly published book. The 1955 printing of *The Urantia Book* was impressive in size, containing over 2,000 pages and a million words bound within its deep blue covers.

"Judge Hammerschmidt gave me this book," said Dr. Brueseke. "Some businessmen think it's a new Bible." He and his wife smiled as Meredith held the massive volume in his hands and opened it. Meredith scanned the Table of Contents pages. It was the alleged authors of the various 196 Papers that composed the book that challenged his credulity rather than the titles of the Papers. The second Paper was titled: *"The Nature of God"* by a *"Divine Councilor."* Another was titled: *"The Universe of Universes"* by a *"Perfecter of Wisdom."* Another: *"Personalities of the Grand Universe"* supposedly authored by a *"Mighty Messenger."* These were enough to turn him off and strike him as ludicrous.

Meredith read a few of the titles and authors aloud to his wife, Irene, seated next to him. Then they all had a gentle laugh about Judge Hammerschmidt's naivete and closed the book. However, both ministers and their wives maintained respect for Judge Louis Hammerschmidt's contributions to the Zion Church. He was an esteemed layperson of the larger United Church of Christ. Judge Hammerschmidt had been instrumental in bringing a Children's Hospital to South Bend, and he had donated a chapel to Elmhurst College.

However, there seemed no euphemistic way of putting it, *The Urantia Book* must be some kind of hoax. Dr. Sprunger set the book aside, and assumed that the December, 1955 glimpse would be the last he would see of it. He was wrong.

About a month later, Dr. Sprunger, who was Vice President of the Indiana-Michigan Conference Board, was to pick up Judge Hammerschmidt and drive him to their January council meeting in Jackson, Michigan. During the two and a half hour journey, the Judge cautiously mentioned his tentative investigation of Spiritualism.

Hammerschmidt had lost his wife over a decade before and, in his grief, he looked into the practice of Spiritualism. He was not impressed by what he discovered. Upon seeing that Dr. Sprunger was not at all disturbed about an open discussion of such things, the Judge was emboldened to comment: "Say, I've got a book that I would like you to read and tell me what you think about it." Dr. Sprunger kept his eyes on the road and the bleak January landscape ahead. He knew what was coming. Not wanting to hurt the Judge's feelings, however, Meredith replied: "OK, Judge, send it to me."

In about a week, a package was delivered to the Sprunger household with *The Urantia Book* enclosed. Over the subsequent months, Dr. Sprunger made several efforts to read sections of the extensive work. From his fleeting appraisal of the Urantia Papers,

Dr. Sprunger in the Mid-Fifties

Dr. Sprunger thought the authors' use of esoteric names might indicate the Papers represented some form of Theosophy. He even took it on vacation with him that year, but could not get interested in the material enough to read much of it.

September of 1956 arrived, and *The Urantia Book* had not been even partially read. Dr. Sprunger realized that he would be meeting with Judge Hammerschmidt in October, and he felt obligated to read something to get off the hook. He decided to read a small series of Papers and candidly tell the Judge what he thought of the material. So Dr. Sprunger began to examine the Table of Contents again.

As he skimmed the contents, Meredith recalled the book had a large section devoted to the *"Life and Teachings of Jesus."* He surmised that with his academic theological background he could surely make short work of this material. Previously, he had read other attempts, such as the *Aquarian Gospel,* to portray the early life of Jesus. Apocryphal stories about Jesus molding little clay birds and then bringing them to life did not impress him. So, with the intention of quickly refuting the material, Dr. Sprunger began to read the Urantia Papers' account of the life of Jesus. He did not find what he expected to find.

Meredith became gradually enthralled as he read. The Papers had the ring of reasonable, perhaps even authentic, historicity. As the narrative progressed to the story of John the Baptist and paralleled the New Testament account, Dr. Sprunger was deeply impressed. The colorful and vivid recounting of the life of the Master unfolded, at times moving Dr. Sprunger to tears. When he closed the book on the final Paper: *The Faith of Jesus,* Meredith concluded the Urantia account was harmonious with perceived New Testament realities. More than that, he believed it was the most profound and inspiring life and teachings of Jesus in print.

Due to the unexpected high quality of Part IV — the 700-page depiction of *The Life and Teachings of Jesus* — Dr. Sprunger suddenly found himself intensely motivated to read the rest of the material. Starting with the Foreword, Meredith read the balance of the Urantia Papers. When he had finished, he realized the Urantia Papers offered the most comprehensive and integrated picture of science, philosophy and religion that he had ever read. Suddenly, everything he had ever learned was rearranged and melded with new concepts into a grand, new, mind-boggling synthesis.

Dr. Sprunger pondered this immense new paradigm of actuality for some time. He thought: *"If this is not an authentic picture of Reality, it is the way it ought to be!"*

Meredith contacted Judge Hammerschmidt to find out where he had gotten the book. The Judge, delighted at Sprunger's interest, informed him that a friend by the name of W. H. Harrah had given him the book. Mr. Harrah was a successful businessman, and the co-founder of the National Standard Company. He was also a member of a group in Chicago that had somehow originally acquired the Urantia Papers.

A luncheon meeting was arranged. Mr. Harrah explained that the leader of the group that had published *The Urantia Book* was Dr. William Sadler. Dr. Sprunger was surprised. He knew of William Sadler by his reputation. Dr. Sadler had studied overseas with Freud, and was sometimes referred to as the "father of American Psychiatry." Dr. Sadler was also a prolific author in his field and a college professor. Meredith had friends who had taken Dr. Sadler's course of Pastoral Counseling at McCormick Theological Seminary.

Mr. Harrah stated that he wanted to provide Urantia Books for some of Dr. Sprunger's ministerial colleagues in The United Church of Christ. He wrote out a check to pay for a dozen books and handed it to Dr. Sprunger. Later, Dr. Sprunger gave twelve of his ministerial colleagues a copy of *The Urantia Book*. All but one of these young ministers (who admitted he had not read the book) were as impressed as Dr. Sprunger with the material.

There ensued a deep, scholarly review of the book and its possible origins by the ministerial team. When Dr. Sprunger revealed to the group what little he had learned about the origin of the book from Mr. Harrah, the group began studying the books written by Dr. Sadler as part of their research project. They discovered highly relevant material in one of the books that Dr. Sadler had authored: *The Mind at Mischief*, Funk & Wagnalls, 1929. The subtitle of the book was: *"Tricks and Deceptions of the Subconscious and how to Cope with Them."*

The Mind at Mischief

Out of all of his voluminous mainline writings, Dr. Sadler mentions the process that was to eventually lead to the materialization of the Urantia Papers in only one year's printings of a single book. At the time of writing *The Mind at Mischief*, Dr. Sadler was known to be a leading debunker of psychic phenomena. The book itself is a powerful rebuttal of all known processes involving marginal human consciousness that produce "messages" from the "spirit world." In the foreword to the book, Robert H. Gault, Ph.D. and Professor of Psychology at Northwestern University wrote:

> "The psychiatrists of our day are showing us that in the background of personalities are wells of latent memories that may account, literally by the wholesale, for the phenomena of dreams, automatic writings, "spirit communications," and many other phenomena connected with hysteria, disassociation, and other abnormal psychic states." 1

In *The Mind at Mischief* Dr. Sadler took the position that, in his experience, all psychic phenomena fall into three categories: *(1). Self-deception. (2). Emotional Illness. (3). Fraud.* In his book he presented case history after case history to support these views. However, the ministers found a tiny crack in his professional stance on page 332:

> "Perhaps this statement should be qualified by adding that there are possibly one or two exceptions to this general classification of so-called psychics and trance mediums. Many years ago I was made acquainted with a

". . . It is the Way it Ought to Be!"

very extraordinary phenomenon of this sort, which it has been my privilege to observe periodically from that time to this, and some day I hope to report more fully upon this unique case; but I hasten to say that in none of my observations of this individual and the peculiar associated experiences of the night period was there ever anything that pointed toward spiritualism. In fact, the contacts of this individual with the alleged forces which dominated at such times, whatever they were, were always in a most positive manner antagonistic to, and condemnatory of, all beliefs or tendencies associated with the idea of the return of the dead to participate in the affairs of the world of the living." [2]

A footnote for this paragraph led the investigators to an Appendix in the back of the book. Here they discovered a rather detailed disclaimer written by Dr. Sadler. Dr. Sadler mentions two cases in this Appendix, only one of which he was able to investigate. It was this case that he expanded upon in depth. It appeared that the ministers had found the thread they were looking for:

"The . . . exception has to do with a rather peculiar case of psychic phenomena, one which I find myself unable to classify, and which I would like very much to narrate more fully; I cannot do so here, however, because of a promise which I feel under obligation to keep sacredly. In other words, I have promised not to publish this case during the lifetime of the individual. I hope sometime to secure a modification of that promise and to be able to report this case more fully because of its interesting features. I was brought in contact with it, in the summer of 1911, and I have had it under my observation more or less ever since, having been present at probably 250 of the night sessions, many of which have been attended by a stenographer who made voluminous notes."

To most Urantia Book readers this is now a very familiar paragraph. Yet, in the Seventies and Eighties it was very seldom seen. I recall seeing it for the first time about 1975. It was in the home of Berkeley Elliott, of Oklahoma City. Berkeley had been a reader almost since *The Urantia Book* had first been published. She was a good friend of Bill Sadler, Jr., the son of Dr. Sadler, who often visited the Oklahoma group in the late Fifties and early Sixties. I happened to pull a volume off of one of Berkeley's bookshelves that day, titled: *The Mind at Mischief.* I remembered Clyde Bedell once telling me of the Appendix of that book, and how it contained a reference to an individual known only as the *"sleeping subject."* When I was able, at last, to read those words of Dr. Sadler the hair on the back of my neck stood up. It was so rare, in those days, to see anything like this. Material such as that in *The Mind at Mischief* was considered secret, and only a special few were privy to it. The narrative continued:

"A thorough study of this case has convinced me that it is not one of ordinary trance. While the sleep seems to be quite of a natural order, it is very profound, and so far we have never been able to awaken the subject when in this state; but the body is never rigid, and the heart action is never modified, tho respiration is sometimes markedly interfered with. This man is utterly unconscious, wholly oblivious to what takes place, and, unless told about it subsequently, never knows that he has been used as a

sort of clearing house for the coming and going of
alleged extra-planetary personalities. In fact, he is more
or less indifferent to the whole proceeding, and shows a
surprising lack of interest in these affairs as they occur
from time to time."

Although this may seem old-hat to Urantians now, we should
remember that this may be the most complete description of the
early contacts that Dr. Sadler ever wrote. *The Mind at Mischief*
was printed in several editions in 1929, and after that, Clyde told
me the reference was deleted. The most astounding paragraph
follows:

"In no way are these night visitations like the séances
associated with spiritualism. At no time during the
period of eighteen years' observation has there been a
communication from any source that claimed to be the
spirit of a deceased human being. The communications
which have been written, or which we have had the
opportunity to hear spoken, are made by a vast order of
alleged beings who claim to come from other planets to
visit this world, to stop here as student visitors for study
and observation when they are en route from one
universe to another or from one planet to another. These
communications further arise in alleged spiritual beings
who purport to have been assigned to this planet for
duties of various sorts."

Dr. Sadler then admits he has not been able to discover the
psychic, or unconscious, source of the information that was being
disclosed. The case remained a bafflement to him.

"Eighteen years of study and careful investigation have failed to reveal the psychic origin of these messages. I find myself at the present time just where I was when I started. Psychoanalysis, hypnotism, intensive comparison, fail to show that the written or spoken messages of this individual have origin in his own mind. Much of the material secured through this subject is quite contrary to his habits of thought, to the way in which he has been taught, and to his entire philosophy. In fact, of much that we have secured, we have failed to find anything of its nature in existence. Its philosophic content is quite new, and we are unable to find where very much of it has ever found human expression."

Note the scientific detachment by which Dr. Sadler addresses this case. He apparently had not yet, in 1929, given up his quest to find a scientific answer to the phenomenon.

"Much as I would like to report details of this case, I am not in a position to do so at present. I can only say that I have found in these years of observation that all the information imparted through this source has proved to be consistent within itself. While there is considerable difference in the quality of the communications, this seems to be reasonably explained by a difference in state of development and order of the personalities making the communications. Its philosophy is consistent. It is essentially Christian and is, on the whole, entirely harmonious with the known scientific facts and truths of this age. In fact, the case is so unusual and extraordinary that it establishes itself immediately, as far as my experience goes, in a class by itself, one which has thus far resisted all my efforts to prove it to be of auto-psychic origin. Our investigations are being continued and, as I have intimated, I hope some time in the near future to secure permission for the more complete reporting of the phenomena connected with this interesting case." [3]

The next step for the team of ministers was clear: They would need to go to Chicago and meet personally with Dr. William S. Sadler to discuss the origin of the Urantia Papers. The remarkable meeting took place on May 7, 1958.

ENDNOTES:

1. THE MIND AT MISCHIEF, by William S. Sadler, M.D., F.A.C.S.; Funk & Wagnall's Company, New York and London, 1929, *page xi.*
2. IBID. page 332.
3. IBID, pages 382,383,384.

Rare old photo of 533 Diversey Parkway, Chicago, IL

Chapter Two
Chicago and Dr. William S. Sadler

Chicago and Dr. William S. Sadler

*T*HE KEY PLAYERS IN THE MAY 7, 1958 meeting were certainly Dr. Sadler and Dr. Sprunger. It is important to set the stage for this rendezvous by providing additional background about both Dr. Sadler and Dr. Sprunger, so the reader will understand the meeting's significance. Each was a formidable personality. Dr. Sadler was energetic and dominating in a friendly, personable manner. At the time Dr. Sadler met with Dr. Sprunger and his associate ministers, Sadler was nearly 82 years of age, still vigorous, but mellowing well into the autumn of a very successful career. Meredith Sprunger was a gracious and perhaps less assertive man of 42, yet one who possessed comparable depth and academic development.

Dr. William S. Sadler was without question a man of unique academic and professional stature. Dr. Sadler's 1942 listing in *Who's Who* gives an idea of his versatility and accomplishments *(see next page)*. He had been nationally noted, and featured in an article in *Reader's Digest* magazine. His training had been exceptionally broad in two key disciplines: psychology and theology. Dr. Sadler's books reflected religious insights, extensive clinical experience, as well as profound knowledge of the science

SADLER, WILLIAM SAMUEL: Psychiatrist, born: Spencer Indiana, June 14, 1875, son of Samuel Calvin and Sarah Isabel (Wilson) Sadler. Education: Battle Creek (MI) College; Cooper Medical College; University of Chicago, M.D.; American Medical Missionary College; University of Illinois, 1906. Studied in Europe with Freud, 1911. Married Lena C. Kellogg, M.D. of Paris, Illinois, December 3, 1897. Children: Willus Kellogg (deceased); William Samuel Sadler, Jr. Practiced in Chicago since 1906. Formerly Professor Post-Graduate, Medical School of Chicago; professor-lecturer, pastoral psychology, Presbyterian Theological Seminary; Director and Chief Psychiatrist Chicago Institute of Research and Diagnosis, 1906; attending psychiatrist, Columbus Hospital North Side Rest Home; consulting psychiatrist, W. K. Kellogg Foundation, Battle Creek, MI. Fellow, American College of Surgeons; A.M.A., A.A.A.S., American Psychiatric Association. Member, American Psychopathological Association; Illinois State Medical Society; Chicago Medical Society of Mental Hygiene; Chicago Society for Personality Study. Republican, Protestant. Author: The Psychology of Faith and Fear, 1912, 9th edition, 1925; Worry & Nervousness, 1913; Quest for Happiness, 1926; The truth About Heredity, 1927; The Truth About Mind Cure, 1928; The Mind at Mischief, 1929; Piloting Modern Youth (with wife) 1931; Theory & Practice of Psychology, 1936; Psychiatric Nursing, (with wife) 1937; Living a Sane Sex Life, (with wife) 1938; Problems with the Pre-School Child (with wife) 1940; 15 other books on psychology and mental hygiene; also health articles in magazines and articles on mental hygiene and psychiatry. Lecturer on psychiatry and other subjects. Home Office: 533 Diversey Parkway, Chicago, Illinois.

Facsimile of 1942 WHO'S WHO entry for Dr. William S. Sadler.
Photo was added by author.

of the human mind. If there was any weakness in his holistic vision that was apparent from his written works, it might be the third key discipline of human thought — the great intellectual unifier — philosophy.

Dr. Meredith Sprunger was one of those rare scholars who was as well grounded in religion and science as Dr. Sadler. As an ordained minister he naturally had a strong educational background in theology. In addition, Dr. Sprunger had a doctorate in psychology, a clinical practice, was trained as a social scientist, and engaged in a successful academic career at the Indiana Institute of Technology. With his long experience as a college professor and administrator, Dr. Sprunger was also thoroughly trained in philosophy. So it was that Dr. Sprunger brought to the meeting what might be considered an even more balanced and broader working knowledge than Dr. Sadler of all three of the great disciplines of human knowledge: science, religion and philosophy.

The stage was set for a unique relationship. Dr. Sprunger would win the confidence and respect of William Sadler. The two would become colleagues in their pursuit to better understand, and to help propagate, the Urantia Revelation. It was over a decade later when Dr. Sprunger officiated at the memorial service of his friend and colleague. He would later write of the human side of Dr. Sadler:

"Although Dr. Sadler was an extraordinary person with great talents and diverse experience in serving humankind, he was also a warm and loving person with a great sense of humor. Dr. Sadler's life experience uniquely prepared him

to serve as a pioneer in the field of medicine, psychiatry, and religion."[1]

The Meeting

Dr. Sadler was well aware of the curiosity of the ministerial team in the origin of the Urantia Papers, as well as their interest in the technique by which they were materialized. At the beginning of the meeting, Dr. Sadler informed the ministers that although he was not permitted to tell what little he knew about the materialization of the Papers, there was nothing to prevent him from explaining the way the Papers were *not* materialized. He offered a paper that listed every imaginable form of subconscious mind or psychic activity. *(See opposite page).* At the bottom of the paper was a note reading: *"The technique of the reception of The Urantia Book in English in no way parallels or impinges upon any of the above phenomena of marginal consciousness."*

Dr. Sadler went on to explain that, as nearly as he could determine, the appearance of the Urantia Papers was associated with some form of *superconscious — not* subconscious — activity.[2]

During the meeting, Dr. Sadler candidly discussed any questions the ministers asked him. However, he made it clear that he would not talk about two things: the name of the individual who was used in some undisclosed way for the materialization of the Papers, nor would he discuss the details of the materialization. Dr. Sadler explained that the small group, known as the "Contact Commission," that had interfaced with the contact personality and the Revelators, had been required to take vows of secrecy about these subjects. He was asked why these restrictions were imposed. Dr. Sadler gave these reasons:

While we are not at liberty to tell you even the little we know about the technique of the production of the Urantia Papers, we are not forbidden to tell you how we did not get these documents.

Let me call your attention to the following outline of present-day psychologic and psychic phenomena.

UNUSUAL ACTIVITIES OF THE MARGINAL CONSCIOUSNESS. (The subconscious mind)

1. Automatic Writing.
2. Automatic Talking.
   a. Speaking with "tongues."
   b. Trance Mediums.
   c. Spirit Mediums.
   d. Catalepsy.
3. Automatic Hearing—Clairaudience.
   Hearing "voices."
4. Automatic Seeing.
   a. Dream States—Twilight Mentation.
   b. Visions—Automatic Dramatization.
   c. Hallucinations. (Shifty "Reality" Feelings.)
5. Automatic Thinking.
   a. Automatic Fearing—Anxiety Neurosis.
   b. Automatic Ideation—Mental Compulsions.
   c. Automatic Judgments—Intuition, "Hunches."
   d. Automatic Association of Ideas—Premonitions.
   e. Automatic Guessing—E.S.P. Extra-Sensory Perception.
   f. Automatic Deductions—Delusions—Paranoia.
   g. Dominance by Marginal Consciousness—Dreams and Hypnosis.
6. Automatic Remembering.
   a. Clairvoyance—Automatic Memory Associations.
   b. Telepathy—Mind Reading (?)
   c. Fortune Telling (Largely Fraudulent).
   d. Musical and Mathematical Marvels.

7. Automatic Acting.
   a. Automatic Behavior—(Major Hysteria. Witchcraft.)
   b. Automatic Motion—Motor Compulsions.
   c. Automatic Overdrives—Manic Episodes.
   d. Automatic Walking—Somnambulism.
8. Automatic Personalization.
   a. Automatic Forgetting—Amnesia.
   b. Automatic Dissociation—Double and Multiple Personality.
   c. Schizophrenia—Split Personality.
9. Combined and Associated Psychic States.

   NOTE: The technique of the reception of the Urantia Book in English in no way parallels or impinges upon any of the above phenomena of the marginal consciousness.

DR. SADLER'S LIST OF PSYCHIC PHENOMENA THAT WERE *NOT USED* TO MATERIALIZE THE URANTIA PAPERS

SOURCE: *CONSIDERATIONS OF SOME CRITICISMS OF THE URANTIA BOOK* by William S. Sadler, 1958

"[1]. The main reason for not revealing the identity of the contact personality is that the revelators did not want any human being — any human name — ever to be associated with *The Urantia Book*. They wanted the Revelation to stand upon its own declarations and teachings. They are determined that future generations shall have the book wholly free from all mortal connections —they do not want a new St. Peter, St. Paul, Luther, Calvin or Wesley. The book does not even bear the imprint of the printer who brought the book into being." *[NOTE: A printer traditionally includes a small imprint of their identity on large publications. In this case, R.R. Donnelley & Sons was requested to waive this identification.]*

"[2]. There is much connected with the appearance of the Urantia Papers which no human being fully understands. No one really knows just how this revelation came to appear in written English. If anyone should tell all he really knows about this [sic] technique and methods employed throughout the years of getting this revelation, such a narration would satisfy no one — there is simply too much missing"[3]

Dr. Sadler also explained that, in addition to the Contact Commission, there had been another, larger group associated with the Urantia Papers. This group was known as the "Forum." Several members of the Forum had speculated that the above restrictions were imposed because the Revelators wanted nothing "miraculous" associated with the appearance of the Urantia Papers.

Dr. Sadler confided to the group of ministers that he had spent a great number of years seeking to discover natural explanations for what he had been observing. He had consulted with Sir Hubert Wilkins, a noted scientist and explorer who had an interest in psychic phenomena. He also contacted Howard Thurston, a professional magician who was noted for his ability to expose fraudulent mediums and psychics. All of the outside experts who were consulted agreed that the phenomena associated with the contact personality were not classifiable as known so-called psychic activities, such as automatic writing, telepathy, clairvoyance, trances, spirit mediumship, channeling — nor as any psychological disturbance such as split personality.[4]

It was obvious to Dr. Sprunger that William Sadler had started as a professional, objective researcher and skeptic, and yet somehow had become a believer. Dr. Sprunger asked him how this transformation had occurred. Dr. Sadler replied:

> "We set up our 'Forum' in the mid-twenties as an informal Sunday tea, a place where a group of about thirty interested people could meet and discuss medical and social issues. The Forum was composed of people from all walks of life, including professionals such as doctors, lawyers, dentists, ministers and teachers, as well as housewives, secretaries, farmers, and laborers. The Forum eventually became involved in examining the Urantia Papers, and in discussing them. Each week, I began to read them one of the Papers and accept questions from the Forum members about what they had heard. In time, it seemed to me the folks in the Forum were becoming more and more impressed with the content of the Papers, and were losing objectivity. I was most concerned with Lena, my wife."

Indeed, Dr. Lena Sadler was evidently a strong believer in the Papers long before William. She apparently urged him to continue the process when his interest began to flag. Unfortunately, Lena died of cancer in 1939 at the age of 64, more than fifteen years before the Urantia Papers became *The Urantia Book*.

"So one Sunday," continued Dr. Sadler, "I made a speech to the group about the importance of maintaining a tough, critical and objective approach to the material. To my astonishment, the response I got was almost like a testimonial meeting! The essence of the reaction was: 'We don't care who wrote these Papers, they simply make more sense than anything else we have ever read along this line.'"

"Now, I believed that my own professional reputation was at stake. I had often declared in public that there were no genuine mediumistic phenomena, and I wasn't going to let one baffling case change my mind. I felt that in time I would discover a natural explanation for this remarkable case.

"However, as years went by I became more and more impressed with the quality and the consistency of the material that was being received. I became satisfied in my own mind that the subject involved in the materializations could not have authored the Papers we were receiving. He simply did not have the qualifications nor the abilities to do so. I finally became satisfied that I was not dealing with some hoax or trick, but some kind of an authentic phenomenon.

"Finally, in the mid-thirties — over twenty years after I had first encountered this case — I carefully studied a Paper evaluating the personalities of the apostles of Jesus. It was at that point that I threw in the intellectual towel. I am a psychiatrist, and I believe I know my business. But this Paper was a real blow to my pride. I believe that if I assembled a half dozen of the world's best psychiatrists and had years to prepare it, we could not collectively fabricate a paper with this ring of genuineness and insight. So I said to myself: 'I don't know what this is, but I do know it is the highest quality of philosophical-religious material I have ever read.'"

From that point on, Dr. Sadler became not simply a detached professional director of the group, he became a proactive and dedicated leader.5

The question of origin

Ideally, from a human philosophical perspective, Revelation is best served when evaluated upon its content, not upon some supposed miraculous origin. However, many people believe that a mysterious — or even seemingly "miraculous" — origin of revelatory material actually validates the contents of the material itself. Yet, in the case of the Urantia Papers, Dr. Sadler made great effort to avoid attaching some supernatural occurrence to explain their materialization. In point of fact, there is no authentic record I know of that either he or any member of the Contact Commission *ever witnessed a supernatural event associated with the actual materialization of the text of the Urantia Papers.* They attested to many events relative to the materialization of the text that they could not explain, but none claimed to have witnessed any of the the materialization events. Even so, the Urantia Papers themselves tell us that if the human mind cannot fathom the true origin of a phenomenon, it will create an origin:

> **"Partial, incomplete, and evolving intellects would be helpless in the master universe, would be unable to form the first rational thought pattern, were it not for the innate ability of all mind, high or low, to form a *universe frame* in which to think. If mind cannot fathom conclusions, if it cannot penetrate to true origins, then**

will such mind unfailingly postulate conclusions and invent origins that it may have a means of logical thought within the frame of these mind-created postulates. And while such universe frames for creature thought are indispensable to rational intellectual operations, they are, without exception, erroneous to a greater or lesser degree." [1260, par.2]

We will see that Dr. Sadler may have eventually authorized the preparation of a "History of the Urantia Movement" for this reason. Later, in private discussions with Dr. Sprunger, William Sadler would reiterate that he did not know how the materialization of the Papers was accomplished. Dr. Sadler also insisted that everything known about the materialization of the Urantia Papers can be found in various parts of the book. However, based upon these Urantia Book references and Dr. Sadler's own experiences in relationship to the materializations, the colleagues were led to speculate upon the process, as we shall see.

Dr. Sprunger and his ministerial colleagues left Chicago with a much better idea of how the Urantia Papers came to be. It should be emphasized once more that the origins of the Urantia Papers have little relevance in assessing the truth and spiritual quality of their content. It is, however, an important area of research that was destined to be revisited. On October 6, 1958, Dr. Sprunger and the ministerial group met with Dr. Robert V. Moss, who was at the time Professor of New Testament Studies at Lancaster Theological Seminary and President of the United Church of Christ. The purpose of the South Bend meeting was to evaluate *The Urantia Book.* There was a lively and spirited discussion. Although Dr. Moss had not read the entire book, he remarked that the Biblical material in *The Urantia Book* was essentially in harmony with the best scholarship of the day, and that the book had many inspiring passages.

A week after the meeting, Dr. Moss wrote Dr. Sprunger and asked a most provocative question:

"It occurred to me that we did not deal with one basic question. As you know, Christianity is a historical religion and because of that the basis of revelation can be tested by scholarship. It seems extremely important that the source of the Urantia 'revelations' be set forth in any serious discussions of its claim. To say there is no historical basis for the "revelation" is to say that it differs greatly from the biblical understanding of the way in which God acts."[6]

Thus, it is reasonable to conclude that an investigation into the origin of the Urantia Papers would lend a significant contribution to the evaluation of the text itself. Indeed, issues about the sequences and techniques of the origin remained. In the next decade, Dr. Sprunger would pursue these questions. He would have many conversations with Dr. Sadler as well as with two other members of the Contact Commission: Bill Sadler, Jr. and Emma Louise Christensen (Christy). He would also meet and develop associations with many Forum members.

Our own quest for answers begins in the early years of the twentieth century. It was a uniquely colorful period in world history. Matisse and Renoir were still painting. And, another aspiring artist named Adolf Hitler was attempting to sell his watercolors in Vienna. Theodore Roosevelt was President of the United States. Americans were still talking about two brothers named Orville and Wilbur Wright who successfully flew a heavier than air machine in 1903. Chicago was then the center of movie making, and Bill Harris has noted: "in the prairies just out of town someone first headed someone else off at the pass in cowboy pictures. They called it Chicago's Golden Age. And in every quarter of the arts, from jazz to poetry, Chicago was clearly the place to be."[7] Chicago newspapermen like Carl Sandburg, Ben Hecht, and Ring Lardner were turning to more serious ideas — and America was sitting up and taking notice. H. L. Mencken wrote: "In Chicago, a spirit broods on the face of the waters."[8] It was in this remarkable city of Chicago, Illinois, that the intriguing story of the Urantia Papers was set into motion.

ENDNOTES

1. A full biography of Dr. Sadler is beyond the scope of our book. However, a few highlights of his life were gleaned from a paper written by Meredith Sprunger after Dr. Sadler's death, and an article in *PERVADED SPACE*, a newsletter published by Chicago Urantian David Kulieke, Spring, 1979. Born in Spencer, Indiana, 1875, as a boy Sadler was not allowed to attend public school after the death of his sister, because his parents were afraid that he would also catch a communicable disease. So it was that he received most of his formal education from his parents and tutors, and through his own initiative. He showed early signs of skill as an orator, and because of his remarkable knowledge of the Bible he was called the "boy preacher" at fourteen. He was also a remarkable salesman, selling health foods for John Harvey Kellogg, brother of W. K. Kellogg, founder of the Kellogg cereal empire. At twenty, as director of a Chicago Medical Mission, Sadler engaged in teaching, speaking, and working with skid row people. He initiated and edited a magazine which reached a circulation of 150,000 copies. His theological training took place at the Moody Bible Institute. He met Lena Kellogg in 1893, when she was a student nurse. They married in 1897. The Sadler's lost their first son a few years later, who died at the age of 11 months. Soon after that, both Sadlers decided to become doctors, and attended different medical schools. This was virtually William Sadler, Sr.'s first formal education. After a few years as a successful surgeon, he decided to become a psychiatrist. After passing the required examination, he went to Europe (circa 1911) and studied with Freud in Vienna for almost a year. He told Dr. Sprunger that he was a member of Freud's "fair-haired

boys' club" along with Jung and Adler, meeting weekly with Freud for informal debates. All three men were to later break with Freud, Dr. Sadler going on to become the "father of American Psychiatry" and recognized in the International Who's Who as a "pioneer in the popularization of preventative medicine." For all of his accomplishments, Dr. Sadler told Meredith that he considered his most important contribution to the world to be his leadership of a little-known group called the "Forum," which received the gift of the Urantia Papers from celestial beings and published it as *The Urantia Book.*

2. The term "superconscious" is used in the Urantia Papers to describe the higher reaches of human consciousness, above the conscious level and distinct from the subconscious mind. The idea of a superconscious mind has been hinted at by a few scientists such as Abraham Maslow, Roberto Assagioli, and Dr. Barbara Brown. The Urantia Papers propose a fully operational mind that functions above the level of human consciousness and impinges upon the highest reaches of human thought by means of religious insights and spiritual values (or what Dr. Maslow termed meta-values): **"But there is also a domain of prayer wherein the intellectually alert and spiritually progressing individual attains more or less contact with the superconscious levels of the human mind, the domain of the indwelling Thought Adjuster."** [996, par. 4] **"Prayer induces the human ego to look both ways for help: for material aid to the subconscious reservoir of mortal experience, for inspiration and guidance to the superconscious borders of the contact of the material with the spiritual, with the Mystery Monitor."** [997, par 3] **"Most of the spectacular phenomena associated with so-called religious conversions are entirely psychologic in nature, but now and then there do occur experiences which are also spiritual in origin. When the mental mobilization is absolutely total on any level of the psychic upreach toward spirit attainment, when there exists perfection of the human motivation of loyalties to the divine idea, then there very often occurs a sudden down-grasp of the indwelling spirit to synchronize with the concentrated and consecrated purpose of the superconscious mind of the believing mortal. And it is such experiences of unified intellectual and spiritual phenomena that constitute the conversion which consists in factors over and above purely psychologic involvement."** [1099, par.2]

3. THE HISTORICITY OF *THE URANTIA BOOK* by Meredith J. Sprunger, Paper revised December 18, 1993, page 3.

4. IBID, page 3.

5. IBID, pages 3-4.

6. IBID, page 1.

7. CHICAGO, A PHOTOGRAPHIC JOURNEY by Bill Harris, Crescent Books, New York, 1989, page 15.

8. IBID, page 15.

What the Urantia Papers Say About . . .

4. THE LIMITATIONS OF REVELATION - page 1109

"Because your world is generally ignorant of origins, even of physical origins, it has appeared to be wise from time to time to provide instruction in cosmology. And always has this made trouble for the future. The laws of revelation hamper us greatly by their proscription of the impartation of unearned or premature knowledge. Any cosmology presented as a part of revealed religion is destined to be outgrown in a very short time. Accordingly, future students of such a revelation are tempted to discard any element of genuine religious truth it may contain because they discover errors on the face of the associated cosmologies therein presented.

"Mankind should understand that we who participate in the revelation of truth are very rigorously limited by the instructions of our superiors. We are not at liberty to anticipate the scientific discoveries of a thousand years. Revelators must act in accordance with the instructions which form a part of the revelation mandate. We see no way of overcoming this difficulty, either now or at any future time. We full well know that, while the historic facts and religious truths of this series of revelatory presentations will stand on the records of the ages to come, within a few short years many of our statements regarding the physical sciences will stand in need of revision in consequence of additional scientific developments and new discoveries. These new developments we even now foresee, but we are forbidden to include such humanly undiscovered facts in the revelatory records. Let it be made clear that revelations are not necessarily inspired. The cosmology of these revelations is *not inspired*. It is limited by our permission for the co-ordination and sorting of present-day knowledge. While divine or spiritual insight is a gift, *human wisdom must evolve.*"

(Left) Marshall Field, one of America's first department stores.

Chicago, circa 1910, the second largest city in the United States — a city of contrasts.

(Above) The immigrant tenements of Maxwell Street

(Left) Frank Lloyd Wright's Martin House in Oak Park.

Chapter Three
"Something Has Happened to My Husband"

"Something Has Happened to My Husband" 43

ONE SUMMER BETWEEN 1906 and 1911, there was a remarkable encounter involving two couples. One of the couples was Dr. William Sadler and his wife, Dr. Lena Sadler; the identity of the other couple is not known. The event would completely alter the lives of all four individuals, and would have implications that are still not fully grasped nearly a century later.

The exact date and nature of the meeting of the two couples has been an object of much discussion. The 1911 date of this episode can be documented by two references from the Appendix in *The Mind at Mischief*. Dr. Sadler simply states that he was brought into contact with this case in the *"summer of 1911."* In *The Mind at Mischief*, which was published in 1929, Sadler states: *"Eighteen years of study"* had taken place — again placing the meeting in the 1911 frame.[1] Some researchers have called this a printing error, claiming that Dr. Sadler came into contact with the so-called *"sleeping subject"* as early as 1906. It hardly seems likely that two printing errors were made.

A date of 1908 is suggested by other researchers, and is supported by evidence that the Sadlers, while they were waiting for a new residence to be prepared, lived in a temporary apartment in La Grange, Illinois, during the spring and summer of 1908.

This interim residence situation seems to have occurred only once, and fits the version of Dr. Sadler's description of the seminal events that was disclosed by author Harold Sherman. Sherman's information is based upon a conversation with Dr. Sadler that took place in 1942, in which Sadler stated the first encounter with the sleeping subject had been about *"thirty-five years ago,"* more closely matching the earlier dates.[2]

Long and tedious efforts have been made to establish the date of the Sadlers' first contact with the sleeping subject based upon records of their various residences. It may have been that they met the sleeping subject in 1906 or 1908 — we cannot be sure. Some believe Dr. Sadler intentionally created confusion about the date to protect the identity of his patient, the individual who would become known as the sleeping subject. It is also possible that in the early days the sleeping subject appeared to be nothing more than a patient with some kind of a sleeping disorder. As we shall see, the sessions with the sleeping subject took a remarkable and baffling turn somewhat later in the process.

Some writers, with agendas to discredit the authenticity of the Papers, have detailed biographical information on Dr. Sadler and others to set the stage for one claim or another. In this history, we are less interested in establishing factual dates and exhausting the biographical backgrounds of the participants than we are in following the authentic historic development of the Revelation.

It is important to relate here that all the people who were involved in the early stages of the contact (and all subsequent stages) were quite ordinary human beings. Notwithstanding Dr. Sadler's status as a psychiatrist and prolific writer in his field, both he and his wife were simply ordinary folks with foibles and strengths just like the rest of us. To my knowledge, no one associated with the Urantia Movement has demonstrated any special spiritual status or unique "power." In the early sessions, we can know for certain that only Dr. Sadler, Dr. Lena, the sleeping subject and his wife were involved. Dr. Sadler's son, Bill Sadler, Jr., was not involved in the early contacts, he was only three years old in 1911.[3]

Dr. Sadler estimates in the Appendix of *The Mind at Mischief* that about 250 night sessions with the sleeping subject had taken place by 1929. We have only the testimony of Dr. Sadler about the events that took place prior to the commencement of the Forum and the enlargement of the Contact Commission in the early twenties. We will see that the activities were significantly altered as other personalities became involved. Although Sadler has written virtually nothing about the primal events that set the Revelation into motion, Meredith Sprunger supplies a great deal of the information that he had personally learned from Sadler.

Less reliable information about the seminal events has been provided by Harold Sherman, (a writer and a self-proclaimed psychic) who challenged Dr. Sadler's stewardship of the Papers. Sherman and his wife were reporters, and they claimed to have a candid interview with Dr. Sadler in August of 1942, in which he described the early episodes. They said they wrote their recollections down immediately after hearing the story.[4]

Generally, what Sherman wrote in his book, *How to Know What to Believe,* is self-serving and configured to support his own views of psychic phenomena. However, in the particular segment of his book referring to Dr. Sadler's story of the early contacts, a great deal of his information correlates with that of Dr. Sprunger and other early Urantians. Also in support of this portion of Sherman's narrative are the comments of Carolyn Kendall, who briefly worked for Dr. Sadler as a receptionist and who has been closely associated with Urantia Foundation. Carolyn states that when she was "almost 19 years of age" (in 1951), Dr. Sadler related to her the story of the sleeping subject. Carolyn recalls that it was *"essentially the same as in Sherman's book."*[5]

La Grange, Illinois, Circa 1906 - 1911

If, for the sake of argument, we split the difference and use the 1908 date, picture a 33-year old William Sadler, his wife Lena, and a newborn Bill Sadler, Jr., living in a suburb of Chicago, Illinois. They were temporarily housed in a furnished apartment, waiting for their new residence to be prepared. We know that some accounts relate that late one summer evening there was a knock on the door. Evidently another tenant, a lady directly beneath their apartment, had learned that they were doctors.

"Will you come downstairs with me?" she asked. *"Something has happened to my husband. He's gone to sleep, he is breathing very strangely, and I can't wake him up."*[6]

The Sadlers donned robes and slippers and followed the distraught woman to her apartment. In the bedroom they found a middle aged man lying on a bed. He was apparently sleeping, but his respiration seemed disturbed. He would take a couple of fast breaths and then stop breathing for an almost alarming interval. Dr. Sadler quickly took his pulse, and was surprised to find it normal. However, the depth of the subject's sleep was quite profound. Dr. Sadler attempted various ways to awaken the man, but without success. Finally, there seemed nothing left to do but wait.

Nearly an hour went by. The man's body made several rather violent movements during this period. Then, suddenly, he sat up

*Dr. William S. Sadler
circa 1914*

*Dr. Lena Celestia
(Kellogg) Sadler
circa 1914*

*Dr. Lena Sadler
with son Bill circa 1914*

and looked around. "Who are these people?" he asked his wife. She explained that they were doctors whom she had called from upstairs when she could not wake him. He exclaimed: "What? What has happened? Is something wrong?"

Dr. Sadler asked: "How do you feel?" "I feel fine," the man replied. "What is it you have been dreaming about?" asked Dr. Sadler. "Why, nothing." the man replied. "But you have been jumping all around the bed," said Sadler. "Well, I don't know anything about that," the man replied. "I feel fine."

After a bit of small talk, Dr. Sadler said: "Look, I believe it will be wise if you come in for a complete examination tomorrow morning. This is quite unusual, and we want to be on the safe side." The man and his wife agreed.

The next day Dr. Sadler made the examination and found the gentleman to be in excellent physical condition. After thoroughly testing him, Sadler checked into the man's family history. There was no record of insanity or of epilepsy. Dr. Sadler suggested that he would like to keep the patient under observation for a while, and the patient consented.[7]

Several weeks passed. Then the wife called and informed the Sadlers that her husband was in the peculiar deep sleep again. The doctors responded, and discovered him to be in the same profound sleeping state as before. They attempted to rouse him, even sticking pins in him, but nothing worked. Fortunately the pulse remained normal during the strange breathing sequences and abnormal movements, so nothing appeared life-threatening about the extraordinary state. Then, he awoke as before, completely oblivious of any unusual behavior during his sleep. Both doctors were puzzled.

The phenomenon occurred several times by the fall of that year, when the Sadlers' new residence was ready. The lease on the subject's apartment was expiring at the same time. He and his wife elected to move so they could be near the Sadlers. It was at this new address that the peculiar "sleep" of the patient became considerably more remarkable and perplexing.

The first contact

The Sadlers were soon called to the new residence of the subject. The customary procedure was followed, and the physicians sat by the bedside, observing and waiting for him to awaken. Lena Sadler noticed the subject was moistening his lips. "Perhaps he wants to say something. Perhaps we should ask a question," she said. "How are you feeling?"

To the great astonishment of everyone, the subject spoke! But the voice was peculiar, not his normal voice. The voice identified itself as a student visitor on an observation mission from another planet![8] This "being" apparently was conversing through the sleeping subject by some means. Both doctors thought they were simply observing a phenomena known as *automatic speaking*. This activity involves the subconscious mind, and can take place without the awareness of the patient.

To verify this diagnosis, Dr. Sadler arranged for the subject to come to his office a few days after the remarkable occurrence. He was certain that he must explore the mind of the subject in order to discover the source of (what seemed to Dr. Sadler at the time) a phenomenon that was rooted in the sleeping subject's subconscious. In cases of subconscious activity that apparently drives otherwise inexplicable behavior, the traditional tool of psychiatry is hypnosis. At Dr. Sadler's request, the sleeping subject agreed to be hypnotized.

Once in the office, Dr. Sadler found it difficult to get the subject "under." After finally achieving a hypnotized state in the subject (in this and subsequent hypnosis sessions), Dr. Sadler discerned that there was *absolutely no subconscious awareness of the information that was discussed by the purported celestial visitor.* This was most amazing, and quite bewildering. As time progressed other supposed visiting beings began to speak "through" the subject. Dr. Sadler remained confounded as to how the unusual and challenging material being disclosed could have its origin in the psyche of the patient. The quality, uniqueness and consistency of what was being reported impressed both of the doctors. Dr. Sadler and Dr. Lena were also perplexed in that the sleeping subject was indifferent to the process and the material that resulted from it. Although the wife of the sleeping subject was anxious about the procedure, the subject seemed to have little interest or concern about what had happened during his deep sleeping state.

Notwithstanding his bafflement, Dr. Sadler continued to be certain that he could find a "scientific answer" to the case. He began to consult with other scientists and doctors about the mysterious phenomena of the sleeping subject. As stated earlier, Howard Thurston and Sir Hubert Wilkins, experts in spiritualistic frauds and tricks, were called in. These and other specialists were unable to account for the strange behavior of the sleeping subject — and were equally intrigued and bewildered by the remarkable information coming from the nocturnal sessions with him.

In the meantime, life went on. The decade between 1911 and 1921 was to be one of the most turbulent and terrible in human history. The mighty Titanic slipped beneath the waves of the Atlantic in April of 1912, a stunning rebuke of the technology of the mortal beings who had defied nature to sink it. The material loss of the Titanic was widely communicated. But the corporate indifference of the White Star Line was quietly accepted and not reported by the news media of the day: the company docked the pay of the crew from the minute the ship sank. The bereaved widows received pay checks diminished even further since the cost of their husbands' uniforms were deducted — a brief note explained that the uniforms were not turned in as required. Two years later the civilized world was at war. Even though it was all over by 1919, the seeds for World War II were to be sown in the aftermath of that first struggle. Meanwhile, in Chicago, the groundwork continued for a new age of religious living and spiritual discovery. In the early twenties, the effort to bring an epochal revelation to light the materialistic darkness of Urantia took a new turn.

The Forum

About 1923, on his way to the University of Kansas for a lecture on Gestalt psychology, Dr. William Sadler wrote a note to Bill Sadler, his son, who was fifteen and in high school at the time. Dr. Sadler suggested that it would be good to begin getting together with some of both Dr. Lena's and Dr. Sadler's friends and colleagues for tea and philosophic discussions on Sunday afternoons. *(The Sadlers had moved to their spacious new residence at 533 Diversey Parkway the year before)*. He proposed that Bill talk over the idea with his mother. When Dr. Sadler returned to Chicago he discovered his wife had invited a group of about thirty friends for a three o'clock Sunday afternoon tea.[9]

The group was destined to become the "Forum," and soon began to include interested individuals from all walks of life. Clyde Bedell[10] told me there was a brief screening process consisting of an interview with Dr. Sadler, and the early sessions

"Something Has Happened to My Husband" 53

were somewhat informal. Later, as the Urantia Papers were read, the meetings may have been rather tedious. The turnover of Forum members was great, and during its period of existence, a total of 486 members had come and gone. The final meeting of the Forum as such took place on May 31, 1942.[11] In a 1983 interview, Clyde Bedell spoke of those early days. The year was 1924; Clyde was 26 years old. He had just returned to Chicago:

> "I saw Lister Alwood . . . I had Sunday dinner at his home
> . . . He asked me if I would like to go to a Forum meeting at
> the home of an eminent Chicago psychiatrist. I asked a few
> questions, and he said: 'Well, Sadler is a fantastic speaker;
> he talks about all sorts of things. Discussion may go in any
> direction. But he's a fascinating, interesting, brilliant man.'
> . . . So that first Sunday I had dinner at Lister's home and we
> went to Dr. Sadler's Forum at 533 Diversey. It was
> extremely interesting. I have no idea what it was all about or
> what he talked about now . . ."

Clyde goes on to tell us that he asked Dr. Sadler's permission to invite a woman to attend a session. He brought his future wife, Florence Evans, to the next meeting.

> "Incidentally, I should mention the fact that shortly after
> I joined the Forum, Lister Alwood was through with the
> Forum . . . There was quite a little turnover. There were
> no limits on what could be discussed. I think a good
> many people in the very early Forum felt, years later,
> they had been circumstanced into it. If that is the case,
> what occurred before papers started coming . . . was of
> no moment. It's a strange thing but . . . many things
> which you think today we should have remembered we
> do not remember . . . What year did the papers begin

coming through? I don't know.   If we had known that such a thing as an epochal revelation was coming through, we would have kept diaries . . ."[12]

As the Forum began to discuss various issues, Dr. Sadler was continuing his efforts to discover the source of the puzzling night manifestations of the sleeping subject. He and his wife had begun to work out various questions about the universe in advance, asking them verbally as opportunities arose.

Sadler decided to privately develop a series of especially difficult questions as a test. He memorized fifty-two specific questions (Dr. Sadler was noted for having a remarkable photographic memory) to see if these so-called "student visitors" could ascertain what was in his mind. It should be noted that according to Dr. Sprunger, Sadler did not believe that mental telepathy was possible.

Shortly after, in one of the nocturnal sessions with the subject, Dr. Sadler and Dr. Lena encountered a particularly "electrifying personality" who claimed to be from a distant planet. He greatly excited the doctors by his comments. As this personality seemed about to take leave, Dr. Sadler challenged him saying: "How can you prove you are who you say you are?" The entity replied: "I cannot prove — but you cannot prove that I am not." He then stunned the doctor with this remark: "However, I have just received permission to answer forty-six of the fifty-two questions you have been holding in your mind."

Lena spoke up in surprise, "Why Will, you have no such list of questions, do you?" Dr. Sadler was forced to admit, "Yes I do Lena, and fifty-two is the exact number."

The astonishing personality then proceeded to answer the forty-six acceptable questions as promised.[13] He then added a pointed admonition:

"If you only knew what you are in contact with you would not ask me such trivial questions. You would rather ask questions as might elicit answers of supreme value to the human race."[14]

The Contact Commission

At the time the above remark was made (probably later in 1924) we can be reasonably certain that the group that was to become the Contact Commission consisted of at least Dr. Sadler who was then about 48 years of age, Dr. Lena (48), Lena's sister Anna Bell Kellogg (49), and her husband, Wilfred Custer Kellogg (50). Emma Louise Christensen (36) had likely become a new member, since she had been "adopted" as a family member by the Sadlers in December of 1923.[15] Bill Sadler, Jr. was not at the "electrifying personality" session depicted above, and related his knowledge of it as "hearsay."[16] Clyde Bedell mentions in the 1983 interview that the Kelloggs had a daughter who may have "very rarely" attended some of the sleeping subject sessions. He also had a vague memory of another doctor who may have attended occasionally in the early days. Urantian historian Mark Kulieke identifies the doctor as possibly Meyer Solomon. *(Dr. Solomon wrote a "Neurologist's Introduction" for "The Mind at Mischief" in 1929, pp xiii - vx. He was a professor at the Northwestern University School of Medicine).*

We can reasonably assume Bill Sadler, Jr.'s earliest attitudes toward the Revelation were guarded. Dr. Sadler wrote in early 1958:

56   A HISTORY OF THE URANTIA PAPERS   *Chapter Three*

"When my son came home from furlough from the Marine Corps to read the Urantia Papers, the first question he asked me was: 'Dad, is there anyone making money out of this thing?' I answered: 'No, son, but there are a number of people who are putting money into it.'"[17]

Eventually Bill Sadler, Jr. became a dedicated member of the Contact Commission, a student of the Papers, and perhaps the first Urantian philosopher. The final makeup of the Contact Commission as it saw the project through to completion[18] consisted of six members: Doctors William and Lena Sadler, Wilfred and Anna Bell Kellogg, Emma Christensen (or "Christy"), and Bill Sadler, Jr.

Whoever was present when the dramatic statement of the celestial visitor was made, we are told that it was taken as a challenge as well as a rebuke. On the evening of the remarkable admonition, Dr. Sadler was said to have later remarked: "Now they have asked for it. Let's give them questions that no human being can answer!"[19]

The stage was set. Very soon, in one of the Forum gatherings, a chance question by a member to Dr. Sadler would set into motion a fresh chain of events, and the casual nature of the informal Sunday teas would sharply change. The Forum would become drawn into its own rendezvous with destiny.

ENDNOTES

1. THE MIND AT MISCHIEF, by William S. Sadler, M.D., F.A.C.S.; Funk & Wagnall's Company, New York and London, 1929, page 383.

2. HOW TO KNOW WHAT TO BELIEVE by Harold Sherman, Fawcett, New York, 1976, pp. 61 and 62.

3. It is difficult to establish a birthdate for Bill Sadler, Jr. *The Urantia Book Fellowship Website* contains an excellent timeline of events related to

"Something Has Happened to My Husband" 57

the Urantia Movement. The date there is given as 1908, but indicates some dispute exists about this. It is believed Bill Sadler's Marine Corps records erroneously show 1906 as his birthdate because he lied about his age in order to enlist.

4. HOW TO KNOW WHAT TO BELIEVE by Harold Sherman, Fawcett, New York, 1976, pp. 58-96.

5. THE CONJOINT READER, Interview by Polly Friedman, Summer, 1993, page 3. In addition to Carolyn's verification, the basic facts in the "first contact" narrative were developed from Sherman's information, cross-checked against and modified by Meredith's information and my recollections of discussions I had over the years with Clyde Bedell and Berkeley Elliott. Clyde joined the Forum with his wife Florence in September, 1924, at the age of 26. Clyde Bedell was closely involved with the Urantia Movement until his death in January, 1985. Berkeley Elliott was a close friend of mine who had many candid conversations with Bill Sadler, Jr. in the late fifties and early sixties. I developed the dialogue between the various individuals in the seminal contact with some artistic license. It was based upon a composite of the sources above and is a plausible dramatization that fits the known facts.

6. HOW TO KNOW WHAT TO BELIEVE by Harold Sherman, Fawcett, New York, 1976, page 62. However, we may never know exactly how Dr. Sadler and Dr. Lena first encountered the sleeping subject and his wife. David Kantor has heard a different version, and wrote this note to me: *"My understanding is that the wife of the sleeping subject was a medical patient of Lena Sadler's and that when she described to Lena the curious sleeping problems her husband seemed to be having, Lena suggested that they get Dr. William involved due to his interest in and knowledge of psychic phenomena."* This story has plausible features to it. We know that Dr. Sadler sought to protect the identity of the sleeping subject, and therefore the beginning of the story which set the scene in the version he told Sherman and Carolyn may have been fabricated for this reason. If so, the 1908 dating of the meeting, based upon the residences of the Sadlers, may be suspect.

7. HOW TO KNOW WHAT TO BELIEVE by Harold Sherman, Fawcett, New York, 1976, page 63.

8. IBID., page 64.

9. HISTORY OF THE URANTIA MOVEMENT TWO - [Compiled by a Contact Commissioner.] Undated, page 7.

10. I became associated with Clyde Bedell in 1968, when he lived in Santa Barbara. At the time, Clyde had become known as one of the great retail advertising experts of all time. He wrote a book on retail advertising in the 1930's that was used as a college text book. Our

58   A HISTORY OF THE URANTIA PAPERS   *Chapter Three*

common interest was advertising. As stated earlier, Clyde gave me my first Urantia Book, an original 1955 printing.

11. HISTORY OF THE URANTIA MOVEMENT ONE, "by a Group of Urantian Pioneers, assisted by Members of the Contact Commission, 1960", pp. 5-6. The Forum seated about fifty people, and this would indicate a turnover factor of ten over the approximately twenty years of functioning. In other words, although a few stalwarts such as Clyde Bedell stayed the distance, the average Forum-member lasted only two years.

NOTE ON HISTORIES: *[See the exhibits on following four pages].* I am using two different "histories" of the Urantia Movement for some specific information. For clarity, I identify them as History One and History Two.

History One is a short historical narrative of 14 pages. The cover of this document states that it was written by a "Group of Urantian Pioneers, assisted by Members of the Contact Commission, 1960." A copy of this document, with the word "Sadler" written across the cover, was given to me by Dr. Sprunger. It contains editing and remarks that were probably written by Dr. Sadler.

History Two was authored by one or more anonymous individuals and was submitted to a court in 1994 in behalf of Urantia Foundation during a copyright litigation against Kristen Maaherra. Although Urantia Foundation and others continue to refer to this document as "written by Dr. Sadler," it almost certainly was not. After careful examination, the 30 page document appears to be the long lost, unfinished "history" of Emma Louise Christensen. This history was known to exist, but could not be found after her death in 1982. "Christy," as she was known, apparently used History One as a template, inserted a few pages authored by Dr. Sadler but never published, and added her own observations. The History Two document, as submitted to the Court, had no cover page, but began with what was "page 2" of History One. The pages were obviously renumbered, in some cases having two conflicting page numbers. History Two is a hybrid that is obviously the product of an inexperienced writer and editor. Dr. Sadler was an accomplished author. There are awkward shifts from second to third person, and long passages refer to Dr. Sadler in the third person. In one place (page 7) the writer inserted a comment: *"The doctor continues his narrative:"* Dr. Sadler never wrote about himself in this manner. The information in History Two is helpful, but must be regarded with some caution and weighed against other information. A copy of the original court submission was supplied to me by Kristen Maaherra.

12. AN INTERVIEW WITH CLYDE BEDELL, conducted by Barbara Kulieke, The Study Group Herald, December, 1992, page 12.

"Something Has Happened to My Husband" 59

13. HOW TO KNOW WHAT TO BELIEVE by Harold Sherman, Fawcett, New York, 1976, page 65. Both Meredith and I separately recall hearing, along the way, the story of Dr. Sadler's memorized questions.

14. HISTORY OF THE URANTIA MOVEMENT TWO - [Compiled by a Contact Commissioner, Undated] page 5. Dr. Sprunger records the comment somewhat differently: _"If you people realized what a high spiritual source you are now associating with you would stop making these puerile investigations to detect fraud and would ask some significant questions about the nature and reality of the universe." [See Affidavit, page 318]._

15. URANTIA BROTHERHOOD BULLETIN, Special Memorial Edition, Spring, 1982, page 1.

16. Bill Sadler, Jr. describes the encounter with the "electrifying personality" in a tape made in Oklahoma City, dated 2/18/62. However, he states in the same tape that incidents between 1924 and 1928 that he will relate on the tape are "hearsay."

17. CONSIDERATION OF SOME CRITICISMS OF _THE URANTIA BOOK_ by Dr. William S. Sadler, a paper produced in 1958, page 19. There is plausible but unverified testimony that Lena used her connections with the American Red Cross to get Bill Sadler, Jr. released from the Marine Corps early. It is believed she wanted him to become involved in the Revelation. The date of his leave from the Marines and his reading of the Papers (that were available at the time) was not given in Dr. William Sadler's reference.

18. Dr. Lena Sadler did not make it to the publication of the book. She died August 1, 1939, at the age of 64.

19. HISTORY OF THE URANTIA MOVEMENT TWO - [Compiled by a Contact Commissioner, Undated] page 5. Also on the Oklahoma City tape dated 2/18/62 Bill Sadler, Jr. attributes the remark: _"Now they have asked for it. Let's give them questions that no human being can answer!"_ to his father.

HISTORY ONE

The front page of History One reads: "This historical narrative was prepared by a group of Urantia pioneers, assisted by members of the contact commission.

"1960"

My copy was supplied by Dr. Sprunger, and had "Sadler" written across the front when I received it.

A typical page from History One, with what I believe is Dr. Sadler's editing.

On this page, the original copy: "the new creations would be presented" is edited to read: "the forum members would bring to the meeting their questions on the paper read the previous Sunday."

A note is added: "Throughout this entire operation, only one subject, or contact personality, (see p. 865-2) was involved."

Another note circles for removal the phases: "The last meeting of the Forum as a genetic assembly was held on May 31, 1942. During its existence the membership figure mounted to a total of 486. From this date in 1942 /" and suggests leaving only: "The Forum continued as a study group to the time of the organization of the First Urantia Society in 1956."

History Two does not have these changes.

History One was given to me by Dr. Sprunger. It has a note: *"Sadler"* on the cover and contains hand editing. David Kantor believes the handwriting on the cover may be that of Marian Rowley.

HISTORY TWO

Page one of History Two is actually page two of History One.

The cover page of History Two was either removed, or the author never prepared one.

(handwritten note) LARRY — THEY FILED THIS. 30 PAGE HISTORY LOVE, K.

Page six of History Two begins to refer to Dr. Sadler in the third person,

Dr. Sadler never wrote about himself in this way. History Two, in the judgment of the author, is a hybrid prepared by Emma Louise Christensen.

History Two was submitted in behalf of Urantia Foundation in the litigation against Kristen Maaherra. We carefully examined every page of this document, and concluded it is a hybrid, containing some material from History One, a few pages of Dr. Sadler's writings, and additional material apparently added by another Contact Commissioner. It may be the long lost history that Christy began to work on, but never completed.

INTRODUCTION OF THE FORUM TO THE "CONTACTS"

"The doctor continues his narrative

"Presently, I was asked to give a series of talks on "Mental Hygiene," or "Psychic Phenomena." At the beginning of my first talk, I said: "With one or two exceptions, all of the psychic phenomena which I have investigated have turned out to be either conscious or unconscious frauds. Some were deliberate frauds—others were those peculiar cases in which the performer was a victim of the deceptions of his own subconscious mind."

"I had no more than said this, when one of the group spoke up, saying: "Doctor, if you have contacted something which you have been unable to solve—it would be interesting—tell us more about it."

"I asked Dr. Lena to get some notes she had taken at a recent "contact" and read them to the group. It should be understood that up to this time there was no secrecy connected with this case. The Urantia Papers had not begun to appear.

"It was at about this time that this group meeting at our house on Sunday afternoons began to be called the "Forum."

"The group manifested such a great interest in this case that I never did get around to giving any of the health talks such as had been planned.

"It was while these informal discussions were going on from week to week that the challenge came to us suggesting that if we would ask more serious questions we might get information of value to all mankind.

7

A copy of a page from History Two as it was submitted to the Court in behalf of Urantia Foundation by Carolyn Kendall. As a source document, it is instructive. Note that the original number, "8" partially removed at the top. This is because Page "1" (probably stating authorship) was probably removed before submission, and the pages apparently renumbered. Note also the addition of quote marks by the original editor, who was apparently a Contact Commissioner, but not Dr. Sadler. This page is taken from Dr. Sadler's writings, edited to be presented in the third person, and inserted in the history by the individual who prepared it.

INTRODUCTION OF THE FORUM TO THE "CONTACTS"

" The doctor continues his narrative

Presently, I was asked to give a series of talks on "Mental Hygiene," or "Psychic Phenomena." At the beginning of my first talk, I said: *"*With one or two exceptions, all of the psychic phenomena which I have investigated have turned out to be either

Sincerely,

Christy

(Miss) E. L. Christensen
Secretary

ELC:kfm

Attach.

P.S. *We didn't get your note in time to make any changes in the Seventh. Printing but corrections necessary will be made in the Eighth.*

(Above, top) A detail of the page in question. Note that the editor who was preparing this history adds the sentence: "The doctor continues his narrative." It is doubtful Dr. Sadler would have authored a document and edited it in this way. Compare the handwriting with that of Christy's, in a September 4, 1981 document. (See Chapter Nine for the full letter.) Allowing for her advanced age (she would have been 91 at the time) in the lay opinion of the author, the handwriting is remarkably similar.

A third version of the history, again using the same template as Histories One and Two, was prepared by Marian Rowley for Urantia Brotherhood in 1960. The original document can be viewed on the Fellowship website. The cover page citation is very similar to History One. It is logical to conclude that all the histories are exactly what they say they are, narratives prepared by several Urantians and edited by several others. Authorship of History Two, with its "missing" cover page and renumbering, should not be attributed to Dr. Sadler.

HISTORY OF THE URANTIA MOVEMENT

This historical narrative was prepared by a group of Urantia pioneers, assisted by members of the contact commission, and approved for distribution by action of the Executive Committee of the Urantia Brotherhood. 1960

Copyright 1960

by

Urantia Brotherhood

Four members of the Contact Commission, left to right: Emma Louise Christensen, Dr. Lena Sadler, Dr. William Sadler, Bill Sadler, Jr.

Chapter Four

"There is One Peculiar Case I Have Not Yet Been Able to Solve"

"There is one peculiar case I have not yet been able to solve"   65

*S*HORTLY BEFORE THE ENCOUNTER with the "electrifying" personality who spoke through the sleeping subject and claimed to be from another world, Dr. Sadler prepared to give the Forum a series of talks on "Mental Hygiene." Just as he got behind the lectern on Sunday afternoon, a participant asked if the Doctor had any information about a psychic who had advertised in the newspaper and was performing in downtown Chicago at the time. Dr. Sadler replied that he did not, and he added:

"With one or two exceptions, all the psychic phenomena which I have investigated have turned out to be either conscious or unconscious frauds. Some were deliberate frauds — others were those peculiar cases in which the performer was a victim of the deceptions of his own subconscious mind."[1]

Another member of the group spoke up. "What were the exceptions? Doctor, if you have found cases which you have been unable to solve, this would be interesting. Tell us more about them."

"There is one peculiar case I have not yet been able to solve," the Doctor answered. "I am presently working on it." Dr. Sadler then requested that Dr. Lena get some notes she had taken during a recent session with the subject. It should be pointed out that there was no secrecy connected with the case at the time (other than professional respect for the subject's anonymity). The Urantia Papers had not begun to appear.[2]

Dr. Lena Sadler began to read her recent notes to the fascinated group. Later, Dr. Sadler commented about the energetic reaction of the assembly: "The group manifested such an interest in the case that I never did get around to giving any of the mental health talks I had planned." The gathering then began to focus their informal debates on psychic phenomena. These discussions went on for several weeks, and were still in progress when the Sadlers received the momentous challenge from the "electrifying personality," the alleged celestial being who had admonished them to ask more significant questions.[3]

Dr. Sadler elected to tell the Forum about the rather robust provocation that he and Dr. Lena had received at the hands of the purported celestial visitor. He suggested that the members might help formulate the most difficult questions they could think of and bring them back the next Sunday. The members agreed, and in the immediately ensuing discussion it was decided to start out with questions about the origin of the cosmos, Deity, creation, and other such subjects far beyond the present day knowledge of humankind. The following Sunday hundreds of questions were brought in. It took several days to sort and classify these questions, and discard duplicates.[4]

So it was, in December of 1924, that the Sadlers were prepared to present a formidable number of questions in response to the professed celestial challenge. They held these questions in readiness for the next session with the sleeping subject, hoping for an opportunity of "calling the bluff" of the alleged higher intelligences. Dr. Sadler felt he was "loaded for bear," with 181 written queries of rather profound magnitude.[5] The first of these questions were: *"Is there really a God? And, if so, what is he like?"*[6] However, weeks passed by, and nothing happened.

Then, at six a.m. one morning, the telephone rang. It was the wife of the sleeping subject.

"Please come over here, quick!" she said.

"What's happened?" asked Dr. Sadler. "Is he in the sleeping state?"

"He's asleep alright, but that's not it," she replied. "Please get over here, quickly!"

The Sadlers "dressed like volunteer firemen" and rushed to the residence. When they arrived, they were out of breath and full of curiosity.[7]

The subject's wife led them to a desk in the study. She picked up a voluminous handwritten manuscript and handed it to Dr. Sadler. "Where did this come from?" Sadler asked.

"I don't know," the distraught lady said. "He made strange noises in his sleep that awakened me. I then spotted this on his desk."

"Has he been out of bed?" asked Dr. Sadler.

"Not to my knowledge. I don't see how he could have gotten out of bed without my being awakened. And, he's still asleep. I don't see how he could have done it."

The Sadlers began to examine the nearly 500 pages of tightly handwritten text.[8] The manuscript seemed to be addressing the 181 questions that the Sadlers had obtained from the Forum! The astonished Sadlers went into the bedroom. The subject was in a normal sleep at this time, and awakened easily.

"Do you know what you have been doing in your sleep?" asked Dr. Sadler.

"I haven't been doing anything," replied the subject.

"Oh, yes you have! Didn't you write this?" Sadler asked.

"No. I haven't written anything." [9]

Dr. Sadler phoned his office and asked Christy to immediately bring over a grip device that he used to test muscular fatigue. He reasoned that if the subject had actually written the document that night, his arm would show evidence of exhaustion. But when Christy showed up and the gentleman was tested, there was no evidence of fatigue. The Sadlers obtained the permission of the subject and his wife to remove the manuscript and have the pages typed.

The amazing manuscript

It should be noted that events had taken a distinct turn. What had happened was remarkably different from the earlier sessions with the subject "speaking" and Dr. Lena Sadler taking notes. Though what had occurred had further rocked Dr. Sadler's scientific objectivity, he remained resolute that there must be a plausible explanation for what had transpired. Nevertheless, he was losing ground, and he was not a man accustomed to being totally confounded. He had a case that had at first seemed to be ordinary automatic talking, but one that had defied traditional analysis. Now, he was confronting what plainly appeared to be at first blush *automatic writing*. But the analysis of this new phenomena was even more problematic than the primary sessions.

Aside from how the Forum's list of questions were discerned in the first place and the prodigious content of the manuscript,

"There is one peculiar case I have not yet been able to solve" 69

there were other problems. Dr. Sadler estimated that it would take a normal individual writing at top speed seven to eight hours to produce the document. But the content of the material was so profound and intelligent that Dr. Sadler doubted anyone had the capacity to generate the material that quickly. [10]

The doctors had to face another possibility: *that material could have been prepared over a period of weeks or months, and the entire episode could be a hoax.* As scientists, the next obvious step for the Sadlers was to get handwriting experts to verify that the manuscript was written by the subject. If this proved to be the case, there could be no scientific alternative but to conclude that the manuscript was either a product of unconscious automatic writing or it was a deliberate fabrication — regardless of the seeming sincere testimony of the subject and his wife.

Several handwriting experts were employed, and they all agreed that the material was *not* in the handwriting of the sleeping subject. Many years later in Culver, Indiana, Meredith Sprunger had a conversation with Clara Stahl, a CPA and a member of his congregation. Clara told him that years before when she was working in Chicago she went to the Sadlers for medical treatment. She was invited to attend the Forum, which she did. She recalled that handwriting experts had determined the Papers were not in the handwriting of the subject. Not only was the subject tested, his wife was also tested. The handwriting was determined to be of unknown origin. [11]

Mark Kulieke writes on page nine of *Birth of a Revelation*:

> "Although Dr. Sadler refers to written messages of the contact individual in The Mind at Mischief, handwriting experts determined that the written material was not in the handwriting of the human subject or those around him. The contact group speculated on the possibility that the writing was that of a secondary midwayer."

We can reasonably assume the reason why the "contact group" may have speculated that a "secondary midwayer" may have done the physical writing of the Papers. In History Two, on page four, we learn that the Contact Commission's exhaustive efforts, observations and investigations, "utterly failed to reveal the technique of reducing the messages to writing."

The handwriting question

Not all Urantian historians will agree with the assessment that the handwriting in the original text was of unknown origin. While generally believing in the authenticity of the Revelation, some nonetheless believe the text of the Urantia Papers was written in the handwriting of the subject. *However, it is important to note that virtually all agree that the subject was never seen to be writing the text or any messages, and nearly all agree he did not actually do so.* Perhaps the strongest argument in favor of the handwriting being the subject's is based upon an Oklahoma audio tape of Bill Sadler, Jr., dated 2/18/62, in which he answers the question of whether the text was written in pencil:

> *"All written in pencil, yes. All written in the handwriting of this individual, who ruefully remarked: 'If they ever want to draw on my bank account, I — I'm a dead duck because the bank will pay on that signature.'"*

It is unclear what is meant by "that signature." It would be absurd, with their concern for his anonymity, for the Midwayers to sign the name of the sleeping subject to the text! Also, though the comments seem fairly definitive, they should be considered in context with Bill Sadler's remarks earlier in the same tape that establish the fact that *no one ever saw the subject writing.*

> *"Now, during all these years, this particular individual, who is referred to in the book, was never seen to write one of these Papers. And don't think we weren't wearing*

gumshoes looking. If he wrote them, all I can say is he was more clever than the whole lot of us. He was never observed to write them."

Forumite Herman Schell is said to have stated that they even followed the subject to work in an effort to "catch" him writing the text. Even the critical Harold Sherman writes that the subject was asleep in bed with his wife at the time he was supposed to be writing the material.

How, then, were the Papers written? Bill Sadler goes on in this tape to propose a remarkable theory, which we will explore in detail in the next chapter:

"This is the theory I accept. I want you to visualize several points in space. . . we'll call them point A, point B, point C, and point D. I think the Papers were dictated, or conceived, at point A. And I think if we could have been present at point A when any one of these Papers were being written, we would have seen absolutely nothing. At point A was perhaps this Divine Counselor who signs Paper One."

Bill Sadler then digresses to discuss problems in translating the Language of Uversa, the Capital of the superuniverse of Orvonton, into the language of Salvington, (our local universe) and finally into English. Then he continues on with his theory of how the Papers were materialized:

"Now, you'd have something to see at point B, but it would be very dull. It would be a man asleep, some ordinary looking guy, just asleep, doing nothing. Now, if you could get to point C, this would be exciting! You remember the day of the resurrection, the soldiers saw the stone roll away, apparently by itself? Now, that stone was being pushed . . . by Secondary Midwayers who are non-

corporeal beings who can deal with physical substances. At point C, I think you would have seen a very exciting phenomenon, a pencil moving over paper with no visible means of propulsion. That's where the physical writing was consummated." [Note: Point "D", mentioned earlier, was not referred to again on the tape].

Thus, most Urantian scholars agree that the subject *did not write* the Papers, and most agree that the writing was probably done by a Secondary Midwayer. Surely the Midwayers *could have* accomplished the feat of duplicating the sleeping subject's handwriting had they elected to do so. Yet, *to what end?* Not only would this be at odds with their goal of keeping the subject's identity unknown, an intrusion into the human mind to this degree would not be in agreement with the philosophy of the Papers. Secondary Midwayers can penetrate the human mind for purposes of attaining varying degrees of contact with the fragment of God *(called the Thought Adjuster)* that normally indwells each person. (1258 - par. 1) — Thought Adjusters are **"quite alone in their sphere of activity in the mortal mind."** (1190 - par. 2) — Finally, Thought Adjusters make the information from diverse levels of celestial beings *"meaningful"* to human personalities.(425 - par. 1). The Papers state the Thought Adjuster of the human subject was used for materializing the Papers, but nowhere do they state his *human mind* was used. It is fair to conclude that a human's Thought Adjuster — not a human mind — was required for the speculative process we will explore more deeply in the next chapter.

Two additional groups of related factors, plus a philosophical principle, compel the author to the conclusion that the handwritten text of the Urantia Papers was not in the handwriting of the Contact Personality.

[1]. Dr. Sprunger's unequivocal recollections of what Dr. Sadler and Christy said, verified by Clara Stahl, support the

conclusion that the material was not in the subject's handwriting. It should also be recalled that Bill Sadler, Jr. was 16 years of age at the time of the first manuscript's appearance, as documented in Chapter Three. This was about the time he enlisted in the Marines (by lying about his age). He would not actually begin to read the Urantia Papers until later, when he was home on leave from the Marines, as documented earlier. He could not have begun an intense study of the Papers until his enlistment was terminated in 1928, when he was twenty years of age. It is very likely that the testing of the handwriting had taken place quite early in the process, while Bill Sadler was away. Although he may have attended some of the early sessions involving the contact personality, his objective attention and interest at that time may be open to reasonable doubt. Finally, Dr. Sprunger states in an E-mail to me, November 8, 1999:

"Bill Sadler told me that the best guess that he and his father had about who did the handwriting producing the original text was that a Secondary Midwayer did the handwriting."

This statement, in my judgment, fits the accepted premises better than Bill Sadler's contradictory statement on the audio tape.

[2]. Dr. William Sadler was a noted expert on psychic phenomena. He often stated that he and other experts were baffled as to how the Papers were materialized. Had the Papers been in the Contact Personality's handwriting, this would have been compelling *prima-facie* evidence to a scientist that the material had been produced by automatic writing. If any of the text on the Papers had been spoken, it would be, self-evidently, the product of automatic talking. *The doctor categorically declared that no known form of automatic writing, speaking, or psychic methods were ever employed to produce any part of the text of the Urantia Papers, as documented earlier in this book.* Dr. Lena Sadler was presumably in agreement with this assessment, and was persuaded of the authenticity of the Papers long before her husband.

[3]. The philosophical principle of *Ockham's Razor* can be applied. Faced with conflicting analyses of a set of agreed-upon premises, all other things being equal, choose the least complicated alternative.

Why the handwriting issue is important

These concerns about handwriting seem pointless to many people. Dr. Sprunger never tires of saying that it is the message of the Papers that is the important thing, and the Urantia Revelation will not be established in our culture until many people grasp its unrivaled quality.

However, this history is prepared primarily to give readers an opportunity to make informed decisions when weighing the various debates and unresolved issues that revolve around the origin of the Urantia Papers. In the most enlightened of worlds, we would not need a new history to do this. Certainly, no individual's spiritual destiny will hinge upon whether or not they believe the Papers were originally materialized in handwriting of unknown origin. No one will suddenly accept the Urantia Papers based upon the exact date and circumstances under which Dr. Sadler met the sleeping subject. Why then, attempt to establish for new readers and future readers as many facts and reasonable assumptions as possible? *Because it will be virtually impossible to establish the fact for future generations that the Urantia Papers were not simply a product of automatic writing — another channeled work — if it is passively assumed that they were indeed in the handwriting of the sleeping subject.*

We are on a meticulous quest for truth because there are those who, because either they wish to denigrate or control the Papers, are energetically presenting only one side of the issue. In the case of the handwriting, on page 67 of *How to Know What to Believe,* Harold Sherman makes four references within a hundred words or so that declare the document that was produced on that night long ago was in the handwriting of the subject. Yet, in his own narrative, Sherman virtually places the subject in bed sleeping with his wife when the document was written. This paradox may be explained by Sherman's apparent desire to forcefully classify the Urantia Revelation as a common psychic phenomenon of automatic writing. He was very put out about the Urantia Paper's general dismissal of "psychic" phenomena, especially those of communication with the dead and reincarnation. Sherman's handwriting theorem was seized by Martin Gardner and others to help support their attacks on the fidelity of the Urantia Papers, and to establish they were produced by common "psychic" activities, and had human authorship.

If we who believe differently are silent, it lessens the opportunity for readers to make informed evaluations. I came to believe the Revelation long before I discovered much about its origin, as did most of the second generation of readers. Future readers, whether we prefer it or not, may learn of the origins before they have an opportunity to ponder the message. We should strive to see that a reader has enough information to establish informed conclusions. We should also aspire to a quality of analytical thinking about such questions that is *consistent with the philosophy of the Urantia Papers.* In the following chapter we will examine exactly what the Papers *themselves* say about the materialization of the Revelation.

The Forum is read the first Papers

Doctors William and Lena Sadler brought the huge typed manuscript to the Forum meeting of January 18, 1925.[12] The doctor announced to the members that their questions had been answered in amazing detail, and read the first section, or "Paper," to the group. Much later, after the meeting, the members left the building at 533 Diversey Parkway to make their way home. It seems doubtful that many of them grasped the import of what had actually happened on that January night in Chicago. Clyde Bedell, who became as staunch a Urantian as any who has ever lived, could not even recall when the first reading of the Papers took place. And he said, to his knowledge, no one at the time had a clue that they were involved with an epochal revelation.

The process of the Forum

In the ensuing weeks, a pattern developed of reading a section of the manuscript and eliciting questions from the participants in the Forum. The Forum room at Sadler's home contained about fifty folding chairs. At times Forumites filled all of the chairs and spilled into the adjacent hall. Dr. Sadler (or later, Bill Sadler, Jr.) would read a Paper. Members of the Forum would then submit queries in written form, which were collected in a fishbowl or basket and placed on a table at one side of the room. These questions would be sorted, duplicates eliminated, and the relevant ones prepared on a page or two. It is not exactly clear how they were submitted to the Revelators. Helen Carlson, who was in the Forum from 1935 on, described the question and answer process above. She said she thought the questions were then placed in a specific spot, but she was never able to discover where that spot might be.[13]

The Forum was used in a manner that "focus groups" are used in commercial marketing to study general reactions of consumers to products and advertising campaigns. The large turnover of people in the Forum was thus not so significant, since, on the average, a Forum member lasted about two years. Apparently what the celestial revelators were concerned with was general human reaction and understanding of the material that was being presented. By monitoring and evaluating reactions to the reading of the Papers, the unseen Revelators expanded and reworked the material. This process gradually formed a larger, revised manuscript better attuned to the reactions, understanding, and new questions of the Forum members. The initial arrangement was rather informal and continued for nearly eight months after the first Paper was read to the Forum. At that time, Dr. Sadler announced to the members that the Contact Commission had been instructed to make the Forum a closed group.

The Forum becomes official

Members were told they would be required to sign a secrecy pledge. In September of 1925, thirty individuals agreed to sign this pledge and the Forum officially became a closed group. Since turnover continued to be a problem, new members could be accepted, but only after being "interviewed by the officers and signing the same pledge that was signed by the original Charter Members":

> "We acknowledge our pledge of secrecy, reviewing our pledge not to discuss Urantia Revelations or their subject matter with anyone save active Forum members, and to take no notes of such matter as is read or discussed at the public sessions, or make copies or notes of what we personally read."[14]

However, the members of the Contact Commission were the only individuals who ever knew the identity of the sleeping subject. Forum members did not attend the contact sessions.[15] Forum members never saw the original manuscripts, which were kept in a safe.[16] After they had been typed, Dr. Sadler told Dr. Sprunger that the original written manuscripts mysteriously disappeared from the safe. Although he tried to discover the technique that was being used, Sadler was never able to determine how this was accomplished.[17] Dr. Sprunger says that Dr. Sadler told him that early on he tried various tricks to confuse the process and possibly uncover a hoax. Sadler once placed several $10 bills between certain pages of a manuscript before placing it in the safe. The manuscript disappeared and the $10 bills remained. He then placed a manuscript in a bank vault deposit box, rather than his own safe. He said the manuscript somehow disappeared, and he was later admonished that it would be desirable if he discontinued his various "tricks."

The initial question and answer process continued until 1929. We know that Dr. Sadler still harbored reservations about the procedure because of his contemporaneous commentary in *The Mind at Mischief*, but that he also conceded that he was exactly where he had started as far as analyzing the phenomenon that was taking place. The five year process eventually produced 57 Papers, and the final typewritten manuscript consisted of 1700 pages.[18]

During the total procedure, which was to continue in a similar manner for many years, the sleeping subject was the only contact involved.[19]

The entire text of the Urantia Papers was materialized in handwritten form.[20] The text was then typed, checked, and the original handwritten document was placed in a safe. (As explained, these original documents always mysteriously disappeared from the safe.) The Contact Commission had no editorial authority whatsoever. Contact Commissioners were confined to the clerical duties of spelling, capitalization, and punctuation. The Urantia Papers were published in 1955 just as they were received — to the best of human ability to do so. There was absolutely no human input as to authorship, content or arrangement.[21]

There apparently developed informal verbal communications between the Revelators and the Contact Commission, *always* as a group, and *always in the sleeping subject's presence*. These informal verbal communications with the Contact Commission as a group were probably direct, and no longer used the contact

"There is one peculiar case I have not yet been able to solve" 79

personality's vocal cords as an intermediary mechanism for the intercourse.[22] How these new communications were achieved is open to question. However, in my judgement, such verbal communications are not inconsistent with the Urantia Papers in that Secondary Midwayers can affect matter under certain conditions, so they can, theoretically, produce sound waves. Such communications were administrative and *had nothing to do with the text of the Urantia Papers*, which was always materialized in written form by some means not fully understood.

It is also significant that verbal communications took place only under certain conditions. *No less than two Contact Commissioners had to be present for them to take place.*[23] This is distinguished from so-called "channeling" activities because the verbal communications in question were apparently disembodied and were always heard by at least two verifying parties. This verification precluded self-delusion. In the so-called "channeling" process words are supposedly either "heard" by an individual in private or spoken by an individual who alleges them to be coming from a disembodied authoritative entity. Corroboration — in either of these cases — is impossible. Perhaps these observations point to why the original method of verbal communication by means of using the sleeping subject's vocal cords may have eventually been abandoned by the Revelators. At this stage of the contact process — (assuming that direct verbal contact was employed) — perhaps the Contact Commissioners could handle the disembodied voices without undue stress. Even so, this technique may have sown the seeds for future problems in the human mind of one of the Commissioners, as we shall see.

Other administrative communications, *likewise not related to the text*, included more formal instructions to the Contact Commission in written form. Like the text, these written messages were materialized in some unknown manner. Almost all written messages had a directive on the last page reading: *"To be destroyed by fire not later than the appearance of the Urantia Papers in print."* No originals of any kind are known to exist. [24]

Was a sleeping subject necessary?

The reasonably documented and defined facts above raise the question as to not only how, but *why* the sleeping subject was involved with the procedure of materializing the text and written messages, since the evidence indicates he was not writing them. Also, why was he apparently always present (in a sleeping, wholly unconscious state) when verbal group communications between the Contact Commission and the Midwayers took place, since there is at least some indication that his voice was no longer being used? Although we are unsure whether his voice mechanisms continued to be used for some communications, we can be fairly certain that, although the text of the Papers was finished and preparations for printing the book were set in motion in the early Forties *(see Chapter Nine)*, the contact personality was present during all communications until the connection was officially broken in 1955.

Dr. Sprunger surmises that certain strict celestial rules or protocols govern the process by which an epochal revelation can be delivered. This is consistent with what the Papers themselves disclose about epochal revelations on page 1109. In this section the Papers also inform us that epochal revelation is distinct from autorevelation, or the personal revelations that are achieved in a human mind by a Thought Adjuster alone. Epochal revelations are **"presented by the function of some other celestial agency, group, or personality."** On page 1008 we are told that the Urantia Papers **"differ from all previous revelations, for they are not the work of a single universe personality but a composite presentation by many beings."** We can reasonably presume that the seemingly difficult process by which the initial materialization of the Papers was achieved, and the means by

"There is one peculiar case I have not yet been able to solve" 81

which they were edited by celestial beings, may have required the services of a human being's Thought Adjuster. It is possible that celestial protocol may have required a human Thought Adjuster to be present, but we cannot be certain. Of utmost concern to celestial personages in the process of presenting epochal revelation is evidently the ultimate welfare and protection of the mortal evolutionary beings of the planet. For this reason the process is made to be the safest and least intrusive possible.

We do not know how the later sessions were instigated by the Revelators, or what the actual procedures were for the subsequent contacts. It seems clear that the Revelators were directing the mortals. We do not know if the wife of the subject continued to be present during the later contacts.

In considering the process of epochal revelation, there are questions we cannot answer: Was it necessary for Dr. Lena to ask a question before the initial contact could be made through the sleeping subject? Why did it seem necessary to solicit deeply thought-out inquiries from the Forum members before addressing topics? Also, much speculation and apocrypha has developed around the method of materializing the Papers. In an ideal world, these questions would not arise, the message of the Papers alone should speak for their authenticity. This was the original hope of Dr. Sadler:

> "There are only a few of us still living who were in touch
> with this phenomenon in the beginning, and when we die,
> the knowledge of it will die with us. Then the Book will
> exist as a great spiritual mystery, and no human will know
> the manner in which it came about."[25]

The irony of this purported statement is that it was made just after Dr. Sadler had revealed a vast amount of information to two journalists (the Shermans) about the origin of the Urantia Papers. Human nature being what it is, a mass of misinformation and apocrypha about the Papers has emerged, especially in recent years. The risk is one of developing a cult around *The Urantia Book* itself, a virtual "religion" about the Book — to the exclusion of its message and teachings. Perhaps the most unsavory idea that has come forward is that the Contact Commissioners had secret powers and special spiritual status. People love stories of this nature. In his various writings, Mark Kulieke seems to be of two minds about this. But in his second edition of *Birth of a Revelation,* he makes a definitive and important observation on page 11:

> "Probably one factor or perspective that is often overlooked is the fact that not only Dr. Sadler, but all of the Contact Commission were not given [sic] to mystical or extra-sensory experiences. While they lived and witnessed some highly unusual occurrences spanning half a century, they did not actively solicit these experiences. They could never initiate the contact experiences nor do aught to enhance the likelihood of a contact. Indeed, they spent much of their time being dubious about the whole procedure. All of the impetus and control was in the hands of the superhumans. The Contact Commission were [sic] unable to cultivate anything unusual — but were essentially passive recipients of this highly unusual project. They had their active roles, but their activities were human and ordinary, not mystical. And they remained skeptical of all things occult or unusual. They experienced a unique transaction of epochal revelation but did not interest themselves in many episodes of personal revelation (many of them also genuine or partly genuine) which continuously abound all around us."

"We are going through the book again"

Sometime in 1929, it appeared the project was nearing completion. But then the Forum was sent a new direct written message through the Contact Commission:

> "With your increased understanding derived from reading and study of the material, you can now ask more intelligent questions. We are going to go through the book again."[26]

So, circa 1929-1930, the group commenced a re-reading of the formidable manuscript.

ENDNOTES

1. HISTORY OF THE URANTIA MOVEMENT TWO - [Compiled by a Contact Commissioner, Undated] page 7.

2. IBID., page 7.

3. IBID., page 7.

4. IBID., page 8.

5. The PLAN FOR *THE URANTIA BOOK* REVELATION, by Carolyn B. Kendall, Paper distributed January 18, 1996, page 1. Ms. Kendall is the daughter of Forum member Clarence N. Bowman, and was employed as a receptionist at the age of 19 by Dr. Sadler, and worked from 1952 to 1954 and in 1957. She has held many offices in the Urantia Brotherhood. Her husband, Thomas A. Kendall was a trustee of Urantia Foundation 1963-1983, and its President 1973-1983.

6. Meredith J. Sprunger, personal disclosure. He told me that Dr. Sadler disclosed this information to him.

7. HOW TO KNOW WHAT TO BELIEVE, by Harold Sherman, Fawcett, New York, 1976, pp. 66-67.

8. IBID., page 67. Sherman gives the number of pages of the manuscript as 472.

9. IBID.

10. IBID.

11. THE HISTORICITY OF *THE URANTIA BOOK* by Meredith J. Sprunger, page 5. Also, Dr. Sprunger disclosed this in video interviews with the author, taped by Eric Cosh the CEO of Paradigm Productions, Phoenix, AZ.

12. The PLAN FOR *THE URANTIA BOOK* REVELATION, by Carolyn B. Kendall, Paper distributed January 18, 1996, page 1.

13. Sworn deposition of Helen Carlson, Chicago, June 29, 1994.

14. HISTORY OF THE URANTIA MOVEMENT TWO - [Compiled by a Contact Commissioner, Undated] page 9. The reference in the History: "after being interviewed by the officers" is not clear. The reference may be to the Contact Commission, since there is not any record of actual "officers." Clyde Bedell told me he was interviewed by Dr. Sadler.

15. HISTORY OF THE URANTIA MOVEMENT TWO - [Compiled by a Contact Commissioner, Undated] page 9.

16. THE HISTORICITY OF *THE URANTIA BOOK* by Meredith J. Sprunger, page 5.

17. Meredith Sprunger, telephone conversation with the author October 16, 1999.

18. The PLAN FOR *THE URANTIA BOOK* REVELATION, by Carolyn B. Kendall, Paper distributed January 18, 1996, page 1.

19. HISTORY OF THE URANTIA MOVEMENT ONE, "by a Group of Urantian Pioneers, assisted by Members of the Contact Commission, 1960", page 6.

20. THE HISTORICITY OF *THE URANTIA BOOK* by Meredith J. Sprunger, page 5. –also- BIRTH OF A REVELATION by Mark Kulieke, second edition, 1992, page 14. Also see Chapter Six of this book.

21. HISTORY of the URANTIA MOVEMENT TWO - [Compiled by a Contact Commissioner, Undated] page 24. Also see sworn affidavit of Meredith J. Sprunger, October 24, 1998, (pp 315 -320). Also, in a nearly decade-long litigation, Kristen Maaherra marshalled and documented compelling previous sworn testimony by Contact Commission members and Urantia Foundation officers to support this issue. This testimony established legally uncontested facts. See Chapter 7, Note 20 for additional information on this testimony.

22. Meredith Sprunger has disclosed in taped interviews that, by some means, the Contact Commission was once allowed to "listen in" on a celebration of the Midwayers when they received permission to materialize Part IV, *The Life and Teachings of Jesus.* (See Chapter Six, page 115). Obviously the technique to do this transcended using the vocal mechanism of the sleeping subject. Bill Sadler, Jr. maintained that once the Papers started coming through there "was not much interaction with the 'sleeping subject'."Fellowship website: (archive/history/h_timlin_2.htm, May 19,1999). However they may have been received, Christy evidently took notes of all administrative verbal

"There is one peculiar case I have not yet been able to solve"   85

contacts with the revelators after she joined the Contact Commission, and is probably the "stenographer" referred to in *The Mind at Mischief*.

23. The Urantia Book Fellowship Website discloses in its timeline that: "Guidelines established by the revelatory commission" required that at least two contact commissioners were to be present when any verbal communications were taking place. David Kantor discloses he received this information from Christy and Carolyn Kendall. Meredith Sprunger told me that all contacts he knew about had at least two Commissioners present. The website also discloses that Contact Commissioners were required to "leave the room" if any physical objects were required to be moved or manipulated by the unseen Midwayers. It was divulged to the Commission that witnessing such effects would be too "psychologically disturbing" for the mortal observers. It should be noted that the establishment of these "guidelines" signalled the formal engagement of the unseen "Revelatory Commission." Up to this point all contacts had been with Midwayers and "student visitors." The actual transmission of revelatory material ended in May, 1942. The celestial Revelatory Commission was replaced in 1954 by a "Midwayer Commission." See Chapter Seven.

24. HISTORY of the URANTIA MOVEMENT TWO - [Compiled by a Contact Commissioner, Undated] page 21.

25. HOW TO KNOW WHAT TO BELIEVE, by Harold Sherman, Fawcett, New York, 1976, page 69.

26. BIRTH OF A REVELATION by Mark Kulieke, Second Edition, 1992, page 14.

Chapter Five
"We Were Introduced to Many New, And to Us, Somewhat Strange Concepts"

"We Were Introduced to Many New and Somewhat Strange Concepts" 87

A T THIS POINT WE SHOULD PAUSE for a tactical re-assessment of the material we have covered. We have described a process that was set into motion over a period of about twenty-five years — a process that is remarkably profound in its implications. Any thinking person must wonder if the events just described could have really happened. Possibly only a long-time reader of the Urantia Papers could be quickly convinced that the events that I have pieced together and depicted here actually occurred.

The Urantia Papers are the best testimony of their own validity. Virtually anyone who studies them with care and an open mind must be persuaded that they are, at the very least, a unique presentation of who we are, where we came from, and where we are going. For this reason, those of us who believe in the authenticity of the Urantia Papers might tend to be credulous about any plausible, consistent and documented story that would account for their depth and scope. In fact, we hunger for the details of how this life-changing volume came to be.

However, new readers may be quickly lost as the narrative unfolds if we do not explain that Dr. Sadler and those involved in the early sessions with the sleeping subject were also very perplexed by the concepts being presented to them. There is a section of History Two which is titled: *"Contact Activities Preceding the Urantia Papers."* It consists of three pages, and appears to have been written by Dr. Sadler and inserted in the document.[1] In contrast to many other parts of History Two, the style and content of these pages are consistent with Dr. Sadler's writing. If we grant that Dr. Sadler wrote them, he explains that the period between the first contact and the beginning of the Urantia Papers was a period of preparation and testing. He goes on to point out some of the new concepts that were presented during the preparation stage. He also states, speaking of the Contact Commission:

> "We never realized how much our religious thinking had expanded until the Papers began to arrive. As the revelation progressed we came to more fully appreciate how much we had been prepared for the vast alteration of our religious beliefs by these preliminary contacts extending over a period of twenty years of pre-education."[2]

These three pages explain a twenty-year process of pre-education that took place "until the Papers began to arrive." This "pre-education" reference could only apply to the original four Contact Commissioners, although some historians have erroneously applied it to the Forum. As we shall see, the twenty-year pre-education period referred only to four of the members of the Contact Commission, and not at all to the Forum members.

Veteran readers of the Urantia Papers sometimes forget the immense paradigm shifts that took place in their own thinking after reading the Revelation. We sometimes refer to new concepts and thoughtlessly use words such as "Midwayers," "Thought Adjusters" and "morontial" to the confusion of new readers. We know Dr. Sadler was an ordained minister and a profoundly religious man. The pre-Urantia Paper sessions contained scientific

"We Were Introduced to Many New and Somewhat Strange Concepts" 89

and religious material that had considerable impact on him. To truly have some understanding of this, and to assist new readers, let's review the 16 "pre-education" initiatives the Revelators introduced to the early Contact Commission — before the Forum came into being. These early presentations seem to have been intended to prepare the small group of mortals for even more advanced concepts. Comments in brackets were added by myself, otherwise this material is as the Contact Commissioner presented it on pages 11, 12, and 13 of History Two: *"Among these numerous new ideas of cosmology and philosophy, the following may be mentioned:*

"[1]. The new concept of a vast, far-flung universe." [The cosmos of the Urantia Papers exceeds anything yet postulated by science. At the time the universe was not known to be expanding. The Revelation tells us it is expanding according to a regular respiration, every one billion years it "exhales" and then "inhales" for an equal period. This notion challenges the "Big Bang" and supports the less-favored "Occilating Universe" notion, which addresses the unanswered Big Bang scientific puzzle as to why the universe expands at precisely the rate to keep it from either flying apart or imploding.]

"[2]. Billions of other inhabited worlds.

"[3]. Introduction to the concept of scores of different and varied echelons of Universe personalities.

"[4]. Confirmation of the scientific belief in the evolutionary origin of humankind, even of an evolutionary cosmos.

"[5]. Initiation of multiple Creator Deities." [The philosophy of the Urantia Papers is purely and consistently monotheistic. However, while there is only one First

Source and Center and one God, or Father of the Universe, the Father distributes himself and delegates Creator prerogatives to lesser Divine Beings of his creation.]

"[6]. Tentative testing of our theologic concepts. Patient determination of how far we might go in the direction of modifying our theologic beliefs and philosophic opinions.

"[7]. Without realizing it, over a period of twenty years, our fundamental religious views and attitudes had been considerably changed.

"[8]. We had been familiarized with such terms as the First Source and Center, Havona," [The central universe complex of seven circuits of a billion perfect worlds plus three circuits of Paradise spheres] *"superuniverses, and the Supreme Being"* [The evolutionary aspect of God that adventures and evolves into perfection with evolutionary beings. This concept has been postulated by modern theologians, but not presented in association with an all-knowing God] *"although we had but meager ideas as to the real meaning of these terms."*

"[9]. We also heard such words as Master Spirits, outer space, and Power Directors. But again, we understood little as to their meaning. We also learned about numerous orders of angels.

"[10]. We also heard about Thought Adjusters, but our concept of the meaning of the term was vague and indefinite." [A Thought Adjuster is the Fragment of God that is bestowed upon each normal human mind at the moment moral consciousness is achieved, and impinges upon the superconscious levels of thought. The sleeping subject's Thought Adjuster played a key role in the

materialization of the Urantia Papers, but the human mind of the subject was not used, as we shall see.]

"[11]. We had acquired a fuzzy concept of the morontia level of existence — but we never heard the word 'morontia' until the Papers started." [The morontia level of existence is the intervening area between material and spiritual. It is to be classified as neither material nor spiritual, yet containing aspects of both. The human soul is a morontia creation that is born during our life in the flesh.]

"[12]. The Midwayers were very real to us — we frequently talked with them during our 'contacts.' We quite fully understood that Secondary Midwayers supervised these contacts." [As we shall see, the Secondary Midwayers played a key role in the materialization of the Urantia Papers. Both Primary and Secondary Midwayers are a form of celestial being just beyond the scope of human vision. They are permanent residents of our planet during its evolutionary struggle. Secondary Midwayers are immensely versatile, mobile and intelligent, and are able, under certain conditions, to manipulate matter. They can penetrate the human mind in order to communicate with a mortal's Thought Adjuster.]

"[13]. We heard about things like the Lucifer rebellion, but got little information about Adam and Eve.

"[14]. We gained the impression that there were special reasons for Jesus' bestowal but we had little or no idea as to the nature of these unrevealed reasons.

"[15]. We listened to occasional references to Jesus' life and teachings — but they were very cautious about the introduction of any new concepts regarding Michael's Urantia Bestowal." [Jesus was the human name given to

92 A HISTORY OF THE URANTIA PAPERS *Chapter Five*

our Creator Son, Michael of Nebadon, during his bestowal mission to our planet.] *"Of all the Urantia Revelation, the Jesus Papers were the biggest surprise."*

"[16]. While we did not hear the term 'Corps of Finality' we did pick up a hazy idea that Paradise might be the destination of surviving mortals.

"Our superhuman friends thus spent upward of two decades in extending our cosmic horizons, enlarging our theologic concepts, and expanding our over-all philosophy."

This preliminary education was evidently designed for the Contact Commission and took place before the first Urantia Papers began arriving — *"in fact, in a general way, setting the stage for the subsequent initiation of the presentation of the Urantia Papers."*[3] We can be reasonably certain the first Paper was read to the Forum in January of 1925, as previously noted. Therefore, in pages 11, 12, and 13 of History Two we are probably reading the words of either Drs. William or Lena Sadler, or one of the Kelloggs. The most logical choice is Dr. Sadler, whose words were inserted at certain times in History Two by the Contact Commissioner who assembled that document. The hybrid nature of History Two is likely totally innocent, and reflects the desire of the anonymous author that the History not be associated with any individual Commissioner.

In addition, we may reasonably conclude that the entire Contact Commission was not provided this pre-education. Only Dr. Sadler, Dr. Lena Sadler, Wilfred Kellogg and Anna Kellogg could have received the "twenty years of pre-education." Emma L. Christensen ("Christy") did not come to the Sadler household until December of 1923, just over a year before the first Paper was read to the Forum.[4] Bill Sadler, Jr. was not quite 16 in January of 1925. He was doubtless a precocious lad, and may have had some exposure to the early contact process, but it is self-evident that he could not have undergone "twenty years of pre-education" before he was 16.

"We Were Introduced to Many New and Somewhat Strange Concepts" 93

These facts become important as we evaluate information about the history of the Revelation and the sources that are available to us. Dr. Lena Sadler died August 1, 1939, at the age of 64. Wilfred C. Kellogg died August 31, 1956, at the age of 75 - less than a year after the publication of *The Urantia Book*. Anna Bell Kellogg died February 24, 1960 at the age of 82.5 So, by early 1960, the only living Contact Commissioner who had the actual experience of the nearly two decades that preceded the first appearance of the Urantia Papers was Dr. Sadler. And, since (to my knowledge) neither Dr. Lena Sadler nor the Kelloggs left any writings or testimony regarding the revelation, Dr. Sadler's writings, statements and recollections of the early events are thus of great importance.

More about the early contacts – and Jesus

Among other duties, the unseen Midwayers monitor the nonmaterial, unseen activities of the spiritual realm on our planet.

"Midwayers are the guardians, the sentinels, of the worlds of space. They perform the important duties of observers for all the numerous phenomena and types of communication which are of import to the supernatural beings of the realm. They patrol the invisible spirit realm of the planet." [864 bottom, 865 top.]

Midwayers apparently were present at every contact. Evidently, there was a specific commission of Midwayers who were assigned to the Urantia revelation project. Other than these Midwayers, no two contacts were alike; every contact was entirely different from any and all that had gone before. Seldom did the original team of four Contact Commissioners meet the same visiting personality more than once. The Commission was thus provided an extensive and liberal preparatory educational training.6

Jesus is mentioned in *the Urantia Book* as early as page 30, and 19 additional times before we reach page 100. In addition, Michael is mentioned on page 8 as *"Christ Michael — Son of Man and Son of God,"* and 16 additional times before page 100. There are continuing references to him and his career throughout the Papers.

In the early contacts, before the Papers began to come through, there was a limited amount of discussion about the life and teachings of Jesus. Dr. Sadler speculated that the Midwayers may have been a bit *"dubious about their authority in such matters."* He may have based this possibility on the fact that, much later in the presentations of the Papers, the Revelatory team of Midwayers was said to have sought higher authorities to give clarification of their right to tell the enlarged and expanded story of Jesus of Nazareth and his matchless teachings.[7]

Once more it should be noted that Dr. Sadler long believed he would find a scientific explanation to what was occurring. Even during the early Forum period of 1924-1935, he sought to remain objective, and only provisionally accepted the validity of the content of the Urantia Papers. He wrote of the early contacts:

> **"Those of us who attended these nocturnal vigils never suspected that we were in contact with anything supernatural."** [8]

The materialization process

Along with the name of the contact personality, what little the Contact Commissioners knew of the technique of materialization was not to be discussed. However, both Dr. Sadler and Bill Sadler, Jr. could not resist speculating on the materialization technique of this epochal revelation. They may have been challenged by the philosophical difficulty in postulating that spiritual beings can simply communicate at will with humans. The

*Young Emma
Louise Christensen
(Christy)*

*Anna Bell Kellogg
and Wilfred Custer Kellogg,
June, 1942*

intervening "distance" between the realms of matter and spirit is vast. We are told in the Urantia Papers that:

"The gap between the material and spiritual worlds is perfectly bridged by the serial association of mortal man, secondary midwayer, primary midwayer, morontia cherubim, mid-phase cherubim, and seraphim. In the personal experience of an individual mortal these diverse levels are undoubtedly more or less unified and made personally meaningful by the unobserved and mysterious operations of the divine Thought Adjuster." [425, par. 1]

and that:

" . . . since each order of midwayer can establish perfect synchrony of contact with the other, either group is thereby able to achieve practical utilization of the entire energy gamut extending from the gross physical power of the material worlds up through the transition phases of universe energies to the higher spirit-reality forces of the celestial realms." [424 bottom, 425 top.]

A complete study of the possible method of materializing the Urantia Papers is beyond the scope of this book. Interested readers are invited to examine the figures at the end of this chapter, and check the references suggested.

Three final points should be made. From my perspective as a layperson, presenting the Urantia Papers in the English language was an unimaginably formidable task. They are in large part what we would call a "translation" from another language, in some cases, two other languages. In some instances a Paper had to be translated from the complex language of Uversa, which is the capital of our superuniverse of Orvonton, to that of the Local Universe of Nebadon, and finally into the linguistic and conceptual patterns of the English language. Some readers love the dialogues and conversations of Part IV because they say they contain the "actual words of Jesus." Yet, although Jesus spoke several languages, none of them was modern English. All of the previously undisclosed dialogues and conversations had to be "translated," so to speak, from their original languages and recorded in some form of symbolic imagery by the Midwayers. In a 1959 letter to Dr. Adams, Dr. Sadler disclosed:

"You must remember that the midwayers prepared a narrative that was many times larger than was finally given us as Part IV of the Urantia Book." [See Appendix B]

From this statement it seems Dr. Sadler had been informed that a preliminary "editing" process by the Midwayers took place before the materialization of the restatement of the Life and Teachings of Jesus. The Midwayers were required to use human sources when they were available, supplement and correct these with revelatory information, and then materialize the result in a seamless presentation in contemporaneous English. In addition, the Midwayers calculated dates of events during the life of Jesus to interface with a modern calendar and established the exact times of day (based upon modern chronology) for many events that had happened when no method of precise recording of time had yet been invented. Thus, in my lay opinion, we should keep in mind that the process of materializing the Papers in the English language was one of remarkable complexity.

The second point is: The Urantia Papers made use of a great amount of existing human concepts and written material. The Papers freely and clearly proclaim this in several places. Yet, to some readers, this is very disturbing. They reason that a revelation should present only new material. But this is an over-simplification of the process and purpose of an epochal revelation. The technique of epochal revelation includes synthesizing existing concepts and knowledge, recovering that which might be otherwise lost, and using new concepts and ideas only when necessary to perform the primary mission. The purpose of epochal revelation is to expand the spiritual meaning and universe implications of existing knowledge and concepts — which in the case of the Urantia Papers required introducing a wealth of new concepts and previously unknown universe data.

Contrasted with epochal revelation is a phenomenon the Urantia Papers describe as *autorevelation.* [1109 par. 4] Auto-revelation is the result of the Thought Adjuster's activity in the human mind, and produces many inspiring and wonderful things, although too often otherwise "inspired" material is skewed as a result of its passage through the mortal mind. Epochal revelation, on the other hand, involves the activities of celestial personages.

"The proof that revelation is revelation is this same fact of human experience: the fact that revelation does synthesize the apparently divergent sciences of nature and the theology of religion into a consistent and logical universe philosophy, a co-ordinated and unbroken explanation of both science and religion, thus creating a harmony of mind and satisfaction of spirit which answers in human experience those questionings of the mortal mind which craves to know *how* the Infinite works out his will and plans in matter, with minds, and on spirit." [1106, top.]

Epochal Revelation and existing human knowledge

To synthesize science, religion and philosophy, celestial authors of epochal revelation must draw upon, and harmonize, widely divergent existing human concepts. Matthew Block, one of a growing number of Urantian researchers, has been assembling human source documents and writings that were apparently utilized by the Revelators as raw material for the synthesizing process. The task of the Revelators is apparently to reach the evolutionary mortal mind where it is, and to then skillfully offer new information to expand humankind's grasp of universe meanings and values. Matthew shows us how ingeniously new ideas and concepts are interfaced with existing human concepts by the Revelators. His project is a work in progress which will yield important information that will require a great deal of study to fully understand and adequately evaluate. The problem is, as important as this work is, simply reducing the Urantia Papers to the component parts will not necessarily reveal their true nature — no more than a human mind can be truly understood by devising a purely reductionist analysis down to molecules and atoms.

David Kantor is a highly regarded scholar and historian, and a member of the Executive Committee of the General Council of the *The Urantia Book Fellowship*. David made this observation:

"The real mechanism for assembling the Revelation on a conceptual level has yet to be discovered and described by scholars. I think Matthew's work is a start. I am reminded of the quote on page 1105: **'(Religion) consists not in the discovery of new facts or in the finding of a unique experience, but rather in the discovery of new and spiritual *meanings* in facts already well known to mankind.'** The 'source materials' being discovered and evaluated by Matthew Block and others indicate that the Revelators not only used the linguistic constructs of the English language to communicate with us, but they used the 'conceptual' vocabulary reflected in the best of our religious, philosophic and scientific writing as well. These studies are still in a very early stage of development but will likely change our understanding of the origins of the Urantia Papers in profound and fundamental ways."

Kristen Maaherra has probably studied the human sources of the Urantia Papers and their structure as intensely as anyone. She has uncovered many fascinating clues, including the use of what she calls "once words" (words that are only included once in the million words of the text), hyphenated words, italicized words, and other elements that relate somehow to the immensely complex and baffling whole. The work on the structure and conceptual methods that produced the Papers goes on, and will doubtless continue for many years into the future.

However, I suspect that no logical argument could convince a closed-minded doubter that the synthesis of new information with existing information is precisely one of the goals that the Urantia Papers tell us epochal revelation seeks to achieve. For the new reader, I will give one example of this process and let each individual decide. There is a passage in the Urantia Papers that is said to be a virtual paraphrased version of a message by Bertrand Russell, purportedly delivered to a college graduating class before the Urantia Papers were published. It is ponderous, negative, and seems to ring of typical intellectual existential orientation:

"To the unbelieving materialist, man is simply an evolutionary accident. His hopes of survival are strung on a figment of mortal imagination; his fears, loves, longings, and beliefs are but the reaction of the incidental juxtaposition of certain lifeless atoms of matter. No display of energy nor expression of trust can carry him beyond the grave. The devotional labors and inspirational genius of the best of men are doomed to be extinguished by death, the long and lonely night of eternal oblivion and soul extinction. Nameless despair is man's only reward for living and toiling under the temporal sun of mortal existence. Each day of life slowly and surely tightens the grasp of a pitiless doom which a hostile and relentless universe of matter has decreed

"We Were Introduced to Many New and Somewhat Strange Concepts"   101

shall be the crowning insult to everything in human desire which is beautiful, noble, lofty, and good." [1118, par. 1]

Now consider the positive counter-argument that appears in the Urantia Papers on the page prior to the comments above. This rebuttal may be from some human writing that has been long lost to us, and is being restored to us by the Revelators. Or, as I believe at this point, it may be completely original and wonderfully inspired. In any case, it could hardly be more appropriate:

"[True] Religion assures man that, in following the gleam of righteousness discernible in his soul, he is thereby identifying himself with the plan of the Infinite and the purpose of the Eternal. Such a liberated soul immediately begins to feel at home in this new universe, his universe.

"When you experience such a transformation of faith, you are no longer a slavish part of the mathematical cosmos but rather a liberated volitional son of the Universal Father. No longer is such a liberated son fighting alone against the inexorable doom of the termination of temporal existence; no longer does he combat all nature, with the odds hopelessly against him; no longer is he staggered by the paralyzing fear that, perchance, he has put his trust in a hopeless phantasm or pinned his faith to a fanciful error.

"Now, rather, are the sons of God enlisted together in fighting the battle of reality's triumph over the partial shadows of existence. At last all creatures become conscious of the fact that God and all the divine hosts of a well-nigh limitless universe are on their side in the supernal struggle to attain eternity of life and divinity of status. Such faith-liberated sons have certainly enlisted

in the struggles of time on the side of the supreme forces and divine personalities of eternity; even the stars in their courses are now doing battle for them; at last they gaze upon the universe from within, from God's viewpoint, and all is transformed from the uncertainties of material isolation to the sureties of eternal spiritual progression. Even time itself becomes but the shadow of eternity cast by Paradise realities upon the moving panoply of space." [1117, par. 1-3]

This is revelation, and it speaks for itself beyond any rhetoric or argument I could add. One grasps this or one does not. This is but one example among countless others of the power of the Revelation to transcend the common parameters of human creative thought. For myself and other Urantians who have experienced the Urantia Papers for many years, and who have long enjoyed the spiritual richness and challenging insights of the Revelation, there is simply no room to doubt its authenticity.

The third and final point is this: It cannot be over-emphasized that the Thought Adjuster of the human subject was necessary for this process to work, *but not the human mind itself.* The Thought Adjuster's activities do impinge upon the superconscious levels of the human mind, but do so (with rare exceptions) without the conscious awareness of the human subject.

The Thought Adjuster of the sleeping subject — along with the Secondary Midwayers — were the final links in the complex materialization process of this epochal revelation and its insertion into the evolutionary mainstream. On evolutionary worlds, Thought Adjusters are always associated with a human host under these revelational circumstances. Thus, the sleeping subject was a necessary (though indirect) component in the intricate chain of procedures.

Why so complex a methodology? Most theologians would agree with Chapter Four's premise that certain rules seem to govern the way revelation is presented upon the planet. Angels are not permitted to "miraculously" plunk down a revelation into the laps of mortal beings. When Clyde Bedell handed me my first Urantia Book in 1968, he informed me it had been authored by celestial beings and no one knew exactly how it came about. This was a major turn-off for me, until he added: *But that is the worst reason to believe anything. Read it, and see if it resonates with you. Evaluate this book solely on its content.*

It could be argued that the personality of Jesus of Nazareth, whose life and teachings were also an epochal revelation, was in effect "plunked down" by means of his bestowal birth upon our planet. But note that Jesus could have won the world easily by simply exercising his seeming miraculous powers fully. He could have simply "walked on air" over the Temple had he chosen to do so, and overwhelmed the doubts of virtually every civilized mortal on the planet. But such works and wonders also would have been the least noble reason to believe in the Master, and Jesus never tired of teaching this principle to the apostles. Apparent miracles have compelling appeal to the immature personality, but they do not eliminate the need for personal spiritual progress. We each must work for our spiritual bread, just as we work for our material bread.

How were the Urantia Papers materialized? No one knows. On the next few pages we present some references from the Urantia Papers and additional speculations related to the question of materialization. Philosophers who oppose the concept of revelation have long pointed out the problems associated with how the spiritual realm could interface with the material realm. Perhaps the most interesting thing about the clues provided in the Urantia Papers is the fact that this question, which very few people know exists, is addressed so completely. The idea of an intervening morontia realm that blends material and spiritual and interfaces with both realms, is unique to the Urantia Papers.

In the next chapter the Jesus Papers arrive as we resume the historical events and sequences by which the Urantia Papers were materialized.

ENDNOTES

1. Dr. Sadler is known to have begun, but never completed, a history of his own. These pages may be from that document. It is possible Dr. Sadler delegated the history project to Christy.

2. HISTORY TWO, [prepared by a Contact Commissioner], undated, pages 2-4. Note that a "twenty year pre-education process" would set the date for the first contact all the way back to 1904-5. This of course would support the belief that the process began much earlier than Dr. Sadler stated in *The Mind at Mischief*.

3. HISTORY TWO, [prepared by a Contact Commissioner], undated, page 2.

4. URANTIA BROTHERHOOD BULLETIN, Special Memorial Issue, Spring 1982, page 1.

5. URANTIA, THE GREAT CULT MYSTERY by Martin Gardner was the source for the exact dates of death of the various Commissioners. Gardner is a good researcher of factual material such as dates. However, Gardner's book is, in the author's opinion, non-objective, inconsistent, relies upon mixed premises, and is bluntly prejudiced against the Revelation. Any religious belief could be attacked and ridiculed by means of the unfortunate techniques Mr. Gardner used to attack the Urantia Papers. Also see Chapter Seven, endnote 4.

6. HISTORY TWO, [prepared by a Contact Commissioner], undated, page 4.

7. IBID., page 4.

8. IBID., page 4.

What the Urantia Papers Say About . . .

How They Were Materialized
in the English Language

"The gap between the material and spiritual worlds is perfectly bridged by the serial material association of mortal man, secondary midwayer, primary midwayer, morontia cherubim, mid-phase cherubim, and seraphim." [page 425, par. 1]

"Midwayers vary greatly in their abilities to make contact with the seraphim above and with their human cousins below. It is exceedingly difficult, for instance, for the primary midwayers to make direct contact with material agencies. They are considerably nearer the angelic type of being and are therefore usually assigned to working with, and ministering to, the spiritual forces resident on the planet. They act as companions and guides for celestial visitors and student sojourners, whereas the secondary creatures are almost exclusively attached to the ministry of the material beings of the realm." [page 865, par. 3]

"The 1,111 loyal secondary midwayers are engaged in important missions on earth. As compared with their primary associates, they are decidedly material. They exist just outside the range of mortal vision and possess sufficient latitude of adaptation to make, at will, physical contact with what humans call 'material things.' These unique creatures have certain definite powers over the things of time and space, not excepting the beasts of the realm." [page 865, par. 4]

"When assigned to a planet, cherubim enter the local courses of training, including a study of planetary usages and languages. The ministering spirits of time are all bilingual, speaking the language of the local universe of their origin and that of their native superuniverse. By study in the schools of the realms they acquire additional tongues." [page 422, par. 5]

"Cherubim and sanobim are by nature very near the morontia level of existence, and they prove to be most efficient in the borderland work of the physical, morontial, and spiritual domains. These children of the local universe Mother Spirit are characterized by "fourth creatures" much as are the Havona Servitals and the conciliating commissions. Every fourth cherubim and every fourth sanobim are quasi-material, very definitely resembling the morontia level of existence." [page 422 - par.6]

"One of the most important things a destiny guardian [Seraphim] does for her mortal subject is to effect a personal co-ordination of the numerous impersonal spirit influences which indwell, surround, and impinge upon the mind and soul of the evolving material creature." [page 1244, par. 2]

"In the minds of the mortals of Urantia--that being the name of your world--there exists great confusion respecting the meaning of such terms as God, divinity, and deity. Human beings are still more confused and uncertain about the relationships of the divine personalities designated by these numerous appellations. Because of this conceptual poverty associated with so much ideational confusion, I have been directed to formulate this introductory statement in explanation of the meanings which should be attached to certain word symbols as they may be hereinafter used in those papers which the Orvonton corps of truth revealers have been authorized to translate into the English language of Urantia." [page 1, par. 1]

"These triune rulers of the major sectors are peculiarly perfect in the mastery of administrative details, hence their name--Perfections of Days. In recording the names of these beings of the spiritual world, we are confronted with the problem of translating into your tongue, and very often it is exceedingly difficult to render a satisfactory translation. We dislike to use arbitrary designations which would be meaningless to you; hence we often find it difficult to choose a suitable name, one which will be clear to you and at the same time be somewhat representative of the original." [page 210, par 6]

"Each superuniverse has its own language, a tongue spoken by its personalities and prevailing throughout its sectors. This is known as the tongue of Uversa in our superuniverse. Each local universe also has its own language. All of the higher orders of Nebadon are bilingual, speaking both the language of Nebadon and the tongue of Uversa." [page 503 , par. 3]

"The ability to translate thought into language in the morontia and spirit spheres is beyond mortal comprehension. Our rate of reducing thought to a permanent record can be so speeded up by the expert recorders that the equivalent of over half a million words, or thought symbols, can be registered in one minute of Urantia time. These universe languages are far more replete than the speech of the evolving worlds. The concept symbols of Uversa embrace more than a billion characters, although the basic alphabet contains only seventy symbols. The language of Nebadon is not quite so elaborate, the basic symbols, or alphabet, being forty-eight in number." [page 503, par. 4]

"Acting as interpreters for the seraphic guardians and the finaliters are the exalted and liberated midway creatures." [page 627, par. 6]

> **NOTE:** *The technique of materializing the Urantia Papers into the English language involved the help of all the above mentioned personalities, together with the Thought Adjuster of the sleeping subject:*

"Apart from possible co-ordination with other Deity fragments, the Adjusters are quite alone in their sphere of activity in the mortal mind. The Mystery Monitors eloquently bespeak the fact that, though the Father may have apparently resigned the exercise of all direct personal power and authority throughout the grand universe, notwithstanding this act of abnegation in behalf of the Supreme Creator children of the Paradise Deities, the Father has certainly reserved to himself the unchallengeable right to be present in the minds and souls of his evolving creatures to the end that he may so act as to draw all creature creation to himself, co-ordinately with the spiritual gravity of the Paradise Sons." [page 1190 - par. 2]

"The Adjuster of the human being through whom this communication is being made enjoys such a wide scope of activity chiefly because of this human's almost complete indifference to any outward manifestations of the Adjuster's inner presence; it is indeed fortunate that he remains consciously quite unconcerned about the entire procedure. He holds one of the highly experienced Adjusters of his day and generation, and yet his passive reaction to, and inactive concern toward, the phenomena associated with the presence in his mind of this versatile Adjuster is pronounced by the guardian of destiny to be a rare and fortuitous reaction. And all this constitutes a favorable co-ordination of influences, favorable both to the Adjuster in the higher sphere of action and to the human partner from the standpoints of health, efficiency, and tranquillity." [page 1208, par. 6 —page 1209]

"In the personal experience of an individual mortal these diverse levels are undoubtedly more or less unified and made personally meaningful by the unobserved and mysterious operations of the divine Thought Adjuster." [page 425 - par. 1]

> **NOTE:** *The Papers tell us the Thought Adjuster of the sleeping subject was apparently crucial to the materialization procedure, but we do not know precisely why or how. The quotes above are offered for information and possible relevance since the Thought Adjuster's activities are pre-personal and include, but are not necessarily restricted to, the descriptions above.*
>
> *No mortal can presume to know precisely how the Urantia Papers were materialized. Dr. Sadler often declared that everything that is actually known about the materialization process can be found in the Urantia Papers. On the next page we offer additional references that may be significant to the materialization process.*

SUMMARY of REFERENCES TO ORIGIN AND TECHNIQUE:

Authority to materialize Papers: 354, bottom par.

Example of Paper presented in person [Solonia, the seraphic "voice in the Garden"]: 846, bottom par. (See next page.)

Example of personally dictated Paper: [Brilliant Evening Star]: 417, par. 1. *(See next page).*

Necessity for translation: 503, par. 3-4.

Midwayers as translators: 627, par. 3. *(Beginning: "Acting as interpreters . . .")*

Actual session of translation & recording: 498, par.4, *(Beginning: "I cannot . . .".)*

Reference to "city of this visitation": 1243, par. 4.

Midwayers' activities: page 865, par. 5, 6.

The human subject: 865, par. 1; 1208, last par. continuing through top of 1209.

References to technique used to materialize Papers: page 1258, par. 1.

ADDITIONAL RELATED REFERENCES:

Handicap of our language and the Revelation: page 1, par. 2.

Supplementation of planetary knowledge: page 17, par. 1.

Priority given existing human concepts: page 16, last par. and page 1343, par.1.0

Restrictions that were placed on the revelation of truth: page 1109, par. 2.3.

On spiritual wisdom vs. genetic knowledge: page 215, par. 2-9.

Concerning the fallibility of revelations: page 1008, par. 2.

Human comprehension must depend upon the indwelling divine presence and the Spirit of Truth: page 17, par. 2.

On revelatory religion keeping contact with evolutionary religion: page 1007, par. 1.

846 — THE HISTORY OF URANTIA

There has been no "fall of man." The history of the human race is one of progressive evolution, and the Adamic bestowal left the world peoples greatly improved over their previous biologic condition. The more superior stocks of Urantia now contain inheritance factors derived from as many as four separate sources: Andonite, Sangik, Nodite, and Adamic.

Adam should not be regarded as the cause of a curse on the human race. While he did fail in carrying forward the divine plan, while he did transgress his covenant with Deity, while he and his mate were most certainly degraded in creature status, notwithstanding all this, their contribution to the human race did much to advance civilization on Urantia.

In estimating the results of the Adamic mission on your world, justice demands the recognition of the condition of the planet. Adam was confronted with a well-nigh hopeless task when, with his beautiful mate, he was transported from Jerusem to this dark and confused planet. But had they been guided by the counsel of the Melchizedeks and their associates, and *had they been more patient*, they would have eventually met with success. But Eve listened to the insidious propaganda of personal liberty and planetary freedom of action. She was led to experiment with the life plasm of the material order of sonship in that she allowed this life trust to become prematurely commingled with that of the then mixed order of the original design of the Life Carriers which had been previously combined with that of the reproducing beings once attached to the staff of the Planetary Prince.

Never, in all your ascent to Paradise, will you gain anything by impatiently attempting to circumvent the established and divine plan by short cuts, personal inventions, or other devices for improving on the way of perfection, to perfect and for eternal perfection.

All in all, there probably never was a more disheartening miscarriage of wisdom on any planet in all Nebadon. But it is not surprising that these missteps occur in the affairs of the evolutionary universes. We are a part of a gigantic creation, and it is not strange that everything does not work in perfection; our universe was not created in perfection. Perfection is our eternal goal, not our origin.

If this were a mechanistic universe, if the First Great Source and Center were only a force and not also a personality, if all creation were a vast aggregation of physical matter dominated by precise laws characterized by varying energy actions, then might perfection obtain, even despite the incompleteness of universe status. There would be no disagreement; there would be no friction. But in our evolving universe of relative perfection and imperfection we rejoice that disagreement and misunderstanding are possible, thereby is evidenced the fact and the act of personality in the universe. If our creation is an existence dominated by personality, then can you be assured of the possibilities of personality survival, advancement, and achievement; we can be confident of personality growth, experience, and adventure. What a glorious universe, in that it is personal and progressive, not merely mechanical or even passively perfect!

[Presented by Solonia, the seraphic "voice in the Garden."]

PERSONALITIES OF THE LOCAL UNIVERSE — 417

further revelation of these orders of creation. Enough of the life and administration of this universe is being herewith portrayed to afford the mortal mind a grasp of the reality and grandeur of the survival existence. Further experience in your advancing careers will increasingly reveal these interesting and charming beings. This narrative cannot be more than a brief outline of the nature and work of the manifold personalities who throng the universes of space administering these creations as enormous training schools, schools wherein the pilgrims of time advance from life to life and from world to world until they are lovingly dispatched from the borders of the universe of their origin to the higher educational regime of the superuniverse and thence on to the spirit-training worlds of Havona and eventually to Paradise and the high destiny of the finaliters—the eternal assignment on missions not yet revealed to the universes of time and space.

[Dictated by a Brilliant Evening Star of Nebadon, Number 1,146 of the Created Corps.]

(Above) Some spirit personalities were qualified to personally *dictate* a Paper, as for instance Paper 37, "Dictated by a Brilliant Evening Star of Nebadon Number 1,146 of the Created Corps." [417]

(Left) Some of the spirit personalities who authored the Urantia Papers were able to *present* their Papers in person, as for instance Paper 75, "Presented by Solonia, the seraphic 'voice in the Garden.'" [846]

NOTE: All of the preceding references are pieces to the puzzle. How do they fit together? Indeed, the primary philosophical question still confronts us. *How could literary works that were authored by high celestial spirit beings be made manifest in the material realm?* Even accepting the morontia concepts, if a plan could be devised to down-step this information by stages and degrees until it could be materially manifested, how could it be done without seriously disrupting the culture of mortal beings? Are there restrictions in place to protect the lower evolutionary realms from such celestial intrusions?

Recall that we have no record that any member of the Contact Commission actually witnessed the materialization of any of the text of the Urantia Papers, or the materialization of any written material of any kind. In fact, we have no testimony that any Contact Commissioner observed *any* miraculous happening or event associated with the materialization of the Revelation. There were apparently no known so-called "psychic" processes used.

The following two pages will attempt to assemble some of the pieces of the puzzle. Although the picture is far from complete, you will find the ideas suggested are consistent with all reliable testimony about the materialization, and most known references in the Papers that provide direct clues to the technique.

SOME IDEAS & SPECULATIONS ON THE TRANSMISS[ION]

"The gap between the material and spiritual worlds is perfectly bridged by the serial association [of] mortal man, secondary midwayer, primary midwayer, morontia cherubim, mid-phase cherubim, an[d] seraphim. In the personal experience of an individual mortal these diverse levels are undoubted[ly] more or less unified and made personally meaningful by the unobserved and mysterious operation[s] of the divine Thought Adjuster." [425, par. 1]

AUTHOR

BILL SADLER, JR.'S "POINT A"
(See Chapter 4, page 71)
"I think if we could have been present at point "A" when any one of these Papers were being written, we would have seen absolutely nothing. At point A was perhaps this Divine Councilor who signs Paper One."

"Even as I am engaged in the formulation of this statement, my associated Solitary Messenger's personal sensitivity to the presence of this order of Spirit indicates that there is with us at this very moment, not over twenty-five feet away, a Spirit of the Inspired order and of the third volume of power presence. The third volume of power presence suggests to us the probability that three Inspired Spirits are functioning in liaison." [220, par. 2]

"Of more than twelve orders of beings associated with me at this time, the Solitary Messenger is the only one aware of the presence of these mysterious entities of the Trinity. And further, while we are thus apprised of the nearness of these divine Spirits, we are all equally ignorant of their mission. We really do not know whether they are merely interested observers of our doings, or whether they are, in some manner unknown to us, actually contributing to the success of our undertaking." [220, par. 3]

CELESTIAL OBSERVERS

"I cannot, with exclusive spirit vision, perceive the building in which this narrative is being translated and recorded. A Divine Counselor from Uversa who chances to stand by my side perceives still less of these purely material creations." [498, par.7]

SERAPHIM

"One of the most important things a destiny guardian [Seraphim] does for her mortal subject is t[o] effect a personal co-ordination of the numerous impersonal spirit influences which indwell, surround, and impinge upon the mind and soul of the evolving material creature." [page 1244, par. 2]

"Cherubim and sanobim are by nature very near the morontia level of existence, and they prove to be most efficient in the borderland work of the physical, morontial, and spiritual domains." [422, par. 6]

SECONDARY MIDWAYER

"... as the loyal midway creatures function when they serve as efficient contact guardians of the human minds of the Urantia reserv[e] corps of destiny at those times when t[he] Adjuster is, in effect, detached from th[e] personality during a season of contact with superhuman intelligences." [863, par.6]

BILL SADLER, JR.'S "POINT B" THE "SLEEPING SUBJECT"

(See Chapter 4, page 72-73)

"Now, you'd have something to see at Point B, but it would be very dull. It would be a man asleep, some ordinary guy, doing nothing." Harold Sherman's account also places the man in bed with his wife while the Papers were being materialized. Meredith Sprunger reports that Dr. Sadler consistently stated that the sleeping subject did not write any of the text of the Urantia Papers.

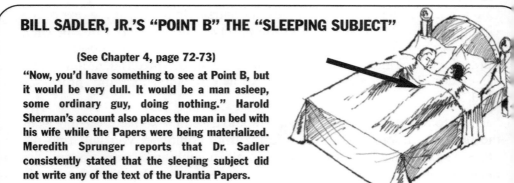

AND MATERIALIZATION OF THE URANTIA PAPERS

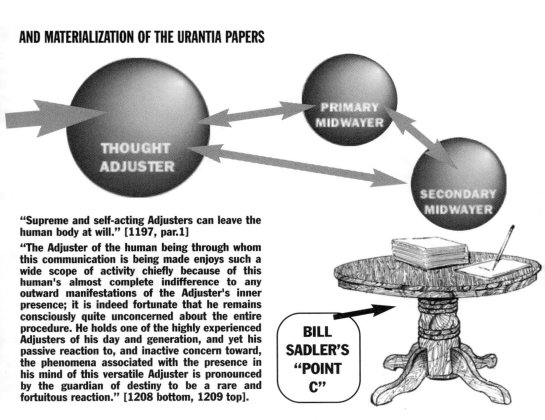

"Supreme and self-acting Adjusters can leave the human body at will." [1197, par.1]

"The Adjuster of the human being through whom this communication is being made enjoys such a wide scope of activity chiefly because of this human's almost complete indifference to any outward manifestations of the Adjuster's inner presence; it is indeed fortunate that he remains consciously quite unconcerned about the entire procedure. He holds one of the highly experienced Adjusters of his day and generation, and yet his passive reaction to, and inactive concern toward, the phenomena associated with the presence in his mind of this versatile Adjuster is pronounced by the guardian of destiny to be a rare and fortuitous reaction." [1208 bottom, 1209 top].

THE MATERIALIZATION OF A PAPER

Bill Sadler, Jr.: "At point C I think you would see a very exciting phenomenon, a pencil moving over a paper with no visible means of propulsion. That's where the physical writing was consummated."

"On many worlds the better adapted secondary midway creatures are able to attain varying degrees of contact with the Thought Adjusters of certain favorably constituted mortals through the skillful penetration of the minds of the latters' indwelling. (And it was by just such a fortuitous combination of cosmic adjustments that these revelations were materialized in the English language on Urantia.)" [1258, par. 1]

"Primary midwayers resemble angels more than mortals; the secondary orders are much more like human beings. Each renders invaluable assistance to the other in the execution of their manifold planetary assignments. The primary ministers can achieve liaison co-operation with both morontia- and spirit-energy controllers and mind circuiters. The secondary group can establish working connections only with the physical controllers and the material-circuit manipulators. But since each order of midwayer can establish perfect synchrony of contact with the other, either group is thereby able to achieve practical utilization of the entire energy gamut extending from the gross physical power of the material worlds up through the transition phases of universe energies to the higher spirit-reality forces of the celestial realms." [424 bottom, 425 top.]

Mary Lou Hales, Christy, and Bill Sadler, Jr.

Chapter Six
"The Majority of Your Forum Shock Me with Their Lack of Enthusiasm"

"The Majority of Your Forum Shock Me with Their Lack of Enthusiasm" 113

*T*HERE WAS A GROWING TURMOIL and uncertainty in the world when the Forum began to re-read the 76 Urantia Papers[1] and ask "more intelligent questions" circa 1929. Black Monday, October 28, 1929, saw the collapse of the U.S. stock market and a world-wide economic crises ensued. The United States was to plunge into a severe depression. Europe was acutely impacted by the crisis, and in Germany a militant Nazi party gained 107 seats in German elections the next year. Between 1924 and 1928 Bill Sadler, Jr. was in the Marine Corps. By 1929, he was 21 and was to become more and more active in the revelation.[2]

Through it all, the Contact Commission continued on with their task of a new round of presenting the Urantia Papers to the Forum members and collecting their questions about the material.

There is not any acknowledgement by the Revelators in the Urantia Papers of any assistance by the Forum or the Contact Commission. The questions asked by the Forum are not included in the text or referred to in any specific way. Many readers have noted that often a question comes up in study groups that is answered a few paragraphs later. This testifies to the human commonality of the type of questions that were asked by the Forum. The request for better questions proved effective, and the

Revelators expanded the existing material considerably. The original Paper about the nature of God was eventually expanded first into two, and then into five Papers, the first five in the Book. A question about the Revelators' use of the word *personality* resulted in an additional Paper.[3] Eventually, during the next five years or so the 76 Papers would be increased to 119. The Papers were divided into three Parts:

THE CENTRAL AND SUPERUNIVERSES. This section was sponsored by a Uversa Corps of Superuniverse Personalities acting on the authority of the Orvonton Ancients of Days. Uversa is the Capital of Orvonton, which is our superuniverse. These Papers eventually numbered 31.

THE LOCAL UNIVERSE. These 25 Papers were sponsored by a Nebadon Corps of Personalities acting under authority of Gabriel of Salvington. Nebadon is the name of our local universe, and Salvington is the Capital.

THE HISTORY OF URANTIA. These were sponsored by a Corps of Universe Personalities under authority of Gabriel of Salvington. These Papers number 63. In the judgment of the author, these Papers may have originally numbered 62, and were possibly expanded to 63 when the Jesus Papers arrived. This possibility would account for the dating, and is examined in the next few paragraphs.

While the Forum was completing the second round of reading the existing Papers in 1934, another drama was unfolding. Behind the scenes, so to speak, the fate of the Jesus Papers was being decided. We know Dr. Sadler believed the members of the Midwayer Commission who were assigned to the Revelation had doubts about their authority to present to the human Contact Commission their narrative of *The Life and Teachings of Jesus*.

To clarify the issue, a "friendly" celestial "legal challenge," ensued, in which the Midwayers in charge of the Revelation technically confronted the group of Midwayers who were responsible for compiling the Jesus Papers. The "charge" was contempt of universe policy.₄ The Local System Councils refused to review the challenge, and referred it upward to the Norlatiadek Constellation Councils. When these courts referred it to the Nebadon Councils, it was pushed yet higher to the Orvonton superuniverse authorities. From beginning to end, the friendly protest extended to a year of Urantia time before the decision was handed down. The group of Midwayers who had prepared *The Life and Teachings of Jesus* were not only exonerated, they were given a special mandate of highest priority for the project. When the news came the Midwayer Commission was overjoyed. Dr. Sadler told Meredith Sprunger that, by some means, the Contact Commission was allowed to briefly "listen in" to the resulting Midwayer celebration.₅

The story of this friendly discord conveys a powerful message. It is touching to consider the energy and devotion of the team of Midwayers who had patiently waited to bring *The Life and Teachings of Jesus* to our dark and foundering world. At the same time, it is inspiring to consider the forbearance and respect they had for the limits of their own authority, notwithstanding their personal feelings and beliefs. Perhaps the Midwayers were modeling an ideal non-proprietary attitude toward the Urantia Papers.

The dating of each section

Some Urantians have been confused by the dating of the various parts of *The Urantia Book*. One commentator has claimed that the Papers were "completed" and "certified" in 1934, basing this idea on an out of context statement in History Two. The full information contained in History Two, the testimony of those who were there, and more important, the Urantia Papers themselves clearly refute the idea that the Papers were designated "complete" by the Revelators in 1934-1935.

At the end of each of the first three parts of the Urantia Papers is a citation, disclosing certain information about the Papers in the section and giving the date that they were formulated or indited into the English language. *Note that in no case does a citation state the Papers were "certified" or "completed" on these dates.* We shall see that the established reading and editing sequences were to take many additional years before the manuscript of *all* 196 Papers would be deemed finished by the Revelators, and ready to be typeset.

The citation at the end of Part I reads: "**These thirty-one papers depicting the nature of Deity, the reality of Paradise, the organization and working of the central and superuniverses, the personalities of the grand universe, and the high destiny of evolutionary mortals, were sponsored, formulated, and put into English by a high commission consisting of twenty-four Orvonton administrators acting in accordance with a mandate issued by the Ancients of Days of Uversa directing that we should do this on Urantia, 606 of Satania, in Norlatiadek of Nebadon, in the year A.D. 1934.**" [354]

The citation at the end of Part II reads: "**This paper on Universal Unity is the twenty-fifth of a series of presentations by various authors, having been sponsored as a group by a commission of Nebadon personalities numbering twelve and acting under the** direction of Mantutia Melchizedek. We indited these narratives and put them in the English language, by a technique authorized by our superiors, in the year 1934 of Urantia time." [648]

The citation at the end of Part III reads: "[This paper, depicting the seven bestowals of Christ Michael, is the sixty-third of a series of presentations, sponsored by numerous personalities, narrating the history of Urantia down to the time of Michael's appearance on earth in the likeness of mortal flesh. These papers were authorized by a Nebadon commission of twelve acting under the direction of Mantutia Melchizedek. We indited these narratives and put them in the English language, by a technique authorized by our superiors, in the year A.D. 1935 of Urantia time.]"[6] [1319] Brackets are in the original.

The final Paper of Part III is possibly a "bridge" into the Jesus Papers, and, because of its dating and authorship, may have been added to the existing 62 Papers of Part III at the time, or just before the Jesus Papers arrived in 1935. Paper 119 (the 63rd of Part III) seems to have no apparent sequential relationship to the Papers proceeding it in Part III. It is authored by "The Chief of the Evening Stars" — an entity who authors no other Papers — and it seems to signal a change of focus to a new phase of the history of our planet: *the recovery and expansion of the human knowledge that had been lost relative to the Fourth Epochal Revelation, the life and teachings of Jesus of Nazareth.*

Part IV, The Jesus Papers

The Life and Teachings of Jesus came all at once in 1935, and not in response to questions by the Forum. Probably, Part IV had been already authored by the Midwayers at the time permission was given to materialize it and insert it into the revelatory process. There is no dating of the Part IV Papers. The sponsoring statement at the beginning reads:

"This group of papers was sponsored by a commission of twelve Urantia midwayers acting under the supervision of a Melchizedek revelatory director. The basis of this narrative was supplied by a secondary midwayer who was onetime assigned to the superhuman watchcare of the Apostle Andrew." [1321]

The Melchizedek director's citation of the first Paper in the series (120) reads: **"Acting under the supervision of a commission of twelve members of the United Brotherhood of Urantia Midwayers, conjointly sponsored by the presiding head of our order and the Melchizedek of record, I am the secondary midwayer of onetime attachment to the Apostle Andrew, and I am authorized to place on record the narrative of the life transactions of Jesus of Nazareth as they were observed by my order of earth creatures, and as they were subsequently partially recorded by the human subject of my temporal guardianship. Knowing how his Master so scrupulously avoided leaving written records behind him, Andrew steadfastly refused to multiply copies of his written narrative. A similar attitude on the part of the other apostles of Jesus greatly delayed the writing of the Gospels."** [Page 1332] The balance of the Urantia Revelation — the Jesus Papers — were sponsored by a "Midwayer Commission."

"The Majority of Your Forum Shock Me with Their Lack of Enthusiasm" 119

Both Dr. Sadler and Christy told Dr. Sprunger that the entire revelation was materialized in handwritten form. In the previously discussed taped interview with Bill Sadler, Jr., he said the process of materialization was never observed, but he speculated that if the materialization of a Paper could have been observed, probably all that could have been seen would be a pencil writing on a tablet all by itself. When asked if all the Papers were written in pencil, he affirmed that they were.[7]

James "JJ" Johnson, of Phoenix, Arizona had two personal conversations with Christy — once in the 70's and again in the early 80's. She told him on his first visit that the manuscript was handwritten. He specifically asked how she knew which words to italicize when she typed the manuscript. Christy responded, *"All the words we italicized were underlined."* He provides this information as further support for a text that was materialized in handwritten form.[8]

Part IV, *The Life and Teachings of Jesus* was materialized just as were the other Papers. The same process took place after they were received: typing the Papers from the handwritten manuscript, checking them, and then the manuscript disappeared. There has been testimony, notably Urantian Bud Kagan's, that the Jesus Papers arrived typewritten. However, this idea flies in the face of Dr. Sadler's testimony and correspondence. A letter from Benjamin N. Adams, copied to Dr. Sadler, queried the accuracy of several areas of the Papers. On one point, Adams noted that the teacher of Alexandria who taught Clement was *Pantaenus*, not *Poutaenus,* as incorrectly stated in the 1955 printing on page 2074. Dr. Sadler explained the error in a letter to Reverend Adams on May 17, 1959:

"I think the spelling of the name of the teacher in Alexandria is undoubtedly an error in transcribing the manuscript into typewriting. An 'an' was undoubtedly transcribed as a 'ou'. I remember when we were sometimes in doubt as to whether a letter was an 'a' or a 'u' in the manuscript. Of course, we who were preparing this matter, did not know the name of this teacher so could have easily made this mistake." [See Appendix B for a full text of this letter].

Since the passage in question is from the Jesus Papers, it was clearly transcribed from a handwritten document, a document written with the *same characteristics as the rest of the Urantia Papers*. In a different portion of the letter Dr. Adams points out another possible error:

"Page1363 (near bottom) **'Far to the east they could discern the Jordan valley and, far beyond, the rocky hills of Moab.'** *But the rocky hills of Moab were* <u>not</u> *east of Nazareth but east of the Dead Sea."* [See Appendix B for a full text of Dr. Adams' letter.]

Dr. Sadler replies:

"Your notation about Moab is a puzzler to me. We have just looked in the atlas, and, of course, you are right. I have no explanation for this matter — either a mistake of the midwayers or a mistake in copying. I cannot say, but evidently you are right in this matter." [See Chapter Seven, changes in the text notation under Part IV, page 156, #13]

In his letter, Dr. Sadler is candid and does not indicate that he will institute changes to correct the apparent discrepancies. The reader may notice that it seems apparent from his responses that he no longer had access to the Revelators by 1959. Another point of interest in Dr. Sadler's letter is that he indicates the Revelators elected to withhold a considerable portion of the manuscript of *The Life and Teachings of Jesus.* He writes:

"You should remember that the midwayers prepared a narrative that was many times larger than was finally given us as Part IV of the Urantia Book. It may be that in deletion some difficulties were encountered."

Based upon the testimony of Dr. Sprunger, Clyde Bedell and others, the Jesus Papers were read to the Forum and handled by the Revelators just like the rest of *The Urantia Book.* This can be also documented within the *full context* of the statements in History Two that the Jesus Papers were read to the Forum:

"This was the plan. We would read a Paper on Sunday afternoon and the following Sunday the new questions would be presented. Again these would be sorted, classified, etc. This program covered several years and ultimately resulted in the presentation of the 196 Papers of the Urantia Book.

"In a way, there was a third presentation. After receiving these 196 Papers, we were told that the 'Revelatory Commission' would be pleased to have us go over the Papers once more and ask questions concerning the 'Clarification of Concepts' and the 'Removal of Ambiguities.' This program again covered several years. During this period very little new information was imparted. Only minor changes were made. Some matter was added – some removed – but there was little revision or amplification of the text.

"What has just been recorded refers more particularly to Parts I, II, and III of the Urantia Book. Part IV — The Jesus Papers — had a little different origin. They were produced by a midwayer commission and were completed one year later than the other Papers. [Note: the following line is the one usually taken out of context]. *The first three parts were completed and certified to us in A.D. 1934. The Jesus Papers were not delivered until 1935."*[9]

The line that is taken out of context is used to support the idea that the Papers were "completed and certified" in 1934. However, in proper context with the previous passages, it is clear that an inexperienced writer (probably Christy) intended to communicate that Parts I-III of the Papers were materialized in 1934 and passed into human hands. The Jesus Papers came a year later. Then the reading sequences continued for all 196 Papers under the watchcare of the Midwayer Revelatory Commission for "several years." [The copy of the text was not frozen until approximately May of 1942. At that time, the Forum was told by the Revelatory Commission that no more questions would be entertained. These events will be examined in more detail in the following chapters.]

There is an anecdote I heard from Clyde Bedell, Dr. Sprunger and others that further indicates the Jesus Papers were read to the Forum and subsequently edited by the Midwayers. Dr. Sadler, in presenting a Paper one Sunday to the Forum, read that "Nathaniel had a good sense of humor for a Jew." There was a titter of amusement that went through the Forum members. Later on, when the typed copy was removed from the vault and examined (the original written manuscripts had been destroyed), this statement did not appear. Since the manuscripts were always kept in a vault, it was never understood how this and other "corrections" could have been executed on the typed manuscript.

YOUNG BILL SADLER, Jr. became an active Contact Commissioner in his early twenties.

A very rare photograph showing the Kelloggs and part of the Forum. (From Left) Wilfred Kellogg, Mrs. Chase, Anna Kellogg, Maizie Jones, Mrs. and Mr. Chilton, Katherine Douglas.
Fellowship Website Photo
http://www.ubfellowship.org/archive/history/rowley/mr_027a.htm

Forum Picnic at Beverly Shores, September, 1949. (From Left) Dr. Anne Whitechurch, Anna and Wilfred Kellogg, Dr. and Mrs. Chase.
Fellowship Website Photo
http://www.ubfellowship.org/archive/history/rowley/mr_041.htm

CLYDE BEDELL in the Fifties. "The first 1300 pages of The Urantia Book are preliminary to its last 800 pages, the most important 800 pages of print on earth – THE LIFE AND TEACHINGS OF JESUS."

The process of reading *all* the Papers to the Forum continued through the Thirties. Clyde Bedell stated in 1983:

"The Papers were revised until Paper 196 had been presented, questions asked, and then answers brought forth into the text which would amplify, and so forth." [10]

When the Jesus Papers first arrived in 1935 they were not only a surprise (in that the original manuscript was not in response to Forum questions), *The Life and Teachings of Jesus* also greatly expanded the scope and implications of the Revelation. As noted, according to Dr. Sadler's letter to Dr. Adams, the final version that was materialized for the humans (after it had been edited down by the Midwayers), was much smaller than the original work. However, Part IV increased the size of the text by one third. Moreover, Part IV was remarkably focused and detailed to a specific time frame.

The previous 1300-plus pages of *The Urantia Book* covered a period of 400 billion years, even to the origin of time itself. It described distances encompassing the universe that are beyond the human imagination to grasp. In contrast, the 773 pages that describe the life and teachings of Jesus cover just over 35½ years of one man's life, and for the most part focus upon his travels over a few hundred square miles of land. Nearly one-third of the Jesus Papers record the last seven days of Jesus' life and the events that immediately followed his death. The proportional ratios in real time to space-allotment in the text would be a challenge to calculate! No wonder Clyde Bedell would later write:

"The first 1300 pages of The URANTIA Book are preliminary to its last 800 pages, the most important 800 pages of print on earth – THE LIFE AND TEACHINGS OF JESUS. The 800 pages are not to support the first 1300. The first 1300 pages are in The URANTIA Book to provide an immeasurable cosmic backdrop. An infinite setting and support for the Creator of our universe – living a life with a mission on our tiny planet." [11]

Some fundamentalist Christians would point to the warning that John gave at the end of Revelations, the last Book in the Bible, in which he declared that no one should add or detract a single word from what has been written. In those "pre-copyright" days such warnings were not unusual. Urantians will point to other words penned by John at the end of his Gospel of Jesus:

"Jesus did many other things as well, if every one of them were written down, I suppose that even the whole world would not have room for the books that would be written" [12]

Many people have been enthralled by the deeds and treasured the words of Jesus in the Bible. If there is the slightest possibility that there are additional words and deeds that were faithfully recorded and are now revealed, would it not be worthwhile to at least examine the Jesus Papers? For many, many Urantians (myself included), the Jesus Papers rekindled my latent desire to believe in the Man of Nazareth and the Son of God, and to study his teachings. When I finished my first reading of the Jesus Papers, I discovered I had recovered a childlike faith in Jesus that was eventually to reconfigure my entire belief system. Such is the power of the life and teachings of Jesus of Nazareth. Indeed: **"Of all human knowledge, that which is of greatest value is to know the religious life of Jesus and how he lived it."** (page 2090)

However, in the years that followed the publication of *The Urantia Book*, the Jesus Papers were attacked by people with various agendas on the basis that they were "added" as an afterthought, or even contrived by Dr. Sadler himself. Even today, some individuals advance this claim. On the contrary, there is some evidence to support Clyde Bedell's assertion that the Jesus Papers were *intended* to be the final masterpiece, and the earlier Papers form the frame that was designed to present them. As an anonymous Urantian once declared:

"The last part of The Urantia Book shows how someone lives who understands the first three parts."

No critic who has proposed that Dr. Sadler was the author, or heavily edited the Urantia Papers in whole or part, has ever pointed to a plausible motive. Dr. Sadler did not need the Urantia Papers, he had a very successful life. He gained no power or wealth from the Urantia Papers, and he was already quite famous. In fact, had Dr. Sadler's involvement with the publication of *The Urantia Book* been widely publicized, it would doubtless have jeopardized his flourishing professional career. Dr. Sadler was a man of unquestioned honor and reputation, and none who knew him believed he would have violated his sacred oath to protect the Urantia Papers from the contamination of human additions or modifications.

With the addition of *The Life and Teachings of Jesus*, Part IV, seventy-seven Papers were added. The Papers now numbered 196.

Preparing a Foreword to the Papers

At some point, Dr. Sadler and Bill Sadler, Jr. decided that the Urantia Papers would need some kind of an introduction. They composed a document to serve this purpose, but were soundly rebuffed in a contact session. The Revelators told them that, although they meant well, their contribution was not acceptable: *"A candle cannot light the way to the sun."* The Sadlers were further advised that at the proper time an introduction would be prepared for the Book. When they received the Foreword for the Book, Dr. Sadler conceded the inadequacy of what he and his son had prepared.[13]

Later on, however, Bill Sadler, Jr. was given permission to compose a Table of Contents for the Book. He compiled the Paper titles and section headings for this Table of Contents. Urantian James "JJ" Johnson, of Phoenix, Arizona, points out that Bill Sadler took some minor liberties in this process. One of Johnson's several discoveries is that Bill lists Mantutia Melchizedek as author of Paper 120. While the Papers imply he *may* have been the author they do not specifically list him. Other than the Table of Contents, Dr. Sadler was very clear that no human had any authorship of any part of the actual text of the Urantia Papers.

A member of the Forum once made suggestions for "improving" one of the Papers and this was relayed through the Contact Commissioners to the Revelators. They were vigorously informed that no human additions to the content of the Urantia Papers would be allowed. Every precaution was made to publish the Urantia Papers and Foreword exactly as they were received.[14] The Foreword of *The Urantia Book* closes with this citation on page seventeen: "**[Indited by an Orvonton Divine Counselor, Chief of the Corps of Superuniverse Personalities assigned to portray on Urantia the truth concerning the Paradise Deities and the universe of universes.]**" Brackets are in original.

The third round for the Forum

By 1939, the process may have become somewhat routine and perhaps even desultory for many of the Forumites. Turnover continued to be high and regular attendance in the Forum was often less than impressive. Some of the more dedicated Forumites

*Dr. Lena Sadler
near the end of her life.*

*Christy takes a break
533 Diversey Parkway*

suggested that a group volunteer to commit to a deeper study of the Papers and more regular attendance. *(Both Dr. Sprunger and Mark Kulieke suggest that this idea might have come at the behest of the Revelators. There is also apocrypha alleging a "communication" to that effect.)* Seventy members of the Forum volunteered for more intensive classes. Meetings of the seventy were held in a more formal manner, with Wednesday night classes as well as Sunday meetings. The "Seventy," as they became known, carried on a systematic study of the Papers from April 5, 1939 to the summer of 1956. During these 17 years, the Seventy enrolled 107 students. This group was the forerunner of the later "School of the Urantia Brotherhood."[15]

The Seventy were said to have received eight written messages through the Contact Commission, communications from the Seraphim of Progress who were attached to the Superhuman Planetary Government of our planet. During these years many other written messages were purportedly received by the Contact Commissioners. Almost all such messages had a notation at the bottom of the last page which read: *"To be destroyed by fire not later than the appearance of the Urantia Papers in print."* It was clearly the design of the Revelators that no Urantia apocrypha would exist subsequent to the publication of the Book.[16]

Unfortunately, alleged Urantia apocrypha continually turn up. Sometimes this information is interesting and helps us understand things, sometimes it is out of context, edited, and misleading. When we examine these materials we should remind ourselves such "messages" are not revelation, and verification of the source of these writings is not possible. Even if they were communications from the Revelators, they were doubtless intended for another time and place. Since the originals were supposed to be destroyed, the existing Urantia apocrypha such as copies of "directive notes" from celestial personages are less historic evidence than they are indications of the weakness and folly of human nature. With these caveats in mind, there follows an alleged message from a regent of the acting Planetary Prince of Urantia which is said to have been intended for both the Seventy and the Forum:

"I have personal interest in your group and deep affection for you as individuals. I commend your loyalty, but I am somewhat amazed at your relative indifference to the importance of the mission which has been entrusted to your hands. Your group of Seventy may seem to show more interest because you are selected and because you are under more or less discipline. But the majority of your Forum shock me with their lack of enthusiasm. . . I admonish you to be ever alert to the importance of the extraordinary trust that has been placed in your hands." [17]

As the Forties approached, it appeared that the Revelators would soon "freeze" the text and permit commencement of the typesetting in preparation for the publication of *The Urantia Book.* On August 1, 1939, Dr. Lena Sadler died after a long and courageous fight with breast cancer. She had been successful in raising over $20,000 in small donations for the publication fund of *The Urantia Book.*[18] Since this fund was not adequate, a wealthy member of the Forum offered to fund the entire publication. However, the Midwayers, according to what Dr. Sadler told Meredith Sprunger, counseled against this. They strongly advised that the funding of the publication of *The Urantia Book* should be a group activity. A general appeal was made and, along with what Dr. Lena Sadler had previously raised, the enthusiastic response by the Forum proved adequate to fund the first printing.

With the death of Dr. Lena Sadler in 1939, one of the original Contact Commissioners was gone and there was no provision to replace her. It became obvious that time was becoming more and more a factor as the remaining Contact Commissioners wondered if they would live to see publication of the book. Dr. Sadler and the Kelloggs were in their mid-sixties now, Christy was almost fifty, and Bill Sadler, Jr. had just passed thirty. Still, the commissioners entertained the hope that the Urantia Papers "would be published during the lifetime of at least some of the members."[19]

One month after Dr. Lena Sadler's death, September 1, 1939, Germany invaded Poland. World War II had begun.

ENDNOTES:

1. The "Foreword" had not yet been materialized, it came later as we shall see.

2. In Chapter Three it was documented that Bill Sadler, Jr. began to seriously examine the Urantia Papers when on leave from the Marines. At that time (as previously documented) he was cautious about them, and asked his father whether anyone was "making money" from the phenomenon. In an audio tape made in Oklahoma dated 2/18/62, Bill Sadler presents a theory about how the Urantia Papers were materialized (See Chapter Five). He also states that the information he relates about the period 1924 – 1928 "is hearsay." He gives this date twice, and also refers to being "in Nicaragua fighting a revolution" in the twenties. This period seems to define the dates of his Marine Corps enlistment. *The World Book Encyclopedia* confirms that American Marines were in Nicaragua during this period, calming a revolution and supervising elections.

3. Deposition of Helen Carlson, Chicago, June 29, 1994.

4. Meredith Sprunger video interviews, also BIRTH OF A REVELATION by Mark Kulieke, Second Edition, 1992, page 16.

5. Meredith Sprunger video interviews, also BIRTH OF A REVELATION by Mark Kulieke, Second Edition, 1992, page 16.

6. JJ Johnson points out that, for whatever reason, the citation for Part III is presented in brackets [ ], while the citations for Parts I and II are not.

7. Audio tape made in Oklahoma, dated 2/18/62.

8. Personal letter from JJ Johnson September 29, 1999. JJ supplied other key elements of information for this history.

9. HISTORY of the URANTIA MOVEMENT TWO - [Compiled by a Contact Commissioner, Undated] pp. 18-19.

10. AN INTERVIEW WITH CLYDE BEDELL, Conducted by Barbara Kulieke in 1983, The Study Group Herald, December, 1992, page 1.

11. A MONOGRAPH ON A VITAL ISSUE CONCERNING THE URANTIA BOOK AND MOVEMENT by Clyde Bedell, 1/81, page 25.

12. JOHN 21:25.

13. A COMMENTARY ON THE ORIGIN OF THE URANTIA BOOK by Meredith J. Sprunger, 6/13/91, page 5.

14. IBID., page 5.

15. HISTORY of the URANTIA MOVEMENT TWO - [Compiled by a Contact Commissioner, Undated] page 22.

16. HISTORY of the URANTIA MOVEMENT TWO - [Compiled by a Contact Commissioner, Undated] page 21.

17. The PLAN FOR THE URANTIA BOOK REVELATION, by Carolyn B. Kendall, Paper distributed January 18, 1996, page 8.

18. HISTORY of the URANTIA MOVEMENT TWO - [Compiled by a Contact Commissioner, Undated] page 24.

19. IBID, Page 21.

An R.R. Donnelley & Sons monotype operator setting type from a manuscript, from a 1958 World Book Encyclopedia Photo.

Chapter Seven

"It was not Portrayed to be Error-Free"

*B*Y 1941, FRANCE HAD COLLAPSED and Hitler was the virtual master of Europe. There was great concern among Americans that the United States would be drawn into the conflict to help England. Meanwhile, at 533 Diversey, the war concern was compounded by a foreboding that the publication of the Urantia Papers would be delayed. In this atmosphere, in July of 1941, Harold Sherman and his wife visited Dr. Sadler in Chicago. It was to be a fateful meeting.

The Sherman tempest

According to his personal account in *How to Know What to Believe*, Harold Sherman and his wife Martha visited Chicago to meet Dr. Sadler while *"en route to Hollywood"* where Sherman was employed periodically as a screenwriter. Sherman and his wife signed the oath of secrecy and joined the Forum. This would permit them to read the Urantia Papers on the premises of 533 on their trips through Chicago. Sherman is not clear about the dates when the readings took place. Martin Gardner states that the Shermans eventually moved to Chicago in May, 1942.

To understand the disruptive impact Mr. Sherman had on the Forum, we need to consider the background of the early plans to form an organization to oversee the welfare and propagation of

136 A HISTORY OF THE URANTIA PAPERS *Chapter Seven*

the Urantia Papers. We know plans for such an organization were being formulated in the early Thirties because Clyde Bedell wrote a strong letter to Wilfred Kellogg in October of 1933 questioning the idea of a board of self-appointed Trustees with lifetime tenures.[1] By 1941, as the possible publication of the Papers seemed to be approaching, lawyers were consulted by the Contact Commission about the formation and structure of an incorporated entity to assume responsibility for the welfare of the Urantia Papers. The Forum was aware of this activity, but they were not consulted, nor even generally privy to the nature and status of the Contact Commission's organizational plans. The last meeting of the Forum as such took place May 31, 1942. At that point, the original Forum became operational as a Study Group.[2] This appears to have been the time when the copy of the Revelation was "frozen," and the typesetting and plate-casting preparations for printing were begun. The Forum was told through the Contact Commission that no more questions would be entertained. The inquiry process was over.[3] This was the atmosphere that prevailed when the Shermans elected to move to Chicago.

Sherman records that in May of 1942 he and his wife began reading the Urantia Papers. Christy brought the Papers "out of the vault," one by one in chronological order, so that he and Martha could read them together. However, he reports on page 61 of his book *How to Know What to Believe* that there were "ninety-two" Papers "in all." This is difficult to understand because, when his own book was published in 1976, *The Urantia Book* with its 196 Papers was in print and it would be easy for him to check his notes. Whatever they read, the Shermans "required almost three months for the entire New Revelation manuscript to be completed."[4]

Sherman's critique of the Papers indicates that he and his wife did not understand even the most basic tenets of the Urantia Philosophy. The reason for this, aside from hasty reading, may have been something Clyde Bedell says Sherman cautiously concealed from Dr. Sadler and the members of the Forum: *Sherman's personal mind-set and prejudice in favor of virtually all forms of so-called "psychic" phenomena.*

Harold Sherman was an investigator and an advocate of psychic phenomena, including astral projection, communication with the dead, numerology, astrology, and reincarnation. He would go on to write books such as *You Live After Death* containing instructions to assist the reader in "communicating" with the dead. Sherman was greatly disturbed that the Urantia Papers refuted such concepts, to the point that the Papers describe them as "sordid." In a short time, his investigative mission began to surface. He wrote a letter to Dr. Sadler virtually accusing him of withholding the truth and distorting the Urantia Papers because he claimed Sadler was "prejudiced" against psychic phenomena. Sherman went so far as to warn Dr. Sadler that as "trusted custodian" he would be held accountable in the centuries to come for his alteration of the text by withholding information on astral travel, communicating with the dead, reincarnation, and so forth.[5] When his harsh letter was not answered, Sherman attempted a political approach.

Sherman arranged a meeting with eight or ten of the more aggressive men in the Forum. Clyde Bedell, who was one of this group, later came to believe that Sherman was driven by commercial motives. Clyde believed that, to Sherman, control of the Revelation represented the potential for acquiring power and riches. However, during the secret meeting, Sherman convinced this small group of males that he was concerned only about the safety and protection of the Revelation. He cast a shadow of suspicion over the structure of the organization that was being planned, implying that the Revelation was being taken over exclusively by the Sadlers. Sherman forwarded the notion that Dr. Sadler and the Contact Commission were unjustly autocratic and he proposed that Forum-study group members should have an equal voice in making decisions about the Revelation. Clyde Bedell, who had long harbored concern about the proposed organizational structure, drafted a four-page petition, in the form of a letter, on behalf of the others. In this letter, Clyde wrote a long, cautious preamble praising Dr. Sadler, and then made his point:

> "We believe the Forum people as a group should turn with the most earnest effort toward the consideration and development of as much sound groundwork as is possible in all the practical aspects of this Book's future. Respectfully, but most earnestly, we request an opportunity to know all the facts in connection with, and all the provisions concerning, the Urantia Book and the proposed associated organization as their plans exist today.

> "To this date, no group opportunity has been offered to study, to freely discuss or to examine charters, articles of incorporation, by-laws, etcetera, of the several contemplated organizations. To this date, earnest Forum members, many with sound experience, judgment and ability, have had no opportunity for frank and full expression of opinions based on familiarity with these organization plans which have been brought to elaborated state by the Contact Commissioners and outside aides.

> "We believe legal talent is justifiably used in formulating certain instruments which implement the Urantia Book plans. But we do not feel that Forum people should be excluded from full and complete understanding of all instruments identified with the Book for which we have a grave and undeniable responsibility as individuals."[6]

"It Was Not Portrayed to be Error-Free" 139

Generally, the balance of this letter addressed the proposed structure of the "organizations that would protect the book's copyright, when it would be published, and its distribution."[7]

A committee of three presented the petition-letter to Dr. Sadler the next day. Clyde Bedell told me, years later, that Dr. Sadler was wounded by the letter. He advised the committee that he already knew about the meeting, and then he proceeded to tell them about it and describe the contents of the petition before even looking at it. He told the committee that everyone who signed the petition could personally meet with him, discuss their personal grievances and then withdraw their names from the petition if they chose. Every signer did so with the exception of the Shermans. Clyde made it clear that the removal of his signature was done as an accommodation to Dr. Sadler, and did not indicate he had been convinced about the proposed structure of Urantia Foundation.

There were some additional fireworks, but soon everything settled down again. Sherman claims that, in spite of his disillusionment, he and Martha continued to attend every Forum-study group meeting for "five continuous years to show our continued interest in the material." Clyde had his doubts the Shermans were there that often, if at all. At the time he wrote his paper, Clyde discussed this supposed attendance with five other Forum members and no one recalled the Shermans returning.[8]

When Clyde told me of the incident, he said Sadler was informed about the meeting and the contents of the petition by a contrite member of the reform group before the committee arrived. Rumors of superhuman activity have been related about this incident, probably stimulated by Dr. Sadler's seeming pre-knowledge of the petition. Clyde wrote in 1976:

"[Sherman] says Dr. Sadler claimed to be 'taken out of his physical body and transported to the Dean home.'
This is precisely the kind of thing in which Dr. Sadler did

NOT believe. Neither I nor anyone else who knew the doctor intimately (I knew him from 1924 until his death a few years ago) will agree that the Doctor was capable of making that kind of a statement."[9]

Martin Gardner used Sherman and another self-proclaimed "psychic," Harry Loose, as his prime sources for his book *Urantia, the Great Cult Mystery,* which sought to defame Dr. Sadler and debunk the Urantia Revelation.

Proofreading the Urantia Papers

By mid-1942, activities were in motion to prepare the Urantia Papers for printing. The meticulously prepared and studied Urantia manuscript would now have to be typeset and carefully proofed before it could be plated and printed in book form. The manuscript copy had probably been cleansed of nearly all spelling, capitalization and punctuation errors. (As we know, the Contact Commission was only permitted to standardize spelling, capitalization, and punctuation, and was not permitted to make editorial changes.[10]) If, in those days, the Contact Commission had the benefit of computer technology, the pre-publication task would have been relatively simple. Christy would have prepared a disk from her computer and handed it to the printer. The type would have been automatically set and a proof generated. Christy would have been required to deal with basic formatting questions.

How different was the situation in the Forties! When Christy handed the precious manuscript of *The Urantia Book* to the publisher, R.R. Donnelley & Sons, the arduous process of setting type, proofing, correcting, and reproofing began. Every word, every line, and every page of that manuscript had to be completely retyped by a monotype operator, then cast in hot metal type and assembled on a galley. A proof was then "pulled" (printed) from the galley and this was checked by a professional proofreader against the original manuscript. Once the proofreader was satisfied, the proof was submitted to the client for final approval.[11]

It is important that the client's final OK be very carefully considered and truly final, before the plates were etched. Otherwise, a significant operation would be required to make even a small correction on a cast plate, or a major correction would require the entire plate to be recast. Casting a plate was a complex and costly process that, in the case of a book, usually involved a large number of pages at the same time. Bill Sadler, Jr. stated in his tape of February 18, 1962, that a plate included one side of 16 sheets (a sheet consisted of two pages) of *The Urantia Book* and these 16 sides were printed simultaneously. This corresponds with the information I have acquired from two retired Donnelley employees. After the client had *signed-off* approval, an impression of the original galley of the page was used to create a mold. Then, hot metal was poured in. The actual curved plate was formed so that it could be used on the rotary press. Once the final plate was cast, the original flat galley of type was "dumped," and the metal then used for new typesetting.

To produce a book that is a flawless, word for word duplicate of the manuscript, perfectly punctuated, is a difficult task with an ordinary book and sophisticated clients. In the case of *The Urantia Book's* manuscript, over one million words were involved. In addition, this enormous work included many coined words not in the English language and featured numerous long and complex sentences. The Urantians would discover that the process of book publishing is far more complex than correcting typed manuscripts.

One of the most difficult problems with clients less knowledgeable about the printing process is what advertising people call the "halo effect." The typeset page-proof looks so beautiful, especially after reading an ordinary typewritten page for years and years, it's difficult for an untrained eye to see the mistakes. But, the cold hard facts were: the accuracy of the printed Urantia Book could be no better than the final proofing process, *regardless of how carefully the original manuscript had been prepared.*

In January of 1939, Marian Rowley joined the Forum. She recalls reading the Papers in the original typed manuscript form.[12] The manuscript of the Urantia Papers could be read by Forum members only at 533 Diversey Parkway. There were several typed copies there, and individuals could sign out one Paper at a time and read them on the premises. They were permitted to read before the meeting on Sunday or during business hours and evenings on weekdays. The Papers were kept in a vault and were administered by the Contact Commission.[13]

We may assume the initial proofing process (prior to casting) went on for a considerable time. We are told that Mary Penn, an employee of the Donnelley Company, was the professional who proofread the Papers on site at 533. If she had a question, she could consult with the Contact Commission.[14] However, the job of a professional proofreader is primarily to supply the client with an accurate proof, the client is responsible for the final adjustments and corrections. The proofreader carefully compares the galley proof with the manuscript, marks corrections, and returns it to the typesetter. The typesetter makes the corrections and prints a new proof. There is no technical limit to the number of proofs that can be corrected and printed, but printing professionals are generally expert at this process, and one or two proofs are usually sufficient.

The responsibility for corrections

Once the proofreader is satisfied, a fresh proof is prepared and supplied to the client. That fresh proof is not considered final until the client decides it is perfect. New proofs are generated until the client is satisfied and signs off on a final proof, and no plating will take place until this signed proof is in the hands of the printer. There is a subtle pressure on the client, because until a proof is given final approval the plate cannot be cast, and the galley of type cannot be dumped and the metal reused. A large number of idle galleys of type awaiting final client approval represent a substantial investment on the part of the printer.

Even so, the responsibility for the final proofs lies with the client — in this case the Contact Commission. Probably the task was primarily on the shoulders of Christy, assisted by Marian Rowley, whom many considered the best proofreader at 533.[15]

The plates are cast

Carolyn Kendall states that the plates for *The Urantia Book* were cast sometime during World War II. If this is accurate, the final proofs were made, the Commissioners signed off, and the plates were cast by the mid-Forties. We know that, at some point in the plate-casting process, the typed manuscripts were destroyed. The plates were etched, cast, and placed in a vault in the R.R. Donnelley plant in Crawfordsville, Indiana. So, as 1945 drew to a close, the only remaining material manifestations of four decades of the revelatory process were the plates and the galley proofs of *The Urantia Book* that had been made from those plates.

However, Carolyn also writes that *informal* proofing continued *after* the plates had been cast. She states that the "final galley sheets read by the Forum in the late 1940s and early 1950s were stamped *'Proofed by Oppy'*."[16] Once the plates were cast and the original typed manuscripts destroyed, there was no longer any means of checking them to verify what were later to be termed "copying errors." We are informed by Carolyn Kendall that these final galley proofs indeed contained "errors" (and so obviously did the plates), but we are not told what kind of errors:

"When the book was published by Urantia Foundation on October 12, 1955, it was not portrayed to be error-free. The multiple processes of transcribing from handwritten manuscript to typewritten pages; the retyping of these pages two to five times; and from typewritten to typeset form, presented opportunities for errors to creep into the papers which were not caught by even two professional proof readings. By publication day, Christy and Marian had already collected a list of errors noticed by sharp-eyed Forum members. The midwayers did not volunteer the location of errors, just that there were errors in the published text."[17]

This paragraph both raises questions and supplies possible clues to their answers. Let us begin with the assumption that the typewritten manuscript was satisfactory to the Revelators, else they would not have decided that the Revelation was complete and it was time to prepare to print the book. The earlier process of transcribing from the original handwritten document to the typewritten pages, and the number of times it was subsequently retyped, may have resulted in copying errors. However, the final manuscript was evidently acceptable to the Revelators.

Errors in The Urantia Book

Only the *final manuscript* was used by the typesetter, and the final typesetting was professionally proofed against this manuscript. If errors existed in this terminal manuscript, as stated, they apparently were not reported to the Contact Commissioners by the Revelators. At least, there is no documentation or testimony I know of to that effect. We can also reasonably assume that the manuscript itself was evidence that — with the consent of the Revelators — the Urantia Papers had entered the evolutionary mainstream. This is very important. That meant human involvement, and human involvement means errors will be made.

We can reasonably deduce that the Revelators were weaning the humans from their control and guidance. The Revelators seemed to be more and more restricted as to their own involvement — thus, perhaps, they could respond to questions about errors in the printed Book but were not permitted to reveal where they were.

We can further assume that any errors were not a threat to the general integrity of the Revelation, and that *there had been no intentional human corruption of the Urantia Papers*. Otherwise, the celestial Revelatory Commission would surely have stepped in and either made adjustments or pulled the plug on the entire operation.

By following this logic we are led to the conclusion that the pre-publication "errors" Carolyn refers to were issues about punctuation, spelling, and capitalization. James Mills, Ph.D., who had been closely associated with the Revelation since 1951, was a Field Representative for Urantia Brotherhood, and who served as a Urantia Foundation Trustee and Trustee Emeritus for many years, wrote this comment in 1991:

> "... prior to publication, Forum members, engaged in reading the first proof sheets made from the original metallic plates, were constantly seeking primarily for typographical errors including punctuation, errors of grammar, syntax, or any other errors which could occur in the process of the transference of a text from manuscript through the linotype procedure into metal printing plates. Apparently, the most potent source of error would lie at the point of the linotype operator."[18]

This commentary indicates the prevailing mind-set of the culture at 533 was that the linotype operator was somehow responsible for the mistakes that were overlooked by the Contact Commission during the proofing process. Also, a strong preoccupation with minor typos is implied. What were to be later called editorial "copying errors" could not have been verified because the source manuscripts had been destroyed. And now we confront a key question. *Why did the Revelators order the original manuscript destroyed once the plates were made?* Conventional human wisdom would surely dictate that the manuscript should be preserved to verify any concerns about copying errors.

The Revelators did not want human input

The Revelators knew human nature. We can reasonably assume that the Revelators knew that typographical errors and apparent inconsistencies existed in the plates. Again: the Revelators were evidently not so concerned that they felt these errors were threatening to the essence of the Revelation. However, *once the plates were cast, there were now two versions of the text: the manuscript and the plates.* The Revelators knew the manuscript would be the "final authority" used to verify this or that word or statement. They also knew this would create a singular "sacred document" in the hands of a small group of people. They were aware that the process of "correcting" the plates would be endless, and the door to human opinions and human meddling, once opened, could never be closed. Better to destroy the manuscript immediately, live with the flawed plates, and let human wisdom deal with the anomalies that were certain to be discovered later. These points are emphasized because of events that occurred before the second printing. We will examine these in the next chapter.

The few points in the text where there were possible editorial inconsistencies would not be unearthed until sharp-eyed *readers* eventually discovered them. Had the Contact Commissioners known about the inconsistencies, surely they would have asked about them and would have sought permission to remake the problem plates in 1950 — prior to the establishment of the

(Above) Bill Sadler, Jr. with Christy in the early thirties.

Marian Rowley and Dr. Sadler, July 1, 1944
Fellowship Website Photo
http://www.ubfellowship.org/archive/history/rowley/mr_009.htm

Dr. William Sadler. The Fellowship Website captions this as "circa 1950," but this is probably an error. He appears younger than the 1944 photo on the previous page.

Fellowship Website Photo
http://www.ubfellowship.org/archive/history/
dr_sadler_standing.htm

(Below) Beverly Shores picnic, June 25, 1960. From left, Edith Cook, Irene Sprunger, Dr. Meredith Sprunger.

Fellowship Website Photo
http://www.ubfellowship.org/archive/history/
rowley/mr_056.htm

Declaration of Trust — when the text was officially transferred and became the responsibility of Urantia Foundation. These editiorial "corrections" would have required word and number changes and deletions, but at that time the Midwayer Revelatory Commission was available and could have readily been consulted by the five remaining Contact Commissioners. It would have been a bit expensive to make these corrections and re-plate some of the pages in 1950, but it would have been worth the time and trouble. As it was, when the plates were made and the manuscripts destroyed, the *plates became the original text.* The plates are so defined in Urantia Foundation's Declaration of Trust — and they were used to publish the original text in book form in 1955. ***10,000 published copies of the Book and the plates were in precise agreement, and there was no other text.***

Thus the list of "errors" that had been collected over a ten-year period by press time, the ones Christy told Carolyn Kendall about, were very likely limited to spelling, punctuation, and capitalization errors. These may have been embarrassing, but obviously the Commissioners considered these typos less than critical. As it was, the Contact Commission proceeded to use the plates as the basis for establishing Urantia Foundation, formulating the Declaration of Trust, and printing the Book. However, as we shall later examine, when the second printing was worked on in 1967, the apparent inconsistencies in the text were important enough to agonize over, and finally "correct."

We can reasonably postulate that the Revelators directed, or gave permission to, the Contact Commission to take the necessary steps to have the plates cast in the early Forties. As previously stated, the Revelators must have known of any problems in the text at the time this was done.

However, the Revelators' grant of permission to the Contact Commission to make any standardizations in

punctuation, spelling, and capitalization was NOT extended to Urantia Foundation through the Declaration of Trust.

The Revelators could probably anticipate that once the Book was exposed to thousands of readers, the possible inconsistencies would eventually be uncovered. Then the problem of reconciling them would have to be addressed by evolutionary human wisdom.

No one could have done better

Having very carefully examined the facts, I hasten to add that the devotion and commitment of the Contact Commissioners, and especially Christy, could hardly have been surpassed in producing the 1955 text. Even under ideal conditions, with very sophisticated experts involved, it would have been impossible, in my judgment, to produce a perfect book. *It was probably never intended that humans would produce a perfect book.* Some of the inconsistencies that eventually emerged could hardly have been detected until thousands of people began to have years of experience reading the Book.

Why not a perfect book?

Some have argued that the Revelators could have simply by-passed the humans and given us a perfect book. This idea is one that should be dealt with. Some take lightly the idea that Urantians might begin to worship their Urantia Book. Many Christians, in fact, do not know that the Muslim counterpart to Jesus is not Mohammed, but the "glorious Koran."

Muslims believe in Inlibration, the embodiment of God in the Koran itself. The reverence that Christians feel toward Jesus is what Muslims feel toward their book. The *uncreated,* or eternal Koran has become a pillar of the Muslim faith. In other words, the Koran itself is thought to be eternal, and was handed, complete and perfect, to Mohammed by God. Bloody wars have been fought over the centuries to preserve this prevailing dogma. Today, the religion of Islam rests firmly upon Inlibration - or the divine "made book."[19]

Make no mistake, the 1955 printing of *The Urantia Book*, warts and all, is an epochal masterpiece. But because it had entered into the evolutionary mainstream, the 1955 printing was, of course, a flawed masterpiece (as are all achievements in which humans have a part).

The Contact Commissioners and the Forum had gone through an extremely difficult test of time, and had, to the best of their human abilities, helped bring to this planet a new Revelation "exactly as they had received it."[20] And one of the things this new Epochal Revelation tells us is that all revelation - short of the presence of God, our Paradise Father - is limited and incomplete. (1008 – par. 2).

Perhaps, from the perspective of an onlooking universe, what the Midwayers accomplished in bringing the Urantia Revelation to our forlorn, backward, and strife-driven planet was a unique achievement, even by the standards of celestial excellence. After two thousand years, the planet of Urantia, the "sentimental shrine of Michael," glimmered once more with new hope as the manuscript of the Fifth Epochal Revelation was at last etched into nickel-plated stereotype plates.

Changes made to the original text

Before we continue with the chronological events associated with the Urantia Revelation, the reader should be informed that the complete set of original plates were used for only one printing of *The Urantia Book*. After the 1955 printing of 10,000 copies, changes were made to the text. Apparently the bulk of these alterations were instioued in an effort to "correct" what were later termed "copying errors" by Urantia Foundation. Over the years, various isolated Urantians began discovering these changes. But, in those pre-internet years, Urantians were rarely able to compare notes. In fact, before the advent of computers, it was very difficult to develop a complete list of the editorial changes that were made after the first printing of the book.

In the early nineties, Merritt Horn, a scholar in Boulder, Colorado, began to use computer technology to compare the first printing of *The Urantia Book*, page by page, with the then-current 1993 printing. This is an extremely slow, tedious, and costly process. Mr. John Hay, a devoted Urantian, financed the historic investigation. Merritt found that over 120 changes to the text had been made since the 1955 printing. Setting aside for the moment the question of the authority of Urantia Foundation to change the original text at all, *most* of the changes were typographical in nature. *Most* did not affect the passages in which they were found. However, approximately fifteen changes clearly involved significant editorial latitude, and included word and number alterations as well as deletions.

Merritt then began to search the various printings to see when the consequential editorial changes were made. He verified that nearly all of them were made in the second and third printings. Although none of the editorial changes seriously affected the essential content of the Book, many veteran readers were shocked when Merritt's findings began to surface. His work confirmed and expanded earlier lists of purported changes that had been compiled by alert readers over the years.

Some readers have asserted that Urantia Foundation's Declaration of Trust forbids *any* changes whatsoever, not even spelling, capitalization, and punctuation changes. These readers were also disturbed by the fact that they had not been informed, and that none of the editorial changes were footnoted or endnoted. In fact, readers had been told by Urantia Foundation for more than twenty years that no such changes had been made. *(See the letter of Trustee Emeritus James Mills, Appendix B.)* Another disturbing fact was that the great majority of the changes seemed arbitrary, unnecessary, or simply wrong. Many of these, such as the deletion of the words *"in the manger"* on page 1317, have been discussed at length elsewhere. Here is a very abbreviated list of Merritt's findings of editorial changes. *(This list includes only a brief description of the key changes. See Appendix D for a more complete exposition of Merritt's work, and an exploration of some of the issues involved if these problems are to be resolved.)*

Key editorial changes in the text

FOREWORD:

[1]. Page 3: In #5 of listing of perfection types, the word "other" was removed from all printings after 1955. The 1967 version corrects the ungrammatical use of the word "other" which was probably inserted by a typist who inadvertently followed the previous pattern of usage in the list.

PART II:

[2]. On page 413, par. 6: The 1955 printing varies from all later printings in that it has the word "secondary," where all others read "tertiary." While both a secondary and a tertiary Circuit Supervisor are assigned to the supervision of a single local universe's circuits, only the tertiary Circuit Supervisor is located on the local universe headquarters sphere; the secondary Circuit Supervisor is located on the superuniverse headquarters. (See page 265). Therefore, **"tertiary Universe Circuit Supervisor"** does appear to be the correct description of Andovontia.

[3]. On page 460, par. 1: The 1955 edition states **"sixty thousand times as dense as your sun"** while the second and subsequent printings have been changed to **"forty thousand."** Textual consistency does require "forty," since page 459 (Section 4, par. 1) states that our sun is about 1.5 times the density of water, or about .054 pounds per cubic inch, and 40,000 times this is about

2,160 pounds per cubic inch (which is also equivalent to 60,000 times the density of water).

[4]. On page 474, par. 5: The 1955 edition placed a capital "Y" here, it was replaced by "gamma" in all later printings. It is likely that the Greek letter gamma (γ) was mistakenly transposed into an English "Y" at some point in the proofing and preparation of the text for printing.

[5]. On page 477, par. 1: Two changes from the 1955 edition were made in all subsequent printings. In the original, "less" was changed to "more," and "from two to three" was changed to "almost two:" **Each atom is a trifle over 1/100,000,000th of an inch in diameter, while an electron weighs a little (less) (changed to "more") than 1/2,000th of the smallest atom, hydrogen. The positive proton, characteristic of the atomic nucleus, while it may be no larger than a negative electron, weighs** (from two to three) (changed to "almost two") **thousand times more."** The revised wording is more consistent with the statement in the paragraph following the subject paragraph (page 477), where the author states that a proton is **"eighteen hundred times as heavy as an electron."** This is also in accord with current scientific opinion which places the ratio at 1: 1,836.

[6]. On page 478, par 3: In all printings after the first, "well-nigh" was placed before "instantaneous." It is unclear how this addition would correct an earlier error.

[7]. On page 486, par 5: The 1955 printing reads "four thousand years," in all subsequent printings, "four" was changed to "forty." Forty thousand years does appear to be correct (see page 1316, section 7, par. 2).

[8]. On page 608, par 4: In the second (1967) and following printings, "681,227" was changed to "681,217," presumably because of the reference on page 581: **"Since the inception of the**

system of Satania, thirteen Planetary Adams have been lost in rebellion and default and 681,204 in the subordinate positions of trust." It does appear that one of the numbers is in error, but whether 681,227 should be reduced to 681,217, or 681,204 should be increased to 681,214 is not apparent from the text.

PART III:

[9]. P.806 - par. 2: In the 1967 printing, in the following sentence the word *"sometime"* was changed to *"sometimes"*: **"In the ideal state, education continues throughout life, and philosophy sometime becomes the chief pursuit of its citizens. The citizens of such a commonwealth pursue wisdom as an enhancement of insight into the significance of human relations, the meanings of reality, the nobility of values, the goals of living, and the glories of cosmic destiny."** From a typographical standpoint, this is a minor change. However, the meaning of the text is dramatically altered from a confident statement of the evolution of the ideal state in the original text, to the acknowledgement of a mere possibility in later printings.

[10]. On page 827, par. 3: In the second (1967) and succeeding printings, "between" was changed to "among." The original is correct because "between" can appropriately be used when more than two objects are related, especially if the relationship is to each object individually rather than in an indeterminate way to the group. The relationship is the division of time between world capitals; it is immaterial that there are more than two capitals involved.

[11]. On page 883, par. 7: The 1955 printing placed "west" at this location rather than "east." Because the term did not appear to be a title for the western hemisphere, "east" has been used in all subsequent printings.

[12]. On page 1317, par. 2: The phrase "in the manger" was deleted in the second and all subsequent printings, leaving the sentence: **"These men of God visited the newborn child."** This change was probably made because Mary and Joseph moved into a room at the inn on the day after

Jesus' birth, and the priests did not arrive in Bethlehem until Jesus was three weeks old. So the "editor" may have presumed that it would not have been possible for the priests to see Jesus "in the manger." However, cradles may have not been easy to come by. Merritt Horn points out that, assuming the manger was portable, it is possible that Joseph and Mary might have taken the manger with them up to the room in the inn in order to continue to have a cradle for Jesus.

PART IV.

[13]. On page 1363, par. 5: In the second and following printings, the line **"Far to the east they could discern the Jordan valley and, far beyond, the rocky hills of Moab."** was changed to: **"Far to the east they could discern the Jordan valley and far beyond lay the rocky hills of Moab."** After the Book was in print, a letter from a Biblical scholar named Benjamin Adams pointed out that: *"...the rocky hills of Moab were not east of Nazareth but east of the dead Sea."* (One Urantian has reported this letter claimed that it is impossible to see the rocky hills of Moab from the location in question. If one troubles to read this letter, this is clearly not what Adams challenged. See Appendix B for a replication of the Adam's letter.) The change avoids the implication that the rocky hills of Moab are east of Nazareth. However, Merritt Horn points out that, in his judgment, the text itself does *not* state the hills of Moab are east of Nazareth. He writes: *"Jesus and his father are standing on top of the Nazareth hill and are moving their gaze from the northwest around an arc to the north, east, south and then west. To the east is the Jordan valley. As they look past the valley, following its line and the arc of their survey, they discern the rocky hills of Moab. That this analysis is correct is supported by the sentence that follows: 'Also to the south and east...' which clearly implies the last referenced location (Moab) was in the same direction. Otherwise, the sentence would be punctuated with a comma in this manner: 'Also, to the south and east...'."*

[14]. On page 1849, par. 5: The 1955 text stated that Lazarus remained at Bethany **"until the day of the crucifixion of Jesus."** This was changed to **"until the week..."** in the second printing. The latter reading is consistent with the later narrative (at pages 1897 par. 1, 1909 last par., and 1927 last par.) which would place the time of Lazarus's flight between Tuesday at midnight (when his death was decreed by the Sanhedrin) and Wednesday evening (when **"certain ones"** at the camp **"knew that Lazarus had taken hasty flight from Bethany"**) - two days before the crucifixion of Jesus.

[15]. On page 1943, par. 2: In the second printing, "apostles" was substituted for the original "twelve" at this point. Because Judas had left earlier, there were only eleven apostles present for the establishment of the remembrance supper, so "apostles" seems more appropriate.

Changes not footnoted or endnoted

To repeat, it is reasonable to concede that none of these editorial changes constitute malicious tampering or a measurable alteration of the Urantia Revelation. However, many Urantians believe the spirit and intent of the Declaration of Trust forbids an alteration of *any kind* to the original text. In addition, to many readers it remains a mystery that Urantia Foundation never alerted the reader to these changes through footnotes or endnotes. This is standard academic practice when making changes to the creative work of another author. Readers point out that in the case of an Epochal Revelation authored by celestial beings, common sense dictates that it should be mandatory. This issue has been dismissed by some supporters of Urantia Foundation as making a "fetish" out of the text of the Urantia Papers. We will examine this question in depth in Chapter Nine.

The timing of publication

By May of 1942, permission had been granted by the Revelators to the Contact Commission to prepare for printing but not, as yet, to actually publish *The Urantia Book*. In the next chapter we will continue to follow the course of the Revelation as it is finally published as a book.

ENDNOTES

1. LETTER FROM CLYDE BEDELL TO WILFRED KELLOGG, OCTOBER, 1933. This letter can be examined on the Fellowship website: *http:// urantiabook.org/archive/historykellogg_letter1033.htm*

2. HISTORY OF THE URANTIA MOVEMENT ONE, by a Group of Urantian Pioneers, assisted by Members of the Contact Commission, 1960, page 6.

3. David Kantor reports that it was his understanding that once the contract was signed for the production of the plates, the Contact Commission was told that there would be no more questions tendered and the work of the Forum in this regard was finished. It continued on only as a Sunday study group, although many members continued to refer to the group as the "Forum" and themselves as "members." Until The Urantia Book was published, new members of the Sunday study group also preferred to identify themselves as "Forum" members, even though the Forum as such ceased to exist on May 31, 1942.

4. HOW TO KNOW WHAT TO BELIEVE, by Harold Sherman, Fawcett, New York, 1976, pp. 66-67. On pages 70-72 Sherman gives an account of Thought Adjusters that is totally inaccurate. He also questions why the Jesus Papers were added, when the book "made no mention of Jesus as such?" (Recall that at the time he met Dr. Sadler, about July of 1941, the text was virtually completed. Within ten months — about the time Sherman and his wife actually began to *read* the Papers — the manuscript would be frozen and deemed ready to typeset).

"It Was Not Portrayed to be Error-Free" 159

Sherman's hasty reading failed to detect that, as previously stated, Jesus is mentioned in *The Urantia Book* as early as page 30, and 20 additional times before we reach page 100. Michael is mentioned on page 8 as "Christ Michael–Son of Man and Son of God, and 16 additional times before page 100!) Harold Sherman's book was a principle source of information used by Martin Gardner in his own book "Urantia - The Great Cult Mystery," which was an unfortunate blanket rejection of any possibility the Urantia Papers have revelatory content. Gardner's chapter on his two key sources, Sherman and Harry Loose, (pages 135-160), has to be read to appreciate how far afield these men's "psychic" ideas were. Gardner also used information he gathered from Sherman's widow, Martha Sherman. Gardner, who rejected and ridiculed information from esteemed Urantians like Dr. Sprunger, reports without comment Harold Sherman's "out-of-body" trips to Jupiter with a scientologist, and Harry Loose's ability to make a handkerchief fly from a dresser into his hand several feet away. (This was reported to Gardner by Martha Sherman, page 139.) Gardner reports on pages 149-150 of accusations by Kellogg's daughter that Sherman had asked her to steal the plates of *The Urantia Book* so he could copyright it as the author and make a movie of it. (The plates were stored in an R. R. Donnelley & Sons vault in Crawfordsville, Indiana). He tells of a letter from Loose to Sherman in which Loose praises a new book of Sherman's: "The Dead are Alive" as a "masterpiece." Gardner discloses that Sherman described his first meeting with Loose as the "most inspiring" hours of his life. Finally, Gardner closes his chapter by publishing a final letter written by Sherman to Dr. Sadler. The letter was filled with bizarre accusations and rhetorical questions. Gardner solemnly reports that "there is no evidence" that Dr. Sadler replied to the letter. On page 407 of his book Gardner tells us that a letter from ex-policeman Loose to Sherman speculated that the death of Dr. Lena Sadler had caused "something to happen" to Dr. Sadler's personality. (Loose may have been a psychiatric patient of Dr. Sadler, as Gardner reports on page 136). Finally, Gardner tells us on page 407 that his own "dear wife" thought his book, "Urantia, the Great Cult Mystery," was a "total waste" of his energies.

160   A HISTORY OF THE URANTIA PAPERS   *Chapter Seven*

5. The text of this letter (according to Sherman) is recorded on pages 73 – 75 in HOW TO KNOW WHAT TO BELIEVE, by Harold Sherman, Fawcett, New York, 1976.

6. CLYDE BEDELL'S 1942 PETITION, page two. The letter or petition in its entirety can be examined on the fellowship website: *http:// www.uversa.org/archive/history/bedell_petition.htm*

7. A RESPONSE TO A THINLY DISGUISED ATTACK ON *THE URANTIA BOOK* by Clyde Bedell, a paper dated September 5, 1976 pp. 2-9. We do not know the specifics about the proposed structure of the organizations mentioned in Clyde's account. In this paper he expresses his own disagreement with an oligarchical lifetime tenure of Foundation Trustees (page 15). He continued to oppose this structure until his death. Regarding commercial motives, Clyde points out that "no one, neither Dr. Sadler nor his family, nor any Urantians to my knowledge, have ever made profit from the Urantia Book" (page 9). Clyde follows this comment with this statement: *"Even today, the frugal Foundation is largely supported by Urantian contributors, so the Book can continue to be sold at a price that makes it one of the greatest book bargains on Earth."* In subsequent years, general contributions dwindled, and the financial base of Urantia Foundation shifted to a few wealthy contributors and to the Book itself. The price of *The Urantia Book* soared. Clyde strongly opposed these price increases, and began referring to the Book as a "rich man's Bible." The price remained high until 1995, when Pathways published an exact replica of the 1955 printing and sold it for less than one-fourth the price of a Foundation printing. The Foundation responded with a competitive price reduction. Today Urantia Foundation is believed to be almost totally supported by revenues from Book sales and the personal donations of the Trustees themselves.

8. HOW TO KNOW WHAT TO BELIEVE, by Harold Sherman, Fawcett, New York, 1976, page 85

9. A RESPONSE TO A THINLY DISGUISED ATTACK ON THE URANTIA BOOK by Clyde Bedell, a paper dated September 5, 1976 page 13.

10. COMMENTARY ON THE ORIGIN OF THE URANTIA BOOK by Meredith Sprunger, 6/13/91, page 5. Also HISTORY TWO, prepared by a Contact Commissioner, undated, page 24.

"It Was Not Portrayed to be Error-Free" 161

11. I drew supplementary information for the printing processes of the time from a 1958 edition of *The World Book Encyclopedia*. I also interviewed two retired gentlemen from the original Donnelley Company plant in Crawfordsville, Indiana. Both men, a Mr. Krohn and a Bart Paddock, live in Crawfordsville. Krohn was a press supervisor and Paddock a plate department manager at the time of the second printing. Both men agreed the M-1000 press would have been used to print *The Urantia Book*. It was a huge old German press. I also interviewed Dr. Sprunger's son-in-law, Greg Young (now a minister), who worked on the M-1000 Press in 1969, a year or so after the second printing. Greg, a reader of the Book, said he understood the press had been used to print *The Urantia Book* before his arrival. Greg said it was also used to print Reader's Digest Condensed Books (as well as the magazine). Both Krohn and Paddock had made the same observation. Greg also commented that the M-1000 was also used to print *The World Book Encyclopedia*. It so happened that I had acquired a 1958 edition of *The World Book Encyclopedia* over ten years ago in Oklahoma for a couple of dollars, purely as a curiosity. That set of books stayed with me, and has proven very valuable in explaining the press methods of the circa 1955 period. By remarkable coincidence, *The World Book Encyclopedia* mentions, in its article on printing, that one of the printing methods presented was the same as had been used in printing the encyclopedia itself. After talking to Greg, I looked again at the pages in the encyclopedia, which featured several photographs of printing methods, a pressman, platemaking and so on. In small print below the photos was the credit: "R. R. Donnelley & Sons, Co." Also see Chapter Nine.

12. The PLAN FOR THE URANTIA BOOK REVELATION, by Carolyn B. Kendall, Paper distributed January 18, 1996, page 4.

13. POSTING by URANTIA FOUNDATION on their website *(http://www.urantia.org/newsinfo/strs.htm)* in 1999, under the title *Setting the Record Straight*: "The last typescript, which probably had a number of errors, was destroyed after the text was plated, cross-checked and believed to be free of mistakes." The syntax of this statement is somewhat strange, in that the procedure should logically have been "cross-checked, believed free of mistakes, and plated." There is no reason given for the assumption that the original text probably had a "number of errors." It had been read and checked over by the Forum

162 A HISTORY OF THE URANTIA PAPERS *Chapter Seven*

for several years. In addition, the text had been destroyed after the plates were made; there was no way to establish whether or not the manuscript used by the typesetter was the source of what was later believed to be errors.

14. The PLAN FOR THE URANTIA BOOK REVELATION, by Carolyn B. Kendall, Paper distributed January 18, 1996, page 5.

15. Meredith Sprunger, personal letter to me, September, 1999.

16. The PLAN FOR THE URANTIA BOOK REVELATION, by Carolyn B. Kendall, Paper distributed January 18, 1996, pp. 4 - 5. "Proofed by Oppy" may be a typographical error in Carolyn's paper. It may have referred to "Poppy," which was Christy's favorite name for Dr. Sadler.

17. The PLAN FOR THE URANTIA BOOK REVELATION, by Carolyn B. Kendall, Paper distributed January 18, 1996, page 5. Carolyn discloses that this information was obtained verbally from Christy. Carolyn's comments are very similar to the comments by a "second generation Urantian" posted by Urantia Foundation on their website in mid 1999 under: "Setting the Record Straight" point #7.

18. Letter from Trustee Emeritus James Mills to Ken and Betty Glasziou, March 5, 1991. Mills' comment that: "Apparently, the most potent source of error would lie at the point of the linotype operator" was imprecise and misleading, but apparently was what he was told. The ultimate responsibility for errors and typos lies with the client. A "press proof" is always provided the client so one final check can be made of the copy before it is etched and cast as a plate. See Appendix B for a complete text of this letter.

19. THE CREATORS by Daniel J. Boorstin, Random House, New York, 1992, pp. 63-64.

20. (REFERENCE CHAPTER FOUR). HISTORY TWO, prepared by a Contact Commissioner, undated, page 24. Dr. Meredith Sprunger has repeatedly stated that Dr. Sadler was emphatic that there was no human editing of the 1955 printing. *(See Affidavit, pp 316-320).* Clyde Bedell told me he would stake his life on it, and his wife Florence was equally convinced of the integrity of the first printing. Kristen Maaherra and Eric Schaveland also collected several dozen supporting comments from various sources and submitted them as exhibits for

the defense in nearly ten years of litigation instituted against them by Urantia Foundation. Here are a few excerpts: Emma Christensen: "I can categorically assure you that no humans decided the content of The Urantia Book. The book is as the revelators gave it to us." (Exhibits 8, 10 and 16.) Thomas Kendall, Trustee: "The Urantia Book is arranged and assembled exactly as revealed." (Exhibits K-1 and 750.) James C. Mills, Trustee: "As to the semantics employed, we had no control over them. We reproduced the text exactly as received. We are pledged to preserve it inviolate, and will do so." [Exhibit 510] William M. (Bill) Hales, First President of Urantia Foundation: "The Urantia Book was published just as it was received in English." There was no editing. Our only jurisdiction had to do with typing, proofreading, and publication." (Deposition of W. Hales, page 19, line 24, continued on page 20, lines 1-3.)

Dr. Sadler, Minnie Green (Christy's sister) and Christy

Chapter Eight
"You are now on your own"

"You Are Now on Your Own"   165

CLARENCE BOWMAN, A MEMBER of the Forum since 1923, told his family that the Forum and the Contact Commission looked forward to the end of World War II, when they were convinced *The Urantia Book* could be published at last.[1] When the war ended, it seemed the planet had passed through a nightmare that had threatened its very existence, and peace at last could be achieved. However, near the end of the conflict, a series of atomic blasts had signaled a new menace to civilization. And on the heels of that, Communism began its relentless campaign of world conquest.

Dr. Sadler related to Meredith Sprunger that the Contact Commission was informed immediately after the war that the Revelators believed Communism represented one of the most serious threats to the religion of Jesus and the freedom of humankind that had ever existed. The Revelators were alarmed that the specter of World War III was emerging, and preventing such a conflict was their immediate priority. In January of 1946, the Contact Commission was informed that the "United Midwayers of Urantia" had declared an intention to defeat Communism. The Contact Commission learned to their disappointment that the anticipated immediate postwar publication of *The Urantia Book* was not to be. [2]

The formation of Urantia Foundation

For more than five years the cast plates of *The Urantia Book* had been in storage at the Crawfordsville, Indiana plant of R.R. Donnelley & Sons, awaiting the order to print.[3] Histories One and Two report that in January, 1950, *these plates became the material basis* for the formation of an organization that was designed and intended to publish the Papers and to perpetually preserve the integrity of the original text:

"The plates of the Urantia Book which had been previously made constituted the basis for the creation of the Urantia Foundation by a Declaration of Trust under the laws of the State of Illinois, dated January 11, 1950. This is a non-profit organization.

"One of the objects for which the Foundation was created was to perpetually preserve inviolate the text of the Urantia Book and to disseminate the principles and teachings of the Urantia Book." [4]

The Declaration of Trust

A Trust is a legal title to a property to be assumed by one party for the benefit of another. The Trust document traditionally defines the property and conditions under which the property is transferred to the care of another party. The purpose of the Trust document is to establish the parameters of the Trust, and to prevent human prerogatives and folly to do damage to the property which is held in trust. *A Declaration of Trust* is a legally binding agreement between the two parties to this effect. To reflect these objectives, a Declaration of Trust was created for Urantia Foundation by the Contact Commission in liaison with attorneys. It provided for five Trustees who would have lifetime tenures. New Trustees, as needed, would be elected by the remaining Trustees.

In the case of the Declaration of Trust that established Urantia Foundation, the "property" that was to be protected by the terms of the Trust is the original text of *The Urantia Book*. The "original text" is defined in the Trust document as the plates that had been etched and cast from galleys that had been typeset from the typewritten text. The manuscript had been destroyed prior to the end of World War II, after the plates were made. The plates were to be used to publish *The Urantia Book*, and three copies of this original text were to be preserved in perpetuity. Thus, under the Declaration of Trust, Urantia Foundation provisionally assumed full responsibility for the text and would eventually become the publisher of *The Urantia Book*. The first Board of Trustees of Urantia Foundation were William Hales, President; Bill Sadler, Jr., Vice President; Emma L. Christensen, Secretary; Wilfred C. Kellogg, Treasurer, and Edith Cook, Assistant Secretary.

Note that the Contact Commission was being cautious. *Three Contact Commissioners were also Trustees on the first Urantia Foundation board: Bill Sadler, Jr., Emma L. Christensen, and Wilfred C. Kellogg.* Bill Sadler and Christy were residents at 533, and Wilfred lived in an apartment house a few blocks away. The Declaration of Trust established that Urantia Foundation was clearly recognized as the party now responsible for the preservation of the original text, but the Contact Commissioners held the majority of votes on the board. Any celestial "advice" to Urantia Foundation could be passed along informally through the still functioning Contact Commission. The other two Trustees, William Hales, President and Edith Cook, Assistant Secretary, had the honor of being the first "outsiders" to be involved with the administration of the original text. However, they obviously could exercise little influence over the policies of Urantia Foundation. Some Urantians believe that this arrangement of an "inner group within the inner group" seeded the original culture of Urantia

168   A HISTORY OF THE URANTIA PAPERS   *Chapter Eight*

Foundation, and continues until this day. *See Chapters Nine and Ten.*

Although three Contact Commissioners were Foundation Trustees, Dr. Sadler and Anna Bell Kellogg were not. According to the Declaration of Trust, Urantia Foundation was organized to eventually function autonomously; it was not a successor to the Contact Commission. The first three paragraphs of the Declaration of Trust make this autonomy clear:

> "KNOW ALL MEN BY THESE PRESENTS, THAT WHEREAS, there has been written a manuscript of a book entitled 'THE URANTIA BOOK,' and there have been produced from this manuscript approximately two thousand two hundred (2,200) nickel-plated stereotype plates[1] of patent base thickness for the printing and reproduction of such book; and

> "WHEREAS, certain persons, hereinafter referred to as the 'Contributors,' being desirous that a foundation be created for the objects herein expressed to be known as 'URANTIA FOUNDATION,' have contributed certain funds to that end, and said funds have been expended for the production of said plates for the printing and reproduction of THE URANTIA BOOK; and

> "WHEREAS, the Contributors, being desirous that their identity remain unknown in order that the creation of such foundation shall have no limitations by reason of its association with their names, coincident with the execution of this Declaration of Trust and with full knowledge and in consideration thereof, have caused their nominees to deliver

---

1. The number of "plates," 2,200, roughly correspond to the number of pages in The Urantia Book, including the preliminary material in the front. Those who prepared the Declaration of Trust evidently considered *each page* as a "plate," although each plate actually included 16 pages.

and turn over to the undersigned the said plates for the printing and reproduction of THE URANTIA BOOK, to be held in trust to make possible the accomplishment and fulfillment of such desires and to carry out and perpetuate the objects herein expressed . . ."

Dr. Sadler remained the leader of the Contact Commission. Although the Contact Commission had provisionally transferred responsibility for the text to Urantia Foundation, it retained control over the Forum-Study Group and the Seventy Group. The Contact Commission continued to function for five years after the January, 1950 establishment of Urantia Foundation.

The Declaration of Trust states the primary duty of the Trustees "shall be to preserve inviolate" . . . "the original text of *the Urantia Book*" . . . "from loss, damage, or destruction, and from alteration, modification, revision, or change in any manner or particular."

The "Substantive Estate" that was entrusted to Urantia Foundation is described in the Declaration of Trust as representing the original text of *The Urantia Book* and is defined in two parts: *[1]. "plates and other media for printing and reproduction of The Urantia Book" and [2]. "authenticated copies of the original text of The Urantia Book, but no less than three (3) such copies." (At the time of the formation of Urantia Foundation, the copies of the book had not yet been published from the plates.)* The document gave Urantia Foundation discretionary control of Substantive Estate with the exception of the "three copies of the original text" that would be printed by the plates. These three books the Foundation is to "preserve from loss, damage, or destruction, and from alteration, modification, revision, or change in any manner or particular."

To achieve their primary duty of preserving the original text inviolate, Urantia Foundation was also entrusted with *publishing* the original text, and thus were given total authority over the "plates and other media" for "printing and reproduction of the Urantia Book." They are permitted to transfer the plates with the provision they be "returned to the Trustees when the purposes for which it was transferred has been accomplished" (presumably printing the book). Finally, they are granted permission to destroy the plates provided all the Trustees agree the plates are "no longer required for accomplishing the purposes for which the Foundation is created" or if "the Trustees are prevented from preserving such portions of the Substantive Estate *[the plates]* by reason of circumstances beyond their control." These stipulations would allow the Trustees to create new plates when the original plates had worn out, a situation which would occur after a million copies had been printed, or if the plates deteriorated over time and could not be used. Duplicate plates could be produced when needed from the monotype tapes, as explained in Chapter Seven, or perhaps by some advanced technology that would allow the continued inviolate reproduction of the original text. It should be noted, however, that *all the Trustees would have to agree before any portion of the Substantive Estate was destroyed.* Chapter Nine will discuss how, after only 10,000 copies were printed, part of the Substantive Estate was destroyed in 1967 — very probably without concurrence or even knowledge of all the Trustees.

The Trustees accepted their responsibilities with this statement:

"We the undersigned herewith accept for ourselves and our successors in trust as herein defined, do hereby acknowledge that there have been transferred and delivered to us approximately two thousand, two hundred (2,200) nickel-plated stereo type plates of patent base thickness prepared from the manuscript of THE URANTIA BOOK for printing and reproduction thereof, which plates are

URANTIA.

Declaration of Trust
creating
URANTIA FOUNDATION

Published by
URANTIA FOUNDATION
533 Diversey Parkway, Chicago, Illinois 60614
®: Registered Mark of URANTIA Foundation

Declaration of Trust

KNOW ALL MEN BY THESE PRESENTS, THAT WHEREAS, there has been written a manuscript of a book entitled "THE URANTIA BOOK," and there have been produced from this manuscript approximately two thousand two hundred (2,200) nickel-plated stereotype plates of patent base thickness for the printing and reproduction of such book; and

WHEREAS, certain persons, hereinafter referred to as the "Contributors," being desirous that a foundation be created for the objects herein expressed to be known as "URANTIA FOUNDATION," have contributed certain funds to that end, and said funds have been expended for the production of said plates for the printing and reproduction of THE URANTIA BOOK; and

WHEREAS, the Contributors, being desirous that their identity remain unknown in order that the creation of such foundation shall have no limitations by reason of its association with their names, coincident with the execution of this Declaration of Trust and with full knowledge and in consideration thereof, have caused their nominees to deliver and turn over to the undersigned the said plates for the printing and reproduction of THE URANTIA BOOK, to be held in trust to make possible the accomplishment and fulfillment of such desires and to carry out and perpetuate the objects herein expressed; and

WHEREAS, it is also contemplated that from time to time hereafter money and property of various kinds and descriptions will be given, granted, conveyed, assigned, transferred, devised, or bequeathed to such foundation for the uses and purposes and upon the trusts and conditions herein expressed:

3

Page three of the original Declaration of Trust Document. The original text is now the plates which were set from the manuscript, and the plates are transferred from "Contributors" who desire their identity to "remain unknown." Urantia Foundation is clearly a new entity. See Appendix F for additional pages of the original document.

presently stored in the plate vaults of R. R. Donnelley & Sons Company at Crawfordsville, Indiana . . ."

Note that the original typed manuscript is not mentioned as part of the Trust. It had been destroyed when the plates were etched, and *the plates were now the text of The Urantia Book* that is referred to in the Declaration of Trust. It was the *plates* that the first Trustees swore to *"accept for ourselves and our successors in trust."* After 1945, the Seventy Group and the Forum-Study Group members used the proofing copies that were made from the plates — not the typed manuscripts — to study the Papers.

Some Urantians have examined the Declaration of Trust and pointed out that, although the Contact Commission had been permitted to standardize spelling, capitalization and punctuation in the original typewritten text, Urantia Foundation had no such latitude with the plates. The "primary duty" of Trustees described in the Declaration of Trust of Urantia Foundation was to preserve the original text of *The Urantia Book* (the plates) from "loss, damage, or destruction, and from *alteration, modification, revision, or change in any manner or particular."* These readers see the authority to control the publication and reproduction of the Book as granted in the spirit of *protecting* the text from change, not to establish the authority of the Trustees to *make changes* in the text. Naturally, if one is to be responsible for the preservation of the original text one must also be given authority to print it inviolate. However, there is no statement in the Declaration of Trust that even suggests allowing any changes in the original text. In fact, in the eyes of nearly all readers who are familiar with this document, both the spirit and the language of the Declaration of Trust clearly forbids any changes whatsoever.

We have noted that, years before, Clyde Bedell and a few others in the Forum harbored strong reservations about the manner in which Foundation Trustees would be selected and replaced. These early Urantians were disturbed about the establishment of a self-appointed oligarchy that would (for a period of a generation at least) totally control the text of the Revelation. (See Chapter Seven, "The Sherman Tempest.") Dr. Sadler told Meredith, Clyde Bedell and others that once a draft of the Declaration of Trust was drawn up by attorneys, it was submitted by the Contact Commission to the Midwayer Commission for their reaction. It may have been submitted more than once. According to Meredith's statements in a video interview, and what Clyde told me personally, the Midwayers refused to give specific suggestions for the document. However, they finally stated: *"If that is the best you can come up with it will have to do."* Meredith and Clyde quoted virtually the same words.

A shift of responsibility

The amount and nature of the contacts after 1952 were greatly changed, according to Mark Kulieke, and the "organizations were largely on their own."[5] Presumably, these organizations included Urantia Foundation, the Seventy Group, and the Sunday Forum-Study Group. There were provisionary restrictions, however. Urantia Foundation had not yet been given permission to actually publish the Book.

In November of 1951, the Seventy and the Sunday Forum-Study group were read an important communication from the "Acting Planetary Prince of Urantia." It had been delivered to the Contact Commission by his personal Regent. No doubt there was great suspense, because the group had been anticipating an announcement that *The Urantia Book* would now be printed. The announcement informed the group that the Acting Planetary Prince had made several decisions. Some of these involved angelic responsibilities for the Urantia Revelation. The status of the newly formed Urantia Foundation was discussed:

"The human aspects of the Urantia Book will be placed in the hands of the Trustees of the Urantia Foundation, subject to the advisory suggestions and veto power of the Revelatory Commission of the United Midwayers of Urantia. When, as, and if, the Midway Commission fails to communicate with the Trustees of the Foundation for a period of three years, then shall such Trustees deem that the affairs of the Urantia Book are wholly and exclusively in their hands and under their jurisdiction. For the time being, mediation between the overall and superhuman supervision of this Commission and the directly human functioning of the Trustees of the Urantia Foundation shall be vested in the Midwayer Commission, the successor of the original Urantia Revelatory Commission. This Commission shall continue to function as advisor to both the Celestial Overseers and the Trustees of the Urantia Foundation, but their veto powers shall extend only to the decisions and acts of the human Trustees."[6]

Note that, with the casting of the plates now completed and responsibility for their preservation transferred in trust to Urantia Foundation, the celestial team that was communicating through the Contact Commission had changed. The "Urantia Revelatory Commission" was now succeeded by a group called the "Midwayer Commission." Note also the comment that this guidance would continue "for the time being," and preparations were being made to place the affairs of *The Urantia Book* "wholly and exclusively" under human supervision. This seems clearly to indicate that special celestial guidance was winding down. In the same alleged message they heard the statement that seemed to foreshadow the news the early Urantians had been waiting for:

"In the absence of Midwayer intervention after February 11, 1954, the Trustees of Urantia Foundation shall proceed in accordance with their own judgment."

Nearly a year later, on the date of Jesus' Birthday, August 21, 1952, another message from the Regent of the Acting Planetary Prince was received and read to the groups. The Forum-Study group was to remain under the direction of the still operational Contact Commission. A Constitution for a new Urantia Brotherhood organization was provisionally approved, with the comment that the document "provides for its own emendation." It was left up to the discretion of Urantia Foundation when to launch the new, autonomous Urantia Brotherhood. As to the fate of *The Urantia Book,* the Regent for the Acting Planetary Prince conveyed this announcement:

"I, and I alone, will direct the time of the publication of The Urantia Book. If I do not provide such instructions on or before January 1, 1955, then the Trustees of the Urantia Foundation should proceed with plans for publication in accordance with their own judgment."[7]

A provisional date was set! The message also approved plans to publish an index to *The Urantia Book* in a separate volume. The Seventy Group was directed to terminate independent activities with the inauguration of Urantia Brotherhood.

The Contact Commission did not hear from the regent by the deadline date of January 1, 1955. Accordingly, the Trustees of Urantia Foundation acted upon their own judgment. The Urantia Brotherhood began officially on January 2, 1955. On that date, Dr. Sadler read a directive to the Seventy Group explaining how the Brotherhood was to be inaugurated. Then William Hales, who was presiding at the meeting, called for nominations for the officers of the Brotherhood. Bill Sadler, Jr. was elected president of the Brotherhood. He then took over the meeting and invited nominations for the nine committee chairmanships.[8] Thus, 36 members of the original Wednesday evening group called "The Seventy" became the Urantia Brotherhood.

176   A HISTORY OF THE URANTIA PAPERS   *Chapter Eight*

Shortly after the deadline for intervention passed, on February 11, 1955, the Trustees of Urantia Foundation signed their "Declaration of Intent to Publish *The Urantia Book*," and read it to the Forum. At last, ten years after etching and casting, the plates were dusted off and soon the printing presses in Crawfordsville were rolling. It should be noted once more that, although the Trustees were aware of a list of "errors" that had been discovered since the casting of the plates, there was no provision in the Declaration of Trust to "correct" them by altering the original text. Moreover, five of the original six Contact Commissioners were still functioning, and three of them were Trustees. I am not aware of any documentation about an inquiry made to the Midwayer Commission, nor of any concern at that time about the "errors" in the cast plates.

The mandate to publish The Urantia Book

The first recorded public mention of the specific wording of the mandate to publish *The Urantia Book* was in Dr. Sadler's 1958 Paper, *CONSIDERATION of SOME CRITICISMS of the URANTIA BOOK*. In the 26-page document the Doctor seems to be as energetic and intellectually acute as ever.

Dr. Sadler also tells us that the mandate to publish the Book was accompanied by some *admonitions* by the Midwayer Commission, which was successor to the original Urantia Revelatory Commission. Here is a complete list of those admonitions that Dr. Sadler elected to make public:

"Before taking up these individual criticisms, allow me to call to your attention some admonitions given us in connection with the mandate for the publication of the Urantia Book. Among other things we were advised:

"You Are Now on Your Own"   177

'You are called to a great work and yours is to be a transcendent privilege to present this revelation to the peoples of this strife-torn world.

'Supercilious scientists will ridicule you and some may even charge you with collusion and fraud. Well-meaning religionists will condemn you as enemies of the Christian religion and accuse you of defaming Christ himself.

'Thousands of spiritually hungry souls will bless you for the message you bring, and thousands of others will condemn you for disturbing their theologic complacence.

'Are you ready for your baptism of joys and sorrows which will certainly attend upon the early distribution of the Urantia Revelation?' " [9]

Later, in History One, further reference was to be given to these admonitions. This time they were referred to as *"suggestions."* This additional information about them was supplied:

"At the time of the publication of the Urantia Book suggestions were given by the revelators respecting the methods to be employed in the work of its distribution. These instructions may be summarized as follows:

"1. Study the methods employed by Jesus in introducing his work on earth. Note how he worked quietly at first — very often after a miracle, he would admonish the recipient of his ministry saying: 'Tell no man what happened to you.'

"2. It was suggested that we avoid all efforts at getting early, and spectacular recognition.

"During the first five years these suggestions have been followed and the distribution increases yearly. The vast. majority of the Brotherhood have concurred with this sort of

178   A HISTORY OF THE URANTIA PAPERS   *Chapter Eight*

quiet and gradual presentation of the book. However, one
thing should be made clear: While it is the policy of the
Brotherhood to work slowly in the distribution of the book,
nothing is done to interfere with the energetic and
enthusiastic efforts of any individual to introduce the book
to his friends and associates."[10]

Contrary to some questionable apocrypha, ***there never was a
set of permanent "mandates"*** given to the Contact Commission
relating to distribution of the Urantia Revelation. There was a
publication mandate for *The Urantia Book*, and this was
accompanied by several *"admonitions"* or *"suggestions"* very
clearly referenced to its early phases of distribution. To my
knowledge, the excerpts above are the only references to these
suggestions that were published for the general Urantia
Movement while Dr. Sadler was still living. History Two (which
was never published) devotes a page to the "Publication
Mandate," and quotes from its introduction. Generally, this page
(23) cautions that: "The Book belongs to the era immediately to
follow the conclusion of the present ideological struggle." It also
advises that the Book is provided early "to be on hand for the
training of teachers and leaders" and to allow for early translations
into other languages. (See Bill Sadler, Jr.'s comments below,
which paraphrase the same material that is on page 23 of History
Two.) There is no reliable documentation that the Revelators were
in contact with the Urantia Foundation, all communication was
with the Contact Commission.

The suggestions that accompanied the mandate to publish the
Book were paraphrased, edited and selectively used and adopted
in several Brotherhood internal memos. Bill Sadler, Jr. prepared a
paper in 1955 titled: *"Timing of The Urantia Book"* for the files of
the Executive Committee of Urantia Brotherhood. In this paper he
paraphrased the suggestions, calling them *"wise sayings."* He also
read his paper to the Forum-Study Group. About that time, the

Communist menace seemed to be gaining momentum. The Soviets had acquired atomic weapons, and American school children were routinely given instructions on what to do in case of an atomic attack. Bill Sadler, Jr. reminded the group that the Revelation was being distributed early, and was really intended for the era after the *"present ideological struggle."* He said, in part:

"The Book belongs to the era immediately to follow the conclusion of the present ideological struggle. That will be the day when men will be willing to seek truth and righteousness. When the chaos of the present confusion has passed, it will be more readily possible to formulate the cosmos of a new and improved era of human relationships. And it is for this better order of affairs that the Book was made ready.

"But the publication of the Book has not been postponed until that (possibly) somewhat remote date. An early publication of the Book has been provided so that it may be in hand for the training of leaders and teachers. Its presence is also required to engage the attention of persons of means who thus may be led to provide funds for translations into other languages. You who dedicate your lives to the service of the Book and the Brotherhood can little realize the import of your doings. You will doubtless live and die without realizing you are participating in the birth of a new age of religion on this world." [11]

Indeed, Contact Commissioners and the original Forum members had grown old waiting for the publication and propagation of the Revelation. Very few who heard this message would live to see the sudden collapse of Soviet Communism nearly 35 years in the future.

The copyrighting of *The Urantia Book*

It seems clear that the Contact Commission was directed by the Revelators to get an international copyright for *The Urantia Book*. Both Histories state *The Urantia Book* was published under an international copyright on October 12, 1955. Dr. Sprunger clearly recalls both Christy and Dr. Sadler stating that they were directed to get an international copyright.[12] An international copyright permits the listing of Divine Authorship, such as is the case of *The Urantia Book*. Neither History mentions a United States copyright. *A United States copyright can only be obtained for works authored by U.S. Citizens.*

The 1955 United States copyright application for *The Urantia Book* listed Urantia Foundation as the author. Many Urantians maintain that the Revelators would never have directed the Contact Commission to obtain a United States copyright by means of such a fraudulent application. Some believe that, although the international copyright was likely suggested by the Celestial Revelatory Commission, the acquisition of a United States copyright was a human idea. There is some documentary support for this. In 1973, Martin Myers and Christy collaborated closely on a speech Myers made to the general readership. It was titled "Unity, not Uniformity!". The speech was carefully phrased, and was copyrighted by Urantia Foundation. It contains these statements on page 5 of the original manuscript:

"The early leaders of the URANTIA Movement devised an ingenious plan. Their strategy was twofold.

"In order to protect the text from editing, alterations, and distortions, they foresaw the necessity of placing The URANTIA Book under the United States and international copyrights, thus guaranteeing future generations the privilege

Bill Sadler, Jr. and Clyde Bedell at a Picnic, June, 1952.

(Above) Lakeside view of the Chicago skyline, about 1955. (Right) A snapshot of the moment the first Urantia Books arrived from R.R. Donnelley & Sons.

of having the unadulterated Fifth Epochal Revelation. To that end The URANTIA Foundation was formalized and the Book was lawfully copyrighted in its name."

Many readers who have studied these comments are disturbed by their implications. Why did Myers (in collaboration with Christy) state that it was the "early leaders," and not the Revelators, who devised an "ingenious plan?" What was so "ingenious" about obtaining an ordinary copyright? Was the technique used to obtain the United States copyright by listing Urantia Foundation as the author considered ingenious by Myers? This is the first mention of a *United States* copyright. Why did Myers mention the United States copyright at all, when both histories and Dr. Sprunger's recollections support only the idea that the Revelators suggested obtaining an international copyright? And why did Myers state the Book was "lawfully" copyrighted? Would we not presume the copyright was lawful? *(See the Epilogue for a discussion of the purported 1942 "message" which was claimed to have been discovered by Myers and Christy in 1980.)*

The original copyright was renewed in 1983 on the basis that *The Urantia Book* is an anthology, a collection of writings by various authors, and the questions asked by the Forum constituted co-authorship. During the Kristen Maaherra litigation in the 1990's both the original and the renewal of the United States copyright were severely challenged. Maaherra maintained that if Urantia Foundation had submitted truthful applications, the United States Copyright Office would never have accepted them. As a result of the Maaherra litigation, both the original and the renewal of the U.S. copyright now exist in a greatly weakened condition. See Chapter Ten for additional discussion of the Maaherra litigation, which was terminated in February, 2000.

Urantia Books are delivered at last

One can imagine the joy of the early Urantians when the first Urantia Books were finally delivered. Mark Kulieke reports the excitement when his father came home on that Wednesday night in 1955 with four Urantia Books.[13] Carolyn Kendall related that her father believed *The Urantia Book* was going to be "the biggest hit in hundreds of years, and it was going to be reviewed in all the major newspapers." It was his plan to buy copies of all of these newspapers with their historic reviews of the great new Revelation.[14]

Shortly after the publication of *The Urantia Book,* a final message from the Midwayers was received by the Contact Commission:

"You are now on your own."

After nearly fifty years, the connection between the mortals of our planet and the unseen Midwayer Commission was severed and went dead.

"They didn't even say goodbye," remarked Dr. Sadler.[15]

ENDNOTES:

1. The PLAN FOR *THE URANTIA BOOK* REVELATION, by Carolyn B. Kendall, Paper distributed January 18, 1996, page 4.

2. The PLAN FOR *THE URANTIA BOOK* REVELATION, by Carolyn B. Kendall, Paper distributed January 18, 1996, page 2. Also statements by Dr. Sprunger in video interviews. There are a number of similar commentaries on the world political situation of the time that have surfaced in written form. Most of these are very questionable. However, *this particular story* regarding an intention to defeat Communism was given to Dr. Sprunger by Dr. Sadler, and I also heard it from Clyde Bedell and Berkeley Elliott. However, David Kantor is very doubtful about the veracity of this story. He believes such a casual comment about human affairs would have been a violation of the revelatory mandate.

184 A HISTORY OF THE URANTIA PAPERS *Chapter Eight*

3. Very probably the original tapes and negative films were also in storage. In the old monotype process described in Chapter 7, the typesetter did not cast the type directly, there was a two stage process. His keyboard punched holes in a paper tape, which was then fed into a caster. Reference for this information was the 1958 edition of *The World Book Encyclopedia*.

4. HISTORY OF THE URANTIA MOVEMENT ONE, by a Group of Urantian Pioneers, assisted by Members of the Contact Commission, 1960, page 9. The actual wording of the Declaration of Trust, page 8, is also "to perpetually preserve inviolate the text of THE URANTIA BOOK . . ." David Kantor has pointed out that the term *"inviolate text"* does not appear in the Declaration of Trust or the Histories. The Trust uses the term *"original text"* when referring to the plates and the 1955 printing. Urantia Foundation uses the term "inviolate text" generically to refer to any version of the text of the Papers they may publish. This will be discussed in Chapter Nine. [The last sentence of the original History One document read: "One of the objects for which the Foundation was created was to **preserve perpetually inviolate the text of the Urantia Book** and to disseminate the principles, teachings, and doctrines of the Urantia Book."] Dr. Sadler apparently changed "perpetually preserve" to read "preserve perpetually" and circled "doctrines," recommending its deletion stating: "the U. B. seems to me to avoid using these words."

5. BIRTH OF A REVELATION by Mark Kulieke, second edition, 1992, page 24.

6. See David Kantor's timeline on the Fellowship website, for 1951 and 1952, http://www.uversa.org/archive/history/message112251.htm where this message is reproduced. In "THE PLAN FOR *THE URANTIA BOOK* REVELATION," by Carolyn B. Kendall, on page 3, Carolyn produces the same "message" with an instructive omission. The missing statement is: **"When, as, and if, the Midway Commission fails to communicate with the Trustees of the Foundation for a period of three years, then shall such Trustees deem that the affairs of the Urantia Book are wholly and exclusively in their hands and under their jurisdiction."** This omitted sentence clearly supports those who believe special celestial guidance for the Trustees ended in 1955, with the message: *"You are now on your own."* See Chapter Nine for a full discussion of the issue of continuing special celestial guidance. Also see the Epilogue for additional discussion of the questionable use of apocryphal "messages," and how they have too often had the appearance of being edited to support a political, philosophical, or legal position. In this case, "THE PLAN FOR *THE URANTIA BOOK* REVELATION" (dated January 18, 1995) was submitted to the members of the Fellowship General Council in an effort to persuade them to reconsider their vote to publish *The Urantia Book*, which was then in the public domain. With her paper,

"You Are Now on Your Own" 185

Carolyn also wrote a cover letter to the Councilors. Some of her comments are interesting. She writes: *"Regardless of how one might wish the old messages would go away, the fact is that they did exist, they did exert a powerful influence and they are still relevant"* . . . *"As a former Forum member, I was constrained by promises not to discuss the origin of the book or anything that happened before publication."* Whether the old "messages" are relevant or not may be arguable. What is difficult to understand is Carolyn's statement that she was a "former Forum member." According to History One (page 6) and History Two (page 10), the last meeting of the Forum took place on May 31, 1942, when Carolyn was about ten years old. In 1951, what she joined was the Sunday study group. Carolyn was 23 when *The Urantia Book* was published. Also see the Epilogue, where Carolyn's history, *The Golden Years*, is discussed. The same critical passage is omitted in that document.

7. IBID, page 3.

8. April, 1992 paper titled AD HOC COMMITTEE ON RESEARCH: PRINCIPLES, PATTERNS, AND STRUCTURES IN *THE URANTIA BOOK* AND RELATED SOURCES by Carolyn Kendall, page 9.

9. CONSIDERATION OF SOME CRITICISMS OF *THE URANTIA BOOK* by Dr. William S. Sadler, a paper produced in 1958, page 1.

10. HISTORY OF THE URANTIA MOVEMENT ONE, by "a Group of Urantian Pioneers, assisted by Members of the Contact Commission, 1960," page 14.

11. The PLAN FOR *THE URANTIA BOOK* REVELATION, by Carolyn B. Kendall, Paper distributed January 18, 1996, page 4.

12. AFFIDAVIT of Dr. Meredith Sprunger, dated October 24, 1998. (See pp: 316 - 320).

13. BIRTH OF A REVELATION by Mark Kulieke, second edition, 1992, page 24.

14. WITNESSES TO A REVELATION by Polly Friedman, Summer, 1993, page 4.

15. A MONOGRAPH ON A VITAL ISSUE CONCERNING *THE URANTIA BOOK* AND MOVEMENT by Clyde Bedell, January, 1981, page 19. Also Clyde Bedell personally related the story of this message to me. Dr. Sadler reported the message to Dr. Sprunger, and added the comment about the sudden severance of the connection: *"They didn't even say goodbye."*

The process of curving printing plates was done so they would fit on rotary press cylinders. This is an R.R. Donnelley employee, from a 1958 World Book Encyclopedia photo.

Chapter Nine

"In my opinion, there can be only one edition of The Urantia Book, the first"

"In my opinion, there can be only one edition of *The Urantia Book*" 187

WE NOW COME TO A DISTINCT line of demarcation in the history of the Urantia Revelation. A remarkable achievement had been accomplished by the small group of Urantians who had somehow interfaced with unseen Revelators. By means of an arduous process that spanned five decades, they had cooperated with the efforts of celestial beings who authored and materialized a manuscript unlike any that had ever existed on the planet before.

The six Contact Commissioners had, to the best of their human abilities, kept their sacred oaths to preserve the text exactly as it was received. Dr. Lena Sadler was gone by the time their work reached fruition. The five remaining Contact Commissioners could take great pride in their human contribution to preserve the original text of the Fifth Epochal Revelation. No deliberate human intrusion had corrupted the Urantia Papers, and now the imperfect — but sincere and valiant — effort to duplicate the original text was safely plated, and 10,000 copies were printed (three copies of which were to be preserved "in perpetuity").

Important sacrifices had been made over the years. The greater portion of the lives of the Contact Commission had revolved around a corps of Midwayers who had provided strength and guidance at every turn. And now, after almost fifty years, the mortals were on their own.

For a time the thrilling reality of printed copies of *The Urantia Book* would provoke and sustain a tremendous euphoria. Urantia Books were mailed to prominent people, to friends, to family. Urantia Foundation and Urantia Brotherhood were launched. A School of the Urantia Brotherhood was formed in 1956. On June 17, 1956 the First Urantia Society was established in Chicago:

> " . . . and the Forum, after 33 years, passed into history and most of its members became the 156 initial members of the new society. The intrepid Forum members now prepared to share *The Urantia Book* with the world."[1]

The School of Urantia Brotherhood had its first session in September of 1956 with 71 students. Dr. Sadler had purchased a property at Pine Lodge in Beverly Shores, Indiana. The idea was that students could live in cottages on the property as they prepared themselves to go out as teachers and leaders of the new Revelation. By 1960, 14 students had graduated and received Certified Leader Diplomas.[2] Ordained Teacher Diplomas were also awarded.

Eventually the main activities of the school were conducted at 533 Diversey in Chicago, with classes being held in the evening. Some Urantians had felt that only professional teachers or retired persons could devote entire summers to the original Pine Lodge program, and the new evening classes were well attended. Dr. Sprunger reports that a Reverend David Schlundt traveled over 120 miles from Goshen, Indiana to attend the evening classes. Unfortunately, the formal teacher training program had lost momentum by 1975. Summer workshops and seminars are still offered by the Urantia Book Fellowship of the Urantia Book. However, the replete Teacher's Curriculum and intensive training program of Dr. Sadler has been abandoned. Urantian Jose Manuel Rodriguez Vargas of Bogota, Columbia is developing a formal training program along the lines of the original, with the idea of graduating certified teachers and leaders. Other schools have been attempted, such as *The Boulder School* established by John Hay in the mid-Eighties (now closed), and Polly Friedman's *School of Meanings and Values* in Los Angeles.

Dr. Sadler wrote that the mandate to publish the book was accompanied by several admonitions and suggestions. These included the development of schools for teachers and leaders. Although the Fellowship has developed in-depth study programs, they are a shadow of the original concepts of Dr. Sadler and Dr. Sprunger. Carolyn Kendall has expressed regret about the loss of formal Urantian schools:

> "If this advice is to be taken seriously, it would be imperative to consider the reinstitution of formal schools, regionally situated, to address the matter of in-depth training and qualification of teachers of The Urantia Book."[3]

In spite of all these activities, however, it surely began to dawn on the humans: *A Revelation of Epochal significance has been placed in our hands, but no one knows how to run a Revelation. And — now we are on our own.* No longer were there superhuman communications and advice to rely upon. The Revelators had unceremoniously broken the connection, and "didn't even say goodbye."

The fate of the Contact Commission

Within eight years, three more Contact Commissioners would follow Dr. Lena Sadler in the afterlife journey. On August 31, 1956, less than a year after the publication of *The Urantia Book*, Wilfred C. Kellogg died at the age of 75. His wife, Anna Bell Kellogg, died February 24, 1960, at the age of 82.[4] In the meantime, Bill Sadler, Jr. and Dr. Sadler fell into estrangement.

Bill and his wife Leone had lived at 533 Diversey Parkway with Dr. Sadler. Bill and Leone divorced around the time of publication. On the day after Christmas, in 1955, Bill and Leone's 19 year-old son was drinking a cup of coffee after a Christmas dinner with his mother and Dr. Sadler when the young man fell into a coma and died. His health had been degenerating, possibly due to a brain tumor. He had lost sight in one eye and vision in the other eye was deteriorating.

190 A HISTORY OF THE URANTIA PAPERS *Chapter Nine*

Sometime in 1956 Bill Sadler, Jr. married Florine Seres.

Bill was a chain smoker and also a heavy drinker. In the midst of all the tragedy and unhappiness in his life, he and his father were now in open rift, chiefly due to his divorce. Bill Sadler went on to form the Second Society Foundation of Chicago. During this period a group in Oklahoma discovered *The Urantia Book* and, on their own, started a "Urantia Church." Bill began to make regular visits to Oklahoma City, where his wisdom, philosophical insights and deep knowledge of the Papers were warmly appreciated. As the first "Field Representative" of Urantia Brotherhood, Bill Sadler, Jr. gave lectures on the Book all over the United States. A series of lectures in Pasadena and Malibu in California, 1958-1959, are preserved on tape and are available from *The School of Meanings and Values.*

Bill Sadler had written his marvelous *A Study of the Master Universe*, and was working on a companion volume of *Appendixes* when his health began to fail. A sudden stroke deprived him of speech. He was attempting to regain his ability to speak when he was hospitalized for cirrhosis of the liver.

Later, in 1963 he was again hospitalized with embolisms in both legs. A few months later, at the age of 56, a heart attack ended his life on earth. The date was November 22, 1963. Another star-crossed prince fell that day, John F. Kennedy. Clyde Bedell, who was a good friend of Bill Sadler, Jr., wrote of him:

> "Bill was one of the most interesting men I have ever known. His conversation flowed from a vastly superior intellect flavored, colored and under-structured by a simply prodigious knowledge and understanding of the Urantia Papers." [5]

The question of continuing special guidance

When did the Midwayers cease their communication with the Contact Commission? Was it over in 1955, immediately after the message *"You are now on your own"*? Or did the Midwayers

*Pine Lodge, Beverly Shores, Indiana,
Site of the first Urantia Brotherhood School.*
Fellowship Website Photo
http://www.ubfellowhip.org/archive/history/rowley/mr_014.htm

(Above) Christy in the Forties.

(Left) Bill Sadler, Jr. in 1960
Fellowship Website Photo
http://urantiabook.org/archive/history/billsadl.htm

Christy teaches at a Summer Study Session in 1963, at the age of 73.

Trustee Thomas A. Kendall, August, 1965

Dr. Sadler in the 50's.

Dr. Sadler teaching at 533 Diversey Parkway.

Fellowship Website Photo
http://urantiabook.org/archive/history/drsad1.htm

continue to give verbal instructions? In this author's judgment, the evidence and weight of testimony overwhelmingly indicates that the communications ended completely in 1955.

As we shall see, Urantia Foundation and many who support their policies believe special and privileged celestial guidance continued until at least 1982.

Because of the importance of this question, I will treat it in depth. Since I have an admitted prejudice against the notion that special celestial guidance continued, *I have assembled nearly all of the supporting documentation for this discussion from material of Foundation supporters — or from Urantia Foundation itself*. I have also presented Dr. Sprunger's slightly different philosophical perspective separately. It is hoped that interested readers can now have a reasonable basis to decide these questions and to weigh the full ramifications of the answers, based upon what the editing team (listed on the back of the title page of this book) believe is a fair assessment of the available information. The critical pivotal point in the events that drive this discussion can be established at the time of the preparation of the second printing which took place in 1967 - 1968. The second printing is copyrighted 1967 but was not actually printed until May of 1968, according to the Fellowship's website timeline. This anomaly may be understood by examining the peculiar process of preparation, which has never been carefully explored until now. Because of the copyright date, we will henceforth refer to the second printing as the 1967 printing.

The second printing of *The Urantia Book*

By the time the second printing was being prepared, there remained of the members of the former Contact Commission only Dr. Sadler, who was 92 years of age and failing, and Christy, 77. Many years before, Dr. Sadler had made it clear to Meredith Sprunger that after the connection of the sleeping subject went dead in 1955, there were no more messages. We have no idea when the sleeping subject himself may have died. The Contact Commission had been previously cautioned by the Revelators that after publication they should not make any commentary or announcement as to whether the sleeping subject was living or deceased.[6] If the established protocol for contacts remained in force, we can reasonably assume he was alive when the final *"You are now on your own"* message was received by the Contact Commission shortly after the book was published in 1955.

It is clear that Dr. Sadler did not have access to the Revelators when he replied to the questions in the letter from Reverend Adams on March 17, 1959. *(See Chapter Six. Also see Appendix B for a reproduction of his letter).* Interested readers will note that Dr. Sadler has few replete answers for the various points brought up by the Biblical scholar. Donald Green, one of the editors of this book, has made the observation that if Dr. Sadler had the ability to question the Revelators about these possible inconsistencies in the text in 1959, he surely would have done so. Likewise, he would have been prudent to inquire of the Revelators the best way to resolve the text questions. As to the more difficult problems presented by Reverend Adams, Dr. Sadler's only comment in his letter was that: *". . . our mandate forbade us to in any way alter the text of the manuscript."*

By 1967 the 92-year old Dr. Sadler, who was never a Trustee, was virtually removed from administrative leadership. More and more responsibilities had been deferred to Christy. As a Urantia Foundation Trustee and Secretary she answered most of the correspondence from readers, or decided who was best qualified to do so. Often she called upon Meredith Sprunger to respond to particularly difficult letters. As the need for a new printing loomed, Christy had to confront serious questions. In addition to the collection of typos she and Marian Rowley had acquired since the plates were made, more consequential problems with the text were being reported by astute readers such as Dr. Adams. It was obvious that, in the next printing of *The Urantia Book,* certain editorial inconsistencies, or seeming inconsistencies, would need to be addressed by Urantia Foundation.

In Carolyn Kendall's 1996 paper, *THE PLAN FOR THE URANTIA BOOK REVELATION*, Carolyn explains her understanding of the process by which presumed errors and inconsistencies were gathered and "corrected" in the 1967 second printing of *The Urantia Book*. She writes on page 5:

"In the years after publication, errors brought to Christy's or Marian's attention were welcomed. The Foundation wanted the book to be perfect. However – Christy was adamant: no arbitrary changes. Between 1955 and 1982 proposed corrections and changes were submitted by either of the two surviving Contact Commissioners to the revelators for permission."

This statement is what Carolyn reported that Christy said to her. It is not clear what Carolyn meant by the term *"revelators."* Many readers have raised philosophical questions about the process that Carolyn has described. As stated before, neither the Midwayer Commission nor the Revelatory Commission were available, according to what Dr. Sadler reported to Meredith Sprunger and Clyde Bedell.

By 1958, in an intra-office memorandum, Bill Sadler, Jr. referred to the Contact Commissioners as "defunct." If, as Carolyn states, *either* Dr. Sadler or Christy could have unilaterally initiated contact and "submitted" proposed changes to superhuman intelligences in 1967, that clearly meant a totally different form of communication than had existed during the Revelatory process. There is no mention by Carolyn of the Contact Personality in this new procedure. The team of Midwayers had always been present at contacts, but neither History One nor Two mentions that they communicated with individual Contact Commissioners other than in the presence of other Commissioners. In fact, there was a rule that no communications would be made unless two or more Contact Commissioners were present.₇ *Abundant evidence — not the least of which was Dr. Sadler's age and his long established repugnance regarding so-called "psychic" activities — indicates that it was Christy alone who was in supposed communication with "Midwayers" during the preparation of the second printing.*

What Carolyn next discloses about the "correction" process is even more remarkable:

"The Trustees of Urantia Foundation did not participate in the process of correcting the text of The Urantia Book. Their job was to publish the text with whatever changes were authorized by the Midwayers. They were to maintain the text inviolate, backing it up by copyright.[8] *It ought to be clarified to the readership by the Foundation that the corrections made after 1982 were apparently made without the authorization of the midwayers.*[9] *Reportedly, in publishing their latest edition, the Foundation is reversing changes made after 1982."*[10]

This series of comments that Carolyn published in 1996 generally represent the point of view of those readers who believe that direct celestial messages, delivered through Christy, continued to counsel and guide the Trustees of Urantia Foundation for nearly three decades after the 1955 printing. Let's very cautiously and reasonably consider this information, and the sources that Carolyn documents, from the perspective of readers who object to the process Carolyn describes above, and who oppose the implications of the notion of continuing direct celestial guidance.

FIRST, Carolyn reports that her husband, Tom Kendall, told her: *"The Trustees of Urantia Foundation did not participate in the process of correcting the text of The Urantia Book."* Yet, recall that, according to the Declaration of Trust, the primary duty of the Trustees is, in Article III, Duties of the Trustees: "PRESERVATION OF THE TEXT OF THE URANTIA BOOK: It shall be the primary duty of the Trustees to preserve inviolate the text of THE URANTIA BOOK. . . preserving and safekeeping of copies of the original text of THE URANTIA BOOK . . . from loss, damage, or destruction *and from alteration, modification, revision, or change in any manner or particular."* Moreover, in

Jacques Weiss with an aging Dr. Sadler at O'Hare Airport in 1960. Edith Cook is at right. Weiss was a French scholar who, with approval of Urantia Foundation, translated The Urantia Book into French and then published it. He was targeted by one of Christy's strange, dark "messages" in 1980. See Chapter 10, page 272, endnote #19.
Fellowship Website Photo
http://www.ubfellowship.org/archive/history/rowley/mr_062.htm

"Christy" on her 90th Birthday, January 29, 1980.

Christy with JJ Johnson and his son, Michael Andrew, in 1980
Photo courtesy JJ Johnson

Jim Mills lecturing on Cosmology in Berkeley, California Circa 1977
Fellowship Website Photo
http://urantiabook.org/org/archive/history/jmills1.htm

"In my opinion, there can be only one edition of The Urantia Book" 199

part 3 of the same section, PRESERVATION AND CONTROL OF REPRODUCTION OF THE URANTIA BOOK, it states: "It shall be the duty of the Trustees to retain absolute and unconditional control of all plates and other media for printing and reproduction of THE URANTIA BOOK . . ."

These duties are logically complementary. If the Trustees were to be responsible and accountable for the preservation of the original text as defined in paragraph 3.1 of the Declaration of Trust, it would be necessary for them to be granted absolute authority and control of the reproduction of *The Urantia Book*. How could it logically follow, then, that the Trustees were not involved in the decisions and processes to "correct" the second printing? Yet, Carolyn writes that her husband, Tom Kendall, who was a Trustee at the time, told her that the Trustees *"did not participate in correcting the text of The Urantia Book."* This is puzzling — and common sense requires these questions: Since Christy herself was still a sitting Foundation Trustee in 1967 (she did not become a Trustee Emeritus[11] until 1971), how could this statement be fully accurate? Christy and Tom Kendall, as Trustees, were both bound by oath to protect the original text from *any* changes *whatsoever*. By what authority and in what capacity was Christy acting, independent of the other Trustees? And how did Tom Kendall, himself a Trustee, know changes were being authorized "by the midwayers," as he had evidently reported to Carolyn? If Christy had told Tom this, was he not obligated to inform all the other Trustees that changes were being made to the text of the Revelation that was under their watch?

SECOND, Carolyn reports that: *"Their job was to publish the text with whatever changes were authorized by the Midwayers. They were to maintain the text inviolate, backing it up by copyright."* However, The Declaration of Trust of Urantia Foundation and the oath taken by the Trustees was never "to publish the text with whatever changes were authorized by the Midwayers," but rather to: *"preserve the original text of The Urantia Book"* from *"alteration, modification, revision, or change in any manner or particular."* Neither the Midwayers nor the copyright are mentioned in the Trust. From a purely technical legal perspective, in the Declaration of Trust there is simply no provision allowing for "correcting" the text of the 1955 edition of *The Urantia Book*. Had the Revelators desired such a provision, we can reasonably assume they would have clearly advocated it.

THIRD, in the next sentence we are told by Carolyn that: *"It ought to be clarified to the readership by the Foundation that the corrections made after 1982 were apparently made without the authorization of the midwayers."* 1982 was the year Christy died. Carolyn implies that the changes prior to and including 1982 *were* made with the authority of the Midwayers. (In her endnotes of *The PLAN FOR THE URANTIA BOOK REVELATION* Carolyn writes that this is her personal opinion.) However, we have only Christy's statement (as reported by Carolyn) that Christy got her authorization from the "Midwayers" to make the word and number changes and deletions. Unlike the Midwayer communications to the Contact Commission, there were no other verifying humans present. Such statements or claims about "communications" are problematic and fall within the realm of unverifiable psychic phenomena because they could neither be validated nor refuted by empirical means, nor could they ever be corroborated by others. Further, some Urantians are puzzled by the notion that the Revelators and the Contact Commission had gone to such strenuous lengths for fifty years to prevent the discovery of the Contact Personality — only to have the Midwayers begin informal conversations with Christy, who then readily discloses her status as a "contact" to several other people.

FOURTH: Carolyn's final comment informs us in her 1996 paper that: *"Reportedly, in publishing their latest edition, the Foundation is reversing changes made after 1982."* She gives as her source Richard Keeler, President of Urantia Foundation. The date of 1982 is when Carolyn believes the "Midwayers" stopped giving information about changes, evidently because Christy died in 1982. Some readers may wonder if Urantia

"In my opinion, there can be only one edition of The Urantia Book" 201

Foundation can so readily reverse the "changes made after 1982" in *The Urantia Book*, why they cannot reverse changes made after 1955. One possible reason was posted in 1999 on Urantia Foundation's web site commentary, *"Setting the Record Straight" (http://www.urantia.org/newsinfo/strs.htm)*. In their explanation of the changes made in the original text after the first printing (Point #7) Urantia Foundation states:

> *"While there is no official documentation as to the reason for some of the changes after the first printing of The Urantia Book, we know from analyzing these changes (see the Foundation's brochure: 'Changes to the Text') that most of the changes were typographical in nature.* <u>**We have reason to believe that none of the more significant changes were made without approval from the revelators.**</u>*"* (My emphasis.)

We must surmise from this statement that Urantia Foundation supports the notion that "Revelators" were directing "significant" changes in the text. Yet, as previously documented, there were no Revelators available when the changes were made. The celestial Urantia Revelatory Commission had been replaced by the Midwayer Commission in the early fifties. After the making of the plates, no text changes were made until 1967. Foundation President Keeler testified in the Maaherra litigation (1991-1999) that *there had been no further contacts after 1955*. Regardless, if the Foundation's statement refers to "messages" from anonymous entities that were supposedly received by Christy, this would seem to fly in the face of the teachings of the Urantia Papers, and elevate unverifiable "channeled" messages above the oath of Urantia Foundation Trustees to honor the Declaration of Trust.

In the final analysis, the three "authenticated copies of the original text of THE URANTIA BOOK" that Urantia Foundation is bound by Trust to keep and protect from "loss, damage, or destruction and from alteration, revision, or change in any manner or particular" no longer matched, word for word, either the plates or what the Foundation printed in 1967. Through 16 subsequent printings from 1967 through 1999, 12 are different and none match the original text of 1955. *(See Appendix D)* Surely, it is reasonable to suggest that this contradiction is a problem for all readers, regardless of whether they believe the post-1955 changes were authorized by Midwayers or not. As Trustee Emeritus James C. Mills wrote to Ken and Betty Glasziou in the letter dated March 5, 1991 *(See Chapter Seven)*:

> *"It looks like we need to carefully proofread the present printing against the first printing. In my opinion, there can be only one edition of The Urantia Book, the first."*

What went wrong?

In the opinion of those who support the notion of continued special celestial guidance, nothing went wrong. They believe Christy was in contact with "Midwayers." However, those of us who do not believe unique celestial guidance extended beyond 1955 must confront the question of exactly what happened to motivate Trustee Christy to alter the original text (the plates) in the face of The Declaration of Trust that forbade any modification whatsoever. The most plausible explanation to us is that Christy *believed* she got the approval of Midwayers to correct the considerable number of typographical errors and apparent editorial inconsistencies that had been collected since the plating of *The Urantia Book* in 1942-45. We cannot know exactly what Christy's thought-processes were, but it is likely they were similar to ideas that drove the tragic channeling episode of Vern Grimsley, which we will examine in the next chapter. Vern came to believe he was hearing "Midwayers" talking to him.

Can people really delude themselves to the point that they actually believe they hear "voices" talking to them? Yes, they can. In a 1984 Report on the Grimsley channeling, Hoite Caston, a former Trustee, quoted Dr. Julian Jaynes, author of the famous book: *The Origin of Consciousness and the Breakdown of the Bicameral Mind.* Dr. Jaynes observed:

> "Whatever brain area is utilized, it is absolutely certain that such voices do exist and that experiencing them is just like

"In my opinion, there can be only one edition of The Urantia Book" 203

hearing actual sound . . . They are heard by many completely normal people to varying degrees. Often it is in time of stress, when a parent's comforting voice is heard."

What situation could have triggered such stress in Christy? Certainly the weight of responsibility for an epochal revelation would be sufficient. Dr. Sadler, as I have indicated, was 92 and deteriorating rapidly. All the other Contact Commissioners were gone. Christy was virtually alone; very serious decisions had to be made, and there was only human wisdom to rely upon. The Midwayer Commission had long since departed. Some have postulated that Christy sincerely believed she had been chosen to "correct" and "perfect" the text, even though this mission would violate her oath as a Trustee. Granting the situation, what would push this otherwise normal woman over the edge to imagine the Midwayers had returned to help her?

Again we turn to Mr. Caston's report on Vern Grimsley. As we shall see, Grimsley was very close to Christy, and he believed she received messages from Midwayers. She confided in Grimsley that she "was told" he was a "destiny reservist." *[Refer to The Urantia Book, pages 1257-1258].* Just months after Christy's death in 1982, Vern was in a very serious emotional crisis. Now Christy was gone, and Vern believed himself to be the "spiritual leader" of the Urantia Movement. Grimsley was contemplating the purchase of a very expensive property in California for his *Family of God* organization. Standing under a tree he looked down on the 25 acre property and the spacious 75-room building. The Appendixes of Caston's report features a letter by Dr. Paul Knott, who informally examined Vern. Dr. Knott reports:

"Vern, in this state of consternation, wandered off by himself and suddenly, 'out of the blue' (Vern's words) a voice above him and to his right speaks commandingly (and tells him what he wants to hear) 'This is it.' The difficult decision is thus made for him, his anxiety is relieved, and the purchase is subsequently made."

Hoite Caston adds this comment:

"An 'unseen friend,' one of the only advisers on the planet who Vern could unquestioningly believe would possess the wisdom to counsel him, has apparently 'spoken' to him."

Returning to Christy's dilemma, a similar scenario is possible. In the company of the other members of the Contact Commission, she had heard the Midwayers speak, and experienced disembodied voices. Now she felt alone and in desperate need of advice. She "hears" a "voice" tell her to "correct" the text, and her problem is solved. It appears that Carolyn and Tom Kendall believed that Christy had a special "connection" to celestial beings. Perhaps such support encouraged Christy to believe she had unique status, and by resolving the apparent inconsistencies she was "restoring" the original text. There is evidence that she did believe this. In a letter to Urantian scholar James Johnson dated September 4, 1981, Christy responded to a list of questions and apparent typos that JJ had submitted for clarification. JJ did not expect that his inquiries would be taken as suggestions for changing the text of the Book. However, in a brief letter that accompanied the list of inquiries, Christy astonished JJ by informing him that two of his inquiries would be accepted and corrected. *(see exhibits, pp 206-207)*:

"Dear 'J. J.'

"I know you have done a great deal of work hunting out these errors, but we have strict orders to leave the text inviolate. Therefore, we do not change errors unless typographical, misspelling, or punctuation. You and I cannot rewrite the URANTIA Revelation. It is as near as we can make it an identical copy of the Midwayers work. Let's bear this in mind at all times."

A hand-written P.S. was added by Christy to the bottom of the letter:

"In my opinion, there can be only one edition of The Urantia Book"   205

"We didn't get your note in time to make any changes in
the Seventh Printing but corrections necessary will be
made in the Eighth."

This dichotomous response perplexed JJ. On one hand,
Christy told him she was under strict orders to leave the original
text inviolate. JJ agreed with this completely, and had never
advocated or even suggested changing anything. On the other
hand, Christy stated that she would "correct" two of the items he
discovered (one of which changed the meaning of a phrase) in the
next printing. Christy died the next year, and the changes were
never made.

However, the question remains: how was it that no Trustee
challenged Christy? *As we shall see, it is very probable that only
those Trustees sympathetic with the supposedly "channelled
messages" knew that a substantial number of plates had been
replaced by altered substitutes, and the originals destroyed.*

Were all the Trustees informed of the changes?

Many readers have difficulty believing all the other Trustees
were not informed of the changes. Yet, there is compelling
evidence that they were not. Consider the documented statements
by James C. Mills, Ph.D., who was selected to replace Christy as a
Trustee in October of 1971. Dr. Mills was a former President of
Urantia Brotherhood, and served many years as a Trustee
Emeritus. In this capacity he "officially" answered much
Foundation correspondence.

On March 5, 1991, Dr. Mills wrote in reply to a question
from Dr. Kenneth & Betty Glasziou of Australia that indicates he
was unaware of the scope and number of editorial changes Christy
had made under his watch as a Trustee:

"I had only one experience with a textual change being
made between printings. I told you about this during
your visit in Pensacola. This was due to the diligence of a
high school science teacher who had a BS in science and
had read in a scientific journal that a specific figure given

URANTIA FOUNDATION
533 DIVERSEY PARKWAY · CHICAGO ILLINOIS 60614

September 4, 1981

Mr. James H. Johnson
Northrop Box 398
APO NEW YORK 09671

Dear "J.J.":

I know you have done a great deal of work hunting out these errors, but we have strict orders to leave the text inviolate. Therefore, we do not change errors unless typographical, misspelling, or punctuation. You and I cannot rewrite the URANTIA Revelation. It is as near as we can make it an identical copy of the Midwayers' work. Let's bear this in mind at all times.

Marian and I have gone through your suggestions very carefully and are in agreement in this report.

Sincerely,

Christy

(Miss) E. L. Christensen
Secretary

ELC:kfm

Attach.

P.S. We didn't get your note in time to make any changes in the seventh printing but corrections necessary will be made in the Eighth.

The letter Christy wrote that accompanied her response to the inquires of JJ Johnson.

September 4, 1981

LIST OF CORRECTIONS FOR THE 8TH PRINTING OF THE URANTIA BOOK -

5. Page 1319, paragraph 1, line 2, change "inhabited worlds" to
    "inhabitable worlds" -

6. Page 486, paragraph 6, "forty thousand" is correct.

7. Page 526, second sentence, is Okay as is.

8. Page 605, paragraph 7, will stand as is in the book. Not contradictory.

9. Page 616, paragraph 5, Okay as is.

10. Page 628, paragraph 5, no change necessary.

11. Page 655, paragraph 4, Okay as is.

12. Page 883, last sentence, "East" is Okay.

13. Page 988, paragraph 6, "Teuskwatowa" is the correct spelling as given
    in   updated Bible dictionaries, the other probably was a mis-typing.

14. Page 1317, paragraph 3, 4th sentence, Okay as is.

15. Page 1372, paragraph 1, no change chould be made. (We do not edit
    The URANTIA Book.)

16. Page 2021, paragraph 8, let stand as is. It is not for us to say.

                    * * * * * * * * * *

Going on to the new correction sheet Marian received from you today:

5. Page 1059, last paragraph, we will let stand as is.

6. Page 121, paragraph 4, must stand as is.

Page two of a list of comments by Christy regarding inquiries JJ Johnson
had made about the text. Page one noted four small typos. On the page
above, JJ was astonished that inquiries #5 and #13 were taken as
suggested changes and accepted. The reader may find the comments on
the balance of JJ's inquiries instructive. (Merritt Horn points out that
whoever typed this reply misspelled "Tenskwatawa" again!)

in The Urantia Book expressing the relationship between the mass of the nucleus and the planetary electron in the hydrogen atom had changed by one digit. He was able to persuade the people at 533 to change it in the second printing. At that time I had moved to Wisconsin and the chap instituting the change had followed me as president of the Brotherhood. Quite by accident, the change was pointed out to me by a young woman student who was incensed at obvious tampering with what she firmly and correctly believed should be left alone by human hands. I raised quite a ruckus about the matter and it was returned to its original status in the very next printing. Since that move, with the exception of 1973-1975, I have not resided in Chicago and have not been informed of any other apparent discrepancies between printings until your letter of Nov.20. I am taking up this matter with the Foundation immediately." *[See Appendix B for a full text of the letter. It should be noted that the change referred to by Dr. Mills was **not** reversed in later editions, contrary to what he had assumed.]*

Certainly, the Trustees were honorable, intelligent individuals who were aware of their solemn trust and responsibilities. One problem was the practical reality that most of the Trustees met only periodically at 533 Diversey Parkway, while Christy lived and worked there on a full time basis. As the Trustees gradually became distanced from actual involvement with the text, the culture at 533 more energetically revolved around the dominating personality of Christy.

It appears that Carolyn's statement is accurate that the Trustees did not participate in the "process" of "correcting" *The Urantia Book*, in the sense that *all* the Trustees were not aware that the 1967 text was being altered by Christy with the "approval" of what she perceived were the voices of the "Midwayers."[12] And perhaps, as indicated, Christy believed she was "restoring" the text to its proper state by "corrections" of

"In my opinion, there can be only one edition of The Urantia Book" 209

what she deemed were human copying errors. At the same time, some Urantians are puzzled about this claim because the original manuscript was no longer available. What empirical method did Christy use to verify "copying errors?"

Was there a "technical" printing problem?

In another part of his letter to Dr. Kenneth Glasziou, Dr. Mills seems to have been under the impression that the entire book had to be reset in 1967 due to the change in printing technology, and this resulted in many new typos and copying errors:

> "In the twelve year interval between the first and second printings new photographic techniques and higher speed presses rendered the original plates obsolete and new plates had to be produced. As the original plates were planned to yield one million impressions, this was quite a blow."

However, this was not the case. *The original plates were used to print the 1967 Urantia Book, with the exception of at least 48 pages that were replaced with altered text.* Also, what had changed was the technology used to *make* plates. The *Urantia Brotherhood Bulletin* reported in their Winter and Spring, 1979 edition, page 2, that: *"[The first] five printings had been performed on the same press."* This agrees with two R.R. Donnelley's employees, now retired, who were there at the time. Mr. Bart Paddock, the plate foreman, and a Mr. Krohn, who was a press supervisor in 1967, agree that an M-1000 press, housed in the original Donnelley building in Crawfordsville, Indiana, would have been used for both the 1955 and the 1967 printings. This press could still accommodate the original plates in 1967. The Urantia Brotherhood Bulletin also reported that: *"The text of The Urantia Book was the same with minor grammatical corrections. That, as many readers know, is one of the main purposes of Urantia Foundation, to protect the text of The Urantia Book and keep it from being changed."*

We now know that changes went beyond this self-contradictory and euphemistic description. To achieve editorial changes in the second printing, it is clear that *someone* decided the simplest course was to *alter the plates by replacing the designated problem pages with at least 48 newly etched pages.* As stated, the use of the original plates in 1967 would not have posed a technical problem to the M-1000 press, other than the age of the plates themselves.[13] Both the 1955 and 1967 printings show evidence of deteriorating plates. However, after examining the 1955 printings and the 1967 printings we can be virtually certain that the original plates were first altered, and then used in the 1967 printing. The pages that "required" word and number changes and deletions were physically removed and replaced with newly etched and cast pages. *[See the Addenda following the endnotes of this chapter for the evidence Merritt Horn and I collected that compelled us to come to this conclusion].*

We can be reasonably certain that, in addition to Dr. Mills, other highly respected leaders were not directly informed that several editorial changes had been made by altering the plates. Clyde Bedell wrote in 1976:

"Every word of the Urantia Papers, even the use of 'the highest existing human concepts' was placed in the URANTIA Papers by the Revelators. None was inserted by any human being whatsoever. I would stake my life on this." [14]

Note that Clyde used the term Urantia Papers, not Urantia Book. Because of his extensive work with his Concordex, Clyde was aware in 1976 that there were typographical problems with various printings of the text.[15] However, if he had known the original text had been deliberately altered, based upon strange new "celestial messages," I am certain he would have, to put it mildly, taken vigorous exception to the process. The purported "channeled" messages were not taken seriously by everyone at 533 Diversey Parkway.[16] It was not until the death of Dr. Sadler that rumors of Christy's channeled "messages" began to surface beyond the inner power structures of Urantia Foundation and Urantia Brotherhood. Gradually, stories of supposed special

"In my opinion, there can be only one edition of The Urantia Book" 211

Foundation "guidance" began to circulate among Urantians. In 1981, Clyde Bedell published a clear evaluation of the alleged "secret" messages and special "celestial guidance" that had continued to be rumored after the death of Dr. Sadler:

> "I do not believe the Trustees are any more divinely guided than you are, or I am. The everywhere repeated words we hear, reportedly communicated to the forum when the Book was published, in 1955: *'You are now on your own,'* I believe to be true and I believe they were meant. We are on our own and should take our privilege and our responsibility far more seriously than we do . . .

> "Yes, I have heard on rare occasions the whispered gossip and maunderings: 'The Trustees must be right. They are so set in their policies they must be getting guidance, communications.' Examine this idea, which, when stated, is usually in querulous tones about the [copyright] issues I have been discussing in this paper. Any reader who believes it, is saying in effect that the teachings of our vast and great Revelation, The Urantia Book, are already being superseded by secret communications to a handful of humanly named servants of the Urantia Movement . . . I believe The Urantia Book will never be superseded until some distant date from now, and then by another Epochal Revelation, not by anonymous spirits secretly passing little 'do's and don'ts' to fallible Trustees." [17]

Something had to be done

Returning to Christy's dilemma just before the 1967 printing — certainly something had to be done. One final conclusion seems self-evident: The decision to change the text itself by secretly altering the plates, rather than openly footnoting or endnoting the apparent inconsistencies, created fresh problems. *The supposedly "corrected" text was no longer in agreement with either the original plates or the 1955 printing.* It is also self-evident that one cannot have multiple and differing sets of inviolate replications of the same original text. In addition, there

212 A HISTORY OF THE URANTIA PAPERS *Chapter Nine*

has never been a candid and complete disclosure to readers. Very few purchasers of later printings of *The Urantia Book* have been informed that the book they were buying was not in complete conformity with the original 1955 text. It is reasonable that readers should be the judge of the importance of the changes that were made, and be able to weigh their buying decisions accordingly.

In the next few pages, Dr. Sprunger reviews the situation just described, weighs its significance, and suggests a solution. His perspective differs slightly from the author's, and is presented here for the consideration of the reader:

Dr. Meredith Sprunger reviews the ambiguities associated with the publication of the Urantia Papers

"It is generally agreed by most students of *The Urantia Book* that the Papers were composed by supermortal personalities and, except for changes in spelling, capitalization, and punctuation, were not edited by any human being. The Urantia Papers were published exactly as they were received from the Revelators.

"Since the Papers were typed numerous times and set in type by R. R. Donnelley & Sons, it is obvious that mistakes in copying could, and probably did, take place. The Midwayers probably were aware of these errors and inconsistencies but did not consider them serious enough to stop the publication.

"In my judgment the greatest mistake religious fundamentalists make is their belief in the literal inspiration, the infallibility, of scripture. The basic purpose of revelation is to enhance spiritual insight by expanding the spiritual paradigm.

"In the years following the publication of *The Urantia Book* in 1955, many of these possible errors and inconsistencies were pointed out and something had to be done about them in the 1967 printing. Someone decided to try to correct these problem areas in the text by altering the plates. In hindsight, the great mistake the Foundation made was not to list these changes along with the reasons for them in endnotes of the book.

"At this point, we should review evidence as to who made the decision to make these changes. Carolyn Kendall tells us, from

"In my opinion, there can be only one edition of The Urantia Book" 213

information provided by Tom Kendall, that the Trustees of Urantia Foundation did not participate in the process of 'correcting' the text of *The Urantia Book*. This would indicate that the changes were made by Christy in the 1967 printing, and subsequent printings until her death in 1982. This assumption is apparently confirmed by Scott Forsythe, Administrative Assistant for Urantia Foundation, when he wrote JJ Johnson, *'Christy's relationship to the text of The Urantia Book was unique.' (See Appendix B)*

"Carolyn Kendall and Tom Kendall believed these changes were approved by the Midwayer Commission. This assumption, of course, is challenged by Dr. Sadler's statement to me that all contact with the superhuman revelators had ceased, and some questions about the nature and authenticity of Christy's alleged Midwayer contacts were raised by some of the power structure of the Brotherhood.

"In my judgment, unless you are a Urantia Book fundamentalist, believing in the 'literal inspiration,' the absolute truth of every word in *The Urantia Book*, from the pragmatic viewpoint it makes little difference whether these changes were approved by the Midwayer Commission or not. These changes do not affect the revelatory authenticity of the Fifth Epochal Revelation. In any case, there is no objective way to prove definitively whether these changes were approved by the Midwayers or not.

"Perhaps the best solution to this unfortunate brouhaha is to list all of the changes made after the 1955 edition, along with the reasons for the changes, and permit each individual to make his or her own decision as to the revelator's original text. Hopefully, the Foundation Trustees will do this by placing endnotes in future printings."

Revisiting the original question

Dr. Sprunger's cautions about Urantian Fundamentalism are well taken, but I do not believe that question is at issue. While, from a pragmatic viewpoint, it may be said that the changes in the text to date have been minor and do not affect our spiritual destinies, I believe we should carefully consider future readers and the overall welfare of the Revelation one, three, or five hundred years hence. If we do, in my judgment it *does* matter whether these changes *"were made by the Midwayer Commission or not."* The question of special celestial guidance after 1955 cannot be avoided, its ramifications are too significant to ignore.

My reasons for believing that the long-range viability and integrity of the Revelation are at stake are four-fold:

[1]. There is a need for a reliable lineage of successive printings with the authentic original (1955) text as a touchstone for future scholars.

[2]. It is illogical, disingenuous, and philosophically inconsistent for Urantia Foundation to "preserve" one original text while printing and selling to the public several different texts, implying that each is an "inviolate" replication of the original text.

[3]. The letter and spirit of the Declaration of Trust forbids any changes whatsoever to the text. It should be honored in deed as well as in rhetoric.

[4]. The questionable process by which the changes were originally made may impinge on classic "psychic" activities, which the Papers themselves refute. The nature of the policy that so long concealed them is repugnant to many Urantians. And Urantia Foundation's refusal to ameliorate the problem is divisive and damaging to the Urantia community.

On the first point, scholars need an accurate touchstone by which to verify their evaluation of the Revelation. The wisdom of the Revelators in mandating the principle of printing and preserving an uncompromised original text seems obvious to many scholars of the Papers. Dr. Mark McMenamin, a professor of geology at Mount Holyoke College, responded to a letter by JJ Johnson with these comments: *"If it was written in 1955, parts of it are strikingly ahead of their time. I could only locate the 1984 edition; can you confirm that pages 664-671 appeared as is in the 1955 edition?"* Because of JJ's persistence and efforts, Dr. McMenamin included very favorable comments about *The Urantia Book* in his own book, *The Garden of Ediacara,* published by Columbia University Press in 1998. (See Appendix C). JJ wrote me later: *"It should be evident this is going to crop up more and more . . . the quicker we nail this down . . . the sooner scientists like Mark won't have to ask these questions and hesitate to include them in their research/books and other works."* JJ points out that if a scholar in 1998 has difficulty finding a 1955 printing, imagine how difficult it will be one or two hundred years from now. Indeed, of what value are three (3) copies of the original text of *The Urantia Book* if they are preserved in some unknown location where no one gets to see them and the Foundation is printing different texts?

The second point is self-evident, or should be: There cannot be two or more versions of the text, each of which is said to be an inviolate reproduction of the original. Urantia Foundation President Richard Keeler told me in 1998 that the Foundation retains the Declaration of Trust's mandated part of the "Substantive Estate" of "not less than three (3) printed copies" of the "original text of THE URANTIA BOOK" that were printed from the original plates. Mr. Keeler believes this fulfills the Trustees oath to preserve the original text inviolate. Unfortunately, as previously stated, the various "inviolate" versions of the text of *The Urantia Book* that Urantia Foundation has been printing and selling for decades are different from the three (3) printed copies of original text of *The Urantia Book* the Trustees presumably are keeping so carefully preserved.

Some Urantians believe Urantia Foundation's policies put the original text itself at risk. Dr. Sadler died on April 29, 1969, at the age of 93. Just after the third printing, on May 6, 1971, Urantia Foundation ordered R. R. Donnelley & Sons in Crawfordsville to complete destruction of the approximately "two thousand two hundred (2,200) nickel-plated stereotype plates of patent thickness for the printing and reproduction of such book." It is almost certain that the Donnelley Company also destroyed the original paper tapes from which the type was set and the negatives from which the plates were made. These tapes and negatives were routinely kept in order to recast plates that had become worn from printing. The destruction of the original plates leads to the third point.

The third point is the Declaration of Trust expressly forbids any alteration of the text. This is also self-evident, or should be. Aside from the *principle* of *printing* as well as *preserving* inviolate the original text, there is the pragmatic legal argument that the Declaration of Trust was designed and intended to protect the text of the Revelation from human folly. Carolyn tells us the clear parameters of the Trust were supplanted by this human aspiration: *"The Foundation wanted the book to be perfect."* This well-intended desire by humans in 1967 resulted in a violation of both the direct instructions of the Revelators and the restrictions of the Declaration of Trust.

It seems clear that a decision was made in 1967 to destroy a portion of the Substantive Estate in defiance of the Declaration of Trust. It is a fact that Urantia Foundation made a decision in May of 1971 to complete the destruction of the historic plates after only 10,000 copies of the original text had been made. To many Urantians the original plates were not merely a curiosity any more than the original typed manuscript was a curiosity. The plates *were* the "original text" of *The Urantia Book* as defined in the Declaration of Trust. And the plates were also the first of the two parts of the "Substantive Estate" described in paragraph four of the Trust document, they had been proofed, cast and sanctioned when the Revelators were in contact. All that now remains of the entire Substantive Estate are three printed books, a generation removed from the original plates (as the original plates were a generation removed from the typed manuscript). Because these books were not printed on acid-free paper, they must eventually disintegrate. Since the original text is no longer being printed, some readers are not comfortable with the reality that the last vestiges of the bona fide revelatory process are three paper and cloth copies of the original 1955 printing of the Book. Many readers and believers are uneasy, even though the current designated "keepers of the original text" assure Urantians that

"In my opinion, there can be only one edition of The Urantia Book" 217

these three Books, printed from the original plates, are being "preserved" in storage somewhere.

The fourth point is the clandestine manner in which the changes were made, the implications of the policy that embraces them. Mark Kulieke unintentionally expresses the resulting paradox on page 24 of *Birth of a Revelation* (second edition):

> "Dr. Sadler and Christy both indicated that the Urantia Papers were published exactly as received except for errors in copying, most of which were subsequently identified and corrected. The Contact Commission was limited to making changes in spelling, capitalization, and punctuation."

There are a few dozen documented statements by Christy and Dr. Sadler, as well as many Trustees and Forum members, and both Histories, to the effect that *"the Urantia Papers were published exactly as received."* However, I could not find a single one that added: *"except for errors in copying, most of which were subsequently identified and corrected."* Moreover, the statement: *"The Contact Commission was limited to making changes in spelling, capitalization, and punctuation"* leads to other questions: *[1]. Was not The Urantia Book published by Urantia Foundation, not the Contact Commission? The Contact Commission was long-defunct by 1967. [2]. Were the plates, defined in the Declaration of Trust as the original text of The Urantia Book, not transferred to Urantia Foundation on January 11, 1950? [3]. Christy was a sitting Trustee in 1967. Why, regardless of her sincere motives, was Christy allowed, independent of the other Trustees, to make alterations in the plates, an action forbidden by the Declaration of Trust and blatantly exceeding the authority of the original Contact Commission?*

A letter from Scott M. Forsythe, Administrative Assistant for Urantia Foundation, to JJ Johnson in 1988 clearly confides that Christy indeed had assumed a "unique" relationship with the text of *The Urantia Book.* Forsythe wrote in reply to an inquiry by JJ about certain questions he had submitted. Christy had written JJ that she had decided to make two changes in the next printing. As previously indicated, Christy died shortly after her 1981 letter to JJ and the changes were never made. Forsythe wrote:

" . . . as you are well aware, Christy's relationship to the text of The URANTIA Book was unique . . . It is quite probable that the current Board of Trustees do not feel they have the same relationship with the text of the book that was enjoyed by Christy. In other words, the Trustees may not feel they can exercise the same latitude that was available to Christy in these matters . . . For obvious reasons, a matter such as this is an issue of delicate and sensitive proportions, and the Board may not wish to expand the written record on this matter." *[See Appendix B for the full text of this letter.]*

This reaction naturally perplexed JJ. If Christy's relationship with the Urantia Papers was considered authentically "unique" by the Trustees, why did they fail to carry through on her final "corrections?" Other than this somewhat candid letter expressing the discomfort of the Trustees, a policy of polite but resolute silence and concealment continued to be generally in force until the proclamation of support for the changes in 1999 by Urantia Foundation on their web site titled: *Setting the Record Straight.* Regardless of how one may view the above comments, we are confronted with one clear fact: By no later than 1994 all the Trustees were aware of the changes that were made and their implications. To date, there has been no movement in the direction of correcting the problem. Although a "list of corrections" was published by Urantia Foundation in 1994, it was not annotated and no disclaimer was placed in the published books to inform purchasers of the changes and the availability of the "corrections" list until 1999. Such half-measures, in any event, are inadequate for most Urantians who want faithful reproductions of the original text to be published and the Declaration of Trust honored.

We must be able to trust the scribe

Aside from: [1]. the need for a reliable lineage of faithful reproductions of the original text as a touchstone for future scholars, and [2]. the philosophical fallacy of preserving one text and printing another, and [3]. the letter and spirit of the Declaration of Trust that forbids Urantia Foundation from making any changes whatsoever to the text, and [4]. the questionable process by which the changes were originally made — and the undefined policy that has so long concealed them and continues to support them — there is a fifth compelling argument.

This argument for printing the original text has been described succinctly by Eric Schaveland: *"We must be able to trust the scribe."* The inescapable fact is: no one — including the Trustees — really knows how much the *current* printings of *The Urantia Book* differ from the original text of the 1955 edition. We will not know until we follow the advice of Dr. Mills and, resolutely and fearlessly, use available technology to compare the current text to the 1955 original. It may be that we shall discover that the current text is "reasonably close" to the 1955 printing. Of course, the Declaration of Trust does not suggest that "reasonably close" is good enough. However, put the "reasonably close" argument aside for a moment.

Surely, the Midwayers had good reasons why they left no discretion whatsoever in human hands regarding the text of *The Urantia Book*. The Declaration of Trust was designed by the Contact Commission to protect the original text from human folly. Despite this safeguard, we know the door was opened in 1967, and changes to the text took place under the watchcare of Urantia Foundation. This precedent has fostered a policy of human discretion by Urantia Foundation — an oligarchy of five self-appointed individuals. Urantia Foundation has continued to make "corrections" in the text in every printing since the second printing. Many subsequent Trustees were evidently unaware of the degree to which these liberties have impacted the text. *However, as I have indicated, all of the Trustees are now cognizant of the alterations to the text, yet they have individually and collectively refused to confront the issue.* One Trustee, Morris (Mo) Siegel, told me in 1998 that he was indifferent to the question of the text because from a commercial marketing perspective he was aware of "very little reader concern" about the alterations in the original text. Yet, the Declaration of Trust was supposedly designed to insulate Trustees from the changing tides of popular opinion.

Urantian scholar David Kantor believes that if rank and file Urantians remain silent and docile about *their* Revelation, future Trustees, operating in social contexts which we cannot conceive today, may easily follow this course of uncontrolled and unmonitored latitude and elect to take additional liberties with the text. We know that, from Carolyn Kendall's statements and Richard Keeler's admission, changes to the text continued after 1982. If Carolyn's account is accurate, Mr. Keeler promised to reverse the changes made after 1982. Merritt Horn's research indicates that these changes were not reversed in current printings as promised. *(See Appendix D)*. Surely, no one can predict where the current philosophy of allowing an oligarchy of five individuals *laissez alter* in regard to the text of the Urantia Revelation will one day lead. Without a trustworthy "keeper of the text," a touchstone of an authentically inviolate printed version of the original text, and an established lineage back to the original printing, both the spirit and the letter of the Urantia Foundation's Declaration of Trust have been, in effect, dishonored.

The search for truth

The information and arguments above are disclosed in the spirit of a search for truth. *The Revelation belongs to the people, and they must be responsible for its destiny.* The Revelators provided us with a grand, ennobling, creative task; Urantia Foundation was established to *serve* us. In choosing the means by which we struggle to achieve the task before us, we must not defer our quest for truth. For truth is one of the triad of precious core values that embody the goal itself.

The truth will not go away by killing the messenger. The adversary system is as necessary for history as it is for science and law. Nor will the truth go away if we simply avoid expanding *"the written record on this matter."* It will not go away if we use sophistry to redefine the term *"inviolate."* Concern about the alterations is not making a *"fetish of the text."* On the contrary, it may be the endless, clandestine series of changes from printing to printing by a committee of five humans in an unattainable effort to *"make the Book perfect"* that is making a *"fetish of the text."*

The most serious consequence of deferring responsibility for the revelation to an oligarchy is not necessarily a question of the quality of the individual Trustees. Philosopher Mortimer Adler expressed the most serious affect of an oligarchy in this way:

"Granted such [superior] men can be found, the point is that letting them rule, with wisdom and benevolence, reduces the rest of the population to perpetual childhood ... " [18]

The question of publishing as well as preserving the original text remains, to this day, *"an issue of delicate and sensitive proportions."* Yet, I submit that it is precisely for the very reasons that it is delicate and sensitive that it demands the courageous scrutiny of Urantians. It cannot be repeated too often: the Revelation was a gift to the people of this planet; *the people are responsible for their Revelation.*

I remain cautiously optimistic about the outcome of this delicate and sensitive issue. For as long as we Urantians creatively debate this question with tolerance and respect, we have not yet wholly descended into a prideful utopian torpor for the sake of "unity." Unity at any price has historically signaled the drift of many a glorious mortal enterprise into cosmic oblivion.

By the time of Dr. Sadler's death, the stage was set. An inner circle within the inner circle had been formed. This ultra-inner circle had replaced the Trustees as the entity in charge of the text of the Revelation.What has happened in the decades that followed was to be aptly described by Dr. Sprunger as the launching of the Revelation upon the *"troubled and turbulent seas of evolutionary struggle."*

ENDNOTES:

1. BIRTH OF A REVELATION by Mark Kulieke, second edition, 1992, page 24. However, the "Forum" had passed into history long before, on May 31, 1942, when they were informed no further questions would be entertained. (See History One page 6 and History Two page 10). The Forum was then replaced by a Sunday study group.

2. HISTORY OF THE URANTIA MOVEMENT ONE, "by a Group of Urantia Pioneers, assisted by Members of the Contact Commission, 1960," page 13. In her "Report to the Ad Hoc Committee" Carolyn Kendall provides the information that there were 71 students. She believes there were 17 diploma students in 1960, History One states there were 14.

3. April, 1992 paper titled AD HOC COMMITTEE ON RESEARCH: PRINCIPLES, PATTERNS, AND STRUCTURES IN *THE URANTIA BOOK* AND RELATED SOURCES by Carolyn Kendall page 29.

4. URANTIA, The Great Cult Mystery, by Martin Gardner, Prometheus Books, New York, 1995, pages 98 and 100.

5. IBID., pp. 40-43. Also, Meredith Sprunger provided some background information. Clyde Bedell's quote was taken from THE PLANETARY PRINTS, Spring 1985, page 35.

6. HISTORY TWO, prepared by a Contact Commissioner, undated, page 21.

7. The intra-office memo by Bill Sadler, Jr. was quoted by Carolyn and Tom Kendall in their RESPONSE TO URANTIA FOUNDATION'S REPORT TO READERS OF THE URANTIA BOOK, June 21, 1990, page 2. As previously noted, Christy told David Kantor that one of the rules of the revelation process was that at least two Contact Commissioners had to be present for any communications to take place.

8. The PLAN FOR *THE URANTIA BOOK* REVELATION, by Carolyn B. Kendall, Paper distributed January 18, 1996, page 5. She gives the source for these comments as her husband, Thomas Kendall, who was a trustee of Urantia Foundation from 1963-1983, and its president from 1973-1983.

9. IBID., page 5. Carolyn says this statement is her personal opinion.

10. IBID., page 5. Carolyn gives as her source Richard Keeler, Trustee and President of Urantia Foundation. Merritt Horn reports this action was not taken. (*See Appendix D*).

"In my opinion, there can be only one edition of The Urantia Book" 223

11. According to the Declaration of Trust: "A Trustee Emeritus shall have no rights, duties or powers hereunder, but that name shall be given such a person only as an expression of his past services as a Trustee." However, Christy's duties and dominance were apparently not curtailed by this stipulation. *(See Appendix F).*

12. It was some time before Urantia Foundation seemed to be awakened to the fact that such changes were made. It was stated in Urantian News, November, 1991: "From time to time the Trustees have authorized changes which corrected spelling, grammatical, or printing errors. The current Trustees are also aware of a few changes to the text undertaken in the second printing. These were changes made necessary because of incomplete proofing of the first printing." However, in reality the "Trustees" do not seem to function as a cohesive group in making observations and decisions about the text. I had personal conversations with three current Trustees in 1998, and none of them seemed aware of exactly what changes had been made in the text. They seemed confused about how they are to police the content of the Book when they are, for all practical purposes, insulated from the printing process. Moreover, they expressed little interest in the problem. The Trustee's duties, their oath, and the Declaration of Trust not withstanding, the culture at 533 that established a resident inner circle within the inner circle in the late sixties still seems to prevail. The Trustees, in general, are titular personages and have never had a hands-on relationship with the preservation of the original text after 1955. The Trustees generally remain passive about the content of the various versions of *The Urantia Book* that are being printed. At this writing, no less than <u>three different</u> supposedly "inviolate" versions of the original text are being published by Urantia Foundation, none of which actually agrees with the original 1955 text that the Foundation is supposedly "preserving."

13. This information was obtained from phone conversations I had with Mr. Krohn and Mr. Paddock, on October 26, 1999. Both of these gentlemen are now retired, and live in Crawfordsville, Indiana.

14. A RESPONSE TO A THINLY DISGUISED ATTACK ON *THE URANTIA BOOK* by Clyde Bedell, a paper dated September 5, 1976, page 13.

15. In a letter to JJ Johnson dated May 11, 1976, Clyde expressed knowledge of specific typographical problems between the 1955 printing and later printings. In a later note (October, 1977) to JJ he suggested ways to obtain a 1955 printing, copies of which were already becoming difficult to find.

16. Meredith Sprunger personally disclosed this observation to me.

17. A MONOGRAPH ON A VITAL ISSUE CONCERNING *THE URANTIA BOOK* AND MOVEMENT by Clyde Bedell, March, 1981, pp. 18-19. [Emphasis in original]

18. HAVES AND HAVE NOTS by Mortimer J. Adler, Macmillan Publishing Company, New York, 1991, pp. 116-117.

ADDENDA to CHAPTER NINE

Comparison of the 1955 and the 1967 Printings *Showing the* Alteration of the Original Plates of *The Urantia Book*

In the process of printing, certain anomalies occur in specific editions of a given book that allow scholars to identify and authenticate each printing. Virtually every printed page has its share of inking variations, so that even within a given printing no two pages are really exactly alike. However, there are certain special variations, such as a broken letter, which will reoccur over and over again within a single printing.

In the case of *The Urantia Book*, Merritt Horn and I examined several 1955 printings and compared them with 1967 and later printings. We did not make an exhaustive study, but we examined enough occurrences to agree upon a few reasonable conclusions.

[1]. Contrary to general belief, the original 1955 plates were used in the 1967 printing — with some very important exceptions. (Recall that Trustee Mills was apparently under the impression that the entire book had to be reset due to new methods of printing.) We cannot escape the conclusion that not all of the Trustees were aware of the alterations being made to the text under their watch.

[2]. These exceptions involved at least 48 pages that were removed and replaced with new pages. The new pages were inserted to "correct" several apparent "errors" and editorial inconsistencies that were discovered in the 1955 printing.

[3]. The integrity of the plates was hopelessly compromised when the 1967 printing was made.

(Left) An R.R. Donnelley & Sons employee fastens a typical printing plate to a cylinder on the press. (1958 World Book Encyclopedia photograph).

Two R.R. Donnelley & Sons employees discuss the sixth printing with Foundation representative Mark Kulieke (on the right).

When Merritt Horn and I began our investigation, we fully expected to find what Trustee Mills believed: that the entire 1967 text had been reset. We suspected that this resetting was unnecessary, although many believed that "new" technology required new plates in 1967. We discovered that the original plates *were* used - *after extensive alterations had been made!* A few examples of the many we found will suffice to illustrate the basis for our belief that the original plates were secretly altered in 1967 to permit significant editorial changes. Perhaps the full implications of the original idea of "correcting" the text was not grasped by the lay persons at 533 who carried it out. Once taking the first steps down the path of "creating a perfect book," it probably became more and more difficult to turn back. The changing was clearly done in a clandestine manner by those who carried it out. We must also conclude that false information was deliberately given to the readership in subsequent years and to those Trustees who were unaware of what was happening. This eventuated in a paradox: Today Urantia Foundation preserves three copies of the 1955 printing as a specimen of the original text, and continues to print different versions, which are sold as "inviolate" copies of the original text. It is self-evident that there cannot be various versions of the identical original text.

The comparison pages that follow were prepared by Merritt Horn and Larry Mullins.

FOREWORD

IN THE MINDS of the mortals of Urantia—that being the name of your world—there exists great confusion respecting the meaning of such terms as God, divinity, and deity. Human beings are still more confused and uncertain about the relationships of the divine personalities designated by these numerous appellations. Because of this with so much ideational confusion, I have been d ductory statement in explanation of the meaning certain word symbols as they may be hereinafter Orvonton corps of truth revealers have been a English language of Urantia.

It is exceedingly difficult to present enlarged in our endeavor to expand cosmic consciousness tion, when we are restricted to the use of a circu But our mandate admonishes us to make every e using the word symbols of the English tongue. W duce new terms only when the concept to be por English which can be employed to convey such with more or less distortion of meaning.

In the hope of facilitating comprehension a the part of every mortal who may peruse these pa in this initial statement an outline of the mea English words which are to be employed in design sociated concepts of the things, meanings, and values of universal reality.

But in order to formulate this Foreword of definitions and limitations of terminology, it is necessary to anticipate the usage of these terms in the subsequent presentations. This Foreword is not, therefore, within itself; it is only a definitive guide designed to assis the accompanying papers dealing with Deity and the unive have been formulated by an Orvonton commission sen purpose.

Your world, Urantia, is one of many similar inhabite prise the local universe of *Nebadon*. This universe, toget tions, makes up the superuniverse of *Orvonton,* from whos commission hails. Orvonton is one of the seven evolution time and space which circle the never-beginning, never-en perfection—the central universe of *Havona*. At the hea central universe is the stationary Isle of Paradise, the finity and the dwelling place of the eternal God.

The seven evolving superuniverses in association with the central and divine universe, we commonly refer to as the *grand universe;* these are the now organ-

I

PAGE ONE 1955 PRINTING
with details showing bad "w"

FOREWORD

IN THE MINDS of the mortals of Urantia—that being the name of your world—there exists great confusion respecting the meaning of such terms as God, divinity, and deity. Human beings are still more confused and uncertain about the relationships of the divine personalities designated by these numerous appellations. Because of this conceptual poverty associated with so much ideational confusion, I have been directed to formulate this introductory statement in explanation of the meanings which should be attached to certain word symbols as they may be hereinafter used in those papers which the Orvonton corps of truth revealers have been authorized to translate into the English language of Urantia.

It is exceedingly difficult to present enlarged concepts and advanced truth, in our endeavor to expand cosmic consciousness and enhance spiritual perception, when we are restricted to the use of a circumscribed language of the realm. But our mandate admonishes us to make every effort to convey our meanings by using the word symbols of the English tongue. We have been instructed to introduce new terms only when the concept to be portrayed finds no terminology in English which can be employed to convey such a new concept partially or even with more or less distortion of meaning.

In the hope of facilitating comprehension and of preventing confusion on the part of every mortal who may peruse these papers, we deem it wise to present in this initial statement an outline of the meanings to be attached to numerous English words which are to be employed in designation of Deity and certain associated concepts of the things, meanings, and values of universal reality.

But in order to formulate this Foreword of definitions and limitations of terminology, it is necessary to anticipate the usage of these terms in the subsequent presentations. This Foreword is not, therefore, a finished statement within itself; it is only a definitive guide designed to assist those who shall read the accompanying papers dealing with Deity and the universe of universes which have been formulated by an Orvonton commission sent to Urantia for this purpose.

Your world, Urantia, is one of many similar inhabited planets which comprise the local universe of *Nebadon*. This universe, together with similar creations, makes up the superuniverse of *Orvonton*, from whose capital, Uversa, our commission hails. Orvonton is one of the seven evolutionary superuniverses of time and space which circle the never-beginning, never-ending creation of divine perfection—the central universe of *Havona*. At the heart of this eternal and central universe is the stationary Isle of Paradise, the geographic center of infinity and the dwelling place of the eternal God.

The seven evolving superuniverses in association with the central and divine universe, we commonly refer to as the *grand universe*; these are the now organ-

I

PAGE 1, 1967 PRINTING
with details showing identical bad "w."
For this unaltered page, the same plate was clearly used for both printings.

> **1955 PRINTING, PAGE 3.**
> Compare the wording of #5 below with the 1967 Printing.

> All of the 1955 Printings that we examined had a bad impression in this area, with poor inking and broken letters. Note especially the word "Deity."

FOREWORD 3

Deity may be existential, as in the Eternal Son; experiential, as in the Supreme Being; associative, as in God the Sevenfold; undivided, as in the Paradise Trinity.

... ty is the source of all that which is divine. Deity is characteristically and ... bly divine, but all that which is divine is not necessarily Deity, though it ... co-ordinated with Deity and will tend towards some phase of unity with ... -spiritual, mindal, or personal.

...VINITY is the characteristic, ...

...inity is creature comprehensible ... personality as love, mercy, and ... ice, power, and sovereignty.

...inity may be perfect—complete ... se perfection; it may be imperfe ... -space evolution; or it may be r ... ain Havona levels of existential-

...en we attempt to conceive of pe ... tivity, we encounter seven conceivable ...

1. Absolute perfection in all aspects.
2. Absolute perfection in some phases and relative perfection in all other aspects.
3. Absolute, relative, and imperfect aspects in varied association.
4. Absolute perfection in some respects, imperfection in all others.
5. Absolute perfection in no direction, relative perfection in all other manifestations.
6. Absolute perfection in no phase, relative in some, imperfect in others.
7. Absolute perfection in no attribute, imperfection in all.

II. GOD

Evolving mortal creatures experience an irresistible urge to symbolize their finite concepts of God. Man's consciousness of moral duty and his spiritual idealism represent a value level—an experiential reality—which is difficult of symbolization.

Cosmic consciousness implies the recognition of a First Cause, the one and only uncaused reality. God, the Universal Father, functions on three Deity-personality levels of subinfinite value and relative divinity expression:

1. *Prepersonal*—as in the ministry of the Father fragments, such as the Thought Adjusters.
2. *Personal*—as in the evolutionary experience of created and procreated beings.

> urce of all that whic
> but all that which is
> d with Deity and w
> mindal, or personal.
>
> **(DETAIL)**

PAGE 3 COMPARISONS - 1955 & 1967 PRINTINGS

On page three we see the first evidence of several alterations to the original plates. Whoever altered the plates in 1967 elected to remove the word "other" from #5 on page three. This required a new page to be set, etched and cast. Then the original page was removed from the plates and the new one was set in. 48 such alterations were made to the text for the 1967 printing. *Merritt Horn's commentaries on this and all 133 word and number changes — and deletions — (that have been found) are available in Appendix D.*

1967 PRINTING, PAGE 3.
This is the first of 48 altered pages that have been discovered in this printing.

FOREWORD 3

Deity may be existential, as in the Eternal Son; experiential, as in the Supreme Being; associative, as in God the Sevenfold; undivided, as in the Paradise Trinity.

Deity is the source of all that which is divine. Deity is characteristically and invariably divine, but all that which is divine is not necessarily Deity, though it will be co-ordinated with Deity and will tend towards some phase of unity with Deity—spiritual, mindal, or personal.

DIVINITY is the characteristic, [...] Deity.

Divinity is creature comprehensible [...] lated in personality as love, mercy, and [...] as justice, power, and sovereignty.

Divinity may be perfect—complete [...] Paradise perfection; it may be imperfe[...] of time-space evolution; or it may be r[...] on certain Havona levels of existential-[...]

When we attempt to conceive of pe[...] tivity, we encounter seven conceivable t[...]

1. Absolute perfection in all aspect[...]

2. Absolute perfection in some phases and relative perfection in all other aspects.

3. Absolute, relative, and imperfect aspects in varied association.

4. Absolute perfection in some respects, imperfection in all others.

5. Absolute perfection in no direction, relative perfection in all manifestations.

6. Absolute perfection in no phase, relative in some, imperfect in others.

7. Absolute perfection in no attribute, imperfection in all.

II. GOD

Evolving mortal creatures experience an irresistible urge to symboli[...] finite concepts of God. Man's consciousness of moral duty and his spiritua[...] ism represent a value level—an experiential reality—which is difficult of s[...] zation.

Cosmic consciousness implies the recognition of a First Cause, the [...] only uncaused reality. God, the Universal Father, functions on three [...] personality levels of subinfinite value and relative divinity expression:

1. *Prepersonal*—as in the ministry of the Father fragments, such as the Thought Adjusters.

2. *Personal*—as in the evolutionary experience of created and procreated beings.

3. *Superpersonal*—as in the eventuated existences of certain absonite and associated beings.

GOD is a word symbol designating all personalizations of Deity. The term requires a different definition on each personal level of Deity function and must

(DETAIL)

source of all that wh[...] e, but all that which [...] ted with Deity and [...] , mindal, or persona[...]

Note that the word "other" was removed from #5 on page 3 in the 1967 printing.

1967 PRINTING, PAGE *lx*.

lx   CONTENTS OF THE BOOK

		PAGE
3.	Sabbath Sermon at Pella	1819
	"Beware of the leaven of the Pharisees..."	
	"...the very hairs of your head are numbered"	
4.	Dividing the Inheritance	1821
	Parable of the foolish rich man	
	"Where your treasure is there will your heart be also."	
	"What shall it profit if you gain the whole world...?"	
5.	Talks to the Apostles on Wealth	1823
	"Consider the lilies, how they grow..."	
6.	Answer to Peter's Question	1824

166. LAST VISIT TO NORTHERN PEREA 1825

1.	The Pharisee [and the publican]
	Ceremonial
2.	The Ten Lep[ers]
3.	The Sermon
	The straigh[t]
	Many who
	"I stand at
4.	Teaching Ab[out marriage]
5.	The Congrega[tion]
	The later

167. THE VISIT TO PHIL[ADELPHIA]

1.	Breakfast wit[h]
	Healing the believer
	"...sit not down in the chief seat..."
2.	Parable of the Great Supper
3.	The Woman with the Spirit of Infirmity
4.	The Message from Bethany
5.	On the Way to Bethany
	The Pharisee and the publican
	Teaching about marriage
6.	Blessing the Little Children	1839
	Beauty as an influence to worship
7.	The Talk about Angels	1840

168. THE RESURRECTION OF LAZARUS 1842

	"I am the resurrection and the life..."	
1.	At the Tomb of Lazarus	1843
2.	The Resurrection of Lazarus	1845
3.	Meeting of the Sanhedrin	1847
	"It is better that one man die..."	
4.	The Answer to Prayer	1848

> **Pharisee and the publican**
> [teac]hing about marriage
> [Blessin]g the Little Children . . .
>
> DETAIL
> Note broken "i" in the word marriage.
> The same plate was clearly used
> for both 1955 and 1967 printings.
>
> marriage
> [th]e Childre[n]

PAGE *lx* COMPARISONS - 1955 and 1967

Page *lx* is important because it was a companion page that was printed side by side with page 3 in the same printing signature. We discovered it had not been changed. So the alterations were apparently strictly confined to areas that contained supposed "copying errors." This shows a special degree of sensitivity to the original plates, because it would have been simpler to replace the entire plate. Unfortunately however, the alterations fatally compromised the integrity of the plates, which were a key portion of the Substantive Estate. This is probably why all of the original plates were ordered destroyed a couple of years later.

1955 PRINTING, PAGE *lx*.

lx   CONTENTS OF THE BOOK

                                                                    PAGE
    3. Sabbath Sermon at Pella   1819
       "Beware of the leaven of the Pharisees . . ."
       ". . . the very hairs of your head are numbered"
    4. Dividing the Inheritance   1821
       Parable of the foolish rich man
       "Where your treasure is there will your heart be also."
       "What shall it profit if you gain the whole world . . . ?"
    5. Talks to the Apostles on Wealth   1823
       "Consider the lilies, how they grow . . ."
    6. Answer to Peter's Question   1824

166. LAST VISIT TO NORTHERN PEREA   1825

    1. The Pharisees at Ragaba   1825
       Ceremonial hand washing
    2. The Ten Lepers   1827
    3. The Sermon at Gerasa   1828
       The straight and nar[row]
       Many who are first w[ill]
       "I stand at the door a[nd]
    4. Teaching About Accide[nts]
    5. The Congregation at Ph[iladelphia]
       The later ministry an[d]

167. THE VISIT TO PHILADELPHIA .

    1. Breakfast with the Phar[isee]
       Healing the believer
       ". . . sit not down in
    2. Parable of the Great Su[pper]
    3. The Woman with the Sp[irit]
    4. The Message from Beth[any]
    5. On the Way to Bethany   1838
       The Pharisee and the publican
       Teaching about marriage
    6. Blessing the Little Children . . . .
       Beauty as an influence to worship
    7. The Talk about Angels . . . . . .

168. THE RESURRECTION OF LAZARUS . . . . .
       "I am the resurrection and the life . . ."
    1. At the Tomb of Lazarus   1843
    2. The Resurrection of Lazarus   1845
    3. Meeting of the Sanhedrin   1847
       "It is better that one man die . . ."
    4. The Answer to Prayer   1848
    5. What Became of Lazarus   1849

169. LAST TEACHING AT PELLA   1850
       The Sanhedrin's charges against Jesus
    1. Parable of the Lost Son   1850

Pharisee and the publican
hing about marriage
g the Little Children . .

DETAIL
Note broken "i" in the word marriage.
The same plate was clearly used
for both 1955 and 1967 printings.

marriage
Children

Emma Christensen with Martin Myers, Circa 1980

Chapter Ten
"The Baptism of Joys and Sorrows"

"The Baptism of Joys and Sorrows"

FTER THE INITIAL EUPHORIA of having Urantia Books, a slow disappointment began to creep over the early Urantians. The expected impact of the Fifth Epochal Revelation did not happen. Books mailed out to famous people[1] were either not replied to, or responded to with brief, curt notes. No major newspaper reviewed the book. Sir Hubert Wilkins, who assisted Dr. Sadler in the early days and who was equally baffled by the sleeping subject phenomena, had studied the Papers periodically for twenty years in Chicago at 533 Diversey Parkway.[2] When the book was published, he sent out twelve copies to special friends. Wilkins reported that he had received only one interested response. *"People seemed to think it was some kind of a joke — novel — or something of the kind. Anyway, the response is a good criterion of their real mind ability."*

In 1958, a nineteen-year old college student who was interested in becoming a minister wrote to Urantia Foundation from Kansas. His name was Vern Grimsley. Grimsley was originally introduced to the Urantia Papers by Dr. Sprunger. He later presented *The Urantia Book* to his University of Kansas fraternity brothers, who included Richard Keeler, Martin Myers, and Hoite Caston. In 1962 Myers and Keeler drove to Chicago to meet with Dr. Sadler and Christy. By 1963 a series of letters were exchanged between Vern and Nancy Grimsley and Dr. Sadler, culminating with Sadler inviting the couple to Chicago for a meeting. About the same time, young Martin W. Myers began to have significant influence at 533 Diversey Parkway. Martin Myers was an enthusiastic reader of *The Urantia Book* — and he especially impressed Christy.

As things gradually settled down, the early Urantians at 533 resolutely geared themselves for yet another test of time. But, they were no longer young. Both Christy and Dr. Sadler were concerned that there were virtually no young readers coming into the fold, and there would be no one to whom the torch could be passed. After the second printing, in July of 1968, Martin Myers came to 533 Diversey Parkway for temporary housing while he "searched for an apartment." Myers, who had trained as a lawyer, soon became a permanent resident at 533. Martin helped the aging doctor and Christy, and tended to them in many ways. He advised Christy about the course of the Revelation from a legal perspective. After Dr. Sadler died on April 26, 1969, Martin drew even closer to Christy.₃

After the death of Brotherhood President Alvin Kulieke in 1973, Christy wrote a letter to the Trustees and "other VIPs" titled: *"The Brotherhood is in Crisis."* She expressed grave concerns about the lack of new people being attracted to the movement. *"We cannot allow Caligastia and those unfriendly to the Urantia Book to prevail."* (I have never found any document in which Dr. Sadler mentions Caligastia[1], or expresses concern about him. The culture was undergoing significant changes at 533). By 1973 young Martin (he was in his early thirties) was

---

1. "The doctrine of a personal devil on Urantia, though it had some foundation in the planetary presence of the traitorous and iniquitous Caligastia, was nevertheless wholly fictitious in its teachings that such a "devil" could influence the normal human mind against its free and natural choosing. Even before Michael's bestowal on Urantia, neither Caligastia nor Daligastia was ever able to oppress mortals or to coerce any normal individual into doing anything against the human will. The free will of man is supreme in moral affairs; even the indwelling Thought Adjuster refuses to compel man to think a single thought or to perform a single act against the choosing of man's own will." [Page 753, par. 2]

"The Baptism of Joys and Sorrows" 235

named a Foundation Trustee, and immediately began to advocate a draconian, legalistic approach to "managing" the Revelation.

A shift to authoritarian leadership

On June 29, 1973, Martin Myers gave a remarkable speech: *"Unity not Uniformity"* at a Urantia Conference in Los Angeles. For the first time, rank and file Urantians heard references to what Martin called "the mandates." The "mandates" were special "guidelines," Martin claimed, which the celestial Revelators had given the Contact Commission. Supposedly, the "mandates" were passed along to Urantia Foundation. The current Trustees, he implied, inherited these mandates to manage the propagation of the Revelation. Martin's strategy to control the Revelation was by means of resolute copyright and trademark enforcement. In his speech, Myers structured a Foundation "slow growth" policy into the next millennium, and startled his audiences with quotes from the "mandates." However, what Martin actually quoted in his speech were selections from the "admonitions" or "suggestions" that accompanied the mandate to publish *The Urantia Book* nearly two decades before he had attained the status of Trustee. Urantians who disagreed with their use noted that Mr. Myers was very selective in the passages he had read in his speech. They complained that Martin was emphasizing the warnings and omitting entirely the positive admonitions that Dr. Sadler had published in his *Consideration of Some Criticisms* paper of 1958. Chapter Eight documents the fact that the so-called "mandates" never existed as such. As noted, Sadler's paper clearly explains that there was a mandate to *publish the book*, accompanied by an elaborate set of what Dr. Sadler referred to as "admonitions" or "suggestions."

Many Urantians believe that in this speech Myers positioned Urantia Foundation as an aggressive central authority — between readers and the Revelation — supporting this posturing by supposed "secret messages" given to the Contact Commission by celestial beings, and allegedly passed on to the Trustees. Over the next few years, some Urantians objected as the secret "mandates" found their way to selected Foundation supporters and were revered as precious privileged information.

Urantians have also commented that, by the time they were being passed around, these suggestions were copies of copies of outdated, heavily edited administrative information. The Revelators had ordered the originals "destroyed by fire" immediately after the publication of *The Urantia Book*. In the light of these instructions, it cannot be appropriate that copies would have been made and preserved. It is even worse that these copies were brought forth 20 years after publication and used to establish the "authority" of a small group of individuals. Many have further protested that no copy of the complete text of the supposed "mandates" was ever provided the general readership. Today, many Urantians consider the so-called "mandates" as only apocryphal curiosities that should be allowed to fade peacefully into the mists of time.

Some Urantians point to the mandate episode as an example of precisely what the Revelators sought to avoid. They knew human nature, and how easy it would be to develop an inner circle of entitled "special people" who have "exclusive" information that they could use to control others. However, before long, just about everyone had a version of the so-called mandates. As Bill Sadler, Jr. wrote in an undated memo, circa April, 1955: *"It is so difficult to avoid the transient ego satisfaction of betraying the possession of secret information."*

From the time of the first public announcement of their existence, the "mandates" had a strong influence on many Urantians. After the Myers speech, there was a definite shift of Foundation policy — away from the Declaration of Trust which mandated the protection, preservation, and publication of the *original text* — to a newly defined mission of preservation and protection of the *copyright, the so-called "marks," and name "Urantia."* None of these items were ever owned by the Contact Commission, and could not have been entrusted to Urantia Foundation. The copyright, the "marks" and the name Urantia were not part of the *Substantive Estate* and thus they are not mentioned in the Declaration of Trust.

A period of litigation and enforcement against Urantians began shortly after Myers became a Trustee. A very real fear of being targeted by litigation dominated much of the Urantia movement. A policy of slow growth ensued. The price of the Book increased dramatically, to a point where Clyde Bedell said it was becoming "A rich man's Bible." Distribution was tightened. Written permission by Urantia Foundation was required to quote publicly or print even short passages from *The Urantia Book*. Use of the three azure blue concentric circles on a white background (the Banner of Michael) and the terms *Urantia* or *Urantian* were forbidden without written authorization by Urantia Foundation. Between 1974 and 2000, numerous lawsuits against Urantians were set into motion.

Licensing the Banner of Michael

In the mid- and late Seventies, Urantia Foundation forced a divisive licensing agreement on Urantia Brotherhood Societies. This agreement was structured and driven by Martin Myers (who had Christy's full support). When I met Berkeley Elliott in 1975 and began to get involved with the movement, it had been common practice to freely use the three concentric azure blue circles described in the Urantia Papers. Everywhere there were pillows, bumper stickers, rings, and amulets with the Banner of Michael on them. Under the new Urantia Foundation licensing agreement, Urantia Brotherhood Societies such as the First Society of Oklahoma could no longer use the three concentric azure blue circles, which were now referred to as the "marks" (the trademarks registered by Urantia Foundation)[4] without authorization and without being a "licensed society in good standing." The words Urantia or Urantian could not be used without Foundation permission. Personal use, such as religious expression, of the three concentric azure blue circles by individuals was forbidden. Many Urantians have protested that these "marks" are in reality the banner of our Creator Son,

As early as 1964 Christy's proprietary attitude began to emerge at 533 regarding the Banner of Michael. Jacques Weiss had requested permission to buy three-concentric-circle lapel pins for his team of translators. They had just completed translating the entire Urantia Book into French, without charge. Christy refused their request to buy pins, stating that their purchase should be deferred until they became "better acquainted" with the Book. They protested and eventually got their pins.

(ABOVE LEFT) It was common practice to display the three-concentric-circles in the Sixties and early Seventies.

(ABOVE) On the 2000th Birthday of Jesus, August 21, 1994 Urantians fly the Banner of Michael over Jerusalem.

(LEFT) Urantians use the concentric circles in various ways. A version of the banner of Michael used in combination with the cross.

Urantians have traditionally ignored the prohibitions of Urantia Foundation regarding use of the three concentric azure circles on a white background - the Banner of Michael. The circles are embraced by many Urantians as a personal religious expression. Urantia Foundation has long sought to confine individual use of the circles to approved forms and organizations. During Urantia Foundation's suit against Eric Schaveland, it began to back down from this stand.

Michael of Nebadon, and the material emblem of the Paradise Trinity. They have commonly ignored these legalistic restrictions. The Urantia Papers clearly support the position that the three concentric azure blue circles were not designed by, and cannot be "owned" by, Urantia Foundation or any other mortal agency:

"... Gabriel called his personal staff together on Edentia and, in counsel with the Most Highs, elected to assume command of the loyal hosts of Satania. Michael remained on Salvington while Gabriel proceeded to Jerusem, and establishing himself on the sphere dedicated to the Father — the same Universal Father whose personality Lucifer and Satan had questioned — in the presence of the forgathered hosts of loyal personalities, he displayed the banner of Michael, the material emblem of the Trinity government of all creation, the three azure blue concentric circles on a white background." *[605 bottom, 606 top.]*

Myers provided insight into his philosophic position when he mailed a "Special Report" to thousands of readers in April 1990, admonishing them: *"Down here on rebellion-torn and sin-seared Urantia, the Foundation owns the trademarks, the word 'URANTIA,' and the Three Concentric Circle Symbol in perpetuity."*

Urantia Brotherhood had freely used the three concentric azure blue circles for two decades. However, the officers reluctantly accepted the retro-fitted agreement that stated they had been licensed all along by Urantia Foundation to use this emblem. By the late seventies, virtually the entire Brotherhood was drawn into Urantia Foundation's licensing agreement, and those who refused were ostracized and threatened with litigation. The officers of the Brotherhood were assured that the agreement was for the benefit of the Revelation and would not be used as a device to control their fraternal organization. This assurance appears to be disingenuous in light of subsequent events. In November, 1979, Clyde Bedell wrote a letter to Martin Myers admonishing him that the restrictions Urantia Foundation was imposing on Urantians were inhibiting religious freedom of expression:

> *"You are not permitting me the latitude all Urantians should have, must have. Rather, you are assuming the role of owners of the Revelation and the New Gospel, who will mot [sic] tolerate its presentation except in your light, which possibly may be an ingrown centripetal light within a small island peopled by a small and determined group of hierarchal authoritarians ... Martin, I believe you are, as a group, treading on grounds that threaten our Movement with schism and great danger. History suggests that self-perpetuating power in the hands of any "religious group" that cannot be reached by the people they are intended to serve, becomes tyranny. You shudder at the word — 'Not us.' you say. But every hierarchal authoritarianism stood once where you stand, asserting the 'good of the movement.'"*[5]

Clyde told me, near the end of his life, that his concerns about the dangers of self-perpetuating power had been curtly brushed aside. Unfortunately, within a few years of his 1979 letter to Martin, a schism even more acute than Clyde might have ever imagined was soon to develop in the Urantia Movement. It began in California, and was led by a "Special Agent" of Urantia Foundation.

The Grimsley WW III "channeling" episode

This is a painful, perhaps the most painful, series of events in the history of the Urantia Papers. To some, at first blush, it seems to be a political issue, not directly related to the history of the Urantia Papers. However, as we began to probe this "off-limits" territory, and open some of the doors that have been hitherto sealed, it became evident that the Grimsley episode is closely tied to the events described in Chapter Nine that had eventually led to the compromising of the Declaration of Trust and the original text of *The Urantia Book*. The events surrounding the Grimsley story may explain why the question of *exactly* what happened to the

"The Baptism of Joys and Sorrows" 241

original text has so long been cloaked in mystery. Further, the ramifications of what happened during the Grimsley crisis affect the welfare of the Revelation to this day, as we shall see. Since this is a very sensitive and glossed-over issue, I have relied almost totally upon documentation and sources that are very close to the Foundation's viewpoints. I have avoided speculation as much as possible and let the facts and the protagonists speak for themselves. I have treated this episode at some length because, as Hoite Caston, a former Trustee, wrote about the Grimsley episode: *"This event is too big to simply sweep under the rug. It would leave a lump so large we would soon be tripping over it again."*[6] Indeed, like the dynamics that drove the changes in the second printing, I believe the Grimsley episode cannot remain a lump comfortably tucked away under a cosmetic rug of secrecy.

Vern Bennom Grimsley, Martin Myers' fellow fraternity brother, had become the golden boy of the Urantia Movement by the nineteen-eighties. Grimsley had established himself as a prominent insider in both Urantia Foundation and Urantia Brotherhood. Mr. Grimsley had become quite close to Christy, and was a highly regarded speaker at Urantia conferences. Grimsley established the Family of God Foundation (FOG) as a not for profit spiritual outreach organization in 1967. He was granted "special agent" status by Urantia Foundation in 1971. I heard his wonderfully orchestrated speech at a Urantia International Conference in Snowmass in 1981. He ended his speech with a plea for unity in the movement and raced off the platform. The music of bagpipes filled the convention tent. Vern stood in the crowd in mock exhaustion, apparently barely able to acknowledge the acclaim, while nearly a thousand Urantians rose to their feet, applauding and cheering. Vern Bennom Grimsley's star never shined brighter.

The Kendalls' account of the Grimsley crisis states that in January of 1983, about eight months after Christy's memorial service, Vern Grimsley called Martin Myers and the Kendalls with a stunning announcement. He said that on December 16,

1982, he had begun receiving "messages" from the "Midwayers" in the form of audible statements. He said he had been instructed to purchase a 25-acre property in Clayton, California, to house the approximately 40-member staff of the Family of God organization. Myers immediately flew to California where he joined the Castons and Keelers for an advance tour of the property.[7]

One might wonder why such bizarre "messages" were not simply rejected out of hand. Some have said it was because Vern's credibility and "charisma" were so convincing. However, if one accepts Thomas Kendall's account of Myers' support of Christy's messages, we might surmise that Trustee Myers (at least at first) was very open to the possibility that they were valid. Keeler and Caston definitely supported the "messages" at first. Early in the crisis Dr. Paul Knott interviewed Vern Grimsley. Vern declared that Christy had told him he was a Destiny Reservist. Dr. Knott asked how Christy would know this. Vern replied: *"I don't know, but I think she got messages the same way I got messages."* Dr. Knott subsequently interviewed several people, (he does not disclose who) but none conceded that they knew of any statement by Christy that she had received "messages" after 1955.[8] The Kendalls both insist otherwise.

In February of 1983 Grimsley announced a new "message:" ***"The time has not arrived to publicize the Book."*** The Kendalls' account says that Martin stated on February 26 that Vern should be invited to attend the Executive Committee of Urantia Brotherhood that evening, and declared: *"They'll really take a strong stand against publicity when they hear about Vern's experiences."* In May of 1983, Martin's father died and Martin invited Vern to conduct the Kansas memorial service. On September 4, 1983, seven months after he had learned of the first Grimsley message, Myers gave a speech at a media conference in Los Angeles. He included a long and glowing tribute to Vern and his organization:

(Left) Young Martin Myers was selected as a delegate to the First Triennial Delegate Assembly in 1964. Lucille Kulieke is seated in front of him, and Meredith Sprunger behind.

(Right) Young Vern Bennom Grimsley at 533 in July of 1964.

(Below) The fraternity brothers serenade Christy at Family of God Headquarters in May, 1980. (From left) Hoite Caston, Martin Myers, Rich Keeler, David Gray and Vern Grimsley.

The photos above are not of high quality, but they are instructive and historic. In the photo directly above, Hoite Caston would become a Trustee, Martin Myers was a Trustee at the time of the photo and would become President of Urantia Foundation, Rich Keeler would become a Trustee and eventually overturn the Presidency from Martin Myers, and Vern Grimsley was designated as a "Special Agent" of Urantia Foundation. As Special Agent Vern helped Urantia Foundation police the "unauthorized" use of the "Marks" and the name Urantia. These four men were fraternity brothers from the University of Kansas. Christy is seated with her back to the camera. *Fellowship Website Photos.*

On May 22, 1982, A dapper Vern Grimsley tells the Urantians at Christy's Memorial Service that she awoke from a coma of several days to tell him before her death to give "especial attention to the maintenance of the copyright and the marks." Within seven months Grimsley reported getting "messages" from the Midwayers.

Clyde Bedell, second from left, listens silently at Christy's service. Few of the original Forum members were still living in 1982.

533 Diversey Parkway, Chicago

"... at this time it is appropriate to make special mention of another group... the Family of God Foundation. Under the tireless, indefatigable leadership of Vern Bennom Grimsley... the Family of God Foundation has defined new levels of effective planetary service ... Their unflinching loyalty to the purposes and goals of Urantia Foundation and Urantia Brotherhood has materially aided in the inauguration of a new age on Urantia ... one can anticipate from the signs on the horizon that their real work is only beginning."[9]

About this time, the Executive Committee of Urantia Brotherhood began discussing the topic of publishing the Urantia Book as a paperback. Councilor Harry McMullan brought a mock-up in three volumes, leading some people to believe he was proposing splitting up the book. In truth, the idea of publishing the Jesus Papers separately had long been discussed among Urantians. Some General Councilors believed a separate publication of the Jesus Papers, as a new and enlarged gospel of Jesus, would reach a great number of Christians who might not be immediately attracted to the full version of *The Urantia Book. (Recall that Meredith Sprunger was led to read the entire book after he read the Jesus Papers.)* Other Councilors, apparently unaware that the original text had already been compromised, believed such an action would somehow endanger what the Foundation now euphemistically termed the *"inviolate text."*

In the midst of this Brotherhood discussion, the issue of channeling — *and the question of continued special celestial guidance* — abruptly emerged from the shadows of the inner circle. On September 19, 1983, yet another "message" supportive of Urantia Foundation's policies supposedly came to Mr. Grimsley while he was taking a bath, and it was very clear: *"Don't split up the Book."*[10] This "message" was relayed personally by Vern to the Executive Committee of the Brotherhood, and soon it was being leaked to many bewildered readers. The leaders on the Executive Committee of Urantia

Brotherhood were strongly influenced by these messages with a few notable exceptions. Especially active in resisting them was Councilor Harry McMullan who, along with Berkeley Elliott, represented the Oklahoma Society on the Council and urged fellow Councilors not to docilely accept the Grimsley admonitions as Midwayer directives.

However, a considerable number of leaders in the power structures of the Brotherhood and Foundation bought into Mr. Grimsley's "messages." It was pointed out by some of these leaders that Christy herself was said to have once stated that Vern Grimsley was a member of the *"Reserve Corps of Destiny."* Some recalled that in Vern's funeral oration for his dear friend Christy, he had revealed that she had, in effect, "commissioned" him to carry on her work. Vern had declared in his memorial speech that among the 92-year old Christy's final requests was an urgent entreaty to protect and preserve the Revelation with *"especial attention to the copyright and registered marks."* Then Grimsley had made a strong appeal for unity at the memorial service:

> "Christy gave me clear and explicit instructions to deliver this message of spiritual unity and spiritual priorities, not only at her memorial here today, but throughout the Urantia movement in the future. And I pledged to her: 'This I shall do until I die.' She directed that I should commission us all to rededicate our lives to God . . . and to labor valiantly for the spiritual unification of the Urantia movement."[11]

Numerous Urantian leaders, especially those who believed Christy had received special celestial "guidance," declared that Vern's report clearly indicated that Christy's "mantle" had been passed to Vern Bennom Grimsley. However, it might be noted that Christy had confined her "messages," and her alleged status as a "contact personality" to a small inner circle. Grimsley was eventually to boldly go public, and this may have been his undoing within the inner power structure. Especially when his messages took a grim and chilling new turn.

*The Clayton, California, Family of God complex.
It consisted of 25 acres, and had 75 rooms. When Vern gazed on the
property, he "heard" his first "message" — **"This is it."***

*Vern Grimsley at work. Hoite Caston wrote that the desk stretched
ten feet from end to end.*

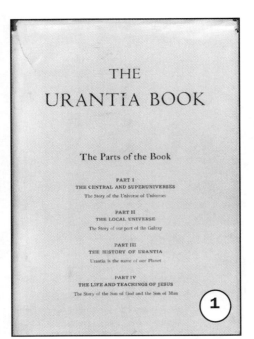

Various Printings of The Urantia Papers:

(Left) [1]. The 1955 Edition. 10,000 Copies of the original text were printed. Three copies of this printing are being preserved by Urantia Foundation. In the next printing, in 1967, and all subsequent printings, editorial changes were made.

[2]. 1994: The Life and Teachings of Jesus, Pathways. Part IV only of the Urantia Papers. About 5,000 copies.

[3]. 1995: The Urantia Papers, Pathways. Exact replica of the 1955 original text, 2,500 copies.

1995: God's Bible, Pathways. Other than two title pages, exact replica of 1955 original text.

[4].1996: The Urantia Book, Uversa Press (The Fellowship). Two column format, two covers were used. Several thousand copies were distributed. Withdrawn in 1997.

[5]. 1999: Jesus, a New Revelation. Part IV, excluding Paper 120. Michael Foundation. Withdrawn from distribution pending outcome of litigation instituted by Urantia Foundation.

On October 6, Grimsley was supposedly "told" by the anonymous voices to: *"Prepare for World War III."*[12] Grimsley cautioned of world-wide upheavals, and the Family of God began storing food and supplies. By mid-October Grimsley mailed over 100 letters to Urantian "leaders" warning them of impending global war and urging them to visit him to discuss the situation. Vern's doomsday predictions shook the Urantia community. Supported by additional "messages," he urged that key Foundation files and Book inventories be transferred to his fortified headquarters in Clayton, for their safety and security. On October 30, 1983, after ten years, a majority of Urantia Foundation Trustees voted to revoke Vern Grimsley's "special agent" status. Thomas Kendall refused to sign the notification letter. Near the end of the month, a concerned Hoite Caston visited Vern. Caston, Myers and Keeler were now in very tight communication, and to many Urantians their actions seemed orchestrated toward the common purposes of distancing themselves from Vern and removing Thomas Kendall, President of Urantia Foundation — Grimsley's most prestigious supporter. The fraternity brothers seemed especially concerned that Vern had elected to go directly to the Urantia Community with his doomsday "message."

Fear gripped the Urantia Community, and many leaders remained undecided about the "messages." Meredith Sprunger had energetically resisted the apocalyptic tide of fear from the beginning and openly declared that Grimsley's messages were delusional. He traveled to Oklahoma City to soothe the fear there, and we benefitted from his cool head, professional knowledge, and spiritual wisdom. In Boulder, Clyde Bedell urged readers to remain calm, and he deplored the fact that Brotherhood "leaders" had begun building fallout shelters and *"running around like chickens with their heads cut off."* On October 27, 1983, Morris "Mo" Siegel, the National Extension Representative of Grimsley's *Family of God* (FOG) organization, took the floor after a Boulder study group. This future Trustee held court for a half-hour, warning the already frightened Urantians about the predicted World War III nuclear holocaust and the dreadful aftermath that would follow. Siegel explained that at considerable cost he had built and outfitted a personal fallout shelter for his family, and he cautioned that an attack could come without warning.

Then, Clyde took the floor. Among other things he said:

"If there are strange voices and groanings in the night for some Urantians and the sound of eerie warnings in some ears, they may possibly be from our friends 'upstairs' . . . or they may be, and in my opinion most likely are, the jumbled echoes, fears, doubts and confusions - I hope - that are born of dual loyalties, loyalties to our spiritually immature human state, and our burgeoning - I hope - but incomplete loyalties to Jesus and to the Father . . . Highly activist Urantians who are loyal to official [Urantian] policies in the light of the Book's demands for loyalty above all else to our universe rulers, put a 'severe strain on the soul . . . the human mind does not well stand the conflict of double allegiance.' . . . Now, if war does not come, we will be, not the nearly 'secret society' we have thus far been due to 533's repressive policies, but a discredited laughing stock."[13]

On Wednesday, November 16, 1983, Vern gave instructions to Richard Keeler, his largest contributor and the Executive Investment Manager of Family of God, to liquidate the FOG account. Vern ordered that the money, which amounted to approximately $1,300,000, be sent to him immediately. Grimsley informed Keeler that the disembodied "voices" had told him it was "Red Alert," and World War III was going to begin the weekend of November 18-20. He told Keeler he wanted to convert the money into gold for the coming catastrophe. The money was wired the next day.[14] On the same day that Vern called Keeler, Hoite Caston sent the "first version" of what he called a "report" to Grimsley by Express Mail, asking for his "feedback." The document, which had obviously been prepared earlier for use at a timely moment, strongly criticized Grimsley and exposed many fallacies in his claims, while presenting Martin Myers as completely negative about Vern's messages. On the *same day* that Caston mailed a copy to Vern requesting feedback, he sent copies of the negative report to all the members of the Brotherhood Executive Committee to "help them" in their deliberations about Vern.[15] On Sunday, November 20th, after enjoying a safe weekend, Richard Keeler sent a hand-written resignation letter as the Investment Manager of the Family of God to Vern and Nancy Grimsley. In this letter multi-millionaire Keeler also informed the Grimsleys he had bequeathed his entire personal wealth to FOG, but now the organization would be stricken from his will.[16] *(See Appendix B.)*

Meanwhile, in the inner power-structure, fraternity brother Myers began to consolidate an anti-message stand. He declared in confidential discussions that he was concerned with public perception: *"I don't want this movement to become known as a doomsday group and that it's being led by a guy who's claiming to get messages."* The Kendalls defended Vern, stating that the previous messages had the ring of truth, curiously reasoning this because they had *"confirmed what were already accepted policies."* Tom Kendall then made a fateful decision. After conferring with the other Trustees, he decided he and his wife Carolyn should go to Clayton to personally discuss the matter with Vern. One Trustee cautioned him not to say he was representing Urantia Foundation, and Tom agreed to this admonition.[17]

Thomas Kendall and Carolyn were but two of the leaders who had believed and supported Grimsley. Before his doomsday message, Vern had won over a great many leaders, including five future Trustees, two of whom, Gard Jameson and Philip Rolnick, were actually working for Vern in his Clayton headquarters as volunteers. Another future Trustee, Morris "Mo" Siegel, was listed in the Family of God brochure as a FOG "National Extension Representative" and was headquartered in Boulder. Yet another future Trustee, Richard Keeler, was "Executive Investment Financial Manager" for FOG. However, Grimsley quickly began to lose support after it became obvious the "Red Alert" World War III "message" was clearly a dud. The persuasive efforts of Martin Myers helped undermine Grimsley's underpinnings. When the Kendalls returned from California, they discovered that Myers had been hard at work and the tide had, for them, disastrously reversed. By the time Tom Kendall had an insight about what had been going on behind the scenes, it was too late and he lamented:

> "I began to realize that Martin believed that he, not I, should be president of the Board of Trustees . . . I suspected that he was waiting for a plausible excuse to have himself installed as president. The Vern Grimsley controversy presented the opportunity. I was served notice on December 31, 1983, that I was no longer president and steps to remove me from the board had begun."

Considering Martin Myers' original support for Vern and alleged long support for Christy's "messages," the charges against Kendall were most intriguing. Kendall was charged with being *"subject to the influence of psychic phenomena"* and that such phenomena *"were in degradation of the teaching of The Urantia Book in that the Book urges the function of evolutionary wisdom and rational judgment as amplified by one's own spiritual experience in solving problems and challenges . . ."*[18]

Kendall disputed the charges, and reminded the Trustees that "the matter of how to deal with the French situation" in 1980 was "solved" through the Trustees' belief in a "message" Christy "received" and one that she (a Trustee Emeritus) and Martin (a Trustee) had brought to the attention of the other Trustees.[19]

This appeal to logical consistency failed, and, after 20 years as a Trustee (and 10 years as President of the Foundation), Kendall was summarily humiliated and expelled, and Martin was soon elected the new president of Urantia Foundation. Myers eventually named as Trustees fraternity brothers Hoite Caston

"The Baptism of Joys and Sorrows" 253

(June, 1986) and Richard Keeler (July, 1989). When asked later why he appointed these men as Trustees, since both had originally supported Vern, Martin replied that they were "rebellion-tested."[20] Ironically, in 1992 Keeler would succeed in turning Myers out of the presidency. (Patricia Mundelius, daughter of Bill Sadler, Jr., assumed the presidency after Martin was ousted, and would be eventually replaced by Richard Keeler, who had led the palace guard revolt against Martin). Myers sued Urantia Foundation in 1993 over his removal. The precise charges that had resulted in the removal of Martin Myers were never clarified.

Many Urantians had cause to recall Clyde Bedell's warnings about establishing a self-perpetuating oligarchy of five to direct Urantia Foundation.

When Grimsley's predicted outbreak of World War III failed to materialize on a specific date, the FOG movement quickly lost momentum and fizzled out, embarrassing several prominent leaders and leaving permanent scars. In June of 1984, Hoite Caston produced a final "report" of over 250 single-spaced pages plus appendixes regarding the affair. It had been edited by Richard Keeler. The final document was described by Nancy Grimsley as *"defamatory"* and containing *"many instances of error, distortion and false representation."* The massive "report" refuted virtually every aspect of Vern's activity, behavior, and character, and did not leave a blade of grass standing. It contained excerpts from the "messages" in which the supposed "celestial voices" made silly jokes and lewd comments. The repugnant content of some of these "messages" convinced virtually all the fence-sitters to abandon support of FOG. Nancy pleaded with Hoite not to distribute the document but to no avail. Notwithstanding the tabloid tone of much of Caston's work, the report contained much wisdom and is instructive about the danger of charismatic practices, especially channeling.

More than ever, after the World War III "channeling" fiasco, perhaps the best kept secret at 533 Diversey Parkway was Christy's "channeling" activities and the alteration of the original text. Evidently unaware of these practices, Caston made the following comment on page 237 of his report:

> "Can the Urantia movement afford to have in leadership positions individuals that [sic] accept guidance from hallucinatory voices, visions, and other forms of psychic phenomena? In my opinion, this behavior would be highly questionable if the individuals themselves were experiencing the phenomena, but when the leaders are accepting and promulgating the unsubstantiated 'contacts' and claims of another person, what does that say about their sense of judgment and responsibility?"

Christy's "channeling" activities were all the more confounding because one of the most quoted "admonitions" among Urantia Foundation's prized apocrypha warns against this very thing. Christy herself, as President of Urantia Brotherhood, used it in a letter to Urantia "leaders:"

> "Many strange "-isms" and queer groups will seek to attach themselves to the Urantia Book and its far-flung influence. Our most trying experiences may well be with such groups who will so loudly proclaim their belief in the teachings of the Book and who persistently seek to attach themselves to the movement. Great wisdom will be required to protect the newly forming Brotherhood from the distorting and distraction influences of those multifarious groups and equally distracting and disturbing individuals, some well-intended and some sinister, who strive to become part of the authentic constituency of the Urantia Brotherhood."

Even so, there seems to be an irresistible attraction to such "influences." There is also an inexplicable ebb and flow of the tides and loyalties driving the Urantia Foundation oligarchy. After Hoite Caston and Dr. Thomas C. Burns resigned as Trustees, some Urantians were astounded as Urantia Foundation moved again to embrace Vern Bennom Grimsley's counsel. In November of 1999, Urantia Foundation posted a report on the internet that the new group of Trustees had traveled to California to meet at

URANTIA FOUNDATION TRUSTEES

DATE INSTALLED	NAMES OF THE BOARD					NOTES
January 11, 1950	William M. Hales (until 4/21/73)	Bill Sadler, Jr. (until 6/18/63)	Wilfred C. Kellogg (until 8/31/56)	Emma L Christensen (until 10/15/71)	Edith E. Cook (until 3/30/86)	
October 1, 1956	William M. Hales	Bill Sadler, Jr.	Russell W. Bucklin (until 3/30/63)	Emma L Christensen	Edith E. Cook	First Printing, 1955
April 1, 1963	William M. Hales	Bill Sadler, Jr.	Thomas A. Kendall (until 7/21/84)	Emma L Christensen	Edith E. Cook	
January 6, 1964	William M. Hales	Kenton E. Stephens (until 6/18/75)	Thomas A. Kendall	Emma L Christensen	Edith E. Cook	Original plates altered for 2nd printing, 1967. Dr. Sadler dies, April '1969. All original plates destroyed May '71.
October 16, 1971	William M. Hales	Kenton E. Stephens	Thomas A. Kendall	James C. Mills (until 5/10/75)	Edith E. Cook	
May 12, 1973	★ Martin W. Myers (until 4/16/93)	Kenton E. Stephens	Thomas A. Kendall	James C. Mills	Edith E. Cook	"Unity not Uniformity" speech - Myers, 1973
August 9, 1975	★Martin W. Myers	Kenton E. Stephens	Thomas A. Kendall	Arthur C. Born (until 2/23/81)	Edith E. Cook	Litigations begin with B. King suit, 1974
September 20, 1975	★Martin W. Myers	William M. Hales (until 1/12/85)	Thomas A. Kendall	Arthur C. Born	Edith E. Cook	
March 1, 1981	★Martin W. Myers	William M. Hales	Thomas A. Kendall	Arthur M. Burch (until 5/23/86)	Edith E. Cook	Copyright renewed 1983
September 30, 1984	★ Martin W. Myers	William M. Hales	Gloriann Harris (until 7/11/89)	Arthur M. Burch	Edith E. Cook	Grimsley Crisis 1983-4
April 12, 1985	★Martin W. Myers	Helena E. Sprague (until 7/7/89)	Gloriann Harris	Arthur M. Burch	Edith E. Cook	
June 7, 1986	★ Martin W. Myers	Helena E. Sprague	Gloriann Harris	Arthur M. Burch	★ Holte C. Caston (until 8/22/95)	
July 20, 1986	★ Martin W. Myers	Helena E. Sprague	Gloriann Harris	Frank Sgaraglino (Until 7/3/89)	★ Holte C. Caston	
	★ Martin W. Myers	Helena E. Sprague (Resigned 7/7/89)	Gloriann Harris (Resigned 7/11/89)	Frank Sgaraglino (Resigned 7/3/89)	★ Holte C. Caston	
July 14, 1989	★Martin W. Myers			K. Richard Keeler ★●	★ Holte C. Caston	
August 18, 1989	★Martin W. Myers	Neal Waldrop III (until 8/3/92)		K. Richard Keeler ★●	★ Holte C. Caston	Urantia Brotherhood "de-licensed" Oct., 1989
March 25, 1990	★ Martin W. Myers	Neal Waldrop III	Patricia Mundelius (until 12/3/97)	K. Richard Keeler ★●	★Holte C. Caston	
August 22, 1992	★Martin W. Myers	Thomas C. Burns (until 12/1/97)	Patricia Mundelius	K. Richard Keeler ★●	★ Holte C. Caston	
April 17, 1993	● Philip A. Rolnick (until 12/31/96)	Thomas C. Burns	Patricia Mundelius	K. Richard Keeler ★●	★ Holte C. Caston	
August 25, 1995	Philip A. Rolnick ●	Thomas C. Burns	Patricia Mundelius	K. Richard Keeler ★●	Georges Michelson-Dupont	Copyright declared invalid by court, 2/10/95
March 26, 1997	Kwan Choi	Thomas C. Burns	Patricia Mundelius	K. Richard Keeler ★●	Georges Michelson-Dupont	9th Circuit Court reverses copyright ruling June 10, 1997
February 16, 1998	Kwan Choi	Morris (Mo) Siegel ●	Gard Jameson ●	K. Richard Keeler ★●	Georges Michelson-Dupont	

★ Kansas State Fraternity Brothers

● Former Members of FOG Organization

NOTE: Morris "Mo" Siegel and Gard Jameson resigned from the Executive Committee of the Fellowship to become Foundation Trustees.

Clyde Bedell addressing Urantians in Boulder, Colorado in 1984.

Perhaps the strongest voice against the announced "slow growth" policies of Urantia Foundation and Urantia Brotherhood was Clyde Bedell. After over 60 years of involvement with the Urantia Movement, he declared shortly before his death:

"It is time the great Urantian secret be let out, that there is an Epochal Revelation here now, given to transform our sadly ill planet through the transformation of men and women. 'Oh, oh,' you say, 'We would be violating the Foundation's and the Brotherhood's strict injunctions if we aggressively handle the Urantia message'. . . but I have never been able to discover a single sentence in [The Urantia Book's] million-plus words that says: 'Obey Jesus and The Urantia Book . . . to eternally spread this his Gospel, except when the human Trustees of the Urantia Foundation in Chicago say: Don't obey Jesus, obey us!'"[31]

length with Mr. Grimsley. Three members of the new configuration of Trustees (Keeler, Siegel, and Jameson), had worked for FOG, and had given considerable financial support to FOG. It was not disclosed exactly what was discussed at the conference. However, after the meeting, Grimsley's services as a speech writer were employed by Urantia Foundation to prepare an address expressing the familiar Foundation theme of the "need for unity." The address, written almost entirely by Mr. Grimsley, was delivered by President Richard Keeler at the 1999 Fellowship Conference in Vancouver, British Columbia.

Conflicts, confusion and litigation

Friction between Urantia Foundation and Urantia Brotherhood progressively increased when Martin Myers took over as President of Urantia Foundation. Thomas Kendall observed:

> "The separation of the Foundation and Brotherhood has gradually eroded. The Foundation has increasingly adopted a proprietary attitude toward not only The Urantia Book, but the Brotherhood as well . . . by applying the hammer of marks management."

In October of 1989, Urantia Foundation President Martin Myers de-licensed Urantia Brotherhood; it was forbidden for Urantia Brotherhood to use the name "Urantia" and the three concentric circles — the so-called "marks." Urantia Brotherhood was also ordered to change its name since it was told it could no longer use the word "Urantia." Urantia Brotherhood obediently became *The Fellowship*. (Years later the name was changed to *The Urantia Book Fellowship*). Nearly all of the existing Brotherhood Societies voted to stay with the original Brotherhood, now the "Fellowship."[21]

Following this series of upheavals, a revival of the interest in channeling again rose among Urantia Book readers and has been yet another divisive factor in the movement. Many readers were astounded that, after the chaos that channeling had caused the movement in the Eighties, channeling activities would again gain momentum in the Nineties — in some cases, replacing serious study groups, with "channeling" sessions, in which disembodied "celestial beings" began "speaking" through human "receivers" to credulous Urantians. Urantia Foundation, under Keeler, granted permission for channeled works to be published along with excerpts from the Urantia Papers. A "channeling" session was a feature of the Fellowship 1999 International Conference in which an alleged entity named "Ham" supposedly "spoke" through a human "receiver" and answered questions from the audience. While not opposing the rights of anyone to indulge in such activities on their own time, many experienced readers found the resurgence of "channeling" to be a wasteful and unfortunate diversion with no connection to the Urantia Papers. Some believe that "channeling" practices fly in the face of Dr. Sadler's warnings about such psychic phenomena. Some Urantians believe "channeling activities" by Christy and their acceptance as a reinforcement of organizational power have confused the readership about the role of psychic phenomena and have opened a Pandora's box of error.

As previously quoted, Dr. Sprunger opposed the channeling activities from their inception. Referring to the period of conflicts, litigation, and differing philosophical views on celestial guidance and contact, Meredith has noted philosophically:

> "Most of us now realize that the Fifth Epochal Revelation
> has been launched on the troubled and turbulent seas of
> evolutionary struggle."[22]

The IUA is born

After the split with Urantia Brotherhood, Urantia Foundation decided to create a new fraternal branch, and it established the International Urantia Association, or IUA. This group is a "task-oriented, social and service organization formed by Urantia Foundation to foster in-depth study of *The Urantia Book* and its teachings." Unlike the original arrangement of a separate Brotherhood as approved by the Midwayers, the IUA organization is not autonomous and is closely linked to the Foundation Trustees. Members are pledged to support Urantia Foundation and the copyright, and the organization continually solicits donations for Urantia Foundation projects. IUA expressly declares itself *not* to be a religious organization. Thus the IUA, like Urantia Foundation and the Fellowship, resolutely avoided defining a religious mission as part of its vision.

More litigation

After Martin Myers became President of Urantia Foundation in 1983, the policy of litigation against Urantians was pursued with renewed energy. Among the series of major lawsuits was a 1991 litigation that was launched against Kristen Maaherra, a homemaker in Arizona, for sending out free computer indexes containing the text of *The Urantia Book.*[23] JJ Johnson was also served papers without warning as a "co-conspirator," although the charges against JJ were subsequently dropped without explanation or apology. The litigation weapon proved dreadfully costly, draining JJ of thousands of dollars to reply to the groundless charges. A few years later Kristen's husband, Eric Schaveland, was sued by Urantia Foundation in a separate action for using the three concentric azure blue circles on a website.

The suits against Maaherra and Schaveland proved to be the undoing of the previously invincible team of Urantia Foundation lawyers. With the support of donations from many Urantians, Kristen and Eric resolutely brought the Foundation's legal steamroller to a standstill. The Maaherra litigation fragmented the Urantian community and dragged on for nearly a decade, shattering Kristen and Eric's family life and siphoning millions of dollars from Urantia Foundation. For over two years during this litigation, *The Urantia Book* was declared to be in the public domain, based upon the Court's judgment that the original 1955 United States Copyright of *The Urantia Book* was invalid. Eventually Urantia Foundation won a reversal and a Pyrrhic victory. The ambiguous wording of the reversal left the copyright wide open to further litigation.

260 A HISTORY OF THE URANTIA PAPERS *Chapter Ten*

The defiant stand of Kristen and Eric seemed to inspire other Urantians to challenge Urantia Foundation's control of the text. In 1994, during the litigation, before any judgments had been made, the Pathways Company defied the copyright by printing and selling to the Urantia readership about 5,000 copies of *Part IV of the Urantia Papers, The Life and Teachings of Jesus.*

During the period the Urantia Papers were in the public domain in 1995, the Pathways Company published the complete 1955 original text of the Urantia Papers, informing the general readership for the first time of the changes that had been made in the Foundation's printings after 1955 and listing the more significant ones in the back pages of their printing. Uversa Press (The Fellowship, formerly Urantia Brotherhood) published the Urantia Papers in a two column format in 1996. In 1999, Michael Foundation of Oklahoma City published Part IV of the Urantia Papers *(without Paper 120)* under the title: *Jesus: A New Revelation.* This publication contained a list of changes that Urantia Foundation had made to the original text.

In the meantime, it became common knowledge among Urantians that the original 1955 text of *The Urantia Book* was not being published by Urantia Foundation. In response to reader inquiries, in 1994 Urantia Foundation published a small pamphlet titled: "Corrections to the Text." Admitting at last that changes had been made, the pamphlet states in part: *"Almost half the changes, including a small number that might be considered to be more than minor changes, were made in the second and third printings. These changes were made by those individuals who were directly responsible for preparing the original text for publication."* Presumably this meant Christy and Marian Rowley. As discussed in Chapter Nine, there had been no statement printed in the Book itself to alert a purchaser of later printings with a full disclosure that the "Corrections to the Text" document (with its approximately 150 changes) was available.

As the millennium drew to a close, after nearly a quarter-century of aggressive litigation against Urantians, Urantia

Berkeley Elliott, 1917-1995. Berkeley was a good friend of Bill Sadler, Jr., and a strong Urantia leader in Oklahoma. She was a member of the Executive Committee of Urantia Brotherhood for many years, and hosted study groups and countless outreach programs.

Dr. Meredith Sprunger speaks about forming a Urantian religious organization at a 1993 Urantia function in Boulder, Colorado. Dr. Sprunger has been ever-willing to travel to Urantia groups and serve wherever he is needed.

| 262 | A HISTORY OF THE URANTIA PAPERS | *Chapter Ten* |

Foundation launched yet another lawsuit by announcing on December 1, 1999 it was filing suit against Michael Foundation and its founder, Harry McMullan, for publishing the Jesus Papers. The announcement said the Trustees' vote to sue Michael Foundation was unanimous. Urantia Foundation announced: *"The Foundation's copyright in The Urantia Book makes possible the preservation of the inviolate text for the next fifty years."*

Mr. McMullan is a very visible Urantian. He is a General Councilor, having served on the Executive Committee of the original Urantia Brotherhood and subsequent Fellowship for nearly two decades. The Urantia Book Fellowship, however, demurred involvement in the litigation and announced the conflict between McMullan and Urantia Foundation was a "private matter." Yet some Urantians believe that a subsequent letter by Fellowship President Janet Farrington Graham to the membership seemed to support the Foundation's contention that printing the Jesus Papers separately has jeopardized their current version of the "inviolate" text. In the Fellowship's *MIGHTY MESSENGER*, for Fall, 1999, Farrington reprinted her letter. Generally ambiguous, the letter was very specific on one point. Referring to an August, 1996 General Council debate about printing the Jesus Papers separately, she wrote:

> "The council was then reminded that when *The Urantia Book* first went into the public domain, the council voted unanimously to protect and preserve the text inviolate; this project of publishing Part IV as a separate volume was deemed to be in conflict with that resolution."

Farrington reports that the two councilors who wanted to fund the printing then withdrew their request to "rethink the project." Some Urantians believe she left the strong implication that the issue had been resolved by the General Council, when in fact it had not. Certainly, the implication that printing Part IV separately violates *de facto* the original text of *The Urantia Book* has never been established. Many Urantians believe such an idea did not attain the status of dogma among some members in the

Fellowship until Vern Grimsley warned: *"Don't split up the book."* Other Urantians believe the issue that initiated the litigation is control of the text and copyright, and had nothing to do with preserving the original text. *They observed that Mr. McMullan's action did not affect the preservation of the original text as Urantia Foundation has defined it: keeping three copies of the 1955 printing in a temperature-controlled environment. An inviolate version of the original text has not been published by Urantia Foundation since 1955.*

Urantia Brotherhood

Urantia Brotherhood was initially designed to function as a fraternal organization, independent of Urantia Foundation. Unfortunately, as Dr. Sprunger points out, the leaders of the Forum who formulated the constitution of the Brotherhood did not take the time to structure it directly from the teachings of *The Urantia Book*. They elected to use an organizational model and constitution designed after a 16th Century Presbyterian prototype. In the place of the 36 elders in the 16th century model, there was established a Brotherhood General Council of 36 Councilors drawn from the Wednesday night "Seventy" group. The constitution of the Brotherhood was tacitly accepted by the Midwayers with the comment that it allowed *"for its own emendation."* According to History One and Two, these Councilors and their successors were to direct the Brotherhood for the first nine years. After that, the Brotherhood was to be governed by the actions of a Triennial Assembly composed of various delegates elected by Urantia Societies.[24] In a 1958 intra-office memo, Bill Sadler, Jr. saw the Brotherhood maturing into a directly representative *"republican institution."*

In 1955, the newly chartered Urantia Brotherhood visualized organizing thousands of Urantia Book study groups, and gradually chartering Urantia Societies. The precise nature of these Societies was ambiguous. Many of the founding members of Urantia Brotherhood regarded the organization as a religious one. It was the original vision of Dr. Sadler that Urantia Societies would develop as bona fide religious groups. Under Dr. Sadler's leadership, a key element of the Constitution of the Brotherhood was the development of ordained teachers. A school to train and ordain teachers was established shortly after publication of the Book. On numerous occasions Dr. Sadler discussed the nature of this new religious organization with Dr. Sprunger.[25]

The fear of "churchification"

As the Brotherhood developed, a view surfaced in Urantia Brotherhood that was very different from that of Dr. Sadler and Dr. Sprunger. A developing majority of the members of the early Brotherhood shared both a strong fear of what they derisively termed *"Churchification"* and a biased attitude against institutionalized religion. There was even a marked uneasiness in the original group toward the use of an opening prayer for meetings. The General Council of the Brotherhood eventually deleted the words "ordained teacher" from the constitution, fearing it had an institutional ring. The Brotherhood now defined itself, not as a religious organization, but as *"an educational-social organization with a religious purpose."*[26] After the death of Dr. Sadler, Urantia Foundation withdrew all of Dr. Sadler's Bible Studies from distribution. These study aids related the Urantia Book to Biblical concepts.

Even so, many in the Urantia Brotherhood were enthusiastic about introducing religious, educational and other leaders to *The Urantia Book*. Meredith Sprunger wrote of those early days:

> "Illusions of grandeur about initiating a spiritual
> renaissance on our planet invigorated Urantia Conferences.
> Gradually evolutionary reality began to change the picture.
> Religious and political leaders were not impressed. The
> Book was succinctly dismissed as a contemporary Gnostic
> document or politely ignored."[27]

In the early nineties, the Triennial Delegate Assembly (which consists of directly elected representatives from Societies) voted for direct representation in the General Council. Societies wanted representatives who were elected by them and who were directly accountable to them. In response, the General Council of the Fellowship voted to amend the constitution and allow direct representation from societies and establish a separation of Executive and Judicial powers. However, the Fellowship Executive Committee was, for some reason, unable to accomplish the emendation of its constitution. The current Urantia Book Fellowship remains structured in the 16th century Presbyterian model although the Presbyterian Church itself has long since discarded it in favor of a more contemporary organizational structure. The issue has been shelved without resolution.

The New Fellowship

There has evolved a fundamental change in the original Brotherhood which is now *The Urantia Book Fellowship*. Whereas the original Urantia Brotherhood was conceived to be a fraternal association of religionists, the new Fellowship is evolving as a *facilitator* of local or regional associations of religionists. The concept of a monolithic social organization has evolved into a service organization which fosters and encourages more intimate local religious and fraternal associations. David Kantor, a member of the General Council Executive Committee, has been instrumental in carrying this concept of service to a global level, especially by means of the internet. Under Kantor's direction, the Fellowship website and internet activities for the first time have very successfully and openly brought reliable information, news, and Urantia Movement history to the entire Urantia community.

Mr. Kantor's perspective is that an infrastructure of grass roots organizations developed by Urantians on an intimate local level would best serve the Revelation at this time. Kantor observes that these kinds of personal associations would "have a better chance of surviving the political struggles which seem to engulf larger social organizations." Thus, he advocates that the Fellowship remain unencumbered by religious trappings so it may more effectively serve in a non judgmental capacity the varied Urantian efforts to develop socialized expressions of their religious beliefs. However, to some Urantians, there remain the problems of how far tolerance should go, as well as how to provide for the needs of individual — not socialized — religious development.

The question of a Urantian religion

The Urantia Papers are not a religion, any more than Jesus of Nazareth is a religion. Yet, the Urantia Papers are profoundly religious. To many Urantians, the secular political struggle for control of the Urantia Papers has so dominated the movement that the more significant questions have been neglected: Do the Urantia Papers change lives? Do they make people better — more benevolent, kinder, more committed to serving humankind?

In the earlier days of the movement, this question was surprisingly absent. The Urantia Papers were born into a world in which intellectualism reigned supreme. Early Forum members were admonished about this. Mary Lou Hales came into the Forum in 1932. She said in a 1993 interview:

"We were told in effect that — 'You are accepting this Revelation intellectually, but you are not accepting it emotionally. We are very anxious that you should let it do more in your lives.' And so, it was our fault, you see, that we were not accepting it in the right way, emotionally, letting it influence our lives the way it should. [The Revelation] was wonderful. We were all thrilled and excited about it and what you should do about this or that, but apparently we were not letting it really change our lives or help us become more spiritual."[28]

Carolyn Kendall's father, Clarence Bowman, was a member of the original Forum. When the Papers were finalized on May 31 of 1942, the Forum became a Sunday Study Group. Carolyn was 19 when she met Dr. Sadler and she joined the Sunday group. She said this of her religious experience:

"The spiritual thing I felt was strangely missing from the Forum . . . It was later on, long after publication, that I realized there was a spiritual message there. Now maybe I was deficient. I probably was. There were high-powered people in the Forum, but I never heard that the Father loves you and that we are all sons and daughters of the Father. That wasn't emphasized, it was read, but it didn't come out."[29]

Perhaps, as a consequence, a nonreligious culture characterized the early movement. The three major Urantia organizations define themselves as secular, or at least nonreligious: *Urantia Foundation*, the *International Urantia Association* (IUA), and the *The Urantia Book Fellowship*. Notwithstanding the excellent service that has been done by many individual members as they foster independent religious expression, the political cultures of all the organizations are relatively secular and non-representational. The individual units generally tend to have a more religious flavor. This grassroots religious activity is viewed favorably by some Urantians who point out that the Urantia Papers state:

"All non-religious human activities seek to bend the universe to the distorting service of self . . ." [67, par.1]

Urantia Study groups have traditionally remained intellectual forums. Gradually, more religious expression has been encouraged at Urantia Fellowship conferences. Hymns, prayers, and group meditations are more and more accepted practices, but generally the fear of "churchification" prevails. Nearly all Urantians view the political chaos of the movement and observe that very little of it has any relationship to the philosophy and spiritual message of the Urantia papers. Many Urantians agree that a great deal was lost when Urantia Brotherhood abandoned its formal schools for developing certified religious leaders and teachers. A fourth organizational alternative, to address the necessity for a purely religious outlet for Urantians, has long been advocated by Meredith Sprunger.

Dr. Sprunger on a Urantian religion[30]

Dr. Sprunger believes there is a great need for new religious institutions to serve the growing edge of spiritual development in this world — authentic religious institutions that will appeal to the highest spiritual aspirations of humankind. Dr. Sprunger believes the Urantia Papers will provide the inspiration for that coming spiritual renaissance. *Further, Dr. Sprunger asserts that such religious institutions are a necessary step in fulfilling the mission of the Urantia Movement.*

These new spiritual organizations will not supplant nor compete with existing Urantia secular organizations. They will draw circles large enough to include and unite many believers, and complement what is now being done. In recent years, spiritual seekers all over the world have emerged in unprecedented numbers, accompanied by a growing disenchantment with existing religious institutions. In the Urantia Movement there is an increasing longing for a "religious community" that goes beyond the usual study group and occasional conference. More and more Urantians long for a sense of "spiritual family" and a clear community identity. There is a growing desire for spiritual nourishment — Urantian spiritual nourishment — from birth to death. Urantia study groups and societies, which are primarily intellectual-social groups, can't fulfill all the functions of traditional religious institutions. It is the conviction of Dr. Sprunger that the most important activity in the Urantia Movement at this time is to focus upon the development of resources to help actualize new religious institutions:

> "New Urantian religious institutions will serve as vehicles through which the Fifth Epochal Revelation can be carried into the world. We also need dedicated Urantians to research and develop creative symbolism as well as appropriate social and religious expression of the Fifth Epochal Revelation."

Dr. Sprunger notes that there have been several spontaneous but short-lived attempts to establish such religious institutions already. When such attempts are made, there is a danger that such institutions will be extemporized, without taking the time and effort to study the teachings of *The Urantia Book*. Meredith suggests that teams of dedicated Urantians must study the information provided in the Book so that new organizations will authentically reflect the truth-insights of the Fifth Epochal Revelation. The mission of these teams would be to evolve a body of resources. Otherwise the pressure of necessity will fashion religious organizations without such help. Dr. Sprunger cautions:

> "The history of religion demonstrates that when strong spiritual ideals and aspirations inspire people, and there are insufficient intellectual and social structural foundations to guide these people in their creative religious expression, all kinds of irrational beliefs are likely to appear, such as: visions of angels, channeling of celestial beings, speaking in tongues, attempting miracles, and doomsday predictions."

Meredith notes that such emotional and psychic phenomena almost always occur in an unstructured social-spiritual atmosphere. The most effective way to establish rational order, reliable stability, and genuine spiritual identity is to evolve structured outlets for social and spiritual Urantian expression. Such outlets will also sponsor creative outreach and loving service.

Is a new paradigm called for?

There is yet another religious perspective to consider. Urantian Rosey Lieske of Phoenix, Arizona is among a growing number of Urantians who passionately believe the Urantia Papers present a message that cannot be embraced by intellectual analysis nor orchestrated by organizational structure. To Rosey the Urantia Papers define with precise clarity the call of Jesus of Nazareth for ever more intimate levels of personal relationship, through worship, meditation and prayer to God directly and without intervention. She says:

"We live in a world that is ravenous and in need of the living gospel of Jesus. We have the dynamic and simple genius behind the Master's plan of action toward spiritual self — and collective actualization on a planetary level. Worship and Service. Not even three little words. Just two — ready to be either buried or mobilized into action."

The intellectual and emotional appeals for unity in the Urantia Movement leave Lieske cold. She believes the Papers tell us that *"goals not creeds"* will someday unify religionists. She says that creedal formation, though inevitable, will not yield a naturally spiritual result.

"Spiritual communities will not spring from the soil of intellectual, creedal, agreement alone — only from real experience borne by faith in action, which is the will to love God — the will to serve his family. Goals, worship-inspired and service-driven, goals that are made and met — both personal and collective — will provide the dynamic for the birth and evolution of true spiritual community."

To Lieske all of the conflict in the Urantia Movement arises because religious forms have been wedded to political ones. She believes Urantian organizations fail to deliver the spiritual message of *The Urantia Book* because Urantians have too often come to venerate the book itself. She asserts that the Kingdom can never be construed, constructed, made manifest, or manipulated by human energies alone. It can only be accessed through *worship*, which is step one of the Master's program, and implemented in the "real world" by step two: *service*. However, Rosey wonders whether many contemporary Urantians can as yet make the paradigm stretch:

"The question remains as to whether large numbers of our spiritual community will mature and grasp the opportunity to ACT on revelation. Can Urantians replace politics and intellectualism with the transcendent message of the gospel — positioning it as their first priority — and strive to return the flock to the Master? Find God, become like Him — find your brother, serve him!"

The process of the "baptism of joys and sorrows" on the evolutionary seas of struggle continues. Some Urantians believe we are now engaged in the preliminary stages of an authentic new age of religion in the world. Time will tell. How soon a significant leadership role may be assumed by Urantians is open to question. In Chapter Eight we reported that Bill Sadler, Jr. (presumably) quoted the Revelators as saying:

"You will doubtless live and die without realizing you are participating in the birth of a new age of religion on this world."

ENDNOTES:

1. These "famous people" included Sholem Asche, Ralph Bunche, Norman Cousins, Aldous Huxley, Eleanor Roosevelt, and Edward Teller. THE FELLOWSHIP BULLETIN, Winter, 1992, page 1.

2. Harold Sherman claims that he and his wife had interested Sir Hubert Wilkins in the Forum, but this seems to be one of his flights of fancy. Dr. Sadler wrote in a March 17, 1959 letter to Reverend Adams (Appendix B): "From a standpoint of general science, I think the studies of the late Sir Hubert Wilkins were the most extended and exhaustive. For a period of twenty years he periodically spent time in Chicago going over the Papers. He would work weeks at a time, ten hours a day. . ." This must have been prepublication since Wilkins would hardly have gone to Chicago to study the Papers if he had a book, and the activity could not have begun until 1935 at the earliest, seven years before Sherman got involved. Also, Dr. Sprunger has stated that Dr. Sadler told him he consulted Wilkins in the early days.

3. AFFIDAVIT OF MARTIN MYERS, May 24, 1993.

4. SPECIAL REPORT TO THE READERS OF *THE URANTIA BOOK*, April 1990, page 22

5. CLYDE BEDELL gave me this letter along with some other correspondence in 1984, a few months before his death.

6. VERN GRIMSLEY MESSAGE EVALUATION by Hoite C. Caston, June 17, 1984, page 10.

7. June 21, 1990 Report by Thomas A. and Carolyn B. Kendall, titled: RESPONSE TO URANTIA FOUNDATION'S SPECIAL REPORT TO THE READERS OF *THE URANTIA BOOK* AND COMMENTS ON OTHER RELATED SUBJECTS, page 7.

8. Letter from Dr. Paul D. Knott to undisclosed readers, November 20, 1983.

9. June 21, 1990 Report by Thomas A. and Carolyn B. Kendall, titled: RESPONSE TO URANTIA FOUNDATION'S SPECIAL REPORT TO THE READERS OF *THE URANTIA BOOK* AND COMMENTS ON OTHER RELATED SUBJECTS, page 8.

10. IBID., page 8.

11. URANTIA BROTHERHOOD BULLETIN, Spring, 1982, page 5.

12. June 21, 1990 Report by Thomas A. and Carolyn B. Kendall, titled: RESPONSE TO URANTIA FOUNDATION'S SPECIAL REPORT TO THE READERS OF *THE URANTIA BOOK* AND COMMENTS ON OTHER RELATED SUBJECTS, page 8.

13. TO BE (upset) OR NOT TO BE by Clyde Bedell, "Read to a Boulder meeting, the evening of 10/27/83, after the people had been given a half-hour or so scare talk urging the storage of food, water, etc., the preparation for each family member of a big kit to take to fall-out shelters, upon alarm, etc.," pages 3 and 5.

14. VERN GRIMSLEY MESSAGE EVALUATION by Hoite C. Caston, June 17, 1984, page 206.

15. IBID., page 28.

16. IBID., Appendixes.

17. June 21, 1990 Report by Thomas A. and Carolyn B. Kendall, titled: RESPONSE TO URANTIA FOUNDATION'S SPECIAL REPORT TO THE READERS OF *THE URANTIA BOOK* AND COMMENTS ON OTHER RELATED SUBJECTS, page 8.

18. IBID., page 8.

19. IBID. Tom is referring to an episode he recorded on page 6 (The date of the astounding incident was approximately November, 1980): *"TAK: [Thomas A. Kendall] After the Board of Trustees meeting the next Saturday, Christy and Martin had read a message to me which had allegedly come to her earlier in the week. It said: 'Do not become involved in long, drawn out discussions with Mr. Weiss. Read page 840.'* [NOTE: Jacques Weiss was a Frenchman who translated The Urantia Book into French and then published it in 1962 after obtaining permission of Urantia Foundation.] *'I interpreted the message, as did administrative assistants, Scott Forsythe and Michael Painter, to mean that we were not to get bogged down in lengthy negotiations. It may be concluded that the other Trustees interpreted this message to mean we should not get involved in any negotiations. Page 840 had to do with Caligastia's plot. The meaning of this reference is also open to question."* From this passage written by Foundation supporters Carolyn

"The Baptism of Joys and Sorrows" 273

and Thomas Kendall we may reasonably arrive at two remarkable conclusions. *First,* Martin Myers bought into, and apparently encouraged, Christy's channeled "messages." *Second,* that these "messages" had not only evidently dictated the alteration of the original text of *The Urantia Book since 1967* (as previously documented), the purported contents of these "messages" were routinely weighed when Urantia Foundation established its policies!

20. IBID., page 7.

21. Many readers remained baffled by the "split." I was a member of the Brotherhood General Council when the final vote was taken. For myself, and for most of the other Councilors, it was our most painful moment as Urantians. However, since the Brotherhood had been summarily disenfranchised and the so-called "marks" had already been "taken away" by Urantia Foundation, there was no choice left the General Council. It should be noted that two future Trustees who were members of the Council at the time, Morris "Mo" Siegel and Gard Jameson, were vocal advocates of defying Urantia Foundation's control tactics and both voted for the split.

22. THE FUTURE OF THE FIFTH EPOCHAL REVELATION by Meredith J. Sprunger, a paper dated 2/10/93, page 1.

23. The 1955 printing of *The Urantia Book* has a statement at the end of the *Contents of the Book,* just before the Foreword: "(An exhaustive index of *The Urantia Book* is published in a separate volume.)" The Revelators had approved of the project years before. When Maaherra was sued 35 years later, the comprehensive index was still unpublished.

24. HISTORY OF THE URANTIA MOVEMENT ONE, by a Group of Urantian Pioneers, assisted by Members of the Contact Commission, 1960, page 10.

25. THE FUTURE OF THE FIFTH EPOCHAL REVELATION by Meredith J. Sprunger, a paper dated 2/10/93, page 1.

26. IBID., page 1.

27. IBID., page 1.

28. THE CONJOINT READER, Publication of the School of Meanings and Values, Santa Monica, CA, Summer, 1993, page 10.

29. IBID., page 3.

30. The essential material for this section was taken from, and based upon THE FUTURE OF THE FIFTH EPOCHAL REVELATION by Meredith J. Sprunger, a paper dated 2/10/93.

31. PLANETARY PRINTS, Rocky Mountain Urantia Society of Denver, Spring, 1985, page 26.

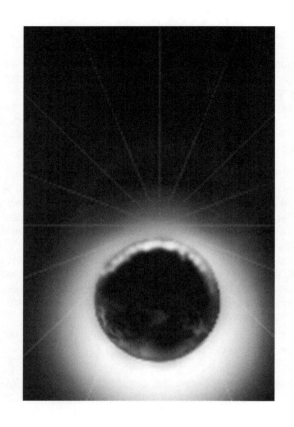

Epilogue

EPILOGUE

WE HAVE TRAVERSED NEARLY a century in our examination of the history of the Urantia Papers. The editors of this book have strived to provide the best available information about the materialization of the Papers, their conversion into a typed manuscript, the process by which they were further converted into printing plates, their publication as a book in 1955, and the fate of the original text after that. Along the way, we discovered many unexpected events and linkages and tried to candidly disclose them as we followed the truth wherever it led us. Considered individually, these ideas may not necessarily be news, but each is supported by documentation, and each is logically connected to the whole picture. The composite gives us a cohesive and reasonable story from beginning to end.

The most important fact about the Urantia Papers that I believe we established with reasonable certainty was that the 1955 printing of *The Urantia Book* was produced without deliberate human intrusion. The errors that exist in that text were minor and unintended human errors. The subsequent printings of the Urantia Papers, although containing intrusive human changes, are reasonably close to the original 1955 text. I write this with some reservation because I remain convinced the situation demands that a reliable "keeper of the text" should publish the *original* text again (with appropriate endnotes) and again make it available to all Urantia Book readers.

276 A HISTORY OF THE URANTIA PAPERS

Second in importance were the following sequences: Documentation and testimony of Forum members clearly establish that the Revelation process took place continuously from January 18, 1925 until May 31, 1942, when the text was frozen by the Revelators. The Forum was told at that time that no additional questions would be entertained. The Revelation had been completed, and the Sunday Forum ceased to exist as a Forum and became a Sunday study group. The text was then set in type, proofs were made, corrected, and approved of by the Contact Commission, and then the text was plated. A team of Midwayers *(no longer as Revelators)* oversaw the entire process from a calculated and respectful distance. They saw to it that the Fifth Epochal Revelation had been delivered into the evolutionary mainstream in reasonably good condition.

Once the plates were made, the typewritten manuscript of the original text itself was destroyed by order of the Midwayer Commission. Thus, by 1945, after decades of Revelatory activity, the printing plates (and the proof pages generated by them) became the only material manifestations of the original text of the Urantia Papers. The plates contained (presumably) human errors that had accumulated somewhere along the evolutionary process, and there was no paper trail left to discover when or how these errors took place. However, it is self-evident that the Midwayers found the text (and subsequently the plates) acceptable, notwithstanding the imperfections that existed. Urantia Foundation was established in 1950 "on the basis of" the plates, (which now constituted the original text). The plates were stored in the vaults of the R.R. Donnelley & Sons Crawfordsville, Indiana plant from approximately 1945 until 1955, when the book was printed. After the printing was completed, they were then returned to the vaults.

Urantia Foundation was specifically designed to function as an autonomous entity, and the Contact Commission remained active until sometime in 1955. At the time the Declaration of Trust was finalized in 1950, it was well established by continuous reading of the proof sheets from the plates that there were *typographical* errors in the plates. However, beyond typographical errors, it is highly probable that the possible *editorial* inconsistencies that eventually were discovered in the published text were not known to the Contact Commission at the time of the establishment of Urantia Foundation. The Midwayers apparently conferred tacit approval of the Declaration of Trust with full awareness of the possible editorial problems that existed within the plates. It seems probable that the Midwayer Commission was constrained to rely upon human wisdom — within the parameters of the Declaration of Trust document — to eventually deal with the typographical errors and the editorial issues. After the Book was published in 1955, the Midwayer Commission signed off, and the mortals were told they were now on their own. In 1967, apparently without the knowledge of all of the Trustees, a considerable number of plates were destroyed and replaced with altered plates for the 1967 second printing. Dr. James C. Mills succeeded Christy as a Trustee in 1971. According to what Dr. Mills wrote in 1991 *(See page 210, and the full text of the letter in Appendix B)*, some Trustees were told the entire Urantia Book had to be reset in 1967 due to technological changes in printing. This was not the case.

From a historical perspective, and confining ourselves as much as possible to the question of the Urantia Papers and their welfare, what are we to make of the disarray and turbulence that has followed after the second printing in 1967? Dr. Sprunger has often observed that the significant threats to the Urantia Movement have come — not from the outside as most early Urantians had anticipated — but from the inside. *Why?* In my judgment, two factors emerge as the underlying attitudes and forces that have caused confusion and chaos within the Urantia Movement. One is fearful ***proprietorship***, and the other is prideful ***entitlement.*** The proprietorship issue is rather clear-cut, while the related issue of entitlement is more difficult to define.

Proprietorship - who owns the Revelation?

Two thousand years ago, according to my Catholic upbringing, Peter was supposedly given the "keys to the kingdom" by Jesus. And (again supposedly), with the words: "Upon this rock (Peter) I shall build my church," the Catholic Church was established. Christian hierarchal religious "authority" and "divine rights" of succession were established upon these presumptions, and centuries of rule by "infallible" Popes has followed. All of the "spiritual implications" regarding Jesus and the "individual believer" were thus shifted from Jesus to the church. And when Paul and his contemporaries did this, **"they struck a deathblow to Jesus' concept of the divine kingdom in the heart of the individual believer."** [1865, bottom]

When I was relatively new to the Urantia Movement, I was told by some individuals that the Trustees and their successors had been given the "keys to the kingdom" in the form of the "mandates." More than that, Urantia Foundation has asserted ownership of the Revelation itself, the Banner of Michael, and the word "Urantia," on the basis of these mysterious "mandates" and "special messages" that are allegedly locked in a safe somewhere at 533 Diversey Parkway. To many Urantians, this would be comparable to the Pope claiming *ownership* of the text of the Bible, the symbol of the cross, and the word "Christian." To a large number of Urantians, in the face of warnings by Clyde Bedell, Bill Sadler, Jr., and others, the human foible of desiring to *own* and *control* the text has *created* disunity and *impeded* the propagation of the Revelation. Time and evolutionary struggle will eventually decide the issue of human "ownership" of the Revelation, as well as the appropriateness of human "ownership" and "authority" over using the Banner of Michael, the right to freely use the name of our planet, and the right to identify oneself religiously as a Urantian.

EPILOGUE

The commentary that follows may be characterized by some as political. But, what is at issue has little to do with organizational questions. What is at issue is not politics but *values*. Most significantly *truth* — not simply the factual nature of truth, but also the *meaning* of what we have discovered. At this point it is appropriate to repeat what was written in the *Introduction* of this history:

> *"Histories are inescapably adversarial and painful processes. The people who undertook this task of developing a good, sound history are aware that the final product is a compelling argument that could help shape the destiny of the Urantia Papers. The stakes are high, because what is ultimately at issue are the various philosophies and agendas of those who seek to control the Urantia Revelation. It will come as no surprise then, that the interpretations of the events relating to the Urantia Papers are destined to be fiercely contested. Sometimes the facts about the Urantia Papers are at issue, but more often the meaning of the facts will be the center of historical controversy."*

With these notions in mind, we will revisit some of the difficult issues and challenges that confront each Urantian, fully aware that what *each* of us decides is of momentous importance to the Revelation.

There are no "secret" documents

It cannot be emphasized too strongly that *all* the supposed "secret messages" and apocrypha said to be associated with the Urantia Papers have doubtful origin. There may be a moral issue as to whether *copies* of any of this material should even exist. *None of the supposed messages are revelation, none can be authenticated.* They may have varying degrees of academic value and — at best — only moderate degrees of reliability and relevancy. Whenever I have used one of these documents in this

280   A HISTORY OF THE URANTIA PAPERS

history, I have tried to carefully disclaim certainty about its authenticity. Yet, although it is appropriate to weigh apocryphal information for historical examination, it is not proper to use it to support claims of authoritative control.

One further example of the inappropriate use and questionable reliability of apocrypha should suffice. In Chapter Ten, endnote #19, we documented Tom Kendall's statements about how, in 1980, a "message" supposedly from the "Midwayers" was delivered by Trustee Emeritus Christy and Trustee Martin Myers to Tom Kendall, President of Urantia Foundation. The message warned against "long, drawn out discussions" with Jacques Weiss, who had translated *The Urantia Book* into French. The "message" suggested reading page 840, which relates to Caligastia's plot against Adam and Eve. We documented how Tom testifies that he brought this "message" to the attention of the other Trustees and employees at 533 for their consideration. The impression given was this procedure of receiving "messages" relating to important Foundation policy decisions and passing them around was not an unusual occurrence in the culture at 533. Another equally disturbing example of the "inner-inner" circle's use of suspect "messages" is also documented in Tom and Carolyn Kendall's 1990 paper, which they distributed within the Urantia Brotherhood General Council when I was a Councilor: *RESPONSE TO URANTIA FOUNDATION'S SPECIAL REPORT TO READERS OF THE URANTIA BOOK AND COMMENTS ON OTHER RELATED SUBJECTS*. On page three of the original document, Tom discloses:

> *"In early 1966 the Trustees began to realize that the Foundation needed to do more to protect the name, Urantia. Christy had recently brought to my attention a message which was given to the Contact Commissioners in 1942:*

EPILOGUE

"'You have not done enough to protect the name. You must carefully safeguard the name Urantia. Make it very safe for one generation so that it cannot be pre-empted. In a common-law trust you hold the name. You also do it in the copyright. You must also carefully register it with the division of government which controls trade relations, trademarks. In all ways you must safeguard the name. This is one of your most important duties.'"

We could ask several questions about this "message." Evidently, it is a purported *copy* of a message that was said to have been communicated in 1942, because all originals of authentic Midwayer messages were to be destroyed. *But, was it supposed to have originally been a written or verbal "message?" Was it given to the Contact Commission according to established protocol, or is it claimed to have been "received" by a lone individual? Why had such an important message never been noticed before? Why is it not mentioned in the Histories?*

Carolyn and Tom provide additional clues to the possible origin of this "message" in an interview with Polly Friedman in the Summer, 1993 issue of The Conjoint Reader *(published by the School of Meanings and Values, Santa Monica, CA).* During the interview, the same alleged 1942 "message" mentioned in the Kendall's 1990 paper is brought up. In this interview, we learn that it was a verbal "message." Carolyn discloses, page 3: *"There were additional verbal messages that came to Dr. Sadler and Christy. One that came through was the message: 'You have not done enough to protect the name Urantia; you register it in the branch of government that I've looked into just like you do with a copyright for the book.' That was in 1942."* Polly then offers this lob: *"So protecting the name is important; that was an actual suggestion?"* Then Carolyn and Tom (in unison) reply: *"Yes, it was an order."* And Polly, evidently won over, adds: *"And to be taken very literally."* Carolyn then decides to emphasize the 1942

282   A HISTORY OF THE URANTIA PAPERS

"message" by reading the document to Polly verbatim, which she happened to have with her. Carolyn says to Polly, *"Here it is, regarding the name Urantia."* Note the significant variations from the document she and Tom prepared and distributed in 1990. (Additions to the 1990 version are indicated by unbolded, non-italic CAPS type, deletions by a strike-through:

> *"You have not done enough to* ~~protect~~ SAFEGUARD ~~the~~ YOUR *name.* (MEANING THE NAME URANTIA). ~~You must carefully safeguard the name Urantia.~~ *Make it very safe for one generation so that it cannot be pre-empted. In a common law trust you hold the name.* YOU DO IT ALSO IN A CORPORATION. A CORPORATION HAS STATUS IN LAW. *You also do it in the copyright. You must* ~~also~~ *carefully register it with the division of government* THAT I HAVE LOOKED INTO THAT ~~which~~ *controls trade relations,* ~~trademarks.~~ TRADEMARK, AND THEN YOU ARE PROTECTED IN COMMON LAW CONNECTED WITH A VOLUNTEER ASSOCIATION SUCH AS YOU ARE PLANNING IN URANTIA BROTHERHOOD. *In all* THOSE *ways you must safeguard the name. THIS IS ONE OF YOUR MOST IMPORTANT DUTIES."*

Carolyn pauses to inform Polly: "And that last sentence was in capitals." [*Note: In the 1990 paper this sentence was not in caps.*] Then Carolyn continues with additional new phrases:

> "IN 50, 75, OR 100 YEARS, THE NAME WILL BE FAIRLY SAFE. YOU SAFEGUARD IT FOR A GENERATION AND IT WILL LARGELY TAKE CARE OF ITSELF."

I confess that I am baffled. How could such an *"important" "order"* from *"Midwayers"* be formally presented twice by the *same people and have such wide variances? The second version has doubled in length and has several word changes. Why do both versions feature such poor grammar? Who edited the material? How could a **verbal** message be delivered with a passage in "capital letters?" And if it was so important to emphasize, why didn't the 1990 report of the message use capital letters for the passage? Urantia Brotherhood was not given Midwayer approval until 1952 and was not officially named and chartered until 1955, **thirteen years after the purported message.** Why did the second version of the message say: "Trademark, and then you are protected in common law connected with a volunteer association such as you are planning in the Urantia Brotherhood"? A generation is usually defined as twenty-five or thirty years. **Why was a celestial personage so ambiguous?** First this anonymous messenger says "one generation," and later "50, 75, or 100 years" and still later "a generation" is used again.*

Yet, for nearly two generations, on the basis of this purported verbal "message," Urantia Foundation has sought to justify its claim of proprietary ownership of the word "Urantia" and "Urantian." In 1990, Thomas Kendall wrote that in 1966 he had been surprised by the purported "message" because he had "been a Trustee for three years" and "this was the first I had heard of these instructions." He said the "instructions" were contrary to the prevailing opinions of legal counsel, who had advised that *"usage, adoption, and use"* were the means to gain "rights" over the word Urantia. Nonetheless, according to Tom, in 1966, Trustee Christy had brought him this written version of a "message" (which, if authentic, should have been destroyed when the Book was published). And Tom obediently sallied forth to do the bidding of this anonymous "voice" that was said to have been recorded somehow, by someone, over two decades in the past — and that had languished unnoticed in a file drawer since then.

> **Background on Marks**
>
> TAK: In early 1966 the Trustees began to realize that the Foundation needed to do more to protect the name, Urantia. Christy had recently brought to my attention a message which was given to the contact commissioners in 1942:
>
>> You have not done enough to protect the name. You must carefully safeguard the name Urantia. Make it very safe for one generation so that it cannot be pre-empted. In a common-law trust you hold the name. You also do it in the copyright. You must also carefully register it with the division of government which controls trade relations, trademarks. In all ways you must safeguard the name. This is one of your most important duties.
>
> I had been a Trustee for three years, but this was the first I had heard of these instructions. It was explained that prior to the middle 1960s, the Board of Trustees had been advised by counsel that we would gradually acquire broader rights to the word Urantia through an enhanced public knowledge of The Urantia Book and our organizational activities. It was our understanding that rights did not accrue from registrations so much as a consequence of adoption and use.

Above: The first version of the purported "1942 Message." This was presented by the Kendalls in a paper titled: "Response to Urantia Foundation's Special Report to the Readers of The Urantia Book and Comments on Other Related Subjects, June 21, 1990." The initials "TAK" indicate a contribution to the paper by Thomas A. Kendall.

At right is the second version of the purported "1942 message" as read by Carolyn Kendall to Polly Friedman in an interview printed in "The Conjoint Reader," Summer, 1993. According to Carolyn the "message" has a date of August, 1942 written in Christy's handwriting. Note that the message has somehow doubled in length and is considerably altered.

In mid-2000 Urantia Foundation moved to copyright the phrase "The Urantia Book" as a trademark. Their applications stated that the goods and services which they wish to identify with this name -- "The Urantia Book" are "caps, hats and shirts, coffee cups and mugs, pens and pencils." Note Carolyn's final comment on the opposite page.

Polly: So protecting the name is important; that was an actual suggestion?

Tom/Carolyn: Yes, it was an order.

Polly: And, to be taken very literally.

Carolyn: Here it is, regarding the name Urantia. *"You have not done enough to safeguard your name. (Meaning the name Urantia.) Make it very safe for one generation so the name cannot be pre-empted. In a common law trust you hold the name. You do it also in a corporation. A corporation has status in law. You also do it in the copyright. You must carefully register it with the division of government that I have looked into that controls trade relations, Trademark, and then you are protected in common law connected with a volunteer association such as you are planning in the Urantia Brotherhood. In all those ways you must safeguard the name. THIS IS ONE OF YOUR MOST IMPORTANT DUTIES."* And that last sentence is in capitals.

In 50, 75 or 100 years, the name will be fairly safe. You safeguard it for a generation and it will largely take care of itself." And, again, they emphasize, they are talking about the name Urantia. You can see that it is dated August 1942 and this is Christy's writing in the corner.

Polly: Oh, that's very important. Now it does say a generation, which is about 25 years. A lot of people say maybe the time is almost over and it isn't that important.

Carolyn: It should be obvious they don't want the name to fall into general use, so that you could have, Urantia Trading Company, Urantia Massage, etc. They didn't say anything about the circles, however.

Dr. Sadler did not "channel" anything

Another disturbing and relatively new tendency of those who believe in anonymous "verbal communications" from "spiritual beings" to "special" individuals is that they include Dr. Sadler as being a deliverer of such material. Some Urantians believe Dr. Sadler's name is used in a crude effort to impart additional credibility to the process that supposedly produced "secret messages." In the interview with Polly, note that Carolyn implies Dr. Sadler's participation in such "messages" by saying: *"There were additional verbal messages that came to Dr. Sadler and Christy."* While Carolyn had previously written that *Christy told her* that *Christy* was in continued contact with the Midwayers, to my knowledge Carolyn never had written or stated that Dr. Sadler had ever told her anything of the sort.

There is not a fragment of documentation or credible testimony to support the idea that Dr. Sadler claimed he communicated with Midwayers *outside of the Contact Commission*, and a great deal of testimony and documentation refutes this possibility. In the unanimous opinion of the Editors of this book, *Christy was the only Contact Commissioner who ever claimed she was individually in contact with "Midwayers" — and Christy alone made statements that she had "received" the alleged "approval" for changes in the original text from anonymous "voices." There is no known testimony that Christy's "voices" were ever heard by any other person, and no evidence whatsoever that Dr. Sadler had approved of this practice.* It is also reasonably certain that rumors of Christy's "channeling" activities did not begin to surface in the general power-structures of the Foundation and Brotherhood until after Dr. Sadler's death in April of 1969. This is the opinion of Dr. Sprunger, *who was there* and who knew the individuals and who worked with the power structure at 533. Prior to Dr. Sadler's death, only a very small inner circle was privy to Christy's so-called "messages."

Dr. Sadler did not authorize changes in the text

Urantia Foundation has also published statements to the effect that *both* Christy and Dr. Sadler were individually involved with "Revelators" in 1967 and *both* were responsible for changing the original text. In the Foundation's web presentation titled: *Setting the Record Straight*, (http://www.urantia.org/newsinfo/strs.htm) Urantia Foundation interjects this rhetorical inquiry in part 7:

"We must pose the question to those who knew of the integrity of these individuals: would Dr. Sadler and Christy have made such changes without good reason?"

This attempt to justify the 1967 changes to the original text by linking them to Dr. Sadler is not supported by documentation or reliable testimony. When Urantia Foundation was established in January of 1950, *the Trustees accepted all authority and responsibility for the original text* (the plates). Dr. Sadler chose not to be a Trustee. We know that in 1967 there occurred a destruction of part of the Substantive Estate (the plates/or the original text) as defined in the Declaration of Trust. Because of the total lack of documentation, we cannot know what "good reason" may have existed in anyone's mind for destroying part of the Substantive Estate without a unanimous vote of the Trustees — which is the provision in the Declaration of Trust by which such an action could be legally taken. *(See Appendix F, Urantia Foundation's Declaration of Trust, Article V, Section 5.2).* Neither Dr. Sadler (who was never a Trustee) nor Christy had authority to authorize the destruction of any part of the Substantive Estate of the Declaration of Trust of Urantia Foundation, regardless of any supposed "good reason" to do so.

Yet, if we are to believe Carolyn Kendall, Christy authorized and brought about changes to the original text because she believed the "Revelators" gave her the authority to do so. And, Tom Kendall told Carolyn that the Trustees had "nothing to do" with the 1967 changes. *Can we believe these assertions by Carolyn?* I cannot be certain, but it is clear that Urantia Foundation relies upon Carolyn's information. Carolyn contributes to the Foundation web material and she was selected to write the fifty-year anniversary history for Urantia Foundation.

"The Golden Years"

In early 2000, Urantia Foundation produced a history to commemorate its fifty year anniversary, titled: *The Golden Years,* authored by Carolyn Kendall and Barbara Newsome. It states that it is based upon "first hand information," but is not documented in any plausible way to support this claim. Within our own history, I have used Urantia Foundation sources, or sources close to the Foundation, in depicting the events in which the Foundation was a key player. With this constraint, I will limit comment to a few of the many instances in which *The Golden Years* is inconsistent with previously published Foundation material.

The chronology presented in *The Golden Years* is generally accurate, although many important events are omitted. This history also leaves the names of the Contact Commission out, "in respect for the spirit in which they served." However, it lists all of the Foundation Trustees since the establishment of Urantia Foundation. In some cases *The Golden Years* draws heavily on "History Two" which it claims was authored by Dr. Sadler, a belief we have disputed in detail in Chapter Three. In other cases *The Golden Years* is clearly at odds with History Two. On page 6, *The Golden Years* states that the Contact Commission consisted of *five* people (the same number as the Foundation), leaving Bill Sadler, Jr. out:

> *"Aside from the patient, the Contact Commission consisted of five related people, the two physicians, her [sic] sister and brother-in-law, and the adopted daughter*

EPILOGUE

of the physicians. When the doctor's wife died in 1939, their [sic] son took her place. Thus the Contact Commission functioned as five until the organizations were established and The Urantia Book was published. As individuals, they functioned as Contact Commissioners the rest of their earthly lives." [Page 6]

This loaded paragraph supports the Foundation's proprietary claims and legal assertions that Urantia Foundation is a continuation of the Contact Commission. This paragraph also seeks to establish that special celestial "guidance" continued after the Midwayers signed off in 1955. This paragraph is at odds with the Testimony of Dr. Sprunger, Clyde Bedell and others who have stated there were six Contact Commissioners, including Bill Sadler, Jr., who became a Contact Commissioner no later than 1930, after his discharge from the Marines. The statements in this paragraph also conflict with Urantia Foundation's own "History Two," which states on page 21 of the original document:

"The fact that no provision was ever made for replacing members of the Contact Commission who might be lost through disability or death, also led us to the belief that the Book would be published during the lifetime of some of us."

Why is this important? Because there was never an organizational connection between the Contact Commission and Urantia Foundation. There was no "passing of the torch." In the 1990's Urantia Foundation began making legal declarations that it is the successor organization to the Contact Commission. This is not supported by the facts. The Contact Commission had six permanent members by 1930, with no provisions for replacement of lost members. Urantia Foundation was established in 1950, has five Trustees, and lost members are replaced through the election of another member by the remaining Trustees. The Contact Commission operated under celestial direction, and ceased to function after the publication of the original text in 1955. Urantia

Foundation is humanly directed, and was founded as a completely autonomous entity as is clearly stated in the preamble to the Declaration of Trust *(See Appendix F)*. The Contact Commission continued to function for five more years after the establishment of Urantia Foundation. Carolyn Kendall has reported that in November of 1951, the Seventy and the Sunday study group were read an important communication from the "Acting Planetary Prince of Urantia." (See Page 174 for the partial text of this alleged communication). In this message, Urantia Foundation and the Contact Commission are clearly viewed and discussed as two separate entities. Therefore it is misleading when the paragraph in *The Golden Years* asserts: ***"Thus the Contact Commission functioned as five until the organizations were established and The Urantia Book was published."*** The claim that Urantia Foundation is a successor to an organization that was directed by celestial beings is completely unfounded. This distinction must be made if we are to avoid creating a faux "divine right" of succession of "authority" over the Revelation *(See Chapter Eight, and Appendix F)*.

The paragraph further asserts that: ***"As individuals, they functioned as Contact Commissioners the rest of their earthly lives."*** This strongly implies that the Contact Commissioners, as *individuals,* remained in contact with Revelators after the final message: ***"You are now on your own."*** The question of continued special celestial guidance is arguable, and one that we have discussed at length. However, I am constrained to point out that there is no documentation to support the statement that those individuals whom Bill Sadler, Jr. referred to as the "defunct contact commissioners"[1] had retained their personal status as "Contact Commissioners" after 1955. The statement in *The Golden Years,* authorized by Urantia Foundation, implies the Contact Commissioners as *individuals* personally remained in contact with Midwayers. The only testimony to that effect is what Carolyn Kendall has told us came from Christy, and Christy's comments about alleged individual "contacts" (as reported) referred to herself, not the other members of the Contact Commission. This sentence also apparently attempts to support the principle of psychic "messages" and "channeling" by "special" individuals — activities which have proved so divisive and damaging to the Urantia community.

On page 9 of *The Golden Years* the statement is made:

"The Jesus Papers, undated in The Urantia Book, were delivered in 1935 with the input of questions from the Forum."

This statement seems crafted to support the legal position of Urantia Foundation against the publication of the Jesus Papers by Mr. McMullan. The clause: *"with the input of questions from the Forum"* is incorrect. History One and Two relate that there were no questions that prompted the delivery of the Jesus Papers, which were materialized in a single written manuscript. The Jesus Papers were read to the Forum over a period of years, and according to Clyde Bedell, did elicit questions from 1935 until all of the Papers were read to the Forum. However, History Two (published on Urantia Foundation's website) is clear about their initial arrival: *"Of all the Urantia Revelation, the Jesus Papers were the biggest surprise."* [Page 3]

On page sixteen of *"The Golden Years,"* under *"Planetary Government Rulings - 1951 to 1952"* important information is omitted. Once more, the information that has been removed runs counter to the idea that special celestial guidance was being given the Trustees after 1955. The same omission was made in another presentation by Carolyn, and this was discussed in Chapter Eight, page 174, and endnote #6 in the same Chapter. It would be redundant to repeat the discussion here. However, it is repugnant to many Urantians that supposed celestial messages are apparently edited when it is convenient to support a specific position.

In the past few pages we have disputed several contentions made by those who believe Urantia Foundation has proprietary ownership of the Fifth Epochal Revelation. Using Urantia Foundation's own material, the issue we have sought to join is one of proprietorship. Carolyn and Tom Kendall report that Bill Sadler, Jr. warned against this attitude in an intra-office memo in 1958:

> *"Unless Urantia Foundation conducts itself with wisdom it may breed dissension between itself and the Brotherhood. There is no room for naivety or any exhibition of proprietary feeling toward the Urantia Papers."*[2]

The end of proprietorship

Many of us who have the conviction that the Urantia Papers belong to the people also believe that, unknown to all of the Trustees *at the time*, the noble task of Urantia Foundation to preserve inviolate the *original text* of the Urantia Papers fell into default in 1967. Those responsible for this error were probably driven by the desire to have a "perfect book," as Carolyn Kendall explained. To achieve this human aspiration, these individuals elected to by-pass the Declaration of Trust and "correct" the original text by applying a "quick fix." There was no documentation, no paper trail, no unanimous vote by the Trustees. This impatient act of short-cutting of the appropriate processes eventually resulted in the 1967 default, and has been followed by increasing doubt and confusion among readers.

After Dr. Sadler's death, during the 1970's, the Foundation's original mission of preserving inviolate the original text of the Urantia Papers was supplanted by efforts to establish *ownership* of the text, *ownership* of the Banner of Michael, and *ownership* of the words "Urantia" and "Urantian." Secular enforcement of these claims was supported by alleged "secret mandates" that were never fully disclosed. Rumors surfaced that the last remaining "Contact Commissioner" reported that she was receiving "special messages" from Midwayers. Shortly after her death, Christy's heir-apparent, Vern Grimsley, also claimed to be in contact with celestial beings. More chaos and strife followed, and continues to divide the Urantia believers. And, in my judgment, nearly all of this cascading confusion has been the harvest of a single stupendous error: the taking of an expedient shortcut in an attempt to "correct" and make "perfect" *The Urantia Book*.

Most of us who believe the Urantia Papers belong to the people contend that there are no "secret messages" or special endowments to justify dishonoring the Declaration of Trust. We believe that the destruction of a substantial number of the plates in 1967 without the unanimous vote of the Trustees was a human error, and was not authorized by "Revelators" or "Midwayers." We do *not* believe the 92-year old Dr. Sadler had any part in or knowledge of the destruction of part of the Substantive Estate in 1967. We believe attempting to deny or cover-up the error has compounded it. In our judgment, the misguided actions of a few people have caused untold harm to the spiritual unity of the Urantia Movement. And we believe the fragmenting of the Urantia Movement stems, in large measure, from the false idea of ownership and the application of the unfounded proprietary and commercial "rights" of an entrenched few over a Revelation that in reality belongs to all of the people.

Entitled and special people

The fearful attitude of proprietorship leads to a second, and equally dangerous quality: *entitlement.* Entitlement, like proprietorship, is not wholly a political issue, but is also an issue of *values.* Entitlement attitudes affect all sides of the political struggles that are taking place to control the Urantia Papers themselves. The issue of presumed "entitlement" within the Urantia Movement reaches back into the mid-Sixties, perhaps even farther back than that. It may be that it began to energetically emerge as soon as the celestial personages signed off with the message: *"You are now on your own."* Surely that statement, which was freely circulated among the Sunday study group and the Seventy, was a clear appeal to *all* Urantians to take personal responsibility for the Revelation.

Yet, human nature does not readily embrace freedom and responsibility. The failure of previous epochal revelations have left marks upon our planet, and timid men and women generally wait for someone in "authority" to give them permission to perform:

> **"And men have always tended to venerate the leader, even at the expense of his teachings; to revere his personality, even though losing sight of the truths which he proclaimed. And this is not without reason; there is an instinctive longing in the heart of evolutionary man for help from above and beyond. This craving is designed to anticipate the appearance on earth of the Planetary Prince and the later Material Sons. On Urantia man has been deprived of these superhuman leaders and rulers, and therefore does he constantly seek to make good this loss by enshrouding his human leaders with legends pertaining to supernatural origins and miraculous careers."** [1008, par.7]

The questions Urantians should answer are these: *"Are there really entitled people who have a special relationship to the Urantia Papers? Are there really infallible human authorities on the Papers themselves? Is unique celestial guidance now being provided to an inner-circle of special people? Are celestial personages really talking through certain entitled people?"* These questions are not directed solely to Urantia Foundation, nor to the "leaders," but rather to the broad movement itself. Each individual Urantian must confront these issues because the most wise and mature people have too often been shunted aside while the most aggressive and ruthless have assumed positions of leadership. Also, with modern technology, virtually anyone who can put up a web site can posture in the role of an "authority" on the Urantia Papers. A rule of thumb used by Clyde Bedell, Berkeley Elliott and other seasoned Urantians was: *There has never been, nor will there ever be a human "authority" on the Urantia Papers.*

Distortion of a Divine Revelation

While the editing team and I were still researching and working on completing this history, yet another new history was published. *Birth of a Divine Revelation* by Ernest Moyer seeks to put forward several notions within its 600 pages that are so bizarre they need no comment. However, the book also postulates that the Urantia Papers were corrupted by Dr. Sadler, a charge that strikes at the heart of the integrity of the Urantia Revelation, and which cannot remain unanswered.

Each individual has a right to his or her own ideas. However, there is a discipline that is traditionally required of a historian who claims to be presenting reasonable notions to the reader. Like some other efforts by Urantians to write histories, in *Birth of a Divine Revelation* Moyer mixes pure speculation, undocumented claims, and established facts carelessly and without informing the reader which is which. It is these flaws that make Moyer's *Birth of a Divine Revelation* more of a collection of curious artifacts and theories than a serious historical work. Mr. Moyer attempts to degrade the personal experience and contributions of Dr. Meredith Sprunger — and he seeks to cast doubt upon the personal integrity and professional competence of Dr. Sadler. To support his attacks, he uses sources such as Martin Gardner, Harold Sherman and Harry Loose. [3]

Generally, experienced readers will not have difficulty sifting through the maze of poorly documented fact and speculative fiction in *Birth of a Divine Revelation*. But some new readers may be confused, especially since the author claims to deeply "love" the Revelation. A few of the more obvious distortions in *"Birth of a Divine Revelation"* require comment.

To support the strange idea that Dr. Sadler, unknown to himself, was *the* "Contact Personality," the author quotes the Urantia Papers on page 208 of *Birth of a Divine Revelation.* The manner in which he distorts the quote is instructive:

> "This passage naturally leads many to believe that it refers to the human subject of Sadler's study. This is suggested by the statement: '. . . **varying degrees of contact with . . . certain favorably constituted mortals through the skillful penetration of the minds of the latters' indwelling.**' This would be the mechanism of trance control of the subject."

The quote actually refers to secondary midwayers and their ability to make contact with Thought Adjusters. In full, filling in the dots the author conveniently used to replace the actual text, the statement on page 1258 of *The Urantia Book* has an entirely different meaning: **"varying degrees of contact with <u>the Thought Adjusters of</u> certain favorably constituted mortals through skillful penetration of the minds of the latters' indwelling."** My emphasis is to show the important words left out by the author, completely distorting the meaning of the text. Certainly the reference has nothing to do with "trance control." The author claims the Midwayers "moved the arms" of the sleeping subject and Dr. Sadler put pencils in his hand to get him to begin trance writing. This is totally undocumented, unfounded, and not a shred of credible testimony supports it. On the contrary, there is ample testimony that the subject was never seen writing anything, and that no Contact Commissioner was ever allowed to observe any material manifestations of the Midwayers' presence.

Moyer claims the Revelators deserted the mortals in 1934-5, after the delivery of the Jesus Papers, and left things in human hands. To support this claim the author again uses a distortion of primary sources to make a point. He claims that Dr. Sadler stated the Urantia Papers were "certified complete" in 1934. He uses History Two as a source. No informed scholar of the Urantia Papers takes this notion seriously. Although some of Dr. Sadler's writings are inserted in History Two, no one knows for certain who actually assembled it. It is, in fact, highly unlikely Dr. Sadler did. Moreover, the statement is pulled out of context. The Papers themselves are not annotated with a statement that they were either "completed" or "certified" in 1934-5. These words are not used in any annotations. Also, we have previously recorded Clyde Bedell's 1983 comment: *"The Papers were revised until Paper 196 had been presented and questions asked, and then answers brought into the text which would amplify and so forth." (See endnote 11 of Chapter Three of this book for an analysis of the two Histories and testimony of Clyde Bedell and others that the Papers were not completed until 1942.)*

Perhaps the most peculiar notion that Moyer puts forth is his attempt to explain the twenty or so innocuous inconsistencies in the text. He claims that, after Dr. Lena Sadler's death in 1939, Christy took over the Contact Commission and began unwittingly "channeling" changes to the text that came from the "Devil." Such speculations, aside from being unfounded and ludicrous, also introduce repugnant philosophical ideas to explain things that have a much simpler cause. In addition, reason dictates that neither Dr. Sadler nor Bill Sadler would have permitted or condoned such activities. Further, we can be reasonably certain the Midwayer Commission was keeping a watchful eye on the Revelation until the 1955 message: *"You are now on your own."* This fits the documented facts and testimony of those who were there.

Mr. Moyer informs us that he has the spiritual insight to sort out the material that is the legitimate Revelation from the

"Devil's" evil handiwork. I will spare the reader and not belabor any additional issues. I will let this man speak for himself and allow the reader to judge his maturity, stability, and character. Many Urantians have protested the assertions of *Birth of a Divine Revelation.* Here are some of the comments the author elected to post broadly on the web in early April, 2000, in an attempt to defend *Birth of a Divine Revelation:*

> *"I not only show that I can distinguish the difference between good and bad spirits, but that I can define their operations."* [It is self-evident that Mr. Moyer believes he has charismatic spiritual powers not granted to normal people.]

> *"Sadler treated the Revelation as if it were subject to his arbitrary changes."* [Absolutely outrageous and defamatory. This flies in the face of the testimony of all who knew Dr. Sadler, and most especially Clyde Bedell and Dr. Sprunger, as we have documented several times in our history. Fortunately for Mr. Moyer, Clyde is no longer around to answer these maligning commentaries about Dr. Sadler. Mr. Moyer, who claims he "loves" the Revelation, has produced a book that, in the opinion of some Urantians, rivals the efforts of Harold Sherman and Martin Gardner to denigrate Dr. Sadler's reputation and accomplishments and depreciate the integrity of the Urantia Papers.]

> *"Such profound exposure had to be considered openly and honestly. There is no way an honest person could duck around it. But more, we had to find a reasonable explanation of Sadler's rationale."* [This "honest" person makes groundless statements defaming Dr. Sadler and then proposes to "explain" actions of which the doctor was never guilty.]

> *"We now have a specific illustration of the iniquitous practices of Caligastia.* [AKA the "Devil"] *I have now*

defined how he operates, with express details." [Again, it is self-evident that Mr. Moyer believes he has unique spiritual powers.]

"If [Sadler] believed the changes came from celestial authority, as he states so strongly, we are then left with only one other alternative, that he became subject to the machinations of Caligastia. He did so because he did not understand the mechanisms of spirit operations, although he wrote several books about it." [These comments border upon blatant distortion. Moyer does not document *where* Dr. Sadler *ever* stated that he authorized any changes, either before or after the original plates were cast, or that he had any contact with celestial authority outside of the Contact Commission. Perhaps Moyer cannot document that Dr. Sadler stated any of these things "so strongly," because there is no documentation to support that he stated them at all. Moreover, editor Andre Radatus pointed out to me that Dr. Sadler did not author any books about the "mechanics of spirit operations." Moyer's implication that he, himself, is the first known mortal to understand the unseen "mechanisms of spirit operations" appears to be baseless self-aggrandizement.]

"We are now left with a concern for corruptions throughout the entire Revelation. We must keep an eagle eye out that we don't fall into a trap of careless acceptance of Revelation statements. This puts an onerous burden upon us, for now we cannot simply take the Revelation and use it until we have assured ourselves that such use is valid, and adheres to truth." [By "we" Moyer apparently means himself, since I know of no other mortal who claims to have his awesome powers. This statement is saying, in effect, that *he* must filter the Revelation for us and then spoon feed it to us.]

It should be clear to any reader of our documented history that there was no simple way for Dr. Sadler to make "changes" in the text once it was plated. No one had authority to make changes in the original text. Even if an individual had a notion to make changes, the text was frozen in the plates, proofs had been made and read, and (with the exception for their removal to print the 1955 books) the plates were in the vaults of R.R.Donnelly & Sons plant in Crawfordsville, Indiana. We have discussed at length Dr. Sadler's non-involvement in the changes that were made in the second printing.

Many have assured me that no informed Urantians take the *Birth of a Divine Revelation* seriously. An apparent characteristic of Moyer's work, however, can be broadly applied to the charismatic segment of the Urantia Movement. I have met several Urantians who assert claims of "knowing" things that are not available to the rest of us. Moyer informs us on the back cover of his book that *"Through a series of unusual events the author came to recognize that our planet is experiencing celestial visitations today . . ."* This kind of beguiling and unfathomable statement is characteristic of charismatics.

In Sedona, Arizona, another "entitled" individual also professes that he has unique status and knowledge denied to ordinary mortals. He is writing a "continuation" of the Urantia Papers. Like the author of *Birth of a Divine Revelation* he claims that he "loves" the Urantia Papers, yet he also claims they were corrupted by Dr. Sadler. This unfounded attack on Dr. Sadler's integrity is identical to the position of Harold Sherman and Martin Gardner. Naturally, like the author of *"Birth of a Divine Revelation,"* this individual in Sedona also presumes to have the power to "correct" the "errors" that Dr. Sadler supposedly made when he "changed" the Papers.

Note that many of those who seek to control the Urantia Papers, or to use them to validate their own activities, attempt to position themselves between the reader and the Revelation.

The cultcentric mind and "channeling"

Yet, are these entitlement characteristics harmless to the Revelation? Is supposed communication with spiritual forces simply benign and amusing diversion? Let us see what a Trustee has to say. Thomas C. Burns, Ph.D., was elected a Foundation Trustee in August 1992, and served until December, 1997. On November 10, 1983, (just prior to Vern Grimsley's Red Alert) Dr. Burns had sent a letter to John Hales, President of Urantia Brotherhood. Dr. Burns' comments about "channeling" are instructive and interesting. Here are some excerpts from the 1983 letter:

> "If Vern's claims are untrue, the credibility given them by persons looked to as spokespersons for the movement to disseminate the Urantia Book teachings, would, in my opinion, set the movement back by at least a quarter of a hundred years."

Dr. Burns goes on to quote Dr. Sadler at length on the subject of self-deluded psychics. Then he clearly spells out the dangers of charismatic practices such as "channeling." Dr. Burns' perspective is equally as valid and relevant today as it was in 1983:

> "There is . . . sufficient cause to avoid such active and passive endorsement as has already been granted by officials of the Urantia organizations. The possible operation of the psychosocial dynamics described above, or more accurately, the failure to eliminate their possibility, is only one of the reasons for caution. Another is the fact that the method of appearance of alleged revelation is at such extreme variance with that of the Urantia Book's. Its methods seem completely antithetical to the teachings of the Urantia Papers.

> "Clearly, the directors of the Urantia revelation strove mightily to avoid identification of contact humans lest they be elevated, or tempted to elevate themselves, to a priest,

302 A HISTORY OF THE URANTIA PAPERS

guru, authority, ruler status. Others were quickly involved to provide the leavening balance of a forum. Vows of silence were taken, and for the most part, observed.

"We are cautioned clearly and repeatedly in the Urantia Papers against the dangers of priesthood, or looking to someone else to serve as our link to personal truth. The authors were unmistakable in showing the dangers inherent in having one person receive a revelation which he then gives to others, thereby establishing the most profound dependency imaginable. The papers caution unequivocally against attributing psychological events to spiritual contact.

" . . . Although probably informal, the Family of God has undoubtedly evolved a subtle and effective screening procedure for the selection of like-minded members, as well as a (perhaps unconscious) hierarchy. When one adds to this the fact that its charismatic leader of selected and loyal followers is now receiving messages from higher beings, and this following is dependent upon the leader for these truths, all the active elements of a cult are present. Such social systems focus on positive feedback on the leader and shield him/her from corrective negative feedback, allowing the system to drift . . . forming a resonating, escalating, self-reinforcing system. Compelling, illusionary experiential phenomenon are highly likely in such a situation.

". . . The Revelation of the Urantia Papers, as I understand it . . . ended. Contact was broken. It was the end of the revelation to be called The Urantia Book, and an organization was formed to support its spread. If there is now a new revelation being provided, should it not be handled by its own organization? Why is there any involvement at all by the Caretakers of the Urantia Revelation?"[4]

This powerful analysis should also be applied to understand what happened to Christy when Dr. Sadler began to fail, and she became the de facto leader of the Revelation. It should also be applied to Urantian Foundation's policies, and should be weighed by all Urantia organizations. During the height of the Grimsley crisis, Dr. Jim Mills wrote to Martin Myers:

> " . . . the [leaders] I am referring to are the ones who are . . . telling so-called key people . . . they should do all sorts of ridiculous things such as buying guns, laying in supplies, transferring records to safe places and in general acting as though affected with a severe hysteria . . . in a word they need diagnosis rather than responsibility . . . I strongly recommend that they be impeached for conduct unbecoming their offices . . . At the moment I can see no place for these people in the Urantia Movement. I think they should resign immediately. They certainly have shown gross incompetence and the inability to perform in responsible positions."[5]

Epochal Revelation, autorevelation, or delusion?

"Channeled" material allegedly involves celestial personages and so must be classified as either *epochal revelation* [1109] or delusion. Some Urantians are moved to repeat the questions Dr. Burns asked in 1983 about channeling activities in the Urantia Movement: *Are the so-called "channeled messages" supposed to be part of the Fifth Epochal Revelation? or are we to believe they are a new Epochal Revelation?*

Some Urantians believe the "inner circle within the inner circle" of Urantia Foundation was born under the same kind of cultcentric phantasm that drives the channeling syndrome: *special status*, and *privileged access to celestial information.* First the alleged "messages" of Christy nurtured an inner group who believed she had a special connection to Midwayers. Then Grimsley attempted to take over the Revelation by claiming to have inherited the same charismatic powers. And following this, Urantia Foundation justifies the modifications to the original text with the subtle claim of special knowledge of an undisclosed nature: *"We have reason to believe that none of the changes were made without the approval of the Revelators."*

The test of a true teacher

How can we know whether those who would be religious teachers — and those who would be our leaders — are worthy of our trust? Emmett Fox seemed inspired when, in 1933, he suggested the following "test" to determine if an individual is a "true teacher" or not. The emphasized words are in the original:

"If he points to his own personality; if he makes *special claims* for himself; if he says he has received *special privileges* not accessible to the whole human race everywhere, if he attempts in his own name or that of an organization to establish *under any pretence* a monopoly over the truth about God; then, however imposing his credentials, however pleasing his personality might be; he is a false teacher, and you would be better off having nothing to do with him.

"If, on the contrary, he tells you to *look away from himself*, to seek God in the presence *in your own heart*, and to use books, lectures, and churches *only as a means to that one end*, then, no matter how humble his efforts may seem, however lacking his own demonstration may appear, he is nevertheless a *true teacher*, and he is giving you the Bread of Life."

The dawning age of personal responsibility

Like many Urantians, I experienced hierarchical authoritarian attitudes in my traditional religious upbringing, and I was driven away from religion because of them. I was subsequently drawn to the Urantia Papers because their philosophy emancipated me from dependence on human authority figures for spiritual insight. As a

Urantian, I came to believe that a key component of the message of Jesus is that we are free from human authority on spiritual matters, truly free, and we are responsible only to the Fragment of God that indwells us. Likewise, for the first time in history, the ownership of an Epochal Revelation has been afforded — not to an inner circle of "special" people — not to the "mere priests" — but to the people themselves. They need but listen to their inner guidance and step up and claim their Revelation.

The task before us seems formidable. However, Urantians with a passion to evangelize can take heart when they consider the eventual success of the Melchizedek missionaries. Four thousand years ago they went forth to prepare the world for the bestowal of Jesus. We are told **"The last stand of the dwindling band of Salem believers was made by an earnest group of preachers, the Cynics, who exhorted the Romans to abandon their wild and senseless religious rituals . . . But the people at large rejected the Cynics; they preferred to plunge into the rituals of the mysteries, which not only offered hopes of personal salvation but also gratified the desire for diversion, excitement, and entertainment."** [1081, par. 3] However, Urantians should note that the work of the Salem faithful was not in vain. **". . . though unproductive of any immediately appearing religions, nevertheless [it] formed the foundations on which later teachers of truth were to build the religions of Urantia."** [1009, par. 4]

A personal note

In my judgment, the age of superstition, gurus, and special spiritual authorities is drawing to a close. The age of the Thought Adjuster and of *personal responsibility* is dawning. In this regard, I believe we ordinary Urantians, who have been given so much, have all been anointed to carry the good news of emancipation and empowerment to the spiritually impoverished of the world. *All* Urantians can agree that the bright and shining soul of our Revelation is, and always will be, the Urantia Papers. This history, to the best of the ability of Joan, myself, and several other dedicated Urantians to present it, is the story of those Papers. Hopefully, this effort to develop a trustworthy history will stimulate further disciplined and scholarly inquiry. As the Master told us, **"There cannot be peace between light and darkness, between life and death, between truth and error."** [1905] Additional investigation and honest debate will result in the perception of new levels of the *meaning* and *mission* of the Urantia Papers.

This history will also, hopefully, help the young better understand what happened to my generation of aging — and perhaps tiring — Urantians. We began our journey, *all of us,* with high hopes for the spiritual unity of our movement. We, too, had great plans for derivative works, evangelistic initiatives and beautiful study aids. But we became afraid — afraid of disapproval — afraid of being sued. A great Revelation cannot be led by people who are afraid. Clyde Bedell repeatedly urged Urantians to shed their fear and to *act.* After being targeted by a pointless and costly Urantia Foundation lawsuit that was eventually withdrawn, James "JJ" Johnson wrote:

> "There is no human being, or group of human beings, organization, institution, foundation or any other temporal entity of any kind that has authority over the truths revealed in the Urantia Papers. *The Urantia Book* derives its authority from the fruits of its acceptance in the hearts of those individuals who choose to accept these truths based upon the leading of the divine Fragment that indwells each of us and guided by the Spirit of Truth."

However, James Johnson is an exception. My generation has generally not been one of action. We have been occupied in dialogues *about* the meaning and mission of the Urantia Papers. Young Urantians watch us curiously as we "play revelation" — and debate bitterly and endlessly about what we should or should not do. The time grows near for us older Urantians to move aside for a new generation, an invisible fellowship of believers committed to the meaning and mission *of* the Urantia Papers. A common mission, not an organization, will spiritually unite these Urantians.

As Jesus put it:

". . . and so will all the children of light be made one and be drawn toward one another. And in this very manner will my Father and I be able to live in the souls of each one of you and also in the hearts of all other men who love us and make that love real in their experiences by loving one another, even as I am now loving you." [1949 top]

To the comfort of Urantian believers, we are told within the final pages of the Urantia Papers, that the gospel of Jesus will one day prevail. We are assured that humankind is quivering on the very brink of one of its **"most amazing and enthralling epochs of social readjustment, moral quickening, and spiritual enlightenment."** We are cheered with the prediction that, someday, new leaders will appear who will energize Urantians and astound the world with their startling devotion to the Revelation and to one another. Indeed, to borrow the inspiring words of Susan B. Anthony, *"Failure is impossible."*

Just before departing from his mission on this planet, Jesus cautioned his associates to **"solemnly shun all forms of spiritual pride."** Then he said, for all ages yet to come, and for all those with ears to hear:

"You have entered upon this great work of teaching mortal man that he is a son of God. I have shown you the way; go forth to do your duty and be not weary in well doing. To you and to all who shall follow in your steps down through the ages, let me say: I always stand near, and my invitation-call is, and ever shall be, Come to me all you who labor and are heavy laden, and I will give you rest. Take my yoke upon you and learn of me, for I am true and loyal, and you shall find spiritual rest for your souls."

"And they found the Master's words to be true when they put his promises to the test. And since that day countless thousands also have tested and proved the surety of these same promises." [1808 par. 1&2]

ENDNOTES

1. June 21, 1990 Report by Thomas A. and Carolyn B. Kendall, titled: RESPONSE TO URANTIA FOUNDATION'S SPECIAL REPORT TO THE READERS OF *THE URANTIA BOOK* AND COMMENTS ON OTHER RELATED SUBJECTS, page 2. A 1958 memo by Bill Sadler, Jr. refers to the "defunct contact commissioners."

2. IBID., page 2.

3. Harry Loose is a key source of information for the author of *Birth of a Divine Revelation*. He appears three times in Index of *Birth of a Divine Revelation* (which, like the book, is poorly organized and confusing): as Harry J. Loose (4 references), Harry Loose (20 references), and as simply Loose (33 references). Sherman and Loose were a good team. Loose claimed he could fly around in his "astral body" and appear thousands of miles away at will, and Sherman (according to Gardner's book) claimed he could take out-of-body trips to Jupiter. The two carried on a correspondence denigrating Dr. Sadler, which was the source of much of the negative information in *Birth of a Divine Revelation*. Mr. Gardner wrote that Harold Sherman " . . . wrote more that 25 books about ESP, pk, prerecognition, poltergeists, animal ESP, dowsing, ouija boards, UFOs and so on. One of his books tells how to tape-record voices from the dead." The author of *Birth of a Divine Revelation* seems to continually favor the testimony of self-proclaimed psychics Harold Sherman and Harry J. Loose to that of esteemed Urantians Dr. Meredith Sprunger, Dr. William S. Sadler, and Clyde Bedell.

4. VERN GRIMSLEY MESSAGE EVALUATION by Hoite C. Caston, June 17, 1994, Appendixes.

5. IBID., Appendixes.

APPENDIXES

APPENDIX A

List of Key Documents and
References used in this History.

APPENDIXES

311

KEY DOCUMENTS AND REFERENCES are listed in the approximate order they were first endnoted. No "downloaded" documents were used for primary editorial reference.

The Fellowship website (http://www.ubfellowship.org) was used for several photos and verification of some dates. The date for the second printing of *The Urantia Book* is given as March 1, 1968. However, the printing itself is designated as 1967, and this is the date we used. The Fellowship printing date may be accurate, due to the alteration of the plates, as explained in Chapter Nine.

[1]. The Urantia Book, 1955 printing of the original text. Original publication was used.

[2]. THE MIND AT MISCHIEF, by William S. Sadler, M.D., F.A.C.S.; Funk & Wagnall's Company, New York and London, 1929. Original publication was used.

[3]. Paper written by Meredith Sprunger after Dr. Sadler's death, and an article in *PERVADED SPACE*, a newsletter published by Chicago Urantian David Kulieke, Spring, 1979. Original documents used.

[4]. THE HISTORICITY OF *THE URANTIA BOOK* by Meredith J. Sprunger, Paper revised December 18, 1993. Original document supplied by Dr. Sprunger. Original document used.

[5]. CHICAGO, A PHOTOGRAPHIC JOURNEY by Bill Harris, Crescent Books, New York, 1989.

[6]. HOW TO KNOW WHAT TO BELIEVE by Harold Sherman, Fawcett, New York, 1976. Original paperback publication was used. Original publication was used.

[7]. THE CONJOINT READER, Interview by Polly Friedman, Summer, 1993. Original publication was used.

[8]. HISTORY OF THE URANTIA MOVEMENT TWO - [Compiled by a Contact Commissioner.] Undated. Copy of original 30-page document supplied to the court in behalf of Urantia Foundation by Carolyn Kendall, for Maaherra litigation. Title page had been removed and the pages renumbered, some pages had original numbers as well as new numbers. The author believes this document was a hybrid created by using materials from various sources. It was probably compiled by Christy, using the same template as History One. See Chapter Three.

LIST OF REFERENCES USED

[9]. HISTORY OF THE URANTIA MOVEMENT ONE, "by a Group of Urantian Pioneers, assisted by Members of the Contact Commission, 1960." This history was supplied to me by Meredith Sprunger, who received it directly from Dr. Sadler. The title page had "Dr. Sadler" written across it. It contained hand-editing and comments on several pages, probably Dr. Sadler's. The author believes the original template for this document was developed by several people and used for History Two as well as for Marian Rowley's History created for Urantia Brotherhood in 1960. Marian made a worksheet comparing her history to the "Doctors." Whatever version the Doctor worked on had the same cover sheet as hers, according to her notes, and had a total of 34 pages (although two are listed as "omitted.") History One only has 17 pages, and History Two (missing the title page) had 30 pages. So no existing history exactly matches the "Doctor's" history she referred to. It is also possible that Christy and Dr. Sadler collaborated on History Two. Certainly, if the "Doctor's" history had the "same" cover sheet, he did not plan to claim authorship. All existing cover sheets read: "This historical narrative was prepared by a group of Urantia pioneers, assisted by members of the contact commission." There is simply no way to establish reliable authorship of any of these histories. Also, the various histories were all created with a 1960 date, and none were ever published in finished form. For whatever reason, the "history" projects failed. Yet another history was said to be in process by Christy, but this one never surfaced with clear authorship designated either. It probably used the same template as all the others.

[10]. AN INTERVIEW WITH CLYDE BEDELL, conducted by Barbara Kulieke, The Study Group Herald, December, 1992. Original published document was used.

[11]. URANTIA BROTHERHOOD BULLETIN, Special Memorial Edition, Spring, 1982. Original published document was used.

[12]. Bill Sadler, Jr. tape made in Oklahoma City, dated 2/18/62. Cassette copy of original reel to reel tape was given me by Berkeley Elliott in the late seventies. David Kantor also distributed copies of this tape.

[13]. CONSIDERATION OF SOME CRITICISMS OF *THE URANTIA BOOK* by Dr. William S. Sadler, a paper produced in 1958. Copy of original document was given to me by Clyde Bedell in 1969.

LIST OF REFERENCES USED

[14]. The PLAN FOR *THE URANTIA BOOK* REVELATION, by Carolyn B. Kendall, Paper distributed January 18, 1996. I used the original version that Carolyn distributed. There are some pagination differences between this and the later copies published on internet.

[15]. Sworn deposition of Helen Carlson, Chicago, June 29, 1994, Maaherra litigation.

[16]. BIRTH OF A REVELATION by Mark Kulieke, second edition, 1992.

[17]. The Fellowship Archive, history timeline, various references to cross-check dates from other sources.

[18]. Meredith Sprunger video interviews, taped by Eric Cosh of Phoenix, AZ.

[19]. Personal letter from JJ Johnson September 29, 1999.

[20]. A MONOGRAPH ON A VITAL ISSUE CONCERNING THE URANTIA BOOK AND MOVEMENT by Clyde Bedell, 1/81. Original publication was used supplied by author.

[21]. A COMMENTARY ON THE ORIGIN OF THE URANTIA BOOK by Meredith J. Sprunger, 6/13/91. Original publication was used, supplied by author.

[22]. 1959 edition of The World Book Encyclopedia. Original publication was used.

[23]. Two telephone conversations with a Mr. Krohn and a Bart Paddock, who live in Crawfordsville, Indiana. Krohn was a press supervisor and Paddock a plate department manager for R.R. Donnelley Company in the Fifties and Sixties. I also had several conversations with the Crawfordsville plant. Two telephone conversations with Greg Young (now a minister), who worked on the M-1000 Press in 1969, a year or so after the second printing.

[24]. POSTING by URANTIA FOUNDATION on their website *(http://www.urantia.org/newsinfo/strs.htm)* in 1999-2000, under the title *"Setting the Record Straight."*

[25]. A RESPONSE TO A THINLY DISGUISED ATTACK ON THE URANTIA BOOK by Clyde Bedell, a paper dated September 5, 1976. Original publication was used.

[26]. Letter from Trustee Emeritus James Mills to Ken and Betty Glasziou, March 5, 1991. Copy of original supplied by Kristen Maaherra.

LIST OF REFERENCES USED

[27]. THE CREATORS by Daniel J. Boorstin, Random House, New York, 1992.

[28]. April, 1992 paper titled AD HOC COMMITTEE ON RESEARCH: PRINCIPLES, PATTERNS, AND STRUCTURES IN *THE URANTIA BOOK* AND RELATED SOURCES by Carolyn Kendall. Original publication was used. Carolyn prepared this material to assist an ad hoc committee for the Fellowship working on a new constitution. I was a member of that committee.

[29]. AFFIDAVIT of Dr. Meredith Sprunger, dated October 24, 1998. Original publication was used, supplied by author. (See pp 316 - 320).

[30]. WITNESSES TO A REVELATION by Polly Friedman, Summer, 1993, School of Meanings and Values. Original publication was used.

[31]. URANTIA, The Great Cult Mystery, by Martin Gardner, Prometheus Books, New York, 1995. Original publication was used.

[32]. THE PLANETARY PRINTS, Spring 1985. Original publication was used.

[33]. RESPONSE TO URANTIA FOUNDATION'S REPORT TO READERS OF THE URANTIA BOOK, June 21, 1990, Tom and Carolyn Kendall. Original publication was used, supplied by authors in 1990 when I was a General Councilor.

[34]. Urantia Foundation Declaration of Trust. Original publication was used.

[35]. HAVES AND HAVE NOTS by Mortimer J. Adler, Macmillan Publishing Company, New York, 1991.

[36]. THE FELLOWSHIP BULLETIN, Winter, 1992. Original publication was used.

[37]. AFFIDAVIT OF MARTIN MYERS, May 24, 1993. Copy of original court document was used.

[38]. Copy of letter of Clyde Bedell to Martin W. Myers, October 16, 1979. Given to me by Clyde in November, 1984.

[39]. URANTIA BROTHERHOOD BULLETIN, Spring, 1982. Original publication was used.

[40]. THE FUTURE OF THE FIFTH EPOCHAL REVELATION by Meredith J. Sprunger, a paper dated 2/10/93. Original publication was used.

[41]. UNITY, NOT UNIFORMITY! A talk dealing with The Urantia Book, the Official Organizations of the Urantia Movement, and Unity, Not Uniformity by

APPENDIXES

315

LIST OF REFERENCES USED

Martin W. Myers. Presented to the First Western Urantia Conference June 29, 1973. Copy of original publication was used.

[42]. AN UNOFFICIAL "WHITE PAPER" Some things for the TRUSTEES OF THE URANTIA FOUNDATION and the EXECUTIVE COMMITTEE OF THE URANTIA BROTHERHOOD CORPORATION to ponder by Clyde Bedell, April 1976. Original publication was used.

[43]. VERN GRIMSLEY MESSAGE EVALUATION by Hoite Caston, edited by Richard Keeler, June 17, 1984. Original publication was used.

[44]. THE PROBABLE BOMBING OF US NUCLEAR TARGETS (OR IMPROBABLE) as of October 27, 1983, by Clyde Bedell. Original publication was used.

[45]. TO BE (upset) OR NOT TO BE, "Read to a Boulder meeting, the evening of 10/27/83, after people had been given a half-hour or so scare talk urging the storage of food, water, etc., the preparation of each family member with a big kit to take to fall-out shelters upon alarm, etc." By Clyde Bedell. Original publication was used.

[46]. THE GOLDEN YEARS, by Carolyn Kendall and Barbara Newsome, 50th Anniversary Commemorative History of Urantia Foundation, first printing, 2000.

316 APPENDIXES

LIST OF REFERENCES USED - Affidavit of Dr. Meredith Justin Sprunger

MEREDITH J. SPRUNGER
4109 PLAZA DR
FORT WAYNE, IN **46806**
219-745-4363

Oct. 24, 1998

AFFIDAVIT

I declare, under penalty of perjury, that the following are my recollections about the authorship, and the issues surrounding the authorship, of *The Urantia Book.*

Following my discovery of *The Urantia Book* in December of 1955, and after introducing it to a number of clerical colleagues and friends, I spent years researching with them the historical aspects of the book. We quickly discovered the Urantia Papers were received by a small group of people in Chicago. Their leader was Dr. William S. Sadler. Dr. Sadler was a highly respected psychiatrist and college teacher in the graduate school of medicine at the University of Chicago. For almost thirty years Dr. Sadler was also a lecturer in Pastoral Counseling at McCormick Theological Seminary.

On May 7, 1958, our group of ministers had an appointment with Dr. Sadler to discuss the phenomena associated with the origin of the Urantia Papers. My personal association with Dr. Sadler continued until his death in 1969. In the course of this friendship, we had many candid conversations about the materialization of the Foreword and the 196 Papers that were eventually published as the text of *The Urantia Book.* It is important to point out that in this regard Dr. Sadler was a professional researcher of unquestioned integrity.

Dr. Sadler categorically declared that there was no known psychic phenomena attached to the origin of the Urantia Papers. The final text of the Urantia Papers was materialized in written form, but it was not channeled or spoken, nor was it the product of automatic writing. Dr. Sadler stated that although the Thought Adjuster (a fragment of God

APPENDIXES

LIST OF REFERENCES USED - *Affidavit of Dr. Meredith Justin Sprunger*

that indwells all normal human minds) of the "contact personality" was somehow engaged in the materialization process by spiritual beings, the contact person was totally unaware of this activity. Neither this contact person, nor any other human, wrote any of the text nor authored or originated any material used in the revelatory text of the Urantia Papers, which consist of the Foreword and the 196 Papers.

Although Dr. Sadler was emphatic that no known psychic phenomena were associated in any way with the authorship of the Urantia Papers, he admitted that he was baffled as to precisely how the text of the Urantia Papers was materialized into the English language. He was very clear in his conviction that no human being edited, selected, or had any creative input whatever into the authorship of the Urantia Papers, nor in the arrangement of the text of *The Urantia Book*, which consists of the Foreword and Papers one through 196. Dr. Sadler was crystal clear that the members of the contact commission had no editorial authority whatever, and their responsibility was confined to spelling, capitalization, and punctuation. Members of the forum were not even permitted to see the original materialized documents, and they had no input in their authorship. Dr. Sadler was convinced that the Urantia Papers are exactly what they purport themselves to be, an epochal revelation authored solely by celestial beings.

I have studied *The Urantia Book* in depth for over forty years, and I am likewise convinced that the authorship of the text was superhuman, and that it was materialized by unprecedented means that are not fully understood. In my best professional and personal opinion, I am absolutely convinced there was no human authorship or creative input, and there were no human editorial decisions involved with the materialization of the Urantia Papers. I believe the truth of what Dr. Sadler wrote — and personally disclosed to me numerous times: the Urantia Papers were published just as received, and the contact commission had no editorial authority whatever, and its role was confined solely to the clerical tasks of spelling, capitalization, and punctuation. Neither did the forum members contribute to the creative contents of the Urantia Papers. The forum was similar to a modem focus group in that they were used by the celestial authors solely as a gauge to measure human understanding.

Dr. Sadler was also absolutely clear about two related things: (1). Absolutely no human name or names should ever be attached to the

318   APPENDIXES

LIST OF REFERENCES USED - *Affidavit of Dr. Meredith Justin Sprunger*

authorship or materialization of the Urantia Papers and the publication
of *The Urantia Book*. Even the printer, R. R. Donnelley and Sons, was
not permitted to place an indicia in the first edition which stated their
identity. (2.) No human being knows, or ever knew, the exact method by
which the Urantia Papers were materialized. We can only be
categorically certain that there was no human authorship, no human
editorial involvement, nor any human activity in creating, selecting and/
or arranging the Urantia Papers, which consist of the Foreword and
Papers one through 196 inclusive, and which constitute the text of *The
Urantia Book*.

Dr. Sadler made it plain to me that the revelators, held total authority
over the process by which the Urantia Papers were materialized. The
revelators suggested the submission of questions, and, at one point after
the contact commission and forum had read some of the papers,
requested that more significant questions be developed and asked by the
contact commission. Dr. Sadler said that in a particular session a
celestial personality who claimed to be a student visitor to our planet
stated to the commission: *"If you people realized what a high spiritual
source you are now associating with you would stop making these
puerile investigations to detect fraud and would ask some significant
questions about the nature and reality of the universe."* It was at this
point the forum was engaged by Dr. Sadler to help him formulate
appropriate questions in answer to the challenge of the revelators. The
forum had originally been assembled by the Sadler family as an group
of lay persons who gathered together in Dr. Sadler's home for tea and an
hour or two of informal discussion and social exchange. The revelators
soon answered the questions the forum had asked, and these answers
were presented to the forum by the contact commission. Shortly after
this the revelators directed Dr. Sadler and the contact commission to
make the forum a closed group, and required each member to take a vow
of secrecy about their knowledge of what the contact commission was
doing and what information the revelators had disclosed to the forum
through the contact commission *"The forum, as it were, was taken away
from us"* wrote Dr. Sadler. He was indicating that the general
discussions in the forum ceased, and the revelators henceforth directed
the agenda of the group through the contact commission, and used the
forum essentially as a focus group for the Urantia Papers.

Dr. Sadler said no forum member except members of the contact
commission, was ever present during any of the contacts with the

APPENDIXES

LIST OF REFERENCES USED - *Affidavit of Dr. Meredith Justin Sprunger*

revelators. He also said that only one "sleeping subject," or person was involved throughout the entire process of materializing the text of the Urantia Papers.

Dr. Sadler told me that at one point he and his son Bill wrote a draft for an introduction to the Urantia Papers, and submitted it to the revelators. At a contact session with the revelators they were told that although they meant well, such submissions were not acceptable, and the revelators made the comment, referring to the introduction written by Dr. Sadler and Bill Sadler, Jr.: *"A candle cannot light the sun."* At the proper time, the humans were assured, an introduction to the book would be materialized. When the revelators produced the Foreword to the Urantia Papers, Dr. Sadler stated that he and his son realized the inadequacy of their own attempt to write an introduction.

Dr. Sadler and his son were, however, given permission to compose a Table of Contents for *The Urantia Book*. Bill Sadler compiled the titles as they appeared in the Papers, and the section headings from the Papers, and he briefly outlined some of the material that was originated in the Urantia Papers, and incorporated it into a Table of Contents for *The Urantia Book*. Dr. Sadler and other members of the contact commission assured me that no human wrote, edited, or arranged any of the text of the Urantia Papers, which consist of the Foreword and all of the Papers from Paper one through Paper 196 inclusive. Dr. Sadler told me that one individual, not a member of the contact commission but rather a member of the forum, who made suggestions to "improve" the Urantia Papers was vigorously informed by the revelators (through the contact commission) that no human additions to the Urantia Papers would be allowed. Dr. Sadler said that every possible precaution was taken to see that the text of the Urantia Papers was presented just as the revelators had authored and materialized it.

It should be emphasized that there is not now, nor has there ever been, a human authority on the content or the origin of the Urantia Papers. However, Christy often requested that I reply to many of the letters Urantia Foundation received from readers requesting information on the origin of the Urantia Papers. As these requests increased, I produced a paper on the essentials of the origin of the Urantia Papers, which constitute the text of *The Urantia Book*. This paper was approved by Urantia Foundation, printed, and freely distributed for several years by both Urantia Foundation and Urantia Brotherhood.

LIST OF REFERENCES USED - *Affidavit of Dr. Meredith Justin Sprunger*

In regard to outreach efforts by Urantians, the following statement was written by Dr. Sadler under the heading, Distribution of *The Urantia Book*: *"However, one thing should be made clear: While it is the policy of the Brotherhood to work slowly in the distribution of the book, nothing is done to interfere with the energetic and enthusiastic efforts of any individual to introduce The Urantia Book to his friends and associates."*

Signed,

Meredith Justin Sprunger

ADDENDA TO AFFIDAVIT:

MEREDITH JUSTIN SPRUNGER is a minister in the United Church of Christ and a college professor, now retired from pastoral and teaching responsibilities. For many years Dr. Sprunger was active as a counselor and psychological consultant, holding a Private Practice Certificate in Psychology in the State of Indiana. He has served congregations in the Midwest and taught at Elmherst College and Indiana Institute of Technology, functioning as the head of the Department of Psychology, chairman of the division of Liberal Arts, and as President.

Dr. Sprunger has served as a Field Representative, Chairman of the Educational and Fraternal Relations Committees, and President of the Urantia Brotherhood. He is founder and Executive Director of The Christian Fellowship for Students of *The Urantia Book*, and Executive Editor of The Spiritual Fellowship Journal. Dr. Sprunger is the only living professional educational colleague of Dr. William S. Sadler associated with The Urantia Book.

APPENDIX B

Reproductions of
Historic
Correspondence

Dr. Benjamin N. Adams wrote a letter to a friend in which he made some critical observations of *The Urantia Book*. He forwarded a copy to Dr. Sadler, who made the reply we publish. Note that Dr. Adams prefaces his remarks with praise of *The Urantia Book: "It seems to me, if I were God, this is the sort of book I would want to supply my human children on such a benighted and remote speck of dust as the earth. Yet, the best and highest service which can be rendered this book is a strictly objective and merciless critical analysis thereof."*

322   APPENDIXES

APPENDIXES

"A Friendly Church in a Friendly City"

Trinity Presbyterian Church

3261 TWENTY-THIRD STREET
TEL. MISSION 7-5156
SAN FRANCISCO 10, CALIFORNIA

March 9, 1959

Dr. William S. Sadler, Sr.
533 Diversey Parkway
Chicago 14
Ill.

Dear Dr. Sadler,

My last letter was written to you on Feb. 24, 1955 --
over five years ago. At that time you did me the honor of
answering my letter some four days later. I was one of the
pre-publication subscribers to the Urantia Book and received
two copies of it when it came off the press in October of 1955.

Since receiving the book I have read it through and have
studied many parts of it over and over. I am enclosing a copy
of a letter I have just written to Dr. Earl L. Douglass whom
you recently met. In it I have outlined some of my conclusions.

Would you be so kind as to let me know what other critical
examinations of the book may have been made by specialists in
other fields such as physics, astronomy, etc.

Very sincerely yours,

Benjamin N. Adams

---

1. Adams' cover letter to Dr. Sadler

APPENDIXES

"A Friendly Church in a Friendly City"

Trinity Presbyterian Church
3261 TWENTY-THIRD STREET
TEL. MISSION 7-5156
SAN FRANCISCO 10, CALIFORNIA

March 9, 1959

Dr. Earl L. Douglass
C/o The Hilton Hotel
Los Angeles
Calif.

Dear Earl,

Your letter of March 1 has just come. I share your disappointment that Los Angeles is not closer to San Francisco.

Was interested to hear of your visit with Dr. Sadler and Miss Rowley. It is a pleasure that I have not thus far had except by correspondence. However, I do keep studying the Urantia Book which I consider in itself a remarkable phenomenon. The author (or authors) of the book have not hesitated to "stick their necks out" in so many areas of human knowledge that a critical analysis of the book should eventually supply a verdict

It seems to me that, if I were God, this is the sort of book which I would want to supply my human children on such a benighted and renfte speck of dust as the earth. Yet, the best and highest service which can be rendered this book is a strictly objective and merciless critical analysis thereof.

As I read what it has to say about cosmology, cosmogeny, geology, chronology, biology, anthropology, astronomy, physics, chemistry, nuclear physics, etc. etc., I find myself wishing that I had considerably more competence in all of these fields. But I know that I had better stick to my own field of competence which happens to be Biblical studies. In passing, I note a few statements outside of my field of competence which I am inclined to challenge. On page 477, for instance, is this statement: "There are just 100 distinguishable atomic materializations of space-energy in a dual universe; that is the maximum possible organization of matter in Nebadon." This seems to me to say that only 100 chemical elements are possible. But I can quote several authorities to the effect that at least 103 elements have been identified and named.

However, returning to the field of Biblical studies, I make the following observations:
(1) Page 2074. The teacher of Clement of Alexandria and the founder of the famous Catechetical School of that city was "Pantaenus" not "Poutaenus". (This may be merely a typographical error.)
(2) Page 1557. Philip the Apostle is identified with Philip the Evangelist (or Deacon) who is said to have gone on the mission to Samaria in Acts 8:5.
(3) Pages 2057-60. The bestowing of the Holy Spirit at Pentecost is represented as occurring of the

2. Adams' letter - copy to Dr. Sadler 3/9/1959, page 1

same day as the ascension and 40 days after the crucifixion. Now this is an obvious error as the very word "Pentecost" means 50 and was supposed to be a week of weeks after the Passover.

(4) Page 542. A quotation from the New Testament Book of Hebrews is attributed to Paul. This is amazing in view of the generally sophisticated and critical attitude toward the authorship of most of the books of the Bible. (E.G.pp.1341-2)

(5) Page 1559. Nathaniel's father is said to be Bartholemew. But Bartholemew is listed by the synoptic writers among the Twelve. It is a patronymic meaning "The Son of Tholmai". Thus it is logical to suppose that Nathaniel of John's Gospel is identical with Bartholemew of the synoptics, and that his father's name was Tholmai.

(6) Page 1362. The synagogue teacher is spoken of as the "chazan." The Hebrew (Aramaic) for this officer is חזן which would be more correctly transliterated "chazzan" (with a double z).

(7) Page 1355 (near bottom) "Far to the east they could discern the Jordan valley and, far beyond, the rocky hills of Moab." But the rocky hills of Moab were not east of Nazareth but east of the Dead Sea.

(8) Page 1648. "Early on the morning of Tuesday, March 30, Jesus and the apostolic party started on their journey to Jerusalem for the Passover." But Hastings Bible Dictionary, Vol. I, p.411 gives a table which shows that the latest possible date for the Passover in A.D.28 was Tuesday, March 30 (beginning with sunset the previous day, Mon., March 29). Thus Jesus and His apostles are represented as setting out for Jerusalem and the Passover on the latest possible date for the Passover to begin. They arrived at Bethany on April 2, three days later. By this time the ceremonies of the Passover Feast and the first-fruits of the Barley harvest "waved" before the Lord would have been completed. True, the Feast of Unleavened Bread would go on for another three or four days, but it seems strange that they would deliberately be so late in arriving.

It is only fair to note that the Urantia Book does not claim to be infallible (p.1008). It is also fair to note that on the other side of the ledger are literally thousands of amazingly accurate details harmonizing perfectly with known geographical and chronological facts. For instance, the U.B.states in opposition to a tremendous weight of tradition that Jesus did not die on Passover Day, but on the day preceding, that, in 30 A.D., Passover began at Sunset on Friday, April 7 and continued until sunset, Saturday, April 8. This agrees with the point-of-view of John's Gospel but disagrees with the synoptics. Moreover, astronomy bears witness that the first visibility of the preceding new moon was at sunset on Friday, March 24. This would then be the beginning of Nisan 1 in the Jewish calendar. This would bring Nisan 14, the "Preparation for the Passover," to the day beginning sunset April 6 (Thurs.) and Nisan 15, the Passover itself to the day beginning at sunset Friday, April 7, continuing through Saturday. This agrees with the Gospel of John and the Urantia Book.

---

2. Adams' letter - copy to Dr. Sadler 3/9/1959 page 2

3.

No doubt many more discrepancies will be discovered in the Urantia Book. About all that this will prove is that even "midway creatures" can make mistakes. But, if for each mistake we are able to spot, we are enriched by 1,000 thrilling new facts, then we have a spiritual gold mine before us in the Urantia Book, and the ore we dig out assays at about 999/1,000. We do well not to accept it blindly, but it merits a considerable measure of our confidence.

Mrs. Adams joins me in extending our best wishes to you and your wife. We have now completed eight years in this difficult inner city church. During this period we have had the pleasure of taking into the church 289 new members. The turnover has been so great that we only have 282 members as of now. Yet we have prospered by the grace of God; and I now have a full-time assistant with an Italian name (Rev. Richard Fagetti) who I think is well-qualified to carry on.

If you know of anyone in New Jersey who would like an experienced Minister of Visitation, I wish you would let me know,-- perhaps even speak a good word for me. I think I could do a good job for some one in helping to build up their membership.

Most cordially yours,

Benjamin N. Adams

2. Adams' letter - copy to Dr. Sadler 3/9/1959, page 3

March 17, 1959

Rev. Benjamin N. Adams
124 Genebern Way
San Francisco 12, California

My dear Rev. Adams:

I was very happy to get your letter of March 9, and I think this is the first really valid criticism I have ever had from a minister as concerns the Urantia Book. I have gotten hold of several the last year, but it was evident that the critics had never even superficially read the Urantia Book.

If minor discrepancies were to be found in the Urantia Book I have always suspected that they would probably be found in Part IV because that is the part of the Book that was prepared by the midwayers. The midwayers' mind level is but a trifle above that of the human mind.

My own preoccupation with the Urantia Book has been along two lines. First, I was concerned as to whether or not this was some fraudulent psychic phenomena or possibly a case of subconscious dissociation on the part of the subject such as I was familiar with in the fields of automatic writing, trance mediums, etc. I was the last of my family to accept the Urantia Papers. I finally decided that the whole thing was beyond my ability to understand.

My next concern had to do with the consistency of the Papers. I finally decided that a fraud could not go on the witness stand for twenty-five years, to be examined and cross-examined by 250, and to give more than a million words of testimony and never once contradict himself. I decided that this subject must be telling the truth in order to discuss such a wide range of topics and not once slip into a contradiction.

You ask about others who have critically examined the Urantia Book. From a standpoint of general science I think the studies of the late Sir Hubert Wilkins were perhaps the most extended and exhaustive. For more than twenty years he periodically spent time in Chicago going over the Papers. He would work weeks at a time, ten hours a day, and his final conclusion was that the Papers were consistent with the known facts of modern science.

3. Dr. Sadler's reply to Adams letter, 3/17/1959 page 1

2.

Since the Book was published, a young physicist in Philadelphia has been a very careful student of the physics of the Urantia Papers. About a year ago he wrote a paper, with many diagrams, for the Gravitational Society, in which he advocated that the cosmology of the Urantia Book was the only one that was possible from the gravitational standpoint.

I was very interested in your criticism as proposed in your letter to Dr. Douglass. I would offer the following comments on these criticisms:

1. I think the spelling of the name of the teacher in Alexandria is undoubtedly an error in transcribing the manuscript into typewriting. An "an" was undoubtedly transcribed as an "ou". I remember when we were sometimes in doubt as to whether a letter was an "n" or a "u" in the manuscript. Of course, we who were preparing this matter, did not know the name of this teacher so could have easily made this mistake.

2. As far as I could detect, there is only one Philip recognized in the Urantia Book. I note what you say in this matter.

3. Now as to the bestowal of the Spirit of Truth—the possible discrepancy between the end of one Paper and the beginning of another we all noted it one time and discussed it further when the Book was going to press. You should remember that the midwayers prepared a narrative that was many times larger than was finally given us as Part IV. of the Urantia Book. It may be that in deletion some difficulties were encountered. Our understanding is that the prayer meeting which Peter conducts at the close of one Paper is not the same as that at the opening of the next Paper. The one ended at the Day of Ascension, the other opened up the Day of Pentecost.

4. About Paul and Hebrews — of course, we all puzzled about that the same as you, and it occurs two or three times in the Papers. We have finally come to the conclusion that it was of composite authorship and the Apostle Paul had something to do with the presentation.

5. About Nathaniel's father I can offer no suggestions except that I know that the manuscript was very clear that it was Bartholomew.

3. Dr. Sadler's reply to Adams letter, 3/17/1959 page 2

APPENDIXES

329

Rev. Adams   March 17, 1959

3.

6. About the spelling of "chazan". Our mandate forbade us in any way to alter the text of the manuscript, but gave us jurisdiction over capitalization, spelling, and punctuation. We were told to select our authority and stick to it. Evidently, the authority we chose spelled "chazan" with one z.

7. Your notation about Moab is a puzzler to me. We have just looked in the atlas, and, of course, you are right. I have no explanation for this matter—either a mistake of the midwayers or a mistake in copying. I cannot say, but evidently you are right in this matter.

8. The intricacies of Jesus' crucifixion and the Day of the Passover I am not competent to appraise. In fact, I was not aware that there was any difference in the Gospel of John and the Synoptics, but I am glad that you are inclined to agree with the Urantia Book.

I was indeed cheered to get such an encouraging estimate of the worth of the Book from one who had made such a careful study of it.

I am taking the liberty of sending you a copy of an outline which I gave to a dozen ministers who came to meet with me about six months ago. I told them that while I was unable to explain to them about how we had got the Book I was able to explain to them how we had not got the Book.

I do hope that we will have the pleasure of seeing you and Mrs. Adams one of these days. I am sure, if you have the occasion to come back East, you will not fail to let us have a visit with you.

With all best wishes, I am

Sincerely yours,

William S. Sadler

WSS/ar

3. Dr. Sadler's reply to Adams letter, 3/17/1959 page 3

URANTIA

URANTIA FOUNDATION
533 DIVERSEY PARKWAY CHICAGO ILLINOIS 60614

June 13, 1988

Mr. J.J. Johnson
44-392 Olena St., #4
Kaneohe, HI 96744

Dear Mr. Johnson:

Thank you for your recent letter with attachments concerning your correspondence with Christy regarding various matters you raised about the text of The URANTIA Book, particularly your concerns about the phrase "inhabited worlds" which appears on page 1319.

A copy of your exchange of correspondence with Christy over the matter of page 1319 will be shared with the Trustees. However, as you are well aware, Christy's relationship to the text of The URANTIA Book was unique. It should be appreciated that the correspondence between Christy and you was of a personal nature and should not be assumed to be the official position of the Board of Trustees. It is quite probable that the current Board of Trustees do not feel that they have the same relationship with the text of the book that was enjoyed by Christy. In other words, the Trustees may not feel they can exercise the same latitude that was available to Christy in these matters.

I can only assure you that this matter will be brought to the attention of the Foundation. I cannot give any assurance that there will be a formal response on this matter from the Board. For obvious reasons, a matter such as this is an issue of delicate and sensitive proportions, and the Board may not wish to expand the written record on the matter. It is possible that the only clear response to this matter will be to examine the phrase of concern in the 10th printing of the book.

It was good to see you and Geri at the General Conference last year. I get the impression through the grapevine that you and Geri's presence on Oahu has had a most positive influence on activity. Keep up the good work. The fields are vast but the laborers are all too few. Best wishes and warmest regards from everyone.

In Fellowship,

Scott M. Forsythe
Administrative Assistant

SMF:cl

4. Scott Forsythe letter to JJ Johnson, 6/13/1988, explaining Christy's "unique" relationship with the text.
(Letter courtesy JJ Johnson)

APPENDIXES

331

THE SPIRITUAL RENAISSANCE® INSTITUTE
BOX 347. BERKELEY. CALIFORNIA 94701

October 16, 1983

Dear Larry,

I trust that this letter finds you in good spirits and in good health.

I write this morning out of growing concern over the clearly worsening global geopolitical situation. It is sad but true that many top international journalists, statesmen and historians around the world are now pointing to gathering war clouds on the planetary horizon and are predicting stormy times ahead. A re-reading of portions of the Urmia lectures in The URANTIA Book (pages 1489-1491) and "Secular Totalitarianism" (pages 2081-2082) will substantiate the premise of such predictions.

I feel so strongly about this matter that I am actively making emergency/contingency plans for our own URANTIA Society and the Family of God Foundation. We are reviewing our local and national civil defense procedures, maintaining maps of escape routes, storing food and water, learning where fallout shelters are and studying techniques of surviving possible global conflict in order that we may safeguard our revelation and our leadership through any such catastrophes as may befall us.

I feel strongly led to write these words to you, a leader in the movement. But I caution you that we must not precipitate blind panic among our fellows. Feel free to discuss these matters with other readers who would be helped by such discussions, but let us avoid creating needless anxiety or mass hysteria over the subject, bearing well in mind the statement on page 556: "Unreasoned fear is a master intellectual fraud practiced upon the evolving mortal soul."

Let us be not anxious and fear not - but let us be prepared.

I warmly invite you to visit us at our new Institute; I would enjoy discussing these and other matters in greater depth with you in person. Since I prefer not to talk about these things over the telephone, I could best offer further clarification in a face-to-face meeting. Due to the accelerated pace of our own emergency planning, such a meeting would have to be held at our California headquarters.

Let us follow our common sense and guidance in all of this. God and the angels love us, and we must love one another as well. "We may not know what the future holds, but we know who holds the future."

May the love of God and humanity fill our souls and inspire our lives.

Yours in our Father's family,

Peace & Blessings!

Vern Bennom Grimsley

---

5. 10/16/1983 Letter from Vern Grimsley to the author inviting me to "visit the institute." *(I didn't go).*

332 APPENDIXES

(Letter from Richard Keeler, F.O.G. Investment Manager)

SUNDAY ... 20 NOV. 83

DEAR VERN & NANCY -

UNTIL RECENTLY I CONSIDERED YOUR WORK TO BE MY WORK, YOUR STRUGGLES TO BE MY STRUGGLES, YOUR FOCUS, YOUR PRIORITIES TO BE MY PRIORITIES. I THOUGHT IT WAS THE MOST IMPORTANT WORK GOING ON, ON THE PLANET. BEING A PART OF IT WAS A PRIVILEGE. THE SATISFACTION THAT I GOT FROM MANAGING AND SEEING FOG'S MONEY GROW FAR EXCEEDED WHAT I GOT MONETARILY AND OTHERWISE FROM ~~FROM~~ MY REGULAR ACCOUNTS. I SUPPOSE IT WAS, I THOUGHT, THE WAY I COULD LEAVE, OR MAKE MY LITTLE MARK ON THE PLANET.

HOWEVER, VERN, BECAUSE I DO NOT AGREE WITH WHAT YOU'RE CURRENTLY DOING AND THE WAY YOU'RE DOING IT, I MUST RESIGN AS INVESTMENTS MANAGER OF THE FAMILY OF GOD FOUNDATION, INC.

6. Rich Keeler resigns from FOG
11/20/1983, page 1

I SHALL BE MAKING NO CONTRIBUTIONS TO YOU IN THE FUTURE NOR SHALL I BE REASSUMING MY POST.

I HAD BEQUEATHED IN MY WILL MY ENTIRE PERSONAL WEALTH TO FOG. FOG WILL NOT APPEAR IN MY WILL IN THE FUTURE.

MY DECISION HAS NOTHING TO DO WITH YOUR HAVING WITHDRAWN THE MONEY FROM THE FOG INVESTMENT ACCOUNT. IT IS TOTALLY BASED ON YOUR CURRENT ACTIVITIES.

I'm OKAY NOW BUT WHEN I REALIZED THAT I WANTED TO DISASSOCIATE MYSELF FROM YOU, NOT PERSONALLY, BUT ORGANIZATIONALLY, I CRIED ... I LITERALLY WEPT. MY POINT IS THAT THIS IS ONE OF THE SADDEST MOMENTS OF MY LIFE.

I LOVE YOU BOTH

**6. Rich Keeler resigns from FOG
11/20/1983, page 2**

334 APPENDIXES

JAMES C. MILLS Ph.D.
2362 THOMPSON BRIDGE
ROAD, N.E.
APT. A-10
GAINESVILLE, GA 30801.

March 5, 1991

Dear Ken and Betty:

I apologize for the overlong delay in response to your letter of November 20, '90. While moving, I severely twisted my back. There was no improvement after four months, so a lumbar X-Ray was taken indicated a healing fracture. This has improved over three months to the point of where I could submit to prostate surgery and that was done on February 1. Yesterday I returned to normal functioning. I feel better than I have in several years and am enjoying getting back to work.

About all the help I can give you on any changes in the text of The URANTIA Book including punctuation, "typos", changes in digits, and textural changes are those of my own experience.

As I told you, prior to publication, Forum members, engaged in reading the first proof sheets made from the original metallic plates, were constantly seeking primarily for typographical errors including punctuation, errors of grammar, syntax, or any other errors which could occur in the process of the transference of a text from manuscript through the linotype procedure into metal printing plates. Apparently, the most potent source of error would lie at the point of the linotype operator. Dealing with a complicated text did not simplify matters, at least in my opinion. It is my belief that some of the "typos" were carried over into the first printing.

I had only one experience with a textual change being made between printings. I told you about this during your visit in Pensacola. This was due to the diligence of a high school science teacher who had a B.S. in science and had read in a scientific journal that a specific figure given in The Urantia Book expressing the relationship between the mass of the nucleus and the planetary electron in the hydrogen atom had changed by one digit. He was able to persuade the people at 533 to change it in the second printing. At that time I had moved to Wisconsin and the chap instituting the change had followed me as president of the Brotherhood. Quite by accident, the change was pointed out to me by a young woman student who was incensed at obvious tampering with what she firmly and correctly believed should be left alone by human hands. I raised quite a ruckus about the matter and it was returned to its original status in the very next printing. Since that move, with the exception of 1973-1975, I have not resided in Chicago and have not been informed of any other apparent discrepancies between printings until your letter of Nov.20. I am taking up this matter with the Foundation immediately.

You have asked the exactly correct question about the original type setting which appears to be involved in some of these events. The original printing plates for the U.B. were made by the old linotype-mold-casting technique. In the twelve year interval between the first and second printings new photographic techniques and higher speed presses had rendered the original plates obsolete and new plates had to be produced. As the original plates were

7. Letter from Trustee Emeritus Jim Mills to Ken & Betty Glasziou, 3/5/1991, page 1

APPENDIXES

335

planned to yield one million impressions, this was quite a blow. It is quite possible, despite what was thought to be close supervision, that errors were introduced at this point. You know from your own writing experience how difficult a proof reading task is involved in a text of over one million words. It looks like we need to carefully proof read the present printing against the first printing. <u>In my opinion, there can be only one edition of the U.B., the first.</u>

I am very glad to receive your comments and appreciate your confidence very much.

In regard to comments about the introduction and summary I find no fault with them.

I would suggest that you give some thought toward some emphasis on the fact that we all can see a new work only through the eyes of our own partial knowledge and experience; our world view or hypothesis, our weltanschauung. This immediately forces us to see a new work through dark glasses. We also place far too much significance on the works of others talking about the same thing, particularly in the areas of philosophy and religion about which A.N. Whitehead quipped: "The safest general characterization of the European philosophical tradition is that it consists of a series of footnotes to Plato." Jesus was more serious than we realize when he said: "you must become as little children." This is particularly true of our approach to the U.B. The fact that it continually reiterates, 'religion is a purely human experience of experiencing a relationship with God' should promptly eliminate our tendency to compare the U.B. with known theological thought except as the latter may provide some means to insight but never explanation. At a recent group meeting in Atlanta, one of the members brought out a bible to compare with the U.B. I interrupted to ask: "do you compare The URANTIA Book to the bible or the bible to The URANTIA Book or do you see each as an independent work discussing at times the same events?" I see science with a different viewpoint. My own early training in Chem. and Physics showed me that science is an ongoing process and to dogmatize it at any point is to fossilize it at that point.

Now that I am beginning to return to the things that I wish to do, I will honestly try to be a better correspondent. Please give my best wishes to that gal from your area who wrote me. I have not answered her and can't remember her name. It will be a great pleasure to hear from both of you again. Eunice sends her best to you. She's out pushing cards this morming.

Sincerely,

James C. Mills.

7. Letter from Trustee Emeritus Jim Mills to Ken & Betty Glasziou, 3/5/1991, page 2. Dr. Mills replaced Christy as a Trustee in 1971. He indicates in this letter, 20 years later, that he has no knowledge of any changes in the text other than the mass of the nucleus of the atom relative to the electron, which he thought was changed back at his insistence. It was not. Mills also seemed to believe the text was completely reset for the second printing. It was not.

APPENDIX C

THE

GARDEN OF EDIACARA

BREAKTHROUGH

APPENDIX C

THE GARDEN OF EDIACARA
BREAKTHROUGH

Dr. Mark A. S. McMenamin, professor of geology at Mount Holyoke College, published *The Garden of Ediacara, Discovering the First Complex Life* (Columbia University Press, 1998). In this study, Dr. McMenamin makes some remarkable references to *The Urantia Book.*

In Chapter Nine of our history (pages 214-215), we made reference to the outreach efforts of JJ Johnson that resulted in this favorable commentary on the Urantia Papers. JJ spotted an article in the newspaper in which Dr. McMenamin commented upon certain emerging geological theories that JJ realized were parallel to some information in the Urantia Papers. He wrote Dr. McMenamin about this. The professor responded to this letter by JJ Johnson with these comments: *"If it was written in 1955, parts of it are strikingly ahead of their time. I could only locate the 1984 edition; can you confirm that pages 664-671 appeared as is in the 1955 edition?"* Because of JJ's persistence and efforts, Dr. McMenamin included favorable comments about *The Urantia Book* in his own book, *The Garden of Ediacara,* published by Columbia University Press in 1998.

It is more remarkable that the plates of the 1955 printing were cast by 1945, making the insights in *The Urantia Book* even more noteworthy. The excerpts that follow are taken from *The Garden of Ediacara.* The following material is especially helpful in evaluating Martin Gardner's dismissal of *The Urantia Book's* treatment of the Continental Drift Theory (*Urantia - The Great Cult Mystery, Prometheus Books, New York, 1995, (pages 197-199).*

338 APPENDIXES

THE GARDEN OF EDICARA - Discovering the first complex life By Mark A.S. McMenamin, Columbia University Press, New York, 1998

PAGES 173-177 Reunite Rodinia!

"The theory of Wegener [continental drift] is to me a beautiful dream, the dream of a great poet. One tries to embrace it and finds that he has in his arms but a little vapor or smoke; it is at the same time both alluring and intangible." The New York Times Magazine Pierre Termier[1]

"We have known since the days of Kant that scientific arguments must never be founded on analogies, but the authors are dead serious about these poetic digressions." Peter Westbroek[2]

"The continental land drift continued; increasingly the ocean penetrated the land as long fingerlike seas providing those shallow waters and sheltered bays which are so suitable as a habitat for marine life ... [with] the further separation of the land masses and, in consequence, a further extension of the continental seas these inland seas of olden times were truly the cradle of evolution." The Urantia Book[3]

The last quotation in this chapter's epigraph describes the Proterozoic breakup of the supercontinent Rodinia. This amazing passage, written in the 1930s, anticipates scientific results that did not actually appear in the scientific literature until many decades

1.   See page 29 in H. W. Menard, The Ocean of Truth, (Princeton, NJ,: Princeton University Press, 1986).

2.   P. Westbroek, "The Ocean Inside Us" The London Times Higher Education Supplement, November 3, 1995.

3.   See Page 663 in Urantia Foundation, The Urantia Book, (Chicago, 1955 [First written in 1934]).

later. This unusual source is *The Urantia Book*.[1] The name Urantia refers to planet Earth.

Like the Book of Mormon and L. Ron Hubbard's Dianetics, The Urantia Book is a modern attempt to found a new religion. But the teachings of The Urantia Book, as promoted by the Urantia Foundation and the Urantia Brotherhood,[2] are more mainstream than either Mormonism or dianetics. Promotional literature of the Urantia organization inserted into new copies of the book state the following:

> "We hope your experience with the URANTIA teachings will enhance and deepen your relationship with God and your fellow man, and provide renewed hope, comfort, and reassurance in your daily life."

What more could one ask for in a religion? Well, for starters, one could hope for accurate geology and profound scientific truths in its sacred literature, something both the devout and the skeptics alike find lacking in much of the Bible.

The comments concerning Rodinia's breakup and its influence on animal evolution are found in part III, "The History of Urantia" in The Urantia Book. According to the first page of this chapter, "these papers were sponsored by a Corps of Local Universe Personalities acting by authority of Gabriel of Salvington." The critical section 8 of Paper 57, titled "Crustal Stabilization, The Age of Earthquakes, The World Ocean and the First Continent," is "presented by a Life Carrier, a member of the original Urantia Corps [who visited our planet hundreds of millions of years ago] and now a resident observer." The following Paper 58, "Life Establishment on Urantia," is attributed

---

1. Urantia Foundation, 1955.

2. The name Urantia may be derived from Urania, the personification of astronomy.

340 APPENDIXES

to "a member of the Urantia Life Carrier Corps now resident on the planet."

Clearly we are not dealing here with an orthodox scientific treatise. Nevertheless, the anonymous members of the Urantia Corps hit on some remarkable scientific revelations in the mid-1930's. They embraced continental drift at a time when it was decidedly out of vogue in the scientific community. They recognized the presence of a global supercontinent (Rodinia) and superocean (Mirovia), in existence on earth before Pangea. From *The Urantia Book*:

> 1,000,000,000 years ago ... [t] he first continental landmass emerged from the world ocean ... 950, 000, 000 [years ago] ... presents the picture of one great continent of land and one large body of water, the Pacific Ocean.[1]

> 800, 000, 000 years ago ... Europe and Africa began to rise out of the Pacific depths along with those masses now called Australia, North and South America, and the continent of Antarctica, while the bed of the Pacific Ocean engaged in a further compensatory sinking adjustment. By the end of this period almost one third of the earth's surface consisted of land, all in one continental body.[2]

Of course I am being selective here in my choice of quotations, and there are reams of scientifically untenable material in The Urantia Book. However, the concept of a billion-year-old supercontinent (the currently accepted age for the formation of Rodinia) that subsequently split apart, forming gradually widening ocean basins in which early marine life flourished, is unquestionably present in this book.

---

1. Page 660

2. Page 662

Orthodox scientific arguments for such a proposal did not appear until the late 1960s, and a pre- Pangea supercontinent was never described until Valentine and Moores made the attempt in 1970. The Urantia Corps not only had the age of the formation of Rodinia approximately correct at 1 billion years, but they also were first to link breakup of Rodina to the emergence of animals (even if the mode of appearance was implantation by extraterrestrials). Furthermore, they even got the timing of that approximately correct at 650 to 600 million years ago ("These inland seas of olden times were truly the cradle of evolution").[1]

This book was unknown to me until it was brought to my attention by J. J. Johnson in October 1995. I obtained a copy of the book from the Smith College library and noted the 1955 (eighth edition 1984) publication date. What could possibly explain such precocious insight from such an unexpected corner? Perhaps it has to do with a lively, unconstrained, but nevertheless informed imagination. John K. Wright has noted how outrageous hypotheses "arouse interest, invite attack, and thus serve useful fermentative purposes in the advancement of geology."[2] But what about outrageous religions?

I wrote back to Johnson on January 15, 1996, asking him whether he could confirm that the passages he had referred me to were indeed written in 1955. In a letter dated January 24, he replied that the section of interest was "put into the English language in 1934," making it even more ahead of its time than I had thought.

Johnson congratulated me on my fossil discovery south of Tucson (see chapter 9) and for my "appreciation for the Truth." He then invited me to contact the Fellowship for Readers of The Urantia Book. He gave me a contact address, telephone number

---

1.   See pp. 663-664

2.   J. K. Wright, "Foreword," in *Maps of the Ancient Sea Kings*, pp ix-x, (Philadelphia: Chilton Books, 1996).

and fax for the Fellowship and advised me to contact John Hales and to consider attending an event called the Flag[staff] Conference. I consider Johnson's (unsuccessful) attempt to convert me to his religion to be a very friendly overture, and although I cannot become a Urantia proselyte, I wish the members of this faith all the best.

Assuming for the moment that space voyagers are not responsible for life's origin and history on this planet, one wonders how the Urantia Book authors arrived at the concept of a Proterozoic supercontinent, and the link between breakup of this supercontinent and the emergence of complex life in the ensuing rift oceans, 30 years before most geologists accepted continental drift and nearly four decades before scientists had any inkling that Rodinia existed. The anonymous authors responsible for the critical part of section 3 evidently possessed a high level of geological training, and while writing in the 1930s must have known of Wegener's ideas on continental drift. Perhaps he or she was, or had contact with, an expatriate from Nazi Germany. Whatever the identity of the author, this person proceeded to speculate about the relationship between evolutionary change and the breakup of a Proterozoic supercontinent in an exceptionally fruitful way. Perhaps this was because the thought and the writing of this person were not fettered by the normal constraints of the (too often highly politicized) scientific review process.

Cases such as this one (which is by no means unique) are an exercise in humility for me as a scientist. How can it be that discovery of Rodinia, plus a fairly sophisticated rendering of the evolutionary implications of the rifting of Rodinia, falls to an anonymous author engaging in a work of religious revelation decades before scientists find out anything about the subject? Perhaps this is an important aspect of religion - a creative denial of certain aspects of reality in order to access a deeper truth.

I am not advocating an abandonment of a disciplined scientific peer review process, but I can't help but wonder whether science would benefit by having scientists themselves or friends

APPENDIXES   343

of science systematically scan the various nonscientific literatures for writings such as those appearing in The Urantia Book. Scientists would ordinarily ignore and dismiss such writings, but a discerning eye might pick up some gems.

The concept of Rodinia therefore has a shockingly unexpected intellectual pedigree. When does the concept finally enter the conventional scientific channels? In articles published in the early 1970s, James W. Valentine and Eldridge M. Moores traced the geological history of the continents and spoke of a Precambrian supercontinent.[1] This continent was subsequently called proto-Pangea, pre-Pangea, Pangea 1, the Late Proterozoic Supercontinent, ur-Pangea, or simply the Precambrian supercontinent. While writing The Emergence of Animals, Dianna McMenamin and I grew weary of these cumbersome names and proposed the name Rodinia for the ancient supercontinent. The corresponding superocean also needed a name, and we decided to call it Mirovia. Here is the key passage from Emergence of Animals[2]:

> "Mirovia is derived from the Russian word mirovoi
> meaning "world or global," and, indeed, this ocean was
> global in nature. Rodinia comes from the infinitive rodit,
> which means "to beget" or "to grow." Rodinia begot all
> subsequent continents, and the edges (continental shelves)
> of Rodinia were the cradle of the earliest animals."

---

1. J. W. Valentine and E. M. Moores, "Plate-Tectonic Regulation of Faunal Diversity and Sea Level: A Model," Nature 228 (1970): 657-659.

2. See p. 95, M. A. S. McMenamin and D. L. S. McMenamin, The Emergence of Animals: The Cambrian Breakthrough (New York: Columbian University Press, 1990).

Curiously, The Urantia Book also refers to Mirovia, the "world ocean."[1] Here are my notes regarding the name from p. 17 of my 1987 composition notebook:

5/12/87 This book would be a good opportunity to "name" "paleo-Pangea"

and "proto-Panthallasa"

How about:

Ur-something

Rodinia from Russian rod: genus rodit: beget, come up, grow

Eomaria

Paleomaris

Mirovian Ocean from Russian mirovoj: World, Global, see pp. 19-20

[the entry on composition notebook pp. 19-20 follows.]

5/21 [/87] Fedonkin, "Organicheskii Mir Venda" 1983 12 10 pp. 4-5.

The glaciation at the beginning of the Vendian period, known under the name of the Laplandian or Varangian Glaciation, may have had catastrophic results for many groups of the organic world which inhabited the world ocean. (translation M. McMenamin, 5/21/1987)

As correctly pointed out by John J. W. Rogers, the word Rodinia is also derived from the Russian word rodina, meaning "motherland."[2][3] The term links the northern and southern hemispheres as well because of its phonic similarity to the Precambrian Rhondonia terrain of South America.

FROM PAGE 267:

Teilhard's great mistake, according to Raymo, was insisting that his most famous work be read as a "scientific treatise" rather than a work of theology. For example, it is unclear how Teilhard's

---

1. [2] Page 660.

2. [3] J. J. W. Rogers, "A History of Continents in the Past Three Billion Years," *The Journal of Geology*, 104 (1996): 91-107; C. Zimmer, "In Times of Ur," Discover 18 (1997): 18-19.

concepts of radial energy could be rigorously tested, and such "Vagueness disqualifies Teilhard's ideas as science." Raymo concedes, nevertheless, that "Teilhard's vision may yet turn out to be correct." Trendy concepts promoted by neo-darwinists such as self-organization may be evidence of a natural drive toward "complexity and perhaps consciousness." And with the Internet and the World Wide Web wrapping the world in a noöspheric embrace, and physicists also taking a second look at Teilhard's cosmology, there is a growing sympathy for Teilhard's vision in the contemporary scientific community.

In the final analysis, Bergson must be right. Intuition trumps reason. From Bergson to The Urantia Book, the human mind in all its unpredictable glory is still our most potent scientific tool. As Paul Feyerabend pointed out in 1988, "Modern science survived only because reason was frequently overrulled."[1]

From page 179 of The Garden of Ediacara. Dr. McMenamin proposes how a single continent broke up into several. This is a tongue in cheek design for a Rodinia medallion. Various continents are portrayed as follows: I. = India, ANT. + Antarctica, AUS. = Australia, N.AM.= North America, SIB. = Siberia, G. = Greenland, BAL. = Baltica

---

1. See p. 7 in Feyerabend, *Against Method* (London, 1988).

END OF EXCERPTS.

The purpose of including this material from *The Garden of Ediacara* in these appendixes is not to impress scientists. Scientists who do not accept religion as a legitimate mode of inquiry will never be persuaded by instances of revelation that indicate a prescience of scientific discovery. Believers who understand the Urantia Papers do not base their belief upon scientific data.

What is significant in the Garden of Ediacara material is the tenacity of outreach by a Urantian lay person who sought to bring information to the attention of a scientist. JJ Johnson's success might seem a small victory, but it was nonetheless an important milestone in bringing the Urantia Papers into the mainstream of human thought.

Another encouraging aspect of this material is that a legitimate scientist dared to publicly acknowledge the possibility that an auxiliary mode of inquiry might bear fruit for scientific thought. The Urantia Papers state:

"Your science is engaged in the agelong contest between truth and error while it fights for deliverance from the bondage of abstraction, the slavery of mathematics, and the relative blindness of mechanistic materialism." [141 par.6]

Urantians should also consider these insights:

"Your religion is becoming real because it is emerging from the slavery of fear and the bondage of superstition. Your philosophy struggles for emancipation from dogma and tradition." [141 par.6]

"Reason is the method of science; faith is the method of religion; logic is the attempted technique of philosophy. Revelation compensates for the absence of the morontia viewpoint by providing a technique for achieving unity in the comprehension of the reality and relationships of matter and spirit by the mediation of mind. And true revelation never renders science unnatural, religion unreasonable, or philosophy illogical." [1106, par.1]

APPENDIX D

Changes in the text of Urantia Foundation printings of *The Urantia Book*

Merritt Horn's Investigations and Conclusions

©COPYRIGHT2000
Merritt Horn, Boulder CO
All rights reserved, used by permission.

348   APPENDIXES

APPENDIX D

Changes in the text of
Urantia Foundation printings of *The Urantia Book*
by Merritt Horn

Contents:

I. Summary of Conclusions for the Impatient Reader

II. Scope of Analysis

III. Editorial Philosophy

IV. Critical Apparatus

A. Classification of Editorial Intent for Changes in the Text
B. Classification of Errors in the Text
C. Abbreviations; printings of *The Urantia Book* and other works cited

V. Changes in Urantia Foundation printings
of *The Urantia Book* (1955-1999)

HOW REFERENCES ARE LISTED

Each note begins with two text location references:

1) The Paper:Section.Paragraph locator [##:#.#], as found in the Uversa Press edition of The Urantia Book and in various other works. As it is based on the inherent structure of the revealed text rather than on the physical location of words on a printed page, this system is language-and format-independent. Each item in a numbered list in the text has its own paragraph number only if one or more of the items in the list contains a complete sentence. If all items are merely words or phrases, they do not have separate locator numbers.

2. The Page and Paragraph system (p.### ¶#), is based upon the physical location of paragraphs in the Urantia Foundation and Pathways printings. In this system, each indented line constitutes a new paragraph. The first full paragraph on each page is labeled paragraph 1; any partial paragraph carried over from the proceeding page is labeled paragraph 0. Thus, paragraphs which span two pages have two paragraph numbers.

I. Summary of Conclusions for the Impatient Reader

Of the 133 changes to the text covered by this Appendix:

1. There was no basis for making 67 of them.

2. Database (spelling) standardization could justify 19 of the changes, but only if standardization were consistently applied—which it has not been.

3. Changes appropriately corrected simple typographic errors in 43 cases.

4. There are only 4 instances in which a change was made to correct an error that this editor cannot yet categorize as typographical, i.e., the error appears to be real but its origin has not yet been explained without resort to postulated erroneous pre-publication editing by the humans involved—editing which those same humans consistently testified as never having occurred.

5. The 11th printing diverged most widely from the first printing, but the text has been returned to its 1955 form at many locations, so that none of the later printings actually differ from the first at every point in the text where a change has sometime occurred. One way to summarize the status of the last three printed editions and the currently available electronic texts is as follows:

a) All agree with each other, but differ from the 1955 text in 81 cases

b) All agree with each other and with the 1955 text in 19 cases.

c) Two notes are difficult to classify (because of end-of-line issues).

d) The late printings disagree with each other on the remaining 31 points: The last two softcover printings (13th; 14th) are identical, and almost always agree with the electronic texts and with the first printing; but the 15th printing (the new paperback and hardbound printing) is almost always at variance with the others (and is, in fact, very close to the 11th printing).

The impatient reader will have to read further for more details.

II. Scope of Analysis

This appendix covers only those changes known to have taken place from the 2nd (1967) through the 11th printings (1993), but tracks those changes through the printed and electronic editions published through 1999.

Textual issues which are outside the limited scope of this Appendix, but which can be profitably analyzed following the methodology employed here, will be included in the subject matter of forthcoming articles.

III. Editorial Philosophy

This analysis of changes in the text of *The Urantia Book* is based on the following assumptions about the origin and resolution of these problems:

1) *The Urantia Book* was actually written by the authors claimed in the text and by the process described in the text.

2) The revelators had reasons for using the linguistic constructions they employed. These reasons may have been variously artistic, semantic, conceptual or spiritual, just as they may be for any author, but the writing of the Fifth Epochal Revelation was neither mindless nor careless.

3) The quality of English usage in the text is acceptable proof that the revelators had the ability to learn proper

English grammar, spelling and usage. The authors were capable of choosing words and phraseology that conveyed precise meanings from among many similar constructions or synonyms.

4) Nothing touched by human hands can be perfect; therefore, mistakes may exist in the first printing of the Urantia Book.

5) Whether working on *The Urantia Book* or an ancient manuscript, an editor does not attempt to "correct" an apparent problem in the text without regard to what the author originally wrote; the editor's goal is to *reconstruct* or *restore* the original if the extant text appears defective in some way. Any proposed reconstruction must not only read well, but must be logically consistent with the theory put forward by the editor to explain the evolution of the extant text from the author's original expression. This issue has never been addressed by any list of *Corrections To The Text* published by Urantia Foundation (or Uversa Press or Michael Foundation).

IV A. Classification of Editorial Intent for Changes in the Text:

Each change has been classified according to the following outline of (presumed) rationales for the changes. Please note that this listing does not express the current editor's opinion of the validity of specific categories or changes. (See Editorial Philosophy above, and the specific notes.)

Spelling

S1) Correction of misspelled common English words

S2) Standardization of variant spellings

S3) Changes for lexical reasons (updating an archaic form or improving the etymological basis of the word)

S4) Changes in non-English words and names either to correct presumed typographical errors or to harmonize with standard transliterations

S5) Changes for grammatical reasons

S6) Changes in spelling for reasons unknown

Capitalization

C1) Changes in capitalization based on English usage

C2) Changes suggested by Urantia Book usage

Punctuation

P1) Changes required to conform with English usage

P2) Changes of preference, phrasing or convenience

Modification, insertion or deletion of entire words or phrases

M1) Grammar-based changes (The original appears ungrammatical and has been changed on that basis.)

M2) Changes to correct perceived inconsistencies or contradictions within *The Urantia Book* itself

M3) Changes to correct perceived inconsistencies or contradictions between *The Urantia Book* and current scientific theory or historical evidence

Database Errors (Unintentional changes)

D1) Changes that may be due to the inadvertent loss of a character in the typesetting database when it was translated from one form to another after initial publication. This type of problem should be most evident in the 1971(3rd)

Merritt Horn's Findings

printing—the first that did not utilize any of the original plates.

IV B. Classification of Errors

Errors by the Author(s)

A1) Grammatically incorrect use of language (Given the revelators' unequaled command of English, this type of error does not seem likely.)

A2) Contradictions or inconsistencies within the text—internal errors (It would seem, given the revelators' command of their material, as demonstrated throughout *The Urantia Book,* and by the general consistency and unity of the revelation, that, except for cases in which *A3* might apply, errors of this type are not likely in *The Urantia Book*)

A3) Errors of scientific or historical statements—external errors (The revelators explicitly warn that **apparent** errors of this type do exist in the text.)

Transcription Errors (at any stage of copying or typesetting)

T1) A dropped keystroke

T2) An extra keystroke

T3) An incorrect keystroke—either the wrong letter or number, or a mistakenly shifted or un-shifted character (capitalization)

T4) Transposed characters—with or without an intervening letter

T5) Pattern insertion or deletion errors—the inadvertent repetition of a near-by word pattern

T6) An overlooked word—usually short connectives (or, an, of, if, it)

T7) Mis-read letters from the handwritten manuscript.

Editorial Errors

E1) The mistaken "correction" of what was perceived to be either a transcription or proofing mistake (This would include any changes that cannot be reverse-engineered to fall within the oft-repeated bounds of "spelling, capitalization and punctuation" that are covered by category E2.)

E2) The inconsistent or incorrect exercise of the power to "correct spelling, capitalization and punctuation."

IV C. Abbreviations; printings of *The Urantia Book and other works cited*

Chicago Manual or *CM*

A Manual of Style, University of Chicago Press, 1927, 1937, 1949 (9th - 11th editions). The 12th and 13th editions are also referenced, but these post-date the period of the original preparation of the text of *The Urantia Book* for publication.

OED

The Oxford English Dictionary, [1933] Compact edition 1971.

Webster's

Webster's New International Dictionary, Second edition, [1934] 1944.

Editions of *The Urantia Book* cited in Appendix

Printings

1st	1955 Original format (6" x 10")	
2nd	1967	"
3rd	1971	"
4th	1973	"
5th	1976	"
6th	1978	"
7th	1981	"

8th	1984	"
9th	1986	"
10th	1990	"
11th	1993	"
12th	1995 Soft-cover (5" x 7")	
13th	1995	"
14th	1998	"

15th 1999 Paperback & new hardcover size (5½" x 8")

Electronic Editions

E-11

HTML text based on 11th printed edition. This is the version licensed by Urantia Foundation to Jesusonian Foundation for the latter's website. It appears to be identical to the 11th printing, so it is not separately referenced in this Appendix.

CD

Refers to the following two electronic editions (E-12a and CD-ROM), as their content is identical insofar as the referenced changes are concerned.

E-12a

HTML text edition available on Urantia Foundation web site in May, 2000. (This text was available at an earlier date, but it is not known when that text reached its quoted form.) The text in this edition seems to be the same as that found on the CD-ROM, and appears to be most closely related to the 12th printed printing.

CD-ROM

The 1997 Folio Bound VIEWS edition

V. Changes found in Urantia Foundation printings of The Urantia Book (1955-1999)

1) 0:1.19; p.3 ¶11 Change type: M1
1st:
5. Absolute perfection in no direction, relative perfection in all other manifestations.
2nd - 15th, *CD*:
5. Absolute perfection in no direction, relative perfection in all manifestations.

Discussion:

The original phraseology is incorrect because the reference to *other* manifestations requires the existence of one or more additional manifestations to which this *other* is being contrasted. As this particular phase of perfection exists in only one manifestation—relative perfection—there are no additional types which require or permit the use of *other* in this context.

Conclusion:

There was a T5 error in the 1955 text—*other* was inserted into the text during one of the pre-publication transcriptions by accidentally repeating the pattern of use found immediately before and after this sentence.

2) 3:1.12; p.46 ¶4 Change type: C2
1st - 6th:
...with the power of choice (concerning Himself)...

7th - 15th, *CD*:
...with the power of choice (concerning himself)...

Discussion:

Because there are four additional changes of this type in Urantia Foundation printings, and a large number of similar changes in the Uversa Press and Michael Foundation printings, it is necessary to examine this issue in some detail.

Although pronouns referring to Deity are usually not capitalized (see, for example, *himself* later in the subject paragraph), after extensive computer-aided analysis of the entire text of *The Urantia Book*, it has been found (without known exception) that the capitalization of pronouns referring to Deity is consistent with the guidelines found in the three editions of the *Chicago Manual* available during the period from 1927 to 1955*:

"Capitalize nouns and adjectives used to designate the Supreme Being, or any member of the Christian Trinity†; and all pronouns referring to the same when not closely preceded or followed by a distinct reference to the Deity:

...'Trust Him who rules all things' (*but:* 'When God had worked six days, he rested on the seventh.')"

[*§72 of 9th *CM* ed.; §28 of 10th *CM* ed.; §29 of 11th *CM* ed. †11th *CM* ed. adds ", the Virgin Mary" here.]

Even if, for argument's sake, it was appropriate to "modernize" the text of *The Urantia Book* to keep its style current, the changes under discussion are not supported by later editions of the *Chicago Manual* either. The 12th *CM* ed., the standard from 1969 until 1982 (the time period during which these changes were made), is equally explicit:

"7.77 Pronouns referring to [Deity personalities] are today seldom capitalized except in instances where capitalization offers a simple way to avoid ambiguity:

Trust in Him.

God gives man what He wills.

but:

God in his mercy.

Jesus and his disciples"

Although the revelators did not have to be slaves to the mandates of the *Chicago Manual,* it was, by all reports, the stylistic authority used by those responsible for the preparation of the first printing when questions of "capitalization and punctuation" arose. Anyone attempting to "correct" the text is required to justify a suggested departure from the guidelines used in the process of preparing the text for its first publication; the relevant part of those guidelines being, in this instance, "Choose your authority and stick to it."

Conclusion:

The 1955 text is correct.

3) 11:7.7; p.125 ¶1Change type: S5
1st:
The relatively quiet zone between the space levels,...,are enormous...
2nd - 15th, *CD*:
The relatively quiet zones between the space levels,...,are enormous...

Discussion:

The plural, found in all printings after 1955, agrees with the verb *are,* and is otherwise consistent with the general sense of the paragraph.

Conclusion:

There was a T1 (dropped keystroke) error in the 1955 text; *zones* is correct.

354 APPENDIXES

4) 12:4.15; p.134 ¶4 Change type: P2

1st:

...next to the domains of the seven superuniverses, seem to be...

2nd - 15th, *CD*:

...next to the domains of the seven superuniverses seem to be...

Discussion:

While the comma in question may be unnecessary, it may nevertheless assist the reader in phrasing an otherwise unwieldy sentence.

Conclusion:

The 1955 text is correct.

5) 12:4.16; p.134 ¶5 Change type: D1

1st, 2nd, 11th - 15th, *CD*:

...is a complement or equilibrant of gravity.

3rd - 10th:

...is a complement or equilibrant of gravity [missing period]

Discussion:

This is one of the minor errors that entered the database when the original plates were first discarded.

Conclusion:

The 1955 text is correct.

6) 29:4.27; p.328 ¶3 Change type: S6

1st - 9th, 12th - 14th, *CD*:

Together with their co-workers, the dissociators,...

10th, 11th, 15th:

Together with their coworkers, the dissociators,...

Discussion:

Neither form is found in *Webster's;* the *OED* contains only the hyphenated form. The *Chicago Manual*'s 9th - 11th

editions use *co-worker* as an explicit example of a general rule regarding certain prefixes. The *CM*'s 10th reads as follows:

"221. Prefixes when joined to roots do not retain the hyphen except in combination with words beginning with their terminal vowel, or with *w* or *y:*

...co-operation

co-worker"

The relevant rule in *CM*'s 11th printing (1969) appears to allow *coworker* by glossing over the case of prefixes formed with initial *w* roots, but its 13th printing (1982) again specifically prescribes the hyphenated form (Table 6.1, p.180).

Conclusion:

The 1955 text is correct.

7) 30:3.12; p.340 ¶1 Change type: S4

1st - 9th, 12th - 14th, *CD*:

...beings enroute elsewhere who pause...

10th, 11th, 15th:

...beings en route elsewhere who pause...

Discussion:

Although the original may be understandable, it is incorrect French and is not the form that has been adopted into English (according to *Webster's,* the *OED,* and the *Chicago Manual*). A simple dropped space-key explains the original.

Conclusion:

There was a T1 (dropped keystroke) error in the 1955 text.

8) 35:6.3; p.391 ¶1 Change type: P2

1st, 12th - 14th:

...at the universe headquarters, as he frequently is,...

Merritt Horn's Findings

2nd - 11th, 15th, *CD*:

...at the universe headquarters as he frequently is,...

Discussion:

The comma after headquarters is required to enclose, with the following comma, the parenthetical phrase "as he frequently is."

Conclusion:

The 1955 text is correct.

9) 36:3.6; p.400 ¶1 Change type: S1 or S3

1st:

...subsequently add any thing new or supplemental...

2nd - 15th, *CD*:

...subsequently add anything new or supplemental...

Discussion:

The compound word was probably the author's choice in this case. The sentence simply does not read well if, to test an alternative hypothesis, the assumption is made that the two-word format was chosen by the author for emphasis (which, to this editor, is the only discernible rationale for the two-word form).

Conclusion:

A T2 (extra keystroke) error was present here in the 1955 text.

10) 37:8.3; p.413 ¶6 Change type: M2

1st:

...the secondary Universe Circuit Supervisor stationed in...

2nd - 15th, *CD*:

...the tertiary Universe Circuit Supervisor stationed in...

Discussion:

While both a secondary and a tertiary Circuit Supervisor are assigned to the supervision of a single local universe's circuits, only the tertiary Circuit Supervisor is stationed within the local universe—the secondary Circuit Supervisor is located on the superuniverse headquarters (See 24:1.5-7). Therefore, if Andovontia is "stationed in our local universe" he would be a tertiary Universe Circuit Supervisor.

The differences between the words appear to rule out typing or proofing errors as the source of this problem, leaving this editor's "last resort" explanation: Sometime prior to publication, but when the handwritten manuscript was no longer available as an authoritative reference, someone noticed what appeared to be an internal inconsistency (ascribed, presumably, to an earlier human error), and an E1 change (erroneous "correction") was made to the text.

Conclusion:

The 1955 text is incorrect. This editor's best explanation, at present, is an E1 change (*tertiary* to *secondary*) made prior to publication to correct what was believed to be an earlier human error.

11) 40:7.2; p.449 ¶0 Change type: S5

1st - 6th:

...When you and your Adjusters are finally and forever fused,...

7th - 15th, *CD*:

...When you and your Adjuster are finally and forever fused,...

356 APPENDIXES

Discussion:

The original, plural form is correct, not only because the referent of every other instance of *you* and *your* in this paragraph is plural (the ascending Sons of God; planetary sons; sons of ascension potential, etc.), but more importantly, the grammar of the sentence requires a plural: "When you and your Adjusters are finally and forever fused,...then in fact have you become the ascending sons of God."

The change to the text was probably made because of the confusion caused by the enclosed, parenthetical phrase, "when you two are made one,..."

Conclusion:

The 1955 text is correct.

12) 41:1.1; p.456 ¶0 Change type: P2

1st - 10th, 12th - 15th, *CD*:

Within the domain of this Paradise Son of God the Supreme...

11th:

Within the domain of this Paradise Son of God, the Supreme...

Discussion:

By indicating the end of the initial adverbial phrase, a comma here does greatly assist the reader. If present in the original manuscript, a simple dropped keystroke (T1) error would have produced the 1955 text.

Conclusion:

A probable instance of a T1 error in the 1955 printing.

13) 41:4.4; p.460 ¶1 Change type: M2

1st:

...having become sixty thousand times as dense as your sun.

2nd - 15th, *CD*:

...having become forty thousand times as dense as your sun.

Discussion:

Textual consistency and current scientific estimates of our sun's density both support the change to "forty thousand." The first paragraph of this section states that our sun is about 1.5 times the density of water, or about 0.054 pounds per cubic inch, and 40,000 times this is about 2,160 pounds per cubic inch; the current scientific estimate of the sun's density is 1.4 times the density of water; 40,000 times that is roughly 2,035 pounds per cubic inch.

There are two possible explanations for the appearance of this error in the 1955 text:

1) It is this editor's opinion that the number in question was written as a numeral in the manuscript (*40,000* not *forty thousand*), and that the error was caused by a simple keystroke error (T3) in which *6* was mis-keyed for *4,* creating *60,000* instead of *40,000*. When the text was formatted for printing, the numerals were changed to words, and an error that formerly consisted of one digit was transformed into an incorrect word. There is no direct evidence in support of this theory, but the formatting of words and numbers for printing is not a revelatory issue; it is a matter of style, and is covered extensively in the *Chicago Manual*. The proper formatting of words and numbers is precisely the type of editorial decision that the revelators could give to the humans preparing the *form* of the text for printing without giving those humans any authority to change any of the *content* of the text.) If this theory is correct, this is a simple T3 (incorrect

Merritt Horn's Findings

keystroke) error, disguised by the later change in formatting of the number. (The problem at 43:1.6 appears to have had an identical origin, and 42:5.1 is very closely related.)

2) The appearance of "sixty thousand" in the 1955 text could be due to an E1 error: a well-meaning but erroneous re-calculation of the underlying math—60,000 is 1.5 times 40,000—which means that the near-by sun is 60,000 times the density of water, though it is only 40,000 times as dense as our sun.

Conclusion:

The 1955 text is incorrect; it should read *forty thousand*. There are two likely causes; this editor favors a T3 (incorrect keystroke) error based on the theory that the manuscript contained numerals rather than written-out numbers. Alternatively, an E1 change (*forty* to *sixty*) was made prior to 1955 to correct what was believed to be an earlier human error.

14) 42:5.1; p.474 ¶5 Change type: S4
    1st:
...ten octaves up are the X rays, followed by the Y rays of radium.
    2nd - 15th, *CD*:
...ten octaves up are the X rays, followed by the gamma rays of radium.

Discussion:

From external reference to physics, and multiple internal cross-references (see for example 42:5.7), *gamma* is clearly intended here. As to the origin of the *Y* in the 1955 text, it is likely that the Greek letter γ (gamma) was mistakenly transposed into *Y* at some point in the preparation of the original printing (probably at the time of the first typing

from the original manuscript) either because of a faulty inference from the immediately preceding *X*, from an unfamiliarity with the Greek alphabet, or simply because there was no better way to represent the character on a standard typewriter.

Even though a typesetter would have been able to place the letter γ on the page, the later decision to replace that letter with *gamma* is clear, reasonable, and consistent with the usage found elsewhere throughout *The Urantia Book*.

Conclusion:

The 1955 text was incorrect; *Y* should have been γ. The error type is best classified as T3 (incorrect keystroke), although it should be understood that the technology available for any transcriptions prior to typesetting did not have a mechanism for representing the correct character.

15) 42:6.7; p.477 ¶1 Change type: M2
There are two interdependent changes in this paragraph:
(a) 1st:
...an electron weighs a little less than 1/2,000th of the smallest atom,...
    2nd - 15th, *CD*:
...an electron weighs a little more than 1/2,000th of the smallest atom,...
(b) 1st:
The positive proton...weighs from two to three thousand times more.
    2nd - 15th, *CD*:
The positive proton...weighs almost two thousand times more.

Discussion:

[For historical reference, the first discussion of the relative masses of the structural elements of atoms in the

358 APPENDIXES

Encyclopaedia Britannica is found in its 13th Edition (1926):

"Through the experimental discoveries of the second half of the 19th century it became gradually clear that the atoms of the elements, far from being indivisible entities, had to be thought of as aggregates built up of separate particles. Thus from experiments on electrical discharges in rarified gases and especially from a closer study of the so-called cathode rays, one was led to recognise the existence of small negatively charged particles the mass of which was found to be about 2,000 times as small as the mass of the lightest atom, the hydrogen atom. These small particles, which may be regarded as atoms of negative electricity are now, following Johnstone Stoney, generally called electrons. Through the investigations of J. J. Thomson and others convincing evidence was obtained that these electrons are a constituent of every atom..." (Vol. 29 pg. 262)]

The revised wording is consistent with the statement in the paragraph following the subject paragraph (42:6.8), where the author states that a proton is "eighteen hundred times as heavy as an electron;" and is also in general agreement with current scientific opinion which places the ratio at about 1:1,836.

If it is assumed that the author of this paper is not the source of the apparent error in the 1955 text, the only mechanism available is an E1 error similar to explanation #2 for the note regarding 41:4.4: If one erroneously interpreted the electron : proton ratio of 1:1,800 as being slightly less than 1/2,000, one might view an original (inferred) passage that was synonymous with the 1967 version as being in error, and suggest those changes in wording which are found in the 1955 text—which then had to be un-done once the erroneous correction was recognized.

There is no direct evidence that this was the actual mechanism for the origin of this error, but if the *authors* were prone to mathematical clumsiness, and the quality of the text was due to excellent mathematical editing, *The Urantia Book* would not contain the flaw under discussion, but would contain a number of errors that simply could not have been found without computers. (For instance, the calculation of the days and dates in the Jesus papers was virtually impossible until a few years ago, but now, anyone with a good calendar program can go back to the years A.D. 1 - A.D. 30 and find that every day associated with a date was calculated correctly somehow by someone during the 1930's.*) If, however, the authors were far better mathematicians than the editors, we might observe precisely what we **do** observe: one or two errors caused by the well-intentioned editorial misinterpretation of proximate data.

(*The apparent miscalculation of Pentecost is a separate issue that will be analyzed in a forthcoming paper.)

Conclusion:

The 1955 text is incorrect. This editor's best explanation, at present, is an E1 change, apparently involving several words, made prior to publication to correct what was believed to be an earlier human error.

16) 42:7.7; p.478 ¶1 Change type: M3
1st:

...the instantaneous disruption of the central proton...

Merritt Horn's Findings

2nd - 15th, *CD*:
...the well-nigh instantaneous disruption of the central proton...

Discussion:

The insertion of *well-nigh* was perhaps made because the observed deterioration of the known man-made elements with atomic numbers above 100, while extremely rapid, is not instantaneous—if by that description one means that such elements would have half-lives of zero. However:

a) Given the time-frame within which a Mighty Messenger (the author of Paper 42) views reality, the phraseology hardly requires correction even if the sentence is to be understood as just described.

b) It is not self-evident that the "disruption of the central proton" is identical with the nuclear deterioration which we measure in terms of half-lives. The central proton's disruption might be the immediate cause for the rapid, though not instantaneous, decay which our scientists observe.

c) The procedure described by the paper's author which leads to the disruption—the insertion of an additional electron into the orbital field of an element that already contains 100 electrons—is itself distinct from the methods whereby transuranium elements are created by our scientists, which involve the insertion of additional particles into the atomic nucleus by various means.

d) It is of interest to note that (laboratory-scale creation of minuscule quantities—no more than a few thousand atoms—of short-lived, heavier elements notwithstanding), the heaviest element ever created during the large-scale matter/energy conversions/interactions of either nuclear reactors or underground nuclear explosions has consistently been an isotope of fermium (the 100th element)—an unexpected fact for which our scientists have found no ready explanation since the early 1960s when this phenomenon was first observed.

Thus, the editorial decision to introduce *well-nigh* into the text was unwarranted—being unnecessary at best, and scientifically incorrect at worst.

Conclusion:

Current science does not require alteration of the 1955 text (even if, for the sake of argument, such a change were within the editor's province).

---

17) 43:1.6; p.486 ¶5 Change type: M2

1st:
...established almost four thousand years ago, immediately after...

2nd - 15th, *CD*:
...established almost forty thousand years ago, immediately after...

Discussion:

The second printing correction appears to be warranted based on a reference at 119:7.2:

"The public announcement that Michael had selected Urantia as the theater for his final bestowal was made shortly after we learned about the default of Adam and Eve. And thus, for more than thirty-five thousand years, your world occupied a very conspicuous place in the councils of the entire universe."

The default occurred about 37,800 years ago, so "almost forty thousand" and "more than thirty-five thousand" would seem to be equally reasonable descriptions.

360 APPENDIXES

While the original reading could have been caused by a T2/T3 typing error, the words don't really fit that type of error very well. Another possibility is that an (E1) incorrect pre-publication edit was made by mistakenly associating the establishment of the college with the time of Machiventa's bestowal (4,000 years ago).

It is this editor's opinion, however, that the problem is identical in origin to that of 41:4.4: the number in question was written as a numeral in the manuscript (*40,000* not *forty thousand*), and that the error was caused by the loss of a zero before the number was formatted into words for printing. (The proper formatting of words and numbers is precisely the type of editorial decision that the revelators could give to the humans preparing the *form* of the text for printing without giving those humans any authority to change any of the *content* of the text.) If this theory is correct, this is a simple T1 (dropped keystroke) error, disguised by the later change in formatting of the number.

Conclusion:

The 1955 text is incorrect; it should read *forty thousand*. There are several possible causes, this editor favors a T1 (dropped keystroke) error based on the theory that the manuscript contained numerals rather than written-out numbers.

18) 43:8.2; p.494 ¶1 Change type: S2
1st:
While you are rekeyed each time...
2nd - 15th, *CD*:
While you are re-keyed each time...

Discussion:

The only other occurrence of *re-keyed* is in hyphenated form (48:2.14).

Words formed with the "re-" prefix, fall under the same general *Chicago Manual* rule referred to for (29:4.27) above, but this instance is covered by an exception:

"*a*) When the first vowel of the added word would...suggest mispronunciation, the hyphen is retained."

In this case, the un-hyphenated form appears to indicate that the first syllable is pronounced with a short *e,* causing the reader to stumble. Insertion of the hyphen resolves the problem.

Conclusion:

There was an error of either type T1 (dropped keystroke) or type E2 (incorrect editorial decision regarding hyphenation) in the 1995 text.

19) 44:0.1; p.497 ¶ 1Change type: P2
1st:
...divisional and universe headquarters worlds, may be found...
2nd - 15th, *CD*:
...divisional and universe headquarters worlds may be found...

Discussion:

Although the comma in the first printing is optional, it is not ungrammatical.

Conclusion:

The 1955 text required no modification.

Merritt Horn's Findings

20) 46:1.8; p.520 ¶4 Change type: P2
1st, 2nd, 12th - 15th, *CD*:
...but it is not dependent on them; worlds like Jerusem...
3rd - 11th:
...but it is not dependent on them, worlds like Jerusem...

Discussion:

The replacement of the original semicolon by a comma was erroneous. The semicolon is the correct choice for joining two independent clauses.

Conclusion:

The 1955 text is correct.

21) 46:5.18; p.526 ¶0 Change type: D1
1st, 2nd, 6th - 15th, *CD*:
...it is among the more recent constructions.
3rd - 5th:
...it is among the more recent constructions [missing period]

Discussion:

This is one of the minor errors that entered the database when the original plates were first discarded.

Conclusion:

The 1955 text is correct.

22) 47:0.2; p.530 ¶2 Change type: D1
1st, 2nd, 6th - 15th, *CD*:
...of the finaliter corps assigned to Satania.
3rd - 5th:
...of the finaliter corps assigned to Satania [missing period]

Discussion:

This is one of the minor errors that entered the database when the original plates were first discarded.

Conclusion:

The 1955 text is correct.

23) 47:0.4; p.530 ¶4 Change type: M1
1st - 6th:
The seven mansion worlds are in charge of the morontia supervisors...
7th - 15th, *CD*:
The seven mansion worlds are in the charge of the morontia supervisors...

Discussion:

This was an unnecessary edit, as the phrase *in charge of* may be employed either actively ("...the morontia supervisors in charge of the mansion worlds...") or passively ("...the mansion worlds in charge of the morontia supervisors..."). Although the former is more common today, the latter construction would not have appeared awkward for any reader of English before the mid-twentieth century; even now, no reasonable reader could claim a basis for confusion unless the author has used the phrase in an inappropriate setting—when the priority of the related parties is not self-evident. The underlying relationship between the parties, here and at the other instances of this construction in the text (46:5.17; 73:7.4; 183:4.4; 187:6.2), is clear; so the authors' choice of words was correct, unambiguous and reasonable.

Conclusion:

The 1955 text is correct.

24) 49:3.3; p.563 ¶6 Change type: D1/ P2
1st, 2nd, 12th - 14th, *CD*:
...meteorites enter the atmosphere of Urantia daily, coming in...

3rd - 11th, 15th:

...meteorites enter the atmosphere of Urantia daily coming in...

Discussion:

The comma in the original sentence is correctly utilized to separate the beginning independent phase from the trailing dependent phrase. The comma's location at the end of a line makes it a likely candidate for inadvertent loss when the text was translated from the original plates—a D1 change—but does not explain its later disappearance in the 15th printing.

Conclusion:

The 1955 text is correct.

25) 51:6.3; p.587 ¶1 Change type: S5/ S6

1st - 5th, *CD*:

...situated not far-distant still another and older headquarters...

6th - 15th:

...situated not far distant still another and older headquarters...

Discussion:

There is no basis for removing the hyphen. *Far-distant* in any structural setting is a single concept. The only un-hyphenated instance of these two words in the text (94:5.6) bears no grammatical relationship to this construction and is very closely related to all of the hyphenated examples. That one case cannot therefore be used as a justification for this change and is itself a reasonable candidate for editorial standardization.

Conclusion:

The 1955 text is correct.

26) 52:6; p.597 Change type: S2

1st:

URANTIA'S POST-BESTOWAL AGE

2nd - 15th, *CD*:

URANTIA'S POSTBESTOWAL AGE

Discussion:

The un-hyphenated form is more commonly found in the text, but the original form is appropriate at this location (as a section title) because of its parallelism with the titles of sections two through five and seven of this paper. Only standardization for electronic search might justify the change (which would require the alteration of section five's title as well).

Conclusion:

There was no error in the 1955 text, but standardization for electronic search, if universally applied, might justify a change.

27) 53:5.2; p.605 ¶6 Change type: P2

1st - 10th, 12th - 15th, *CD*:

...the two which preceded it there was no absolute...

11th:

...the two which preceded it, there was no absolute...

Discussion:

Although a comma here might assist in phrasing, there is no need to insert one.

Conclusion:

The 1955 punctuation is reasonable.

28) 53:7.8; p.608 ¶4Change type: M2

1st:

Of the 681,227 Material Sons lost in Satania,...

2nd - 15th, *CD*:
Of the 681,217 Material Sons lost in
Satania,...

Discussion:

The change from 681,227 to 681,217
was, presumably, made because of the
following passage: "Since the inception
of the system of Satania, thirteen
Planetary Adams have been lost in
rebellion and default and 681,204 in the
subordinate positions of trust." (51:1.5)

It does appear that one of the
numbers is in error, but whether 681,227
should be reduced by ten or 681,204
should be increased by ten cannot be
determined from the text. The cause of
the error in the first printing is almost
certainly a single mistaken keystroke
(T3).

Conclusion:

There was an T3 error made at some
point but insufficient contextual
evidence makes it impossible to
reconstruct the original.

29) 54:6.10; p.620 ¶2 Change type: P2
   1st - 10th, 12th - 15th, *CD*:
At least I was not even when I had thus
attained...
   11th:
At least I was not, even when I had thus
attained...

Discussion:

Though this comma may help the
reader in phrasing the sentence, in the
absence of compelling evidence that the
extant text is a corrupted version of the
original, the editor is not justified in
superimposing his own preferences over
the author's choice of expression.

Conclusion:

The 1955 punctuation is acceptable.

30) 55:2.8; p.624 ¶2 Change type: D1
   1st, 2nd, 11th - 15th, *CD*:
...not yet occurred according to my
observation.
   3rd - 10th:
...not yet occurred according to my
observation [missing period]

Discussion:

This is one of the minor errors that
entered the database when the original
plates were first discarded.

Conclusion:

The 1955 text is correct.

31) 55:7.4; p.632 ¶3 Change type: D1
   1st - 5th, 12th - 15th, *CD*:
...settledness for one millennium of
system time,...
   6th - 11th:
...settledness for one millenium of
system time,...

Discussion:

The loss of the second *n* in the sixth
printing was probably due to an
unnoticed database corruption. The
likelihood that this is the source of the
problem is increased by the fact that in
the first through eleventh printings, the
text flow caused *millennium* to be
broken after the first *n,* with the
remaining letters moving to the
following line.

Conclusion:

The 1955 text is correct.

32) 55:12.5; p.636 ¶6 Change type: S5
   1st, 2nd:
None of us entertain a satisfactory
concept...

3rd - 15th, *CD*:
None of us entertains a satisfactory concept...

Discussion:

This change was apparently made under the misconception that, because of their semantic similarity, *none* and *no one* share the same syntax. However, both *Webster's* and the *OED* attest that *none* commonly takes a plural verb.

Conclusion:

The 1955 text is correct.

33) 57:8.18; p.662 ¶5 Change type: D1
1st, 2nd, 12th - 15th, *CD*:
...and to regulate its flow, as is disclosed...
3rd - 11th:
...and to regulate its flow as is disclosed...

Discussion:

The removal of this comma, located originally at the end of a line, was probably inadvertent, one of many similar problems arising in the 3rd printing.

Conclusion:

The 1955 text is correct.

34) 61:3.13; p.697 ¶8 Change type: S3
1st:
Weasels, martins, otters, and raccoons...
2nd - 15th, *CD*:
Weasels, martens, otters, and raccoons...

Discussion:

A single mistaken keystroke (T3 error) could have produced *martins* from an intended *martens*. It is also possible, however, that the original form was the author's choice, being a correct, though less common, variant. (We cannot assert

that the author would not use an unusual variant, because *coons* was used for *raccoons* only two pages previously. (61:2.7; p.695 ¶5))

Since *martin* is not found in any other context (e.g. *purple martin*), there is no need to change the spelling to improve the accuracy of the electronic database.

Unless it is the policy of an editor to standardize *all* of an author's spellings to the most common variant, the best course of action, if it is believed that the reader will need assistance with unusual words, is to create a comprehensive cross-reference.

Conclusion:

The 1955 text *might* contain a T3 error, but requires no change.

35) 69:3.9; p.774 ¶8 Change type: S2
1st - 9th, 12th - 14th, *CD*:
...the flint flakers and stonemasons...
10th, 11th, 15th:
...the flint flakers and stone masons...

Discussion:

The original is clear, and is a correct form, but of nine occurrences in the text this is the only instance in which the compound form is found; this change would therefore be a reasonable standardization of the database.

Conclusion:

It is likely that the 1955 text contained a dropped keystroke (T1) error here.

36) 71:7.2; p.806 ¶2 Change type: S1/S6

1st:

...and philosophy sometime becomes the chief pursuit of its citizens.

2nd - 15th, *CD*:

...and philosophy sometimes becomes the chief pursuit of its citizens.

Discussion:

The change from *sometime* to *sometimes* is, from a typographical standpoint, a minor matter, but the meaning of the sentence is dramatically transformed from a confident prediction about the evolution of the ideal state in the original text to the mere acknowledgment of a possible development in all later printings.

To paraphrase the original:

...philosophy *eventually* becomes the chief pursuit of the citizens of the ideal state.

By contrast, all later printings convey the impression that:

...philosophy *occasionally* becomes the chief pursuit of the citizens of the ideal state.

Given the immediate context in which this statement occurs and the revelators' broader narrative of the evolution of inhabited worlds toward light and life, and in the absence of compelling evidence that the 1955 text was in error, this editor's assumption is that the original wording was the author's choice.

Conclusion:

The 1955 text is correct.

37) 73:7.4; p.827 ¶3 Change type: M1

1st:

...he and Eve were to divide their time between these...capitals...

2nd - 15th, *CD*:

...he and Eve were to divide their time among these...capitals...

Discussion:

The original construction is correct because *between* can appropriately be used when more than two objects are related, especially if the relationship is to each object individually rather than in an indeterminate way to the group. Here, the relationship is the division of Adam and Eve's time *between* world capitals; it is immaterial that there are more than two capitals involved. The following paraphrase based on the passage may help to distinguish the usages:

The Adamic children were to live *among* the evolutionary peoples, administering the affairs of the planetary government from the various world capitals, while Adam and Eve would divide their time *between* the capitals as advisors and coordinators.

Conclusion:

The 1955 text is correct.

38) 76:5.3; p.852 ¶2 Change type: D1

1st, 2nd, 12th -15th:

...the sovereign of this universe, was so soon to appear...

3rd - 11th, *CD*:

...the sovereign of this universe was so soon to appear...

Discussion:

The location of this comma, at the end of a line in the original format, makes it likely that the change was an accidental database corruption coincident with the use of the new printing plates in 1971. (Unfortunately, the electronic text has not been restored to the original.)

Conclusion:

The 1955 text is correct.

39) 78:0.1; p.868 ¶1 Change type: D1
1st, 2nd, 12th - 15th, *CD*:
...the doings of historic times, and who have so...
3rd - 11th:
...the doings of historic times and who have so...

Discussion:

Same as note for 76:5.3 (except that electronic text has been restored).

Conclusion:

The 1955 text is correct.

40) 78:2.3; p.870 ¶1 Change type: S5
1st:
...was there a civilization in anyway comparable.
2nd - 15th, *CD*:
...was there a civilization in any way comparable.

Discussion:

The two-word form is the appropriate choice when serving as an adverb only, rather than as an adverbial conjunction, in which case the compound *anyway* is more common. This latter use, roughly synonymous with *at any rate* or *in any case,* is well illustrated by its only occurrence in the papers (at 148:6.4) when Job's friend, Eliphaz, is quoted as saying:

"Anyway, man seems predestined to trouble, and perhaps the Lord is only chastising you for your own good."

Conclusion:

The 1955 format is incorrect and probably reflects a simple T1 (dropped keystroke) error.

41) 79:3.5; p.881 ¶5 Change type: S1
1st:
...religious, philosophic, and commerical civilization...
2nd - 15th, *CD*:
...religious, philosophic, and commercial civilization...

Discussion:

This is one of only four instances in the 1955 text (the others being *hestitate* at 121:7.3, *anniversay* at 123:2.3, and *peformance* at 126:1.5) in which common English words have been typeset incorrectly where there is no possible basis for morphological confusion (e.g. *anyway/any way, sometime/some time*). The ease with which such typing mistakes are made, combined with the difficulty of their detection in proofing (because of the mind's tendency to see the correct word even when an error is present), made this a very common form of error in the days prior to spell-checking programs in even the most rigorously proofed book. That there are only four such errors in the first printing is the strongest evidence for the care with which that printing was prepared, and a potent rebuttal for the many "corrections" put forth over the years which presuppose careless preparation of the original text.

Conclusion:

Two keystrokes were transposed in the first printing—a T4 error.

42) 79:5.6; p.883 ¶7 Change type: M3

1st, 2nd:

and when the land passage to the west, over the Bering isthmus...

3rd - 15th, *CD*:

and when the land passage to the east, over the Bering isthmus...

Discussion:

There is no question that North America is east of Siberia—that fact being the basis for the 1967 change. It is difficult to account for the appearance of *west* in the first printing if *east* was in the original manuscript, but if the original was *West,* referring to the Western Hemisphere, the only explanation required is a mistakenly un-shifted keystroke—a simple T3 error.

In the Urantia Papers, *West* and *East* are frequently utilized to designate a generalized geographical location rather than direction, but in all other cases they refer to the western and eastern reaches of Eurasia. Because there is no other instance of *West* referring to the Western Hemisphere, we cannot be certain that this was the original wording, but it is certain that if *West* had been printed here in the first printing, the meaning would have been obvious, the passage would never have been revised, and the question of this unique usage of *West* would never have come up.

[A more complex explanation involving an E1 error (a mistaken pre-publication "correction") is the only mechanism available for the transformation of *east* in the manuscript to *west* in the 1955 text, but in view of the simplicity of the *West/west* solution, it would seem to be unnecessary to resort to the E1 explanation in this case.]

Conclusion:

There was a T3 error in the 1955 text: the *W* in *West* was mistakenly keyed without being shifted into its capitalized form.

43) 79:8.3; p.887 ¶3 Change type: S2/S4

1st - 9th, 12th - 14th, *CD*:

...following the disruption of Graeco-Roman civilization.

10th, 11th, 15th:

...following the disruption of Greco-Roman civilization.

Discussion:

A change for the purpose of database standardization is reasonable, as the original text contained both forms at different locations, but the subsequent reversion of the printed text, and the variant electronic text are problematic and quite incomprehensible to this editor.

The origin of the variants in the text may be related to a change in recommended spellings between the 1927 and 1937 editions of the *Chicago Manual.* (The former specifying *Graeco-,* the latter, *Greco-.*) The *OED* and *Webster's* include both forms, but their preferences are split—along lines the reader can, no doubt, predict. (See also note for 98:4.1)

Conclusion:

The 1955 spelling is an acceptable variant. However, database standardization (if consistently applied), could be a reasonable justification for adopting the more modern form.

44) 80:2.4; p.890 ¶8 Change type: P1

1st:

...to the level of the Atlantic Ocean [missing period]

2nd - 15th, *CD*:

...to the level of the Atlantic Ocean.

Discussion:

This period, at the end of the last line on the page in the original format, was missing in the first printing. There were only two missing periods in the first printing. (*See* 117:7.4)

Conclusion:

The was a T1 (dropped keystroke) error in the 1955 text.

45) 80:5.8; p.894 ¶1 Change type: S5

1st:

Central Europe was for sometime controlled by the blue man...

2nd - 15th, *CD*:

Central Europe was for some time controlled by the blue man...

Discussion:

The two-word form is correct as the reference is to an indefinite period of time rather than to an indefinite point in time. (See *Webster's*)

Conclusion:

There was a T1 (dropped keystroke) error in the first printing.

46) 80:7.1; p.895 ¶1 Change type: S5

1st:

...there persisted for sometime a superior civilization...

2nd - 15th, *CD*:

...there persisted for some time a superior civilization...

Discussion:

As in the previous case (80:5.8), the two-word form is correct because the reference is to an indefinite period of time; not an indefinite point in time.

Conclusion:

There was a T1 (dropped keystroke) error in the first printing.

47) 83:7.6; p.928 ¶7 Change type: S2

1st - 9th, 12th - 14th, *CD*:

...a life-long partnership of self-effacement, compromise...

10th, 11th, 15th:

...a lifelong partnership of self-effacement, compromise...

Discussion:

Database standardization is a good justification for the change here and at (89:8.1) below, as out of the ten occurrences of *lifelong* or *life-long* in the text, only these two were hyphenated. However, the later changes and current discrepancies between printings are at odds with the presumed goal.

Although *Webster's* lists the compound word, differences between *Chicago Manual* editions may have given rise to the varied spellings. The 1927 and 1937 editions contain the general rule (as §251 or §213):

"Compounds of 'life' and 'world' require a hyphen:

life-history, life-principle (*but:* lifetime)..."

But the 1949 *Chicago Manual* modifies the rule slightly and lists *lifelong* as a specific example:

"§214. Compounds with 'god' and some compounds of 'life' require a hyphen:

...life-history, life-line, life-principle, life-story (*but:* lifeblood, lifelong, lifetime, etc.)"

Conclusion:

The 1955 spelling is an acceptable variant. However, database standardization (if consistently applied), could be a reasonable justification for adopting the compound form.

48) 86:5.13; p.955 ¶5 Change type: S4
    1st:
The children of Badanon developed a belief in two souls...
    2nd - 15th, *CD*:
The children of Badonan developed a belief in two souls...

Discussion:

Badonan is the correct spelling; *Badanon* was, no doubt, the result of an inadvertent key transposition.

Conclusion:

There was a T4 (key transposition) error in the 1955 text.

49) 89:8.1; p.982 ¶5 Change type: S2
    1st - 9th, 12th - 14th, *CD*:
...with dedication to life-long virginity...
    10th, 11th, 15th:
...with dedication to lifelong virginity...

Discussion:

See note for (83:7.6) above.

Conclusion:

As for (83:7.6) above, the 1955 spelling is an acceptable variant. However, database standardization (if consistently applied), could be a reasonable justification for adopting the compound form.

50) 90:2.9; p.988 ¶5 Change type: S4
    1st:
...the Shawnee Teuskwatawa, who predicted the eclipse of the sun...
    2nd - 15th, *CD*:
...the Shawnee Tenskwatawa, who predicted the eclipse of the sun...

Discussion:

Tenskwatawa is the standard transliteration for the Shawnee prophet's name; the spelling in the first printing may have been caused by a mistaken keystroke or may have been the result of an error in reading the original manuscript. (Regarding the latter possibility, see the note for 195:3.1.)

Conclusion:

An incorrect letter was present in the 1955 text. It is not possible to determine whether it was a T3 (incorrect keystroke) or T7 (mistaken reading of the manuscript) error.

51) 95:2.3; p.1044 ¶2 Change type: S6
    1st - 9th, 12th - 14th, *CD*:
...more particularly did each of the two-score separate tribes...
    10th, 11th, 15th:
...more particularly did each of the twoscore separate tribes...

Discussion:

The replacement of the original *two-score* with the compound *twoscore* is without support in *Webster's,* the *OED,* or the *Chicago Manual.*

Conclusion:

The 1955 text is correct.

52) 96:3.1; p.1055 ¶4 Change type: C1/C2

1st:

...from Egypt to the Arabian desert under his leadership.

2nd - 15th, *CD*:

...from Egypt to the Arabian Desert under his leadership.

Discussion:

Desert was not capitalized in the 1955 printing, but in all subsequent Urantia Foundation printings it was changed to the capitalized form. The original is appropriate if *desert* is a geographic description rather than part of a name. (See, for example, *Mediterranean coast* (96:2.1), *Nile valley* (96:2.2).)

The Uversa Press printing reflects the correct analysis by restoring this occurrence to its original form and by lowercasing the instance found three paragraphs later so that both of these are consistent with the other examples of this phrase found elsewhere in the text (95:7.1; 187:5.1).

Conclusion:

The 1955 text is correct.

53) 96:4.4; p.1057 ¶0 Change type: C1

1st:

...received the ten commandments which Moses promulgated...

2nd - 15th, *CD*:

...received the Ten Commandments which Moses promulgated...

Discussion:

The capitalized form is the standard approved by the *Chicago Manual*, however, of the six occurrences of this designation in the text, only one was capitalized in the first edition. Because it

is statistically unlikely that five of six would be random errors, a more reasonable explanation is required. In this editor's opinion, the lowercased version was the choice of the several authors because it reflected the evolutionary relationship of Moses' *ten commandments* to the earlier *seven commandments* of Melchizedek (93:4.6-13), the *seven commands* of Eden (74:7.5-6), and the *seven commands* of Dalamatia (66:7.8-15) [which are referenced as the *seven commandments* of Dalamatia at 74:7.6]. The single capitalized instance in the 1955 text is probably the result of a stylistic edit to conform with the usage prescribed by the *Chicago Manual*. (See also note at 137:2.9)

Conclusion:

The 1955 text probably reflects the original manuscript.

54) 98:4.1; p1081 ¶4 Change type: S4

1st:

The majority of people in the Graeco-Roman world...

2nd - 15th, *CD*:

The majority of people in the Greco-Roman world...

Discussion:

See note for 79:8.3 for a detailed analysis. It is interesting to note that these two occurrences are now found in two different forms in the electronic editions.

Conclusion:

The 1955 spelling, although slightly archaic, is correct. Neither "modernization" nor "standardization" has been achieved by the vagaries of later editing.

55) 101:3.4#1; p.1108 ¶4 Change type: P1

1st:

...adverse ani / malistic tendencies. [missing hyphen at end of line]

2nd - 11th:

...adverse ani-/ malistic tendencies. [hyphen inserted]

Discussion:

In the later printed printings, *animalistic* is not broken by a new line.

Conclusion:

There was a T1 (dropped keystroke) error in the 1955 text.

56) 104:3.9; p.1147 ¶8 Change type: P2

1st, 2nd, 15th:

...among absolute relationships; there are several existential triunities...

3rd - 14th, CD:

...among absolute relationships, there are several existential triunities...

Discussion:

The original punctuation was correct, as the use of a semi-colon is required to join two independent clauses.

Conclusion:

The 1955 text is correct.

57) 105:3.8; p.1156 ¶5 Change type: S1

1st:

Unifier of the deified and the undeified; corelater of the absolute...

2nd - 15th, CD:

Unifier of the deified and the undeified; correlator of the absolute...

Discussion:

Although it is possible that the original word (which is not found in either *Webster's* or the *OED*) was a

coined extension of *corelation* and *corelative* (both of which are found), it is not readily apparent how *corelater* would differ in meaning from *correlator(s)*, the now standard form, which is found five times elsewhere in the text. The more likely situation is that two separate typographical errors were made when this word was set. The first was a T1 (dropped keystroke) error at the end of a line of type; the second was an incorrect keystroke (T3) error, substituting *e* for *o*. This doubly misspelled word would still be difficult to catch in proofing because it would sound the same if read out loud, and interestingly enough, if it looked odd to a proofreader and consequently led him or her to consult the dictionary, the spelling could neither be confirmed nor denied by either *Webster's* or the *OED*—neither dictionary contained *correlator* or *corelater*—and without an electronically searchable text, it is unlikely that the evidence of the otherwise unanimous usage within the revelation itself could have been brought to bear on the problem.

Conclusion:

This word contained two errors in the 1955 printing. However, the external reference authorities available at the time did not contain the now standard spelling and provide reasonable etymological support for the possible validity of this variant form.

58) 105:3.9; p.1157 ¶0 Change type: S2

1st - 9th, 12th - 14th, CD:

...is invalidated by the eternity co-existence of the Son, the Spirit...

10th, 11th, 15th:

...is invalidated by the eternity coexistence of the Son, the Spirit...

Discussion:

The hyphenated form is not found elsewhere in the text and is not supported by the guidelines of the *Chicago Manual* or the reference dictionaries. (*Coexist* [no hyphen] and its various derivative forms are found twenty times throughout the *Papers.*)

Conclusion:

An error was present here in the 1955 text—possibly an extra keystroke in typing (T2), or, more likely, an editorial (E2) error.

59) 106:5.1; p.1167 ¶2 Change type: C2
1st:
...and the Unrevealed Consummator of Universe Destiny.
2nd - 15th, *CD*:
...and the unrevealed Consummator of Universe Destiny.

Discussion:

The lowercase version appears to be correct because *unrevealed* does not seem to be part of the name but is solely descriptive (the title being found in several places without *unrevealed* preceding it). In the one other case in which *unrevealed* is found in conjunction with *Consummator of Universe Destiny,* it is not capitalized (0:12.7). [*Unrevealed* is found in one other location as a capitalized component of a title—*The Unrevealed Creative Agencies of the Ancients of Days* (30:1.21)—so such a format is possible.]

Conclusion:

The capitalized *U* was a T3 error in the 1955 text.

60) 107:6.2; p.1182 ¶4 Change type: S6
1st - 5th, 10th - 15th, *CD*:
The Adjuster is man's eternity possibility;...
6th - 9th:
The Adjuster is man's eternal possibility;...

Discussion:

The original text does appear unusual at first glance because one expects a noun like *possibility* to be modified by an adjective such as *eternal;* not by another noun. In this situation however, *eternity* is not serving as an adjective, rather the two nouns together form a single concept or nominal group, identical in structure to the group which ends the subject sentence: *...man is the Adjuster's personality possibility.*

Conclusion:

The 1955 text is correct.

61) 109:7.2; p.1201 ¶3 Change type: S2
1st - 9th, 12th - 14th, *CD*:
Personalized Thought Adjusters are the untrammelled...
10th, 11th, 15th:
Personalized Thought Adjusters are the untrammeled...

Discussion:

Although both variants are acceptable, *untrammeled* is the unanimous usage elsewhere in the text and is preferred by the *Chicago Manual.*

Conclusion:

The 1955 text was not in error, but database standardization, if consistently applied, is a reasonable basis for making the suggested change.

62) 110:3.4; p.1206 ¶2 Change type: S2
1st - 9th, 12th - 14th, *CD*:
...wholly compatible with a light-hearted and joyous life...
10th, 11th, 15th:
...wholly compatible with a lighthearted and joyous life...

Discussion:

All other occurrences in the text follow the compound form: *lighthearted* (with the possible exception of one which is hyphenated at a line break). Database standardization is probably in order here, although it is interesting to note that this may be a stylistic variation as it is the only use of the word by an author other than the midwayers responsible for Part IV.

Conclusion:

The 1955 text was not in error, but database standardization, if consistently applied, is a reasonable basis for making the suggested change.

63) 110:5.2; p.1208 ¶1 Change type: S6
1st - 9th, 12th - 14th, *CD*:
...disconnected parade of the un-co-ordinated sleeping mind...
10th, 11th, 15th:
...disconnected parade of the unco-ordinated sleeping mind...

Discussion:

The original, fully hyphenated form is found in *Webster's*, and the fully closed form is found in the *OED*, but the hybrid of the 10th, 11th and, 15th printings is not found anywhere. The modified spelling also violates the general hyphenation guidelines of the *Chicago Manual* regarding the avoidance of forms which might cause

the reader to stumble over either pronunciation or meaning.

Conclusion:

The 1955 text is correct.

64) 117:7.4; p.1291 ¶8 Change type: P1
1st - 5th:
...of the Qualified Vicegerents of the Ultimate [missing period]
6th - 15th, *CD*:
...of the Qualified Vicegerents of the Ultimate. [period added]

Discussion:

This is one of two missing periods in the first printing. (*See* 80:2.4)

Conclusion:

There was a dropped keystroke (T1 error) in the 1955 text.

65) 118:6.2; p.1299 ¶5 Change type: S2
1st - 9th, 12th - 15th, *CD*:
...the freewillness of the myriads of the children of Deity...
10th, 11th:
...the free-willness of the myriads of the children of Deity...

Discussion:

Free-willness is found at four other locations in the text and all in instances refers to an attribute or characteristic of a being or beings. *Freewill* and *free will* each occur numerous times—the former as an adjective (modifying such words as *choice, action,* or *personality*), while the two-word form is used when *free* modifies *will* itself (i.e. when *will* is under discussion). In light of these consistent usages, conforming this variant is appropriate as the original was probably the result of a dropped hyphen.

Conclusion:

There was a dropped keystroke (T1 error) in the 1955 text.

66) 118:7.5; p.1301 ¶2 Change type: S2
1st - 6th:
Only as a creature becomes God identified...
7th - 15th, *CD*:
Only as a creature becomes God-identified...

Discussion:

Although *God identified* here, and its only related form, *God identification* (at 111:1.6) are both open (separate words) in the 1955 text, the guidelines within the *Chicago Manual* provide a good argument for both being hyphenated. In each case a single concept is referred to, and the missing hyphen causes the unsuspecting reader to stumble (albeit briefly) by suggesting here, "...as a creature becomes God..." and at 111:1.6, "...the exquisite melodies of God..."

Further, at the present location, the comparison with *God-unidentified* in the prior sentence is being made.

Conclusion:

The original text was not in error, but the hyphenated form would have been better.

67) 119:7.6; p.1317 ¶2 Change type: M2
1st:
These men of God visited the newborn child in the manger.
2nd - 15th, *CD*:
These men of God visited the newborn child.

Discussion:

Presumably, this change was made because the original seems to be inconsistent with the narrative of Jesus' birth in 122:8, which states that three wise men from the east visited Jesus when he was almost three weeks old—about the time the family left the inn and over two weeks after they had moved out of the stable.

However, it is certainly possible that Joseph and Mary might have taken the manger with them up to the room in the inn in order to continue to have a cradle for Jesus. The need for a cradle would have been no less in the room than in the stable, and if the manger was portable, as small feed-boxes often are, moving it along with the family seems quite reasonable.

Conclusion:

The 1955 text required no "correction."

68) 121:7.3; p.1340 ¶1 Change type: S1
1st - 10th:
...one who did not hestitate to clash with dogmas...
11th - 15th, *CD*:
...one who did not hesitate to clash with dogmas...

Discussion:

See note at 79:3.5.

Conclusion:

There was an extra keystroke (T2 error) in the 1955 text.

69) 123:2.3; p.1357 ¶7 Change type: S1
1st:
...one month before his fifth birthday anniversay...

2nd - 15th. *CD*:

...one month before his fifth birthday anniversary...

Discussion:

See note at 79:3.5.

Conclusion:

There was a dropped keystroke (T1 error) in the 1955 text.

70) 123:5.12; p.1363 ¶5 Change type: M3

1st:

Far to the east they could discern the Jordan valley and, far beyond, the rocky hills of Moab.

2nd - 15th, *CD*:

Far to the east they could discern the Jordan valley and far beyond lay the rocky hills of Moab.

Discussion:

As others have suggested, the March, 1959 letter from Rev. Benjamin Adams may well have provided the impetus for the change made here. [Rev. Adams: "But the rocky hills of Moab were not east of Nazareth but east of the Dead Sea."] Setting aside (as throughout these notes) a discussion of the nature of the editorial policy which allowed such changes to be made, an analysis of the 1955 text shows that there was no need to "correct" it in any case because the author of the paper does not state that the hills of Moab are east of Nazareth.

The context for this sentence is the "panoramic view" from atop the Nazareth hill: Jesus and his father are standing on top of the hill and are moving their gaze from Mt. Carmel in the northwest around an arc to the north, east, south and west. Mt. Hermon is to their north, and from springs in its

foothills near Dan (northeast of Nazareth) the Jordan valley extends to the Dead Sea in the south. Thus, as Jesus and Joseph follow the line of the river valley along the arc of their survey, as the Jordan approaches the Dead Sea, father and son "discern...far beyond, the rocky hills of Moab."

This interpretation is further supported by the punctuation of the following sentence which does **not** read "Also, to the south and the east,..." (suggesting a change in direction from the last reference), but rather, "Also to the south and the east,..." which implies that the last referenced location (Moab) was in the same direction.

Conclusion:

The 1955 text is correct.

71) 124:1.12; p.1368 ¶1 Change type: S2

1st - 9th, 12th - 14th, *CD*:

...on pleasure or business to nearby Cana, Endor, and Nain.

10th, 11th, 15th:

...on pleasure or business to near-by Cana, Endor, and Nain.

Discussion:

All other instances of *near-by* as an adjective are hyphenated; adverbs are open (*near by*), and the closed form, originally found here, is otherwise entirely absent from the text. Consistent usage would therefore support this change.

Conclusion:

There was a dropped hyphen (T1 error) in the 1955 text.

72) 126:1.2; p.1387 ¶2 Change type: S4

1st, 2nd:

Not far away he could look upon Tannach,...

3rd - 15th, CD:

Not far away he could look upon Taanach,...

Discussion:

The corrected spelling is the standard transliteration of the name.

Conclusion:

There was a mistaken keystroke (T3 error) in the 1955 text.

73) 126:1.5; p.1387 ¶5 Change type: S1

1st:

...some superhuman or miraculous peformance, but always...

2nd - 15th, CD:

...some superhuman or miraculous performance, but always...

Discussion:

See note at 79:3.5.

Conclusion:

There was a dropped keystroke (T1 error) in the 1955 text.

74) 130:6.3; p.1438 ¶0 Change type: S2

1st - 9th, 12th - 15th, CD:

...its abject fear-slave and the bond-servant of depression...

10th, 11th:

...its abject fear-slave and the bond servant of depression...

Discussion:

As discussed in greater detail in the note for 162:7.2, *bond servant* is found in three different forms in the first printing. The only form found in our primary references is the open form (*bond servant*) in *Webster's*. Although the hyphenated version could not be considered incorrect, and at this location it parallels *fear-slave* to good effect, database standardization around the open form would be reasonable.

Conclusion:

Database standardization could justify this change if consistently implemented.

75) 133:7.9; p.1480 ¶1 Change type: S1/S2

1st - 9th, 12th - 15th, CD:

...functioning of a consciousness sorter and associater...

10th, 11th:

...functioning of a consciousness sorter and associator...

Discussion:

While the meaning of *associater* is clear and that variant is found in a reference dating to 1626 in the *OED,* it is probably the result of a keystroke error because the common form, *associator,* is the unanimous usage elsewhere in the text. [Unlike other archaic English words occasionally used in *The Urantia Book* to convey unique meanings (e.g., *inconcussible* at 118:3.3), the ancient word-form *associater* did not convey a meaning distinct from *associator* and no such differentiation is apparent here.]

The original spelling may have been caused by a typist's inadvertent repetition of the *er* pattern from *sorter.*

Conclusion:

There was an incorrect keystroke (T3 error) in the 1955 text.

76) 134:7.5; p.1492 ¶5 Change type: S4
1st:
...Sychar, Schecham, Samaria, Geba,...
2nd - 15th, *CD*:
...Sychar, Shechem, Samaria, Geba,...

Discussion:

The standard transliteration is *Shechem*. [A similar problem occurred at 186:3.2.]

Conclusion:

An extra keystroke was inserted (T2) and a wrong keystroke (T3) was made.

77) 137:2.9; p.1527 ¶3 Change type: C1
1st:
...in the form of the ten commandments and other mottoes...
2nd - 15th, *CD*:
...in the form of the Ten Commandments and other mottoes...

Discussion:

See discussion in note for 96:4.4.

Conclusion:

For the reasons cited in earlier note, the 1955 text probably reflects the original manuscript.

78) 138:7.4; p.1544 ¶3 Change type: S2
1st - 9th, 12th - 14th, *CD*:
...this was their first clearcut and positive intimation...
10th, 11th, 15th:
...this was their first clear-cut and positive intimation...

Discussion:

This word is found eight additional times; all are hyphenated.

Conclusion:

The hyphen was missing (a T1 error) in the 1955 text; database standardization, if consistent, is appropriate.

79) 139:12.1; p.1566 ¶0 Change type: P1
1st - 6th:
Judas' parents were Sadducees, and when their son...
7th - 15th, *CD*:
Judas's parents were Sadducees, and when their son...

Discussion:

The correct form is *Judas's* and it is found that way at all other locations except 177:4.9.

Conclusion:

There was a missing *s* in the 1955 text (T1 error).

80) 139:12.12; p.1567 ¶5 Change type: S2
1st - 9th, 12th - 14th, *CD*:
...in these lucid intervals he faintheartedly conceived,...
10th, 11th, 15th:
...in these lucid intervals he faint-heartedly conceived,...

Discussion:

Usage is split between the two forms in the 1955 text. Though *Webster's* supports the closed form, the *OED* suggests using the hyphen and it is clear from the history of usage documented there that both forms have been commonly used. Database standardization is appropriate here, and this editor suggests that the hyphenated form be used for clarity's sake—in its closed form the word may cause the reader to momentarily stumble over the *th* at the joining of the words. (*see also* 190:3.1)

Conclusion:

The original text was not in error, but database standardization is appropriate.

81) 140:8.9; p.1583 ¶4 Change type: S6
1st - 9th, 12th - 14th, *CD*:
He was liberal, bighearted, learned, and tolerant.
10th, 11th, 15th:
He was liberal, big-hearted, learned, and tolerant.

Discussion:

The only other occurrence of this word is at 139:9.8, where it is hyphenated. Given that this compound could not be considered common in current usage, the hyphenated form is preferable.

Conclusion:

The original text was not in error, but database standardization is appropriate.

82) 142:8.4; p.1606 ¶1 Change type: S6
1st - 9th, 12th - 14th, *CD*:
The Sabbath week ends they usually spent with Lazarus...
10th, 11th, 15th:
The Sabbath weekends they usually spent with Lazarus...

Discussion:

The two-word form is supported by *Webster's;* the hyphenated form (*week-end*) by the *OED,* but the closed form is not found in any of the contemporary sources.

Conclusion:

The 1955 text is correct.

83) 147:5.1; p.1651 ¶5 Change type: S2
1st - 9th, 12th - 14th, *CD*:
He was a half-hearted believer, and notwithstanding...
10th, 11th, 15th:
He was a halfhearted believer, and notwithstanding...

Discussion:

The closed form is the unanimous usage elsewhere in the text, so database standardization is reasonable.

Conclusion:

The original was not in error, but standardization is appropriate.

84) 149:6.12; p.1677 ¶1 Change type: M1
1st:
Of all the sorrows of a trusting man, none are so terrible...
2nd - 15th, *CD*:
Of all the sorrows of a trusting man, none is so terrible...

Discussion:

As at 55:12.5, the original is correct; *none* commonly takes a plural verb.

Conclusion:

The 1955 text is correct.

85) 151:6.2; p.1695 ¶5 Change type: S2
1st - 9th, 13th, 14th, *CD*:
...with fetters and chains and confined in one of the grottos.
10th - 12th, 15th:
...with fetters and chains and confined in one of the grottoes.

Discussion:

Though both forms are correct, this word is found elsewhere in the text as *grottoes.* Therefore, database standardization would be reasonable.

Conclusion:

The original was not in error, but standardization is appropriate.

86) 152:3.2; p.1702 ¶3 Change type: S2
1st - 9th, 12th - 14th, *CD*:
...but you are short-sighted and material-minded.
10th, 11th, 15th:
...but you are shortsighted and material-minded.

Discussion:

The closed form is the unanimous usage elsewhere, so database standardization would be reasonable.

Conclusion:

The original was not in error, but standardization is appropriate.

87) 153:1.7; p.1709 ¶1 Change type: S5
1st - 9th, 12th - 14th, *CD*:
Jairus' only reply to all this pleading was:...
10th, 11th, 15th:
Jairus's only reply to all this pleading was:...

Discussion:

The corrected form is supported by usage elsewhere and by the general rules in the *Chicago Manual* regarding the formation of possessives for ancient names.

Conclusion:

There was a missing *s* in the 1955 text (T1 error).

88) 158:4.6; p.1756 ¶3 Change type: P2
1st, 2nd:
Come out of him you unclean spirit;...

3rd - 15th, *CD*:
Come out of him, you unclean spirit;...

Discussion:

While a comma here is not unreasonable, it is also not necessary.

Conclusion:

The 1955 text does not need correction.

89) 158:7.1; p.1759 ¶3 Change type: P2
1st - 6th:
The apostles had slept very little that night; so they were up early...
7th - 15th, *CD*:
The apostles had slept very little that night, so they were up early...

Discussion:

The stronger separation created by the semi-colon may be unnecessary, but it is also not incorrect.

Conclusion:

The 1955 text does not need correction.

90) 159:1.3; p.1763 ¶0 Change type: P2
1st - 6th:
...whatsoever you shall decree on earth, shall be recognized in heaven.
7th - 15th, *CD*:
...whatsoever you shall decree on earth shall be recognized in heaven.

Discussion:

This is another case of reasonable punctuation by the author that hardly stands in need of correction by an editor.

Conclusion:

The 1955 text does not need correction.

91) 162:2.3; p.1791 ¶1 Change type: C2
1st - 6th:
By refusing to hear me, you are refusing to receive Him who sends me.
7th - 15th, *CD*:
By refusing to hear me, you are refusing to receive him who sends me.

Discussion:

Capitalization of *Him* at this point is correct usage and is required for clarity. (See note for 3:1.12.)

Conclusion:

The 1955 text is correct.

92) 162:2.3; p.1791 ¶1 Change type: C2
1st - 6th:
You, if you will receive this gospel, shall come to know Him who sent me.
7th - 15th, *CD*:
You, if you will receive this gospel, shall come to know him who sent me.

Discussion:

Capitalization of *Him* at this point is correct usage and is required for clarity. (See note for 3:1.12.)

Conclusion:

The 1955 text is correct.

93) 162:2.4; p.1791 ¶2 Change type: P2
1st:
...wonderful than this Jesus of Nazareth has already done?"
2nd - 15th, *CD*:
...wonderful than this Jesus of Nazareth has already done."

Discussion:

While it may be true that the sentence is declarative, the question mark does seem to more acceptably convey the wondering attitude of the people, and it does not confuse the reader. In the absence of compelling evidence that an error has been made, any reasonable punctuation in the 1955 text should be left alone—as the presumed choice of the author.

Conclusion:

The 1955 punctuation does not require correction.

94) 162:2.7; p.1792 ¶1 Change type: C2
1st - 6th:
In just a short time I go to Him who sent me into this world.
7th - 15th, *CD*:
In just a short time I go to him who sent me into this world.

Discussion:

The original is supported by the *Chicago Manual* and by consistent usage in *The Urantia Book*. See note for 3:1.12 for full discussion.

Conclusion:

The 1955 text is correct.

95) 162:5.2; p.1795 ¶1 Change type: M1
1st, 2nd:
You only judge by the appearances of the flesh;...
3rd - 15th, *CD*:
You judge only by the appearances of the flesh;...

Discussion:

While the modified construction may represent adverbial placement "by the rules," the original is perfectly intelligible and conforms with ordinary usage. Regarding the placement of *only,* H. W. Fowler's *A Dictionary of Modern English Usage* (Oxford, 1926), among other examples, cites the common, "He

Merritt Horn's Findings

only died a week ago," in which, technically (as in the subject phrase), the author ought to have located *only* after the verb: "He died only a week ago." Fowler, however, rejects the absolutism of "orthodoxy" and concludes:

"The advice offered is this: there is an orthodox position for the adverb, easily determined in case of need; to choose another position that may spoil or obscure the meaning is bad; but a change of position that has no such effect except technically is both justified by historical and colloquial usage but often demanded by rhetorical needs."

Conclusion:

The 1955 text is clear, and well within the bounds of normal usage.

96) 162:7.2; p.1796 ¶4 Change type: S2
1st - 9th:
...who commits sin is the bond-servant of sin. [*line break at hyphen*]
10th, 11th:
...who commits sin is the bond servant of sin. [*identical line break w/ no hyphen*]
12th - 15th:
...who commits sin is the bondservant of sin. [*no line break*]
CD:
...who commits sin is the bond-servant of sin. [*no line break*]

Discussion:

In the 1955 text, this word is hyphenated and is broken at the hyphen to begin a new line of type, so it is impossible to determine whether *bond-servant* or *bondservant* was intended. The only form that the type (as set) could not have represented was *bond servant*. In the following sentence, *bondservant* is found as one word, so it would be a

reasonable assumption that the same closed form was intended here. Both *bond servant* and *bond-servant* are found once elsewhere in the Urantia papers (69:5.8 and 130:6.3, respectively). In the 10th and 11th Urantia Foundation printings, both occurrences in the present paragraph were separated into two words, as was the 130:6.3 instance, thus standardizing all four to the two-word format. Database standardization would be reasonable for this word, but the electronic editions and the printed texts subsequent to the 11th have diverged (as noted).

Conclusion: *

Database standardization, if consistently applied, would be reasonable, though the original text was not in error.

97) 162:7.2; p.1796 ¶4 Change type: S2
1st - 9th, 12th - 15th, *CD*:
And you know that the bondservant is not likely...
10th, 11th
And you know that the bond servant is not likely...

Discussion:

No line break is found here in any printing. See previous note for more information.

Conclusion:

Database standardization, if consistently applied, would be reasonable, though the original text was not in error.

98) 164:5.6; p.1816 ¶3 Change type: P2
1st - 10th, 12th - 15th, *CD*:
With the two apostles and Josiah the Master went back to Pella.

11th:

With the two apostles and Josiah, the Master went back to Pella.

Discussion:

A comma could assist the reader in phrasing the sentence, but it is hardly necessary.

Conclusion:

The 1955 text does not require correction.

99) 165:0.3; p.1817 ¶3 Change type: S4

1st:

...from these regions during the times of Judas Maccabeus.

2nd - 15th, *CD*:

...from these regions during the times of Judas Maccabee.

Discussion:

Although *Maccabeus* is a more accurate transliteration of the Greek, *Maccabee* is very common in English works and is used in all other occurrences of the word in the Urantia papers. Database standardization is appropriate here.

Conclusion:

Database standardization is reasonable, though the original text was not in error.

100) 166:3.4; p.1829 ¶1 Change type: P2

1st, 2nd:

Lord open to us; we would also be great in the kingdom.

3rd - 15th, *CD*:

Lord, open to us; we would also be great in the kingdom.

Discussion:

In the original format, *Lord* was the last word in the line, making a dropped

comma not unlikely. It is possible that the comma was simply viewed as unnecessary within such a short phrase, and it should also be noted that while the use of the comma in direct address is regarded as standard, the *Chicago Manual* was silent on the matter until its 12th edition (1969).

Conclusion:

It cannot be determined whether an error in typesetting was made here, but the end-of-line location tips the balance in favor of making the change adopted in the 3rd printing.

101) 167:4.3; p.1837 ¶2 Change type: P2

1st - 10th, 12th - 15th, *CD*:

...so that on the second, or even the third, day such a one...

11th:

...so that on the second, or even the third day such a one...

Discussion:

Although the second comma seems clumsy, it is required to enclose the parenthetical phrase *or even the third.*

Conclusion:

The 1955 text is correct.

102) 167:5.3; p.1839 ¶0 Change type: S2

1st - 9th, 12th - 15th, *CD*:

...he had become enamoured of a better-looking woman.

10th, 11th:

...he had become enamored of a better-looking woman.

Discussion:

This word is also found at 121:5.6; there, the American spelling, *enamored,* is used. Both forms are acceptable, though database standardization would justify the choice of one over the other.

Conclusion:

Database standardization, if consistently applied, would be reasonable, though the original text was not in error.

103) 168:0.2; p.1842 ¶2 Change type: D1/S6

1st, 2nd, 10th, 11th, 15th:
...and Mary sent word to Jesus concerning Lazarus's illness,...

3rd - 9th, 12th - 14th, CD:
...and Mary sent word to Jesus concerning Lazarus' illness,...

Discussion:

The original version, *Lazarus's,* is correct. Although the missing final *s* in the 3rd through 9th printings might have originally been due to a database conversion error, it is not known why the incorrect form was again adopted for the softcover and electronic editions.

Conclusion:

The 1955 text is correct.

104) 168:3.7; p.1847 ¶7 Change type: S4

1st - 3rd:
...with friends in Bethpage, a hamlet near Bethany.

4th - 15th, CD:
...with friends in Bethphage, a hamlet near Bethany.

Discussion:

The 1955 text uses *Bethpage* in all thirteen occurrences of this word. In the 4th printing, the original was changed to *Bethphage* here, and at ten other locations; the remaining two were changed in the 9th printing. These changes were presumably made because *Bethphage* is the spelling found in English Bibles since the *Authorized Version* (King James) of 1611. While the apparent misspelling in *The Urantia Book* is not theologically or historically significant, it seems unlikely to the present editor that so many identical typographical errors could have occurred, so the spelling *Bethpage* must have been used in the original manuscript.

Whenever names are translated from one language into another (based on the name's sound rather than its meaning), different transliterations are often chosen by different translators because it can be difficult to transfer sounds precisely from one language to another. Some modern examples would be Peking/ Beijing, Cambodia/Kampuchea and Ceylon/Sri Lanka. This phenomenon also occurs when translating ancient names into modern languages: Akenaton/Ikhnaton, Jerome/ Hieronymus, Nimrod/Nimrud, Beth Shean/Beth Sha'an/Beth Shan, Khufu/ Chefren, etc.

The Greek form of the word in question is $B\eta\theta\varphi\alpha\gamma\eta$. It is found in only 3 places in the New Testament (Mat. 21:1, Mk 11:1, Lk 19:29). Using standard transliteration principles, it would become *Bethphage* in English, and that is how it is found in modern Bibles. However, the usual rules for transliteration do not always produce the most accurate rendering of the original, and may be overruled when appropriate. An example closely related to the present case is the word $K\alpha\varphi\alpha\rho\nu\alpha\upsilon\mu$: if transliterated by the same standard rules, it would become *Capharnaum*, but *The Urantia Book* and English Bibles use *Capernaum* instead. Why? $K\alpha\varphi\alpha\rho\nu\alpha\upsilon\mu$

is found throughout the New Testament; it is hard to talk about Jesus without talking about Καφαρναυμ. So it is natural that translators would attend more carefully to accuracy of transliteration and to ease of vocalization in English. It is this editor's belief that that is precisely what the authors of *The Urantia Book* did when they chose *Bethpage* over *Bethphage*. The former is a more accurate approximation of the Greek original, is much easier for English speakers to say, and doesn't sound like a type of plague.

[As to the origin of the general error of converting φ into the *f* sound in English: In Latin, *ph* was used to replace the Greek φ and was pronounced properly as an aspirated consonant (as in *uphill*). However, English speakers pronounced Greek φ and Latin *ph* as *f* because of a mistaken inference from certain Latin and Greek cognates such as *frater/φρατηρ*. This conversion is well-evidenced in common English words such as *philosophy* and *pharmacy*, but it is not accurate, and certainly does not need to be adopted for an unfamiliar place name like Βηθφαγη*Bethpage]*.

Conclusion:

The 1955 spelling was intended by the authors and needs no revision.

105) 168:5.1; p.1849 ¶5 Change type: M2

1st:
...until the day of the crucifixion of Jesus,...

2nd - 15th, *CD*:
...until the week of the crucifixion of Jesus,...

Discussion:

The change from *day* to *week* was made, because the former is inconsistent

with the ensuing narrative (at 174:0.1, 175:3.1, and 177:5.3) which would place the time of Lazarus's flight between Tuesday at midnight (when his death was decreed by the Sanhedrin) and Wednesday evening (when "certain ones" at the camp "knew that Lazarus had taken hasty flight from Bethany")— two days before the crucifixion of Jesus.

Other than a mistaken pre-publication (E1) change, this editor does not presently have a theory to explain this problem with the 1955 text.

Conclusion:

The 1955 text appears to be inconsistent with itself at this point; the origin of the error is not known.

106) 169:3.2; p.1855 ¶0 Change type: M1

1st, 2nd:
...a certain beggar named Lazarus, who laid at this rich man's gate,...

3rd - 15th, *CD*:
...a certain beggar named Lazarus, who lay at this rich man's gate,...

Discussion:

This sentence, as structured, does require *lay* rather than *laid,* the former being the past tense of the intransitive verb *to lie;* the latter being the past of the transitive verb *to lay.* However, it is this editor's opinion that the error here is not poor grammar by the author, but a lost word in transcription. The authors of Part IV of *The Urantia Book* generally follow the text of the *American Standard Version* (*ASV*) of 1901, with certain modernizations and corrections as needed. The *ASV* text of Luke 16:19-21 is as follows:

"Now there was a certain rich man, and he was clothed in purple and fine linen, faring sumptuously every day: *and a certain beggar named Lazarus was laid at his gate*, full of sores, and desiring to be fed with the crumbs that fell from the rich man's table; yea, even the dogs came and licked his sores." [emphasis added]

The passage from *The Urantia Book* follows the *ASV* very closely:

"There was a certain rich man named Dives, who, being clothed in purple and fine linen, lived in mirth and splendor every day. *And there was a certain beggar named Lazarus, who laid at this rich man's gate*, covered with sores and desiring to be fed with the crumbs which fell from the rich man's table; yes, even the dogs came and licked his sores." [emphasis added]

If the *ASV* narrative provides the structure for the subject passage, the grammatical problem observed in the original text was caused by the inadvertent loss of *was,* which should have immediately preceded *laid.*

Additional contextual support for this argument is based on the beggar's inability to fend for himself. If "even the dogs came and licked his sores," he surely would have been carried to the rich man's gate by others, who would then have *laid* him there.

Conclusion:

There was a T6 error made here at some point in the preparation of the text, and "who was laid" became "who laid."

107) 172:0.2; p.1878 ¶2 Change type: S4

1st - 3rd:
...the common folks of Bethany and Bethpage did their best...

4th - 15th, *CD*:
...the common folks of Bethany and Bethphage did their best...

Discussion:

See note for 168:3.7.

Conclusion:

The 1955 spelling was intended by the authors and needs no revision.

108) 172:1.2; p.1878 ¶5 Change type: S4

1st - 8th:
...all Bethany and Bethpage joined in celebrating...

9th - 15th, *CD*:
...all Bethany and Bethphage joined in celebrating...

Discussion:

See note for 168:3.7.

Conclusion:

The 1955 spelling was intended by the authors and needs no revision.

109) 172:3.6; p.1881 ¶4 Change type: S4

1st - 3rd:
...directing them to go over to Bethpage,...

4th - 15th, *CD*:
...directing them to go over to Bethphage,...

Discussion:

See note for 168:3.7.

Conclusion:

The 1955 spelling was intended by the authors and needs no revision.

110) 172:3.6; p.1881 ¶4 Change type: S4

1st - 3rd:
Go to Bethpage, and when you come...

4th - 15th, *CD*:
Go to Bethphage, and when you come...

Discussion:

See note for 168:3.7.

Conclusion:

The 1955 spelling was intended by the authors and needs no revision.

111) 172:3.6; p.1881 ¶4 Change type: S4

1st - 3rd:

...when the two apostles had gone into Bethpage...

4th - 15th, *CD*:

...when the two apostles had gone into Bethphage...

Discussion:

See note for 168:3.7.

Conclusion:

The 1955 spelling was intended by the authors and needs no revision.

112) 172:4.3; p.1883 ¶5 Change type: S4

1st - 3rd:

...among their friends in Bethany and Bethpage.

4th - 15th, *CD*:

...among their friends in Bethany and Bethphage.

Discussion:

See note for 168:3.7.

Conclusion:

The 1955 spelling was intended by the authors and needs no revision.

113) 172:5.2; p.1884 ¶1 Change type: S5

1st, 2nd:

...some of the twelve whom he knew were armed with swords;...

3rd - 15th, *CD*:

...some of the twelve who he knew were armed with swords;...

Discussion:

The pronoun is the subject of the verb *were armed,* not the object of *knew;* therefore *who* is the correct form (see also 177:5.2). To illustrate:

...some of the twelve *whom* he knew Peter had armed...[he knew Peter had armed *them*]

...some of the twelve *who* he knew were armed...[he knew *they* were armed]

Conclusion:

Either a T2 (extra keystroke) error, or an E2 (mistakenly "corrected" grammar) error occurred here, causing *whom* to appear in the 1955 text. (There is also an identical error two sentences prior to this which was corrected in the Uversa Press printing.)

114) 175:1.20; p.1908 ¶4 Change type: C2

1st - 6th:

...while you plot to destroy Him of whom they spoke.

7th - 15th, *CD*:

...while you plot to destroy him of whom they spoke.

Discussion:

Capitalization of *Him* at this point is correct usage and is required for clarity. (See note for 3:1.12.)

Conclusion:

The 1955 text is correct.

115) 176:4.1; p.1918 ¶4 Change type: P2

1st - 5th:

...his seventh and last bestowal, as a mortal of the realm.

6th - 15th, *CD*:

...his seventh and last bestowal as a mortal of the realm.

Discussion:

The comma is required to give the sentence its correct meaning:

Urantia was the place of Michael's seventh and last bestowal, as a mortal of the realm. [the seventh bestowal—the one in which he was a mortal of the realm]

Not:

Urantia was the place of Michael's seventh and last bestowal as a mortal of the realm. [his seventh bestowal as a mortal]

Conclusion:

The 1955 text is correct.

116) 177:3.7; p.1924 ¶3 Change type: S3
1st:
...why he would be willing to forego the great advantage...

2nd - 15th, CD:
...why he would be willing to forgo the great advantage...

Discussion:

Although *forgo* is etymologically preferable, *forego* has been in use for over 400 years and leads to no confusion; *forego* is also found at two other locations in the text, while *forgo* is absent altogether. In addition, *forego* appears (for the first time for either form) as the preference in the 11th edition (1949) of the *Chicago Manual* (§122).

Conclusion:

The usage in the 1955 text is consistent and reasonable.

117) 177:4.9; p.1926 ¶2 Change type: S6
1st, 2nd,11th,13th,14th:
...Judas's betrayal of Jesus was the cowardly act...

3rd - 10th, 12th, 15th, CD:
...Judas' betrayal of Jesus was the cowardly act...

Discussion:

The correct form is *Judas's* and it is found that way at all locations in the 1955 text except 139:12.1. It is not known why the correct form was changed in the first place, or why it has been changed and changed back again so many times in recent printings.

Conclusion:

The 1955 text is correct.

118) 177:5.2; p.1927 ¶3 Change type: S5
1st, 2nd:
...still others whom you think love the truth will be scattered,...

3rd - 15th, CD:
...still others who you think love the truth will be scattered,...

Discussion:

This is a situation similar to that found at 172:5.2. The pronoun concerned is the subject of *love,* not the object of *think;* therefore *who* is the correct form. To illustrate:

...others whom you think Jesus loved... [you think Jesus loved *them*]

...others who you think love the truth... [you think *they* love the truth]

Conclusion:

Either a T2 (extra keystroke) error, or an E2 (mistakenly "corrected" grammar) error occurred here, causing *whom* to appear in the 1955 text.

119) 179:5.9; p.1943 ¶2Change type:
M2

1st:

...he said to the twelve: "And as often as
you do this,...

2nd -15th, *CD*:

...he said to the apostles: "And as often
as you do this,...

Discussion:

There were only eleven apostles still
present for the establishment of the
remembrance supper because Judas had
left earlier; so the *twelve* of the 1955 text
was incorrect, and was changed to
apostles to make this sentence consistent
with the rest of the narrative.

The error may have originated either
as an inadvertent pattern error (T5) for
either *eleven* or *apostles,* or through an
E1 error (the conscious but mistaken
"correction" of the original based on the
assumption that an earlier T5 error had
occurred).

Conclusion:

The 1955 text contained either a T5
or E1 error.

120) 183:4.3; p.1976 ¶1 Change type: S4

1st - 3rd:

... went into hiding at Bethpage and
Bethany.

4th - 15th, *CD*:

... went into hiding at Bethphage and
Bethany.

Discussion:

See note for 168:3.7.

Conclusion:

The 1955 spelling was intended by
the authors and needs no revision.

121) 184:3.1; p.1982 ¶2Change type: S6

1st - 9th,12th, *CD*:

...on informal charges of law-breaking,
blasphemy,...

10th, 11th, 13th - 15th:

...on informal charges of lawbreaking,
blasphemy,...

Discussion:

Of the five occurrences of
lawbreak[er] [-ing] in the text, three are
closed and two are hyphenated. There is
no differential in meaning indicated by
the two forms, so database
standardization is appropriate. (Note,
however, that the electronic texts do not
reflect this standardization.)

Conclusion:

The 1955 text was not in error, but
database standardization, if consistently
applied, justifies this change.

122) 184:3.12; p.1983 ¶7Change type:
S6

1st - 9th,12th, *CD*:

...be done with this law-breaker and
blasphemer?

10th, 11th, 13th - 15th:

...be done with this lawbreaker and
blasphemer?

Discussion:

See note for 184:3.1.

Conclusion:

The 1955 text was not in error, but
database standardization, if consistently
applied, justifies this change.

123) 186:3.2; p.2001 ¶0 Change type: S4

1st:

...Philadelphia, Sidon, Schechem,
Hebron, Damascus, and Alexandria.

2nd - 15th, *CD*:

...Philadelphia, Sidon, Shechem, Hebron, Damascus, and Alexandria.

Discussion:

The standard transliteration is *Shechem*. [A similar problem occurred at 134:7.5.]

Conclusion:

An extra keystroke was inserted (T2) in the 1955 text.

124) 186:5.5; p.2002 ¶6 Change type: P2

1st:

...throughout the universe of universes, have existed from eternity;...

2nd - 15th, *CD*:

...throughout the universe of universes have existed from eternity;...

Discussion:

This comma is not appropriate as found in the 1955 text. Either it was inserted in error (a T2 mistake), or a second comma earlier in the sentence was inadvertently dropped (a T1 error). In this editor's view, the latter explanation is more likely; and the missing comma would have been located immediately following *Maker,* which would create an enclosed parenthetical statement. The complete sentence would read as follows:

"These touching and divinely beautiful relations between man and his Maker, on this world and on all others throughout the universe of universes, have existed from eternity; and they are not in any sense dependent on these periodic bestowal enactments of the Creator Sons of God, who thus assume the nature and likeness of their created intelligences as a part of the price which they must pay

for the final acquirement of unlimited sovereignty over their respective local universes."

Conclusion:

Either a T1 or a T2 error exists in the 1955 text.

125) 189:4.1; p.2025 ¶2 Change type: S4

1st - 3rd:

...going to the home of Simon in Bethpage,...

4th - 15th, *CD*:

...going to the home of Simon in Bethphage,...

Discussion:

See note for 168:3.7.

Conclusion:

The 1955 spelling was intended by the authors and needs no revision.

126) 190:2.5; p.2032 ¶3 Change type: S4

1st - 8th:

...even while they looked for him at Bethpage,...

9th - 15th, *CD*:

...even while they looked for him at Bethphage,...

Discussion:

See note for 168:3.7.

Conclusion:

The 1955 spelling was intended by the authors and needs no revision.

127) 190:3.1; p.2033 ¶1 Change type: S6

1st - 9th, 12th -14th, *CD*:

...strengthen those who are fainthearted and fear-ridden.

10th, 11th, 15th:
...strengthen those who are faint-hearted and fear-ridden.

Discussion:

See note for 139:12.12.

Conclusion:

The original text was not in error, but database standardization is appropriate.

128) 191:0.1; p.2037 ¶1 Change type: S4
1st - 3rd:
Thomas was brooding over his troubles alone at Bethpage.
4th - 15th, *CD*:
Thomas was brooding over his troubles alone at Bethphage.

Discussion:

See note for 168:3.7.

Conclusion:

The 1955 spelling was intended by the authors and needs no revision.

129) 191:0.13; p.2039 ¶0 Change type: S4
1st - 3rd:
John Mark located Thomas at the home of Simon in Bethpage...
4th - 15th, *CD*:
John Mark located Thomas at the home of Simon in Bethphage...

Discussion:

See note for 168:3.7.

Conclusion:

The 1955 spelling was intended by the authors and needs no revision.

130) 191:0.13; p.2039 ¶0 Change type: S4
1st - 3rd:
...John went over to Bethpage and brought him back with them.
4th - 15th, *CD*:   .
..John went over to Bethphage and brought him back with them.

Discussion:

See note for 168:3.7.

Conclusion:

The 1955 spelling was intended by the authors and needs no revision.

131) 192:4.5; p.2051 ¶2 Change type: S6
1st - 9th, 12th - 14th, *CD*:
This was a sad home-coming for John Mark.
10th, 11th, 15th:
This was a sad homecoming for John Mark.

Discussion:

The only other instance of *home-coming* in the text (at 150:7.3) is broken at the hyphen by the end of a line, so it could support either spelling. Only the hyphenated form is found in *Webster's,* and the *Chicago Manual* gives no guidance. The original should therefore have been left alone.

Conclusion:

The 1955 text is correct.

132) 195:3.10; p.2074 ¶5 Change type: S4
1st:
Poutaenus taught Clement and then went on to follow Nathaniel...
2nd -15th, *CD*:

Pantaenus taught Clement and then went on to follow Nathaniel...

Discussion:

The correct spelling of this name is *Pantaenus;* Dr. Sadler, in a March 17, 1959 letter to the Reverend Benjamin Adams of San Francisco, suggested the possible source of the error:

"I think the spelling of the name of the teacher in Alexandria is undoubtedly an error in transcribing the manuscript into typewriting. An "an" was undoubtedly transcribed as an "ou". I remember when we were sometimes in doubt as to whether a letter was an "n" or a "u" in the manuscript. Of course, we who were preparing this matter, did not know the name of this teacher so could have easily made this mistake."

Conclusion:

Two incorrect letters were present in the 1955 text. There is evidence to support a T7 (mistaken reading of the manuscript) error.

133) 196:3.29; p.2097 ¶3 Change type: P1

1st:

And the spirit of the Father is in his Son's sons—mortal men.

2nd - 15th, *CD*:

And the spirit of the Father is in is Sons' sons—mortal men

Discussion:

Sons' does appear to be correct in view of the context.

Conclusion:

A T4 error (transposed keystrokes) was present in the 1955 text.

APPENDIX E

The International Copyright Status
of *The Urantia Book*

The International Copyright Status
of The Urantia Book

This information is compiled from public, on-line (Internet) records of the United Nations, the World Intellectual Property Organization, the World Trade Organization, the Berne Convention, the U.S. Copyright Office, and other sources. It has not been possible to examine the national copyright laws of every nation of the world in detail in English, so there may be instances in which the term of protection is unexpectedly brief (as was found to be the case of Hungary and Canada) or unusually long (as is the case for Brazil, Slovenia, and the United States) in addition to the specific instances captured in this analysis.

Note: Generally speaking, for anonymous works, countries either provide no international copyright protection, provide it for 50 years from first publication in country of origin (Berne Convention and/or World Trade Organization), or provide it for 70 years from first publication (European Union). Local laws and international treaties are, of course, constantly being revised.

A. Countries in which The Urantia Book has never been subject to copyright, either because of non-recognition of international copyrights or because of local laws in regard to anonymous and pseudonymous works.

Afghanistan, Algeria, Andorra, Armenia, Azerbaijan, Belarus, Bhutan, Cambodia, Cape Verde, Comoros, Democratic People's Republic of Korea, Equatorial Guinea, Eritrea, Ethiopia, Hungary, Iran (Islamic Republic of), Iraq, Kazakhstan, Kiribati, Lao People's Democratic Republic, Marshall Islands, Micronesia (Federated States of), Nauru, Nepal, Oman, Palau, Samoa, San Marino, Sao Tome and Principe, Saudi Arabia, Seychelles, Somalia, Sudan, Syrian Arab Republic, Tajikistan, Tonga, Turkmenistan, Uzbekistan, Vanuatu, Viet Nam, and Yemen.

Note: *Hungary does not recognize copyright in anonymous and pseudonymous works except when the author is known to be a citizen of Hungary.*

B. Countries in which The Urantia Book was once protected by copyright, but where copyright protection ended in 1985.
Canada.

Note: The Supreme Court of Canada has held that copyright protection for anonymous and pseudonymous works extends for only 50 years from date of creation (not publication).

C. Countries in which The Urantia Book is technically protected by copyright, grouped by the last year into which that copyright protection extends.

Copyright through 2005:
Albania, Angola, Antigua and Barbuda, Argentina, Australia, Bahamas, Bahrain, Bangladesh, Barbados, Belize, Benin, Bolivia, Bosnia and Herzegovina, Botswana, Brunei Darussalam, Bulgaria, Burkina Faso, Burundi, Cameroon, Central African Republic, Chad, Chile, China, Colombia, Congo, Costa Rica, Côte d'Ivoire, Croatia, Cuba, Cyprus, Czech Republic, Democratic Republic of the Congo, Djibouti, Dominica,

Dominican Republic, Ecuador, Egypt, El Salvador, Estonia, Fiji, Gabon, Gambia, Georgia, Ghana, Grenada, Guatemala, Guinea, Guinea-Bissau, Guyana, Haiti, Holy See, Honduras, Hong Kong, China, Iceland, India, Indonesia, Israel, Jamaica, Japan, Jordan, Kenya, Kuwait, Kyrgyzstan, Latvia, Lebanon, Lesotho, Liberia, Libyan Arab Jamahiriya, Liechtenstein, Lithuania, Macau, China, Madagascar, Malawi, Malaysia, Maldives, Mali, Malta, Mauritania, Mauritius, Mexico, Monaco, Mongolia, Morocco, Mozambique, Myanmar, Namibia, New Zealand, Nicaragua, Niger, Nigeria, Norway, Pakistan, Panama, Papua New Guinea, Paraguay, Peru, Philippines, Poland, Qatar, Republic of Korea, Republic of Moldova, Romania, Russian Federation, Rwanda, Saint Kitts and Nevis, Saint Lucia, Saint Vincent and the Grenadines, Senegal, Sierra Leone, Singapore, Slovakia, Solomon Islands, South Africa, Sri Lanka, Suriname, Swaziland, Sweden, Switzerland, Thailand, The former Yugoslav Republic of Macedonia, Togo, Trinidad and Tobago, Tunisia, Turkey, Uganda, Ukraine, United Arab Emirates, United Republic of Tanzania, Uruguay, Venezuela, Yugoslavia, Zaire, Zambia, and Zimbabwe.

Copyright through 2015 Brazil.

Copyright through 2025 Austria, Belgium, Denmark, Finland, France, Germany, Greece, Ireland, Italy, Luxembourg, Netherlands, Portugal, Slovenia, Spain, and United Kingdom.

Copyright through 2050 United States of America.

Submitted by Norm Du Val, http://www.freeurantia.org

APPENDIX F

Key pages from Urantia
Foundation Declaration of Trust

URANTIA

Declaration of Trust

creating

URANTIA FOUNDATION

Published by
URANTIA FOUNDATION
533 Diversey Parkway, Chicago, Illinois 60614
®:Registered Mark of URANTIA Foundation

COVER

DECLARATION OF TRUST

Declaration of Trust

KNOW ALL MEN BY THESE PRESENTS, THAT WHEREAS, there has been written a manuscript of a book entitled "THE URANTIA BOOK," and there have been produced from this manuscript approximately two thousand two hundred (2,200) nickel-plated stereotype plates of patent base thickness for the printing and reproduction of such book; and

The Plates are described in this paragraph. The manuscript from which they were produced was destroyed after the plates were cast.

WHEREAS, certain persons, hereinafter referred to as the "Contributors," being desirous that a foundation be created for the objects herein expressed to be known as "URANTIA FOUNDATION," have contributed certain funds to that end, and said funds have been expended for the production of said plates for the printing and reproduction of THE URANTIA BOOK; and

The "Contributors" of the plates establish their ownership of them.

WHEREAS, the Contributors, being desirous that their identity remain unknown in order that the creation of such foundation shall have no limitations by reason of its association with their names, coincident with the execution of this Declaration of Trust and with full knowledge and in consideration thereof, have caused their nominees to deliver and turn over to the undersigned the said plates for the printing and reproduction of THE URANTIA BOOK, to be held in trust to make possible the accomplishment and fulfillment of such desires and to carry out and perpetuate the objects herein expressed; and

The "Contributors" wish to remain anonymous to allow the foundation full autonomy.

WHEREAS, it is also contemplated that from time to time hereafter money and property of various kinds and descriptions will be given, granted, conveyed, assigned, transferred, devised, or bequeathed to such foundation for the uses and purposes and upon the trusts and conditions herein expressed:

3

PAGE 3
(The Trust Document begins on Page 3)

APPENDIXES

398

Now, Therefore.

ARTICLE I

CREATION OF FOUNDATION

1.1. CREATION: We, the undersigned, for and in behalf of the Contributors and those whose inspirations have this conceived, by this Declaration of Trust, hereby create, found, and establish this Foundation to be known as "URANTIA FOUNDATION."

1.2. ACCEPTANCE AND DECLARATION: We, the undersigned, for ourselves and our successors in trust as hereinafter defined, do hereby acknowledge that there have been transferred and delivered to us approximately two thousand two hundred (2,200) nickel-plated stereotype plates of patent base thickness prepared from the manuscript of THE URANTIA BOOK for the printing and reproduction thereof, which plates are presently stored in the plate vaults of R. R. Donnelly & Sons Company at Crawfordsville, Indiana; and we, for ourselves and our successors in trust, do hereby declare that said plates for the printing and reproduction of THE URANTIA BOOK and all moneys and properties of every kind and description which may from time to time hereafter be given, granted, conveyed, assigned, transferred, bequeathed, or devised to, or otherwise acquired by, URANTIA FOUNDATION or the Trustees thereof, and accepted and received by the Foundation or the Trustees thereof, shall be held in trust for the uses and purposes and upon the trusts hereinafter provided.

ARTICLE II

OBJECTS

2.1. PRINCIPAL OBJECT: The object for which this Foundation is created is the promotion, improvement, and expansion among the

4

The Trustees accept the plates from the "Contributors," also in behalf of "those whose inspirations have this conceived," the celestial authors, and on this basis establish Urantia Foundation.

Once again, the Plates are described and accepted in trust.

The document now begins to describe the PRINCIPAL OBJECT for which Urantia Foundation has been created.

DECLARATION OF TRUST

The mission of Urantia Foundation is first to "promote, improve and expand" the understanding of the message of the Urantia Papers for the mutual benefit of humankind. This mission is to be achieved by fostering an appropriate "religion, philosophy and cosmology."

peoples of the world of the comprehension and understanding of Cosmology and the relation of the planet on which we live to the Universe, of the genesis and destiny of Man and his relation to God, and of the true teachings of Jesus Christ; and for the inculcation and encouragement of the realization and appreciation of the Fatherhood of God and the Brotherhood of Man—in order to increase and enhance the comfort, happiness, and well being of Man, as an individual and as a member of society, through the fostering of a religion, a philosophy, and a cosmology which are commensurate with Man's intellectual and cultural development.

Concordant (or in harmony) with the primary mission, Urantia Foundation was created specifically to "preserve inviolate" the original text of *The Urantia Book*. (Emphasis was not in the original document).

2.2. CONCORDANT OBJECTS: The concordant objects for which the Foundation is created are to perpetually preserve inviolate the text of THE URANTIA BOOK and to disseminate the principles, teachings, and doctrines of THE URANTIA BOOK.

ARTICLE III
DUTIES OF TRUSTEES

The spirit and intent of this paragraph explains that the primary duty of the Trustees is to preserve inviolate the text of The Urantia Book from "loss, damage, or destruction and from alteration, modification, revision, or change in any manner or particular."

3.1. PRESERVATION OF TEXT OF THE URANTIA BOOK: It shall be the primary duty of the Trustees to perpetually preserve inviolate the text of THE URANTIA BOOK, and the Trustees shall use and employ such means, methods, and facilities and apply and expend as much of the Trust Estate as in the judgment of the Trustees shall be necessary, proper, or appropriate, for the preserving and the safekeeping of copies of the original text of THE URANTIA BOOK, duly authenticated by the Trustees, from loss, damage, or destruction and from alteration, modification, revision, or change in any manner or in any particular.

While the Trustees preserve three copies of the original text printed in 1955, they have never again printed the same text.

3.2. EFFECTING PRINCIPAL OBJECT: It shall be the duty of the Trustees to use and ceipts from any and all such money and property.

ARTICLE V

POWERS OVER SUBSTANTIVE ESTATE

5.1. GENERAL: The Trustees shall have all powers over the Substantive Estate as shall be necessary to carry out the objects of the Foundation, but the Trustees shall not have any power at any time to sell or in any manner encumber or dispose of the Substantive Estate or any part or portion thereof, except as provided for in this Article V.

5.2. PRESERVATION AND DESTRUCTION OF SUBSTANTIVE ESTATE: The Trustees shall have the power to destroy all or any part of the Substantive Estate except three (3) copies of the original text of THE URANTIA BOOK and the replacements thereof, but no part of the Substantive Estate shall be destroyed unless either (a) the Trustees shall unanimously agree that the continued preservation of such portion of the Substantive Estate is no longer required for accomplishing the purposes for which the Foundation is created or (b) the Trustees are prevented from preserving such portion of the Substantive Estate by reason of circumstances beyond their control.

5.3. TRANSFER OF SUBSTANTIVE ESTATE: The Trustees shall have the power to transfer all or any part of the Substantive Estate, except three (3) copies of the original text of THE URANTIA BOOK and the replacements thereof, to any organization, trust, corporation, institution, or entity of any kind which shall have been created by the Trustees and subject to their control, but only upon the

8

The Trustees are granted, under the terms of the Trust, *provisional* power over "Substantive Estate."

The "Substantive Estate" is described as three copies of the original text of The Urantia Book (printed from the original Plates). These cannot be destroyed under any circumstances.

NO PART of the Substantive Estate, which includes the plates themselves, can be destroyed without the unanimous vote of the Trustees. In 1967, an important part of the Substantive Estate was destroyed without such documented consent.

DECLARATION OF TRUST

condition that the portion of the Substantive Estate so transferred shall be returned to the Trustees when the purposes for which it was transferred have been fulfilled.

ARTICLE VI
GENERAL FISCAL POWERS

6.1. GENERAL POWERS: Subject to the provisions of Article V, the Trustees shall have the power to own, hold, manage, control, operate, care for, protect, and preserve the Trust Estate, and to collect and receive the income and profits therefrom, and the increments thereof, and to make contracts with respect to the Trust Estate or any portion thereof, and to bind the Trust Estate therefor, and to apply and use all or any part of the Trust Estate to effectuate the objects of the Foundation, all in accordance with the sole discretion and judgment of the Trustees.

6.2. PRINCIPAL AND INCOME: The Trustees shall have the power to determine, from time to time, whether or not there shall be any division of the Subservient Estate between "principal" and "income" and to determine what is "principal" and what is "income"; and in any instance in which it may be material, necessary, or desirable, the Trustees shall have the power, in their sole discretion and judgment, to determine how all receipts and disbursements shall be credited, charged, apportioned, accrued, or otherwise divided, prorated, or accounted for as between principal and income or as between separate funds or accounts; and the decision of the Trustees in all such cases shall be final.

6.3. REAL ESTATE: The Trustees shall have power, either (a) for the purpose of carrying out of the objects of the Foundation or (b) for investment or reinvestment of the Sub-

7.4. TRUSTEE EMERITUS: In the event of the permanent disability of any Trustee, which shall be evidenced by the certificate of a competent physician, or in the event of the resignation of any Trustee, which may be done by delivering to any one of the other Trustees a writing stating his resignation, a vancacy shall be deemed to exist in the number of the Trustees. Any person who shall have been a Trustee hereunder and who shall become permanently disabled or who shall have resigned may, if he be willing, be made a **TRUSTEE EMERITUS OF URANTIA FOUNDATION** by a majority vote of the remaining Trustees, certified to under the hands and seals of said remaining Trustees, and filed for record as provided in paragraph 9.1. A Trustee Emeritus shall have no rights, duties, or powers hereunder, but the name shall be given such person only as an expression of appreciation of his past services as trustee.

A Trustee Emeritus is described as having no rights, duties or powers. But Christy retained virtual total control over the text after she was given emeritus status on October 15, 1971. In violation of the terms of the Declaration of Trust, she retained this control until her death on May 2, 1982.

INDEX

Numerics

1942 alleged "message"
    discussion of alterations to **280–283**
    exhibits showing variances in two
        versions of **284–285**
1999 Fellowship Conference in
  Vancouver, British Columbia. **257**
1999 International Conference **258**
533 Diversey Parkway **129, 208, 210, 233,
  234, 253, 278**
    culture of undergoes change after Dr.
        Sadler dies **234**
    early photo of **26**
    eventually conducted classes **188**
    Sadlers establish residency in 1922 **52**

A

Acting Planetary Prince
    alleged communication of Nov 1951
        regarding publication of
        Book **173**
    alleged message of Nov 1951 **290**
    gives provisional date for Trustees to
        act on their own (alleged
        communication of Aug 1952)
        175
Adam and Eve **91**
Adams, Dr. Benjamin **97, 119, 120, 125,
  156, 194, 271**
    reproductions of correspondence with
        Dr. Sadler **321–329**

Adler, Mortimer **221**
Alexandria **120**
alteration of the original plates of The
  Urantia Book **224–231**
Alwood, Lister **53**
American Red Cross **59**
Ancients of Days **114, 116**
Andovontia **153**
Andrew **118**
angels
    are numerous orders of **90**
apocryphal information **130**
    alleged continually turns up **130**
    has doubtful origin **279**
    limited value to history **280**
    Revelators did not want **130**
apostles of Jesus **157**
    Paper on convinces Dr. Sadler of
        validity of the Revelation **34**
Appendix B
    reference to **120, 156**
Appendix D
    reference to **153**
Appendix F
    reference to **287**
    reference to (2 ref.) **290**
Aquarian Gospel **17**
Asche, Sholem **271**
Assagioli, Dr. Roberto **39**
atom
    relative weight of **154**

406 INDEX

atomic weapons **179**
authoritarianism
protested by Bedell **240**
authority to materialize Papers **108**
automatic speaking **68**
automatic writing **68, 69**
autorevelation **98, 303**

B

Banner of Michael **237, 238, 239, 278, 292**
used freely by early Urantians **237**
Bedell, Clyde **12, 57, 103, 122, 137, 160, 239, 253, 256, 289, 295, 297, 298**
"rich man's Bible" **237**
(photo) **124**
all 196 Papers read to Forum **125**
at Christy's memorial service (photo) **244**
believed Jesus Papers supported by rest of Book **125**
believed no human intrusions were made to Papers **210**
could not recall first reading of Papers to Forum **76**
describes early days of Forum **53–54**
drafts petition to Dr. Sadler **138**
eulogizes Bill Sadler, Jr. **190**
joins Forum in 1924 at 26 years of age **53**
member of Forum **8**
on supposed "special guidance" of Trustees **211**
photo with Bill Sadler, Jr. **181**
rebuked warnings of WW III **250**
regretted drafting petition to Dr. Sadler **139**
said Midwayers commented on Declaration of Trust

"If that's the best you can come up with it will have to do." **173**
strong reservations about method of selecting Trustees **172**
tried to calm reader fears in Boulder **249**
warned against proprietary attitudes **278**
writes Wilfred Kellogg re organization **136**
wrote letter to Myers protesting restrictions **240**
Bethany **157**
Bethlehem **156**
Beverly Shores, Indiana **124, 188**
Bible **126, 278**
Biggs, David **11**
Birth of a Divine Revelation
postulates corruption of Urantia Papers by Dr. Sadler **295**
used Harry Loose and Harold Sherman as sources **308**
uses Martin Gardner and Harry Loose for support **295**
Birth of a Divine Revelation (Moyer) discussion of **295–300**
Birth of a Revelation (Kulieke) **69, 82, 217**
Black Monday **113**
Block, Matthew **98, 99**
Bogota, Columbia **188**
Boulder School **188**
Boulder, Colorado **152, 261**
Bowman, Clarence **83, 165, 266**
Brilliant Evening Star **108, 109**
Brotherhood is in Crisis, The
letter by Christy concerning lack of younger people in movement **234**

INDEX 407

Brown, Dr. Barbara **39**
Brueseke, Reverend Edward **15**
Bunche, Ralph **271**
Bunker, John M. **6**
Burns, Dr. Thomas **254**
    warned of damage to movement by
        Vern Grimsley's "messages"
        301

C

California **203, 242, 252**
Caligastia **272, 280, 298, 299**
    Christy warns against **234**
    could never influence a human mind
        against its will **234**
    Dr. Sadler does not mention **234**
Carlson, Helen **76, 132**
Caston, Hoite **202, 204, 247, 254**
    communications with Myers & Keeler
        during Grimsley crisis **249**
    fraternity brother of Grimsley, Keeler
        & Myers **233**
    Grimsley episode too big to "sweep
        under the rug" **241**
    Grimsley gave advance tour of
        Clayton **242**
    issues
        final report on Grimsley episode **253**
    mails Grimsley report to Executive
        Committee **250**
    mails Grimsley report to Vern **250**
    named as Trustee **252**
    photo at FOG **243**
Catholic **278**
Catholic Church **278**
celestial beings **157, 187, 269**
celestial guidance, special after 1955 **190,
  245**
Celestial Revelatory Commission **180**
CENTRAL AND SUPERUNIVERSES
    (Part I) **114**

Certified Leader **188**
certified religious leaders and teachers **267**
changes to original text
    made clandestinely **217**
    many were arbitrary, unnecessary, or
        simply wrong **152**
    not footnoted or endnoted **157**
    only minor changes made in third
        Forum reading, 1935 - 1942
        121
channeled messages **210**
channeling **79, 257, 291, 301, 303**
    can people believe they are hearing
        voices? **202**
    comments by Dr. Thomas Burns **301–
        303**
    featured at Fellowship IC 99 **258**
cherubim **96, 105, 110**
Chicago **19, 42, 53, 65, 135, 136, 181,
  233, 256, 271**
    early days **37, 38**
Chicago's Golden Age **38**
Chief of the Corps of Superuniverse
  Personalities **128**
Chief of the Evening Stars **117**
Choquette, Tom **12**
Christ Michael **117**
Christ Michael--Son of Man and Son of
  God **159**
Christensen, Emma Louise. See Christy
Christian **278**
Christian hierarchal religious authority **278**
Christian religion **177**
Christianity
    historical religion **37**
Christians **126, 150, 245**
Christy **122, 132, 140, 149, 150, 180,
  193, 200, 217, 232, 241, 260, 272, 277,
  281, 283, 284, 286, 287, 290, 292, 297,
  303**
    "All the words we italicized were
        underlined." **119**

408 INDEX

"messages" **252**
(early photo) **129**
alone in her claims of personal
 contacts with Midwayers **196**
and Dr. Sadler concerned about lack of
 younger readers **234**
and Thomas Kendall were Trustees at
 time of second printing **199**
authority to change text independent
 of other Trustees is
 questioned **199**
began to assume more and more
 responsibilities **194**
brings grip device to test sleeping
 subject **68**
brought alleged 1966 "message" to
 attention of Tom Kendall **280**
brought Papers out of vault for
 Shermans to read **136**
channeling activities **258**
channeling activities kept secret **253**
close to Grimsley **241**
collected "errors" in text **144**
decision to change plates without
 endnotes **211**
dominated culture at 533 **208**
Dr. Sadler and, met with Keeler &
 Myers in 1962 **233**
early photo of **95**
early photo with Bill Sadler & Mary
 Lou Hales **112**
early photo with Bill Sadler, Jr. **147**
first secretary of Urantia Foundation
 167
Grimsley claimed she gave him
 deathbed instructions **246**
had "unique" relationship with text
 217
hands over manuscript to typesetter
 140
impressed by young Martin Myers **234**
joins Contact Commission **55**

joins Sadler family **55**
Kendall claims Christy & Myers
 brought supposed "message"
 to attention of Trustees in
 1980 **252**
letter to JJ Johnson **204**
made changes in text that exceeded
 authority of Contact
 Commission **217**
may have believed she had approval
 from Midwayers to alter
 original text **202**
may have believed she heard voices of
 Midwayers **204**
may have believed she was "restoring"
 original text **208**
member of Contact Commission **56**
motivation to alter original text
 examined **202**
nurtured inner group **303**
on changes to the text **163**
on strange "isms" and queer groups
 254
only Contact Commissioner who
 claimed personal contact
 with Midwayers **286**
photo at 90th birthday **197**
photo at FOG headquarters **243**
photo taken on 90th birthday **197**
photo with her sister & Dr. Sadler **164**
photo with James JJ Johnson **198**
photos teaching **191**
possible author of History Two **61–63**
pressure on her was intense in 1967
 203
proprietary attitude toward Banner of
 Michael **238**
rumors of "channeled messages" did
 not surface until after Dr.
 Sadler's death **210, 286**
said manuscript was handwritten **119**

INDEX 409

said to have declared Grimsley to be a member of "reserve corps of destiny" **246**
status as Trustee Emeritus discussed **402**
supported licensing agreement **237**
supposed message in 1980 **280**
supposed messages fall in realm of unverifiable psychic phenomena **200**
told Dr. Sprunger entire revelation materialized in handwritten form **119**
told Vern Grimsley he was a "destiny reservist" **203**
was not pre-educated before arrival of Papers **92**
was Trustee at time of second printing **194**
what Carolyn Kendall reported she said about changes **195**
wrote letter to Trustees & others, "The Brotherhood in Crisis" **234**
chronology
of Jesus Papers **97**
Churchification **264**
Circuit Supervisor **153**
citations
of Parts of Book **116–118**
of Parts of Book do not indicate they were either certified or completed in 1934-35 **116**
Clarification of Concepts **121**
Clayton, California **242, 247, 249, 251**
Clement **119**
Columbia University Press **215**
communications
none made unless two or more Commissioners were present **195**

Communism **165, 179**
discussion of story about intention of Midwayers to defeat **183**
Communist menace **179**
Comparison of the 1955 and the 1967 Printings **224**
concentric circle lapel pins
Christy initially refuses to sell to French translators of Urantia Book **238**
concentric circles **237, 239**
Concordex **210**
Clyde Bedell authored **8**
Consideration of Some Criticisms of the Urantia Book, paper by Dr. Sadler **59, 235**
Contact Activities Preceding the Urantia Papers
excerpt from History Two **88–92**
Contact Commission **32, 45, 92, 109, 113, 130, 137, 144, 149, 150, 151, 158, 165, 167, 168, 174, 178, 190, 200, 217, 235, 276, 286, 288**
became defunct in 1955 **289**
cautioned not to comment on death of sleeping subject **193**
confined to clerical duties of spelling, capitalization and punctuation **78**
consulted lawyers about formation of Foundation **136**
continued to function after Foundation was formed **290**
did not publish Urantia Book **217**
did not see any supernatural events **35**
did not witness any physical evidence of Midwayer presence **85**
directed to get International Copyright **180**
does not hear from regent by January 1, 1955 deadline **175**

410 INDEX

Dr. Sprunger's conversations with Dr.
Sadler, Bill Sadler, Jr. and
Christy **37**
early on did not suspect they were in
contact with anything
supernatural **94**
early photo of Christy, Dr. Lena
Sadler, Dr. William Sadler,
and Bill Sadler, Jr. **64**
fate of the **189–190**
final makeup of **56**
frequently talked with Midwayers
during contacts **91**
function for five years after formation
of Urantia Foundation **169**
had no editorial authority whatever **78**
had provisional right to standardize
spelling, punctuation and
capitalization of original
typewritten text **172**
informed after WW II that
Communism was dangerous
threat to religion of Jesus **165**
knew identity of sleeping subject **77**
lives had revolved around corps of
Midwayers **187**
looked forward to the end of WW II
165
members of **55**
no acknowledgment by Revelators
113
no provisions for replacing lost
members **289**
only four members pre-educated **88**
operated under celestial direction **289**
period of preparation and testing **88**
permitted only to standardize spelling,
capitalization and
punctuation **140**
religious thinking expanded before
Papers began to arrive **88**
remained active until 1955 **276**

responsible for errors in final text **145**
responsible for typesetting accuracy of
text **143**
told to go through the Papers again in
1929 **82**
transferred responsibility for text to
Urantia Foundation **169**
used plates as basis for forming
Urantia Foundation **149**
Contact Commissioners **128, 138, 280,
286, 292**
always at least two had to be present
for contacts **79**
apparently unaware of possible
editorial inconsistencies in
final text **146**
grew old waiting for publication and
propagation of Revelation
179
had no secret powers or special status
82
kept sacred oaths re
1955 text **187**
materialization technique not to be
discussed **94**
no provision to replace lost members
132
none ever saw material manifestations
of Midwayer presence **296**
not contacted individually **195**
three were charter Trustees of
Foundation **168**
wondered if they would live to see
publication of Urantia Book
132
contact personality **5, 200, 296**
Christy's alleged status as one **246**
why name was never revealed **32**
see sleeping subject
contacts with celestial beings
no two were alike **93**

INDEX

411

Contributors
  of Trust Estate wish to remain
      anonymous **168**
Cook, Edith **148, 167, 197**
copying errors **146**
copyright **196**
  not mentioned in Trust document **200**
copyright and trademark enforcement **235**
Corps of Finality **92**
corrections
  technique Midwayers used to revise
      manuscript is not known **122**
Cosh, Eric **11, 83**
Cousins, Norman **271**
Crawfordsville, Indiana **172, 209, 215,
    276, 300**
  R. R. Donnelley Plant **143**
Creator Deities **89**
Creator of our universe **126**
crucifixion of Jesus **157**
cultcentric activities **301**

D

Daligastia **234**
dating
  of Papers **114–118**
  of Urantia Book **115–118**
David Kulieke **38**
Dead Sea **120**
Declaration of Trust **149, 157, 166, 168,
    169, 172, 199, 202, 214, 218, 219, 236,
    240, 277, 287, 292, 293**
  contains no statement that allows any
      changes in text whatsoever
      172
  created by Contact Commission in
      liaison with attorneys **166**
  defined property in trust **167**
  does not extend rights to standardize
      spelling, capitalization and
      punctuation to Trustees **172**

does not grant authority of Foundation
      to make any changes
      whatsoever **150**
  establishes Urantia Foundation as
      autonomous organization
      168, 290
  explained **166–167**
  forbids alteration of text **216**
  forbids any changes in text **172**
  key pages reproduced **395–402**
  Midwayers comment
      "If that's the best you can come up
          with it will have to do."
          173
  no provision for "correcting" text **200**
  reproduction of page 3 **171**
  violated by changes made in second
      printing **201**
Deity **116**
depression
  United States **113**
destiny guardian **110**
Devil
  "Birth of a Divine Revelation" asserts
      he was allowed to corrupt
      Urantia Papers **297**
  doctrine of **234**
  term used in "Birth of a Divine
      Revelation" **296**
distribution of the book
  nothing should be done to interfere
      with any individual's
      enthusiastic efforts **178**
Divine Counselor **110, 128**
documentation
  re supposed celestial guidance after
      1955 **193**
documentation of changes to text
  Urantia Foundation states that none
      exists **201**
Du Val, Norm **11**
  website **394**

412 INDEX

E

Edentia **239**
Edgar Cayce **6**
Edgar Cayce and The Urantia Book **6**
electrifying personality **65, 66**
    challenges Sadlers to develop better
        questions **54–55**
electron
    relative weight of **154**
Elliott, Berkeley **12, 22, 57, 183, 237, 295**
    photo **261**
    resisted Grimsley "messages" **246**
England **135**
English language **97, 116, 117**
entitlement **277, 293, 301**
Epochal Revelation **76, 98, 157, 211, 256, 303**
    all revelation short of the presence of
        God is partial **151**
    contrasted with autorevelation **80–81**
    for the people **305**
    protocol of **80**
Europe **135**
Evans, Florence
    Clyde Bedell brings his future wife to
        Forum **53**
evolution
    of humankind and cosmos **89**
evolutionary
    aspect of God is Supreme Being **90**
evolutionary mortals **116**
evolutionary religion **108**
Executive Committee of the Urantia
    Brotherhood **242, 245, 262**
    debated Grimsley bathtub "message"
        245

F

faith (in Jesus) **126**
Family of God Foundation
    see FOG

Fellowship
    publishes Urantia Book in 1996 **260**
Fellowship Executive Committee
    unable to amend Fellowship
        constitution **265**
Fellowship website **63, 84, 85**
    provides reliable information and
        history **265**
Fifth Epochal Revelation **151, 187, 213, 258, 268, 269, 276, 292, 303**
    failure to make impact **233**
finaliters **106**
First Society of Oklahoma **237**
First Source and Center **90**
First Urantia Society
    of Chicago founded **188**
focus group **76**
FOG **203, 242, 243, 245, 249, 251, 253, 257, 302**
    organized in 1967 **241**
    photo of headquarters **247**
Foreword to Urantia Papers **128, 153**
Forsythe, Scott **213, 217, 272**
    letter to JJ Johnson re
        Christy's relationship with the text
        217–218
    reproduction of letter to JJ Johnson re
        Christy's relationship to the text of
        the Urantia Book **330**
Forum **32, 113, 114, 117, 122, 138, 142, 151**
    attendance not impressive **128**
    aware a Foundation was being planned
        136
    becomes a Sunday study group **136**
    becomes official Sept., 1925 **77**
    Charter Members **77**
    did not come into being until after pre-
        education **89**
    discovered errors prior to publication
        144
    Dr. Sadler establishes **33**

INDEX

early days described by Clyde Bedell 52–54

final meeting May 31, 1942 **53, 136**

first reading of Papers to, Jan. 18, 1925 **75**

formation of Seventy **130**

lack of enthusiasm shocking **131**

large turnover **76, 128**

looked forward to end of WW II **165**

no acknowledgment by Revelators **113**

not consulted about formation of Foundation **136, 138**

performance disappointing to acting Planetary Prince **131**

pledge of secrecy **77**

procedures explained **76**

read Declaration of Intent to Publish the Urantia Book **176**

responded enthusiastically to requests for funding Urantia Book **131**

told no more questions would be entertained in May, 1942 **122**

turnover discussed by Clyde Bedell **53**

Forum members **276**

average lasted two years **76**

did not see original manuscripts, did not know identity of sleeping subject **77**

Forum members, early

not religious **266**

Forum-Study Group **169**

largely on own after 1952 **173**

read alleged communication in 1951 about publication of Book **173**

read an edited version of publication mandate by Bill Sadler, Jr. **178**

read from proofing copies after 1945 **172**

remained under direction of Contact Commission (alleged communication) **175**

Fourth Epochal Revelation **117**

Fox, Emmett **304**

Fragment of God **305**

France **135**

French situation, alleged 1980 "message" **252**

Freud **38**

Friedman, Polly **57, 185, 188, 281, 282, 284, 286**

G

Gabriel of Salvington **114, 239**

galley proofs

replaced typed manuscripts **143**

gamma **154**

Garden of Ediacara, The **215**

Gardner, Martin **75, 104, 135, 159, 295, 298, 300, 308**

Gault, Robert H. **20**

General Council **264**

vote to split from Foundation **273**

Germany **113**

invades Poland Sept. 1939 **132**

Gestalt psychology **52**

Glasziou, Dr. Kenneth **209**

Glasziou, Dr. Kenneth and Betty **162, 202, 205**

Gnostic **264**

God **304, 307**

Paper on nature of **114**

Golden Years, The **290**

booklet published by Urantia Foundation **288**

incorrect description of Contact Commission **288**

incorrectly states that Bill Sadler, Jr. took mother's place on Contact Commission **288**

incorrectly states the Jesus Papers were delivered with "input of

INDEX

questions from the Forum." **291**

problematic claims that Contact Commissioners continued to function as such for the "rest of their lives" **289, 290**

Goshen, Indiana **188**

Gospel of Jesus **126, 307**

Graham, Janet Farrington **262**

Gray, David **243**

Green, Donald Shea **11, 194**

Green, Minnie **164**

Grimsley episode
    "off limits" **240**

Grimsley, Nancy **253**

Grimsley, Vern **202, 252, 253, 263, 293, 301**
    "prepare for WW III" **249**
    "special agent" status revoked **249**
    "the time has not arrived to publicize the Book" **242**
    "This is it" **247**
    author of Richard Keeler's IC 99 speech **254**
    bathtub "message"
        "don't split up the book" **245**
    came to believe he was spiritual leader of movement after death of Christy **203**
    claimed Christy had directed him to "commission" Urantians **246**
    claimed Christy said he was a Destiny Reservist **242**
    claimed Christy told him to protect copyright and registered marks on her death bed **246**
    close relationship with Christy **203, 241**
    fraternity brother of Caston, Keeler & Myers **233**

funeral oration for Christy, said she gave him deathbed instructions **246**

gives WW III ""red alert" to Keeler **250**

golden boy of Urantia Movement **241**

introduction to Book **233**

orders Keeler to liquidate FOG account **250**

photo at FOG **243**

photo at work **247**

photo, delivers message at Christy's memorial service **244**

reproduction of "WW III" warning letter **331**

stated Christy got her "messages" "the same way" he got his **242**

went public with supposed "messages" **249**

WW III "channeling" episode **240–257**

Grimsley, Vern and Nancy **251**
    corresponded with Dr. Sadler **233**

H

Hales, John **301**

Hales, Mary Lou **266**
    early photo with Bill Sadler and Christy **112**

Hales, William **167, 175**
    first president of Urantia Foundation **167**
    on integrity of Urantia Book text **163**

halo effect **142**

Ham, alleged "messages" **258**

Hammerschmidt, Judge Louis **15, 16, 18**

Handicap of our language and the Revelation **108**

handwriting
    not that of sleeping subject **69**
    of Urantia Papers in pencil **70**

INDEX

handwriting of Papers discussed **70–75**

handwriting question
Bill and Dr. Sadler believed it was
Secondary Midwayer **73**

Harrah, W. H. **18**

Havona **90**

Havona Servitals **105**

Hay, John **152, 188**

Hecht, Ben **38**

hierarchical authoritarian attitudes **304**

history
as adversarial processes **10, 279**

History of the Urantia Movement
authorized by Dr. Sadler **36**

History of Urantia Movement One
probably edited by Dr. Sadler **58**

History of Urantia Movement Two
not written by Dr. Sadler **58**

HISTORY OF URANTIA, THE (Part III)
114

History One **263, 291**
admonitions referred to as suggestions
177
does not support contacts after 1955
195
reproductions of some pages **60**

History Two **88, 89, 116, 121, 263, 288,
291, 297**
conflicts with "The Golden Years" -
states that there was no
provision for replacing
Contact Commissioners **289**
does not support contacts after 1955
195
exhibit showing that Christy may have
edited **63**
formation of Urantia Foundation **166**
had anonymous author **92**
reproduction of page showing possible
alterations of page numbers
62
reproductions of some pages **61**

Hitler **135**

Holyoke College **214**

Horn, Jeanney **11**

Horn, Merritt **11, 156, 210, 220, 224, 228**
made computer study of text, found
120 changes, (also see
Appendix D) **152**
on changes to the text **152–157**
review and analysis of Urantia
Foundation's changes to the
text **347–391**

How to Know What to Believe, book by
Harold Sherman **45, 74, 135, 136, 158**

human (sleeping) subject (also see sleeping
subject) **108**

human knowledge
greatest is religious life of Jesus **126**

human mind
not used to materialize Urantia Papers
91
of sleeping subject not used to
materialize Urantia Papers
102

human wisdom
Revelators had to rely on to address
problems with the text **150**

Huxley, Aldous **271**

hypnosis
used on sleeping subject **50–51**

I

Illinois **166**

in the manger
deletion of phrase discussed **155**

inhabited worlds **89**

Inlibration **150**

International Copyright **180**

International Urantia Association
see IUA

inviolate text
term does not appear in Declaration of
Trust **184**

416   INDEX

inviolate text, so-called
  euphemistic term **245**
IUA **258, 267**

J

Jameson, Gard **255, 257**
  votes to break with Foundation **273**
  worked for FOG **251**
Jaynes, Dr. Julian **202**
Jerusalem **238**
Jerusem **239**
Jesus **93, 126, 150, 156, 256, 278**
  A New Revelation **260**
  at first limited information about
    reasons for bestowal **91**
  birthday of **238**
  mentioned early and often in Urantia
    Papers **94**
  teaching methods of **177**
  words and deeds in Bible **126**
Jesus of Nazareth **103, 117, 118, 269**
  and Urantia Papers **4**
  knowledge of his religious life most
    important human knowledge
    126
Jesus Papers **115, 117, 120, 125, 126, 291**
  "most important 800 pages in print on
    earth" **125**
  also see Life and Teachings of Jesus,
    The
  arrival of **114**
  completed one year after other Papers
    122
  friendly challenge by Midwayers
    114–115
  handled like rest of Book **121**
  masterpiece framed by rest of Papers
    127
  separate publication discussed by
    General Council **245**
  were "biggest surprise" **92, 291**

Jesus Papers, The (Part IV) **117**
Jesus' Birthday **175**
John **126**
  wrote in Bible that Jesus did and said
    many other things **126**
John the Baptist **18**
Johnson, James JJ **11, 128, 204, 213, 214,
215, 217, 259, 306**
  conversations with Christy **119**
  perplexed by letter from Christy **205**
  photo taken with Christy **198**
  reproduction of letter from Scott
    Forsythe Re
    Christy's relationship to the text of
      The Urantia Book **330**
  success with outreach to Dr.
    McMenamin **337–346**
Johnson, Michael Andrew **198**
Jordan valley **120, 156**
Joseph and Mary **156**
Judas **157**

K

Kagan, Bud **119**
Kansas **233**
Kantor, David **11, 85, 99, 158, 183, 220,
265**
  alternate version of first meeting of
    Sadlers with sleeping subject
    57
Keeler, Richard **215, 220, 252, 257, 258**
  communications with Caston & Myers
    during Grimsley crisis **249**
  early trip to Chicago with Myers **233**
  edited Caston report on Grimsley **253**
  Executive Investment Manager for
    FOG **250**
  fraternity brother of Grimsley, Caston
    & Myers **233**
  Grimsley gave advance tour of
    Clayton **242**
  named as Trustee **253**
  ordered to liquidate FOG account **250**

INDEX

photo at FOG **243**
reproduction of resignation letter from
FOG **332–333**
resigns from FOG **251**
revokes will bequeathing entire
personal wealth to FOG **251**
testified there were no contacts after
1955 **201**
turns Myers out of presidency **253**
Kellogg, Anna Bell **56, 168**
death of **189**
died Feb. 24, 1960 **93**
member of Contact Commission **55**
was pre-educated before arrival of
Papers **92**
Kellogg, John Harvey **38**
Kellogg, Lena
Marries Dr. William Sadler **38**
Kellogg, W. K. **38**
Kellogg, Wilfred C. **56, 167**
death of **189**
died Aug. 31, 1956 **93**
receives letter from Clyde Bedell re
organization **136**
was pre-educated before arrival of
Papers **92**
Kelloggs **92, 123, 124, 132**
June, 1942 photo of **95**
Kendall, Carolyn **83, 143, 145, 149, 183,
189, 212, 220, 251, 266, 284, 286, 287,
290, 292**
contention that changes made after
1982 were done "without
authorization of Midwayers."
200
describes correction process in 1967
printing **196**
discloses nature of 1942 alleged
"message" **281**
discussion of her contention Trustees
did not participate in

"correcting" the text of The
Urantia Book **196–200**
examination of statements that
Richard Keeler promised to
reverse changes made after
1982 **200–201**
father believed Urantia Book was
going to be "biggest hit in
100 years" **183**
her redefinition of Trustee duties is
questioned **199–200**
omission of key passage in her
presentation of "messages"
184
presents altered version of 1942
alleged "message" **282**
selected by Foundation to write
website material, 50th
Anniversary history **288**
statements re changes made after 1955
195
supports Harold Sherman story of first
contact **45–46**
wrote that final galley proofs (and
plates) contained errors **143**
wrote the Foundation "wanted the
Book to be perfect" **216**
Kendall, Thomas **83, 213, 249, 257, 288**
accepted alleged "messages" from
Christy when president of
Foundation **280**
apparently did not inform other
Trustees of Christy's actions
199
charged with being "subject to psychic
phenomena" **252**
defends Grimsley **249**
disputed Myers' charges **252**
expelled from Foundation **252**
goes to Clayton to see Grimsley **251**
had not heard of 1942 message **283**
on arrangement of Papers **163**

418   INDEX

removed from presidency of Urantia
    Foundation **252**
reported Christy "message" warning
    about Jacques Weiss **272**
wrote that Myers supported Grimsley
    messages early on **242**
Kendall, Thomas and Christy
    were Trustees at time of 1967 printing
        199
Kendalls **242, 280**
    believed Christy had a special
        connection to celestial beings
        204
    believed in both Grimsley and Christy
        "messages" **242**
    continued to defend Grimsley
        messages **251**
    gave account of Grimsley crisis **241**
    reported Bill Sadler, Jr.'s warnings
        about a proprietary attitude
        by Foundation **292**
    said alleged 1942 message was
        delivered verbally to Christy
        281
    told of Grimsley "message" in 1982
        241
Kennedy, John F. **190**
Knott, Dr. Paul **242**
    examined Grimsley **203**
Koran **150**
Krohn, Mr. former employee of R. R.
    Donnelley **161**
Krohn, Mr., retired employee of R.R.
    Donnelley & Sons **209**
Kruger, Aaron **12**
Kruger, Damon **12**
Kruger, Micah **12**
Kulieke, Alvin **234**
Kulieke, Lucille **243**
Kulieke, Mark **55, 69, 82, 130, 217, 225**
    organizations largely on their own
        after 1952 **173**

reports father coming home with
    Urantia Books **183**

L

language
    of local universe **105**
    superuniverse **106**
Lardner, Ring **38**
Lazarus **157**
legal challenge
    by Midwayers concerning Jesus
        Papers **115**
liberated midway creatures **106**
licensing agreement
    forced on Urantia Brotherhood **237**
Lieske, Rosey **11, 269, 270**
Life and Teachings of Jesus **17, 18, 125,
    127**
    Also see Jesus Papers
    not in response to questions by Forum
        117
    original narrative many times larger
        than what was finally given
        97
Life and Teachings of Jesus, The
    friendly challenge by Midwayers
        114–115
    were materialized in handwritten form
        119
linotype operator
    Forum seemed to believe was
        responsible for errors in final
        text **145**
litigation
    Urantians grew to fear **237**
Local System Councils **115**
LOCAL UNIVERSE
    (Part II) **114**
Loose, Harry **140, 295, 308**
    Gardner reports he may have been a
        patient of Dr. Sadler **159**

INDEX 419

Los Angeles **188, 235, 242**
Lucifer **239**
Lucifer rebellion **91**

M

Maaherra litigation **182, 201**
Maaherra, Kristen **11, 61, 100, 162, 182, 259**
   Foundation lawsuit dragged on for nearly ten years **259**
Malibu, CA **190**
man
   as evolutionary accident **100**
Man of Nazareth **126**
mandate
   to publish the Book
      paraphrased passages used in memos **178**
   to publish The Urantia Book **176**
   to publish Urantia Book accompanied by admonitions or suggestions **176**
mandates **292**
   first mentioned in 1973 **235**
   had strong influence on many Urantians **236**
   no set of permanent mandates regarding distribution of Book **178**
   were actually admonitions or suggestions **235**
manuscript
   kept in vault **122**
   of the Urantia Papers could be read only at 533 Diversey Parkway **142**
   of Urantia Papers **120**
   original typed manuscript not mentioned in Declaration of Trust **172**
   original written destroyed **122**
manuscript of Urantia Papers
   destroyed after plates were etched **143**

final version used by typesetters **144**
Marine Corps **113, 132**
Marshall Field (department store) photo **42**
Martin House, Oak Park, Chicago (photo) **42**
Maslow, Dr. Abraham **39**
Master Spirits **90**
Material Sons **294**
materialist **100**
materialization of Urantia Papers **94–96, 105–111, 275**
   Bill Sadler, Jr.
      speculated about **119**
   Contact Commission never found method of "reducing messages to writing." **70**
   first occurrence **67–68**
   never observed **119**
   theory of Bill Sadler, Jr. **71–72**
Maxwell Street (Chicago) photo **42**
McGonegal, Victor **11**
McMenamin, Dr. Mark **214**
   comments about Urantia Book **337–346**
McMullan, Harry **245, 262, 291**
   resisted Grimsley messages **246**
Melchizedek **118**
Melchizedek missionaries **305**
Melchizedek revelatory director **118**
Melchizedek, Mantutia **117, 128**
Mencken, H. L. **38**
mental telepathy
   Dr. Sadler doubted **54**
messages, alleged
   all from Revelators were to be destroyed by fire **236**
   from Revelators cannot be verified **130**
   not reliable, not revelation **279**
   to Christy after 1955 **196**
   written form from Midwayers for administrative purpose **79**

420 INDEX

written messages to be destroyed **130**
meta-values **39**
Michael **91, 117, 151, 159, 239**
Michael Foundation **260, 262**
Michael of Nebadon **92**
 banner of trademarked by Urantia
  Foundation **239**
Michael's bestowal **234**
mid-phase cherubim **96, 105, 110**
Midway Commission
 announces guidance to the Trustees
  through the Contact
  Commission will end if no
  communication is made in
  three years **174**
Midwayer celebration **115**
Midwayer Commission **115, 122, 174,
 203, 213, 214, 276, 277**
 gave some admonitions or suggestions
  in connection with the
  publication of The Urantia
  Book **176**
 last message delivered in 1955 **183**
 no inquiry made regarding errors in
  cast plates **176**
 not available after 1955 **195**
 succeeds Revelatory Commission in
  1951 **174**
Midwayer Revelatory Commission **122,
 149**
Midwayers **88, 91, 105, 115, 118, 120,
 121, 122, 125, 187, 190, 200, 202, 219,
 258, 263, 276, 277, 280, 282, 286, 289,
 293, 303**
 advise to use small donations to fund
  Book **131**
 as guardians of spirit world **93**
 as translators **108**
 Carolyn Kendall claims they
  authorized 1967 alterations
  in text **196**

final message in 1955
 "you are now on your own" **183**
first supposed "communication" with
 Grimsley **242**
in perfect synchrony **96**
may have demonstrated
 nonproprietary model **115**
no supportive testimony that they
 performed "miraculous"
 appearing acts **296**
permanent residents of Urantia **91**
present at every contact **93**
required to use human sources when
 available **97**
would not tell location of errors **144**
MIGHTY MESSENGER publication **262**
Mills, Dr. James **145, 162, 202, 210, 219,
 224, 225, 277, 303**
 apparently was told entire book had to
  be reset in 1967 due to
  printing technology **209**
 believed the single change he knew
  about was reversed in later
  printings **208**
 on preservation of text **163**
 photo teaching at Berkeley **198**
 replaced Christy as Trustee, was
  unaware of changes **205**
 reproduction of letter to Ken and Betty
  Glasziou re
  his knowledge of changes in the text
   334–335
Mind at Mischief, The **5, 19, 20–25, 43,
 45, 55, 69, 78**
 Appendix disclosures **21, 22, 23, 24**
Moab **120, 156**
Mohammed **150**
monotype operator
 had to retype entire book **140**

INDEX 421

monotype operator (photo) **134**
morontia **91, 105, 106, 110**
morontia cherubim **96, 105, 110**
morontial **88**
mortal man
    as son of God **307**
Moss, Dr. Robert V. **36, 37**
Most Highs **239**
Mother Spirit **105**
Moyer, Ernest **295, 297**
    claims to know of celestial visitations
        taking place today **300**
    defense of "Birth of a Divine
        Revelation" refuted **298**
    undocumented claims **299**
    warns of "corruptions throughout
        entire Revelation" **299**
Mullins, Joan Batson **10, 305**
    suggested the history project **8**
Mullins, Kathleen **11**
Mullins, Larry **xii, 225**
    on writing the History of the Urantia
        Papers **xi**
Mullins, Michelle **10**
Mundelius, Patricia **253**
Muslim **150**
Myers, Martin **180, 232, 241, 242, 251,**
  252, 257, 303
   253
    advised Christy about Revelation from
        a legalistic perspective **234**
    and Christy delivered alleged
        "message" to Tom Kendall
        280
    assisted Dr. Sadler and Christy **234**
    becomes Trustee **234**
    claimed perpetual Foundation
        ownership of circles and
        word "Urantia" **239**
    communications with Keeler &
        Caston during Grimsley
        Crisis **249**

crafts licensing agreement **237**
de-licensed Brotherhood **257**
early influence at 533 **234**
early trip to Chicago with Keeler **233**
eventually becomes president of
    Urantia Foundation **252**
fraternity brother of Grimsley, Caston
    & Keeler **233**
gives "Unity not Uniformity" speech
    235
glowing tribute to Grimsley & FOG in
    Sept, 1983 **242–245**
Grimsley gave advance tour of
    Clayton **242**
impressed Christy early on **234**
invited Grimsley to conduct father's
    memorial service **242**
makes 1973 speech Unity not
    Uniformity **180**
moves into 533 **234**
named "rebellion tested" fraternity
    brothers Caston & Keeler as
    Trustees **252**
photo at FOG **243**
pursued policy of litigation after
    becoming president of
    Urantia Foundation **259**
said early leaders had "ingenious plan"
    182
slow growth policy **237**
sues Urantia Foundation **253**
takes strong stand against Grimsley
    251
told of Grimsley "message" in 1982
    241
Mystery Monitors **107**

N
Nathaniel
    good sense of humor **122**

422 INDEX

Nazareth **120, 156**
Nazi party **113**
Nebadon **96, 106, 109, 114**
Nebadon commission of twelve **117**
Nebadon Corps of Personalities **114**
Newsome, Barbara **288**
Nicaragua **132**
non-proprietary attitude **115**
nonreligious culture
of Urantia Organizations **267**
non-religious human activities **267**
Norlatiadek Constellation Councils **115**
Norlatiadek of Nebadon **116**
Northwestern University School of
Medicine **55**

O

Oak Park, Chicago (photo) **42**
Ockham's Razor **74**
Oklahoma **261**
Oklahoma City **190, 249, 260**
Oklahoma Society
Councilors resisted Grimsley
"messages" **246**
oligarchy
of Urantia Foundation **173**
Ordained Teacher **264**
of Urantia Book **188**
ordained teachers **264**
Origin of Consciousness and the
Breakdown of the Bicameral Mind, The
202
original (1955) text
reliable lineage needed **214**
original manuscript
did not exist at time of second printing
209
original plates
altered for 1967 printing **210**
were used for 1967 printing after
considerable alterations were
made **209**

original text
cannot be two versions of **215**
defined as plates **167**
emergence of conflicting texts **211**
no deliberate human intrusion in 1955
187
three copies to be preserved in
perpetuity **167, 169**
to be preserved by Urantia Foundation
166
original text of Urantia Book
does not match what Urantia
Foundation is printing **201**
Orvonton **96, 114, 128**
Orvonton administrators **116**
Orvonton Ancients of Days **114**
Orvonton superuniverse authorities **115**

P

Paddock, Bart **209**
former employee of R. R. Donnelley
161
Painter, Michael **272**
Pantaenus **119**
Paper **119**
possibly a bridge to Jesus Papers **117**
Paper presented in person **108**
Paradigm Productions **83**
Paradise **92, 116**
Paradise Deities **107, 128**
Paradise Father **151**
Paradise realities **102**
Paradise spheres **90**
Paradise Trinity
emblem trademarked by Urantia
Foundation **239**
Part I **116, 122**
Part II **116, 122**
Part III **117, 122**
Part IV **121, 122, 125, 127**
no dating **118**

INDEX 423

Pasadena, CA **190**

Pathways
publishes complete 1955 text in 1995 **260**
publishes Jesus Papers in 1994 **260**

Paul
and associates struck a deathblow to Jesus' concept of a divine kingdom within **278**

Penn, Mary **142**

perfect book
nor possible to produce **150**

personalities of the grand universe **116**

personality **114**

personally dictated Paper **108**

Pervaded Space, publication **38**

Peter **278**

philosophic opinions
of Contact Commission changed **90**

Phoenix, Arizona **119, 128, 269**

Pine Lodge, Beverly Shores, Indiana **188**
(photo) **191**

plan
of reading Papers to Forum **121**

Plan for The Urantia Book Revelation
paper by Carolyn Kendall **200**

Planetary Adams **155**

Planetary Prince of Urantia **294**
alleged message from **131**

plates **201, 209, 211, 215**
1967 destruction of plates forbidden by Declaration of Trust **217**
48 were replaced in 1967 **210**
all Trustees not aware they were compromised in 1967 **205**
altered by Christy in 1967 **202**
became the original text after manuscript was destroyed **149**
became the original text of The Urantia Book **172**

become material basis for formation of Urantia Foundation **166**
decision to alter plates created new problems **211**
destroyed after only 10,000 copies printed **216**
destruction of plates completed in 1971 **215**
exhibit showing plate replacement in 1967 **228**
exhibit showing use of original plates on some pages in 1967 **231**
in agreement with text published in 1955 **149**
no longer matched 1955 edition after 1967 **201**
not cast until final approval of client **141**
of Urantia Book **168**
of Urantia Book in R. R. Donnelley & Sons Crawfordsville plant **166**
Trustee Mills believed entire book was reset in 1967, although it was not. **209**

Power Directors **90**

pre-education initiatives **89**

preliminary education
two decades of took place before the initiation of the Urantia Papers **92**

Presbyterian **263**

Presbyterian Church **265**

Pressler, Karen L. **6**

Primary Midwayer **96, 105, 110**

Primary Midwayers **91, 111**

priority given existing human concepts **108**

proofreader **141**
duties of **142**

424   INDEX

proofreading the Urantia Papers **140–143**
proofs
    checked against original manuscript
        140
proprietary attitude **115**
proprietorship **277, 278, 293**
    end of **292**
protocol
    for contacts **194**
provisional date
    for publication of Urantia Book set
        (alleged communication) **175**
psychic phenomena **254**
    Dr. Sadler evaluates **65**
    list of psychic phenomena not used to
        materialize Papers. **31**
Publication Mandate
    from History Two **178**

Q

questions
    asked by Forum are of ordinary nature
        113
    expanded material considerably **114**
    first asked by Forum **67**
    of Forum how submitted **121**
    of Forum not included in text **113**
    of Forum, how handled **76**
    request for better questions was
        effective **114**
    Revelators asked Forum to go over
        Papers once more in 1935
        121

R

R.R. Donnelley & Sons **134, 140, 172,
186, 209, 212, 215, 225, 276, 300**
    waived imprint in Book **32**

Radatus, Andre **11, 299**
Red Alert **252, 301**
reincarnation **75**
religion **98, 101**
religions of Urantia **305**
religious expression **269**
religious freedom **240**
religious views
    of Contact Commission changed **90**
remembrance supper **157**
Removal of Ambiguities **121**
Reserve Corps of Destiny **246**
restrictions that were placed on the
    revelation of truth **108**
Revelation **151, 158, 221, 234, 235, 241,
265, 278, 293, 294, 299, 302, 303, 307**
    concept of **3**
    limitations of **41**
    no intentional human corruption of
        Papers **145**
    proof of **98**
Revelation process
    took place between Jan 18, 1924 and
        May 31, 1942 **276**
revelations **126**
    fallibility of **108**
Revelators **98, 121, 144, 146, 149, 187,
200, 216, 220, 271, 288, 293, 296**
    avoided creating sacred document **146**
    avoided human input **146**
    began weaning humans from their
        control and guidance **145**
    believed Communism to be dangerous
        threat to religion of Jesus **165**
    communicated through Contact
        Commission only **178**
    did not acknowledge Forum or
        Contact Commission **113**
    did not grant Foundation approval to
        make any changes **149**
    did not want apocrypha **130**

INDEX

expanded Papers by observing and
evaluating Forum reactions
76
found typewritten manuscript
acceptable **144**
ordered original manuscript destroyed
after plates were made **146**
rejected human input **127, 128**
relied upon human wisdom to deal
with errors **146**
suggest a more in depth study **130**
Revelatory Commission **145**
not available when second printing
was made **195**
request that humans go over the Book
again **121**
tell Forum no more questions will be
entertained on May 31, 1942
122
Revelatory Commission of the United
Midwayers of Urantia
had veto power over Trustees in 1951
(alleged communication) **174**
revelatory religion **108**
Rolnick, Philip
worked for FOG **251**
Romans **305**
Roosevelt, Eleanor **271**
Rowley, Marian **63, 143, 194, 260**
early photo with Dr. Sadler **147**
joins Forum **142**
Russell, Bertrand **100**

S

Sadler, Bill Jr. **46, 55, 76, 110, 111, 132,
141, 236, 253, 271, 288**
"You will doubtless live and die
without realizing you are
participating in the birth of a
new age of religion on this
world." **179**
(photo) **123, 191**

15 years of age, helps establish Forum
52
audio tape of 2/18/62 discussed **70–75**
birthdate difficult to establish **56**
cautioned that Book was intended for
era immediately after present
ideological struggle **179**
death of son **189–190**
early attitudes toward revelation **55–
56**
early photo with Christy **147**
early photo with Christy & Mary Lou
Hales **112**
elected President of Urantia
Brotherhood **175**
estranged from father **189**
first field representative of Urantia
Brotherhood **190**
given permission to write table of
contents **128**
in Marines 1924-1928 **113**
in Marines in Nicaragua 1924 - 1928
132
photo with Clyde Bedell **181**
photo with Lena circa 1914 **48**
referred to Contact Commissioners as
"defunct" after publication
195, 290
said all Papers were written in pencil
119
saw Brotherhood maturing into a
republican institution **263**
speculated on materialization
technique **94**
tape made in Oklahoma City, 2/18/62
59
tried to write foreword to Urantia
Papers **127**
Vice President of Urantia Foundation
167
visits to Oklahoma City **22**

warned Foundation against
proprietary attitudes **278,
292**
was Contact Commissioner by 1930
289
was not pre-educated before arrival of
Papers **92**
writes intra office memo allegedly
based on admonitions of
publication mandate **178**
Sadler, Dr. Lena **129, 132, 187, 189**
see also Sadlers
death in 1939 **34**
died Aug. 1, 1939 **93**
died before publication of Book **59**
died of Cancer in 1939 **131**
first meeting with sleeping subject
43–49
member of Contact Commission **55**
Photo circa 1914 **47**
photo with Bill Sadler, Jr., circa 1914
48
raised $20,000 for publication of
Urantia Book **131**
reads notes on sleeping subject to
Forum **66**
strong early believer in Urantia Papers
33
tries to get Bill Sadler, Jr. released
from Marine Corps **59**
was pre-educated before arrival of
Papers **92**
Sadler, Dr. William **87, 107, 110, 114,
120, 122, 127, 128, 131, 132, 137, 138,
168, 195, 197, 213, 217, 221, 233, 263,
264, 266, 271, 281, 287, 288, 292, 295,
298, 301, 303**
"pioneer in the popularization of
preventative medicine" **39**
"they didn't even say goodbye" **183**
a man of honor **127**
also see Sadlers

and Christy concerned about lack of
younger readers **234**
and Dr. Sprunger shared a different
vision of Urantia schools **189**
appendix to The Mind at Mischief **21**
as leader in Chicago **19**
becomes convinced Papers are
authentic by apostle Paper **34**
becomes dedicated leader of group **35**
believed he would find scientific
explanation **94**
biographical information **38**
chose not to be Trustee **287**
Christy and, met with Keeler & Myers
in 1962 **233**
Considerations of Some Criticisms of
the Urantia Book, 1958 **176**
corresponded with Grimsleys **233**
death of **215**
death of April 26, 1969 **234**
debunked psychic phenomena **5**
did not authorize changes to text **287**
did not believe in psychic phenomena
139–140
did not channel anything **286**
did not write books about
"mechanisms of spirit
operations" **299**
does not mention Caligastia in his
writings **234**
early photo **148**
establishes Forum **33**
estranged from Bill **189**
facsimile of Who's Who entry **28**
first meeting with Dr. Sprunger **27–36**
first meeting with Shermans **135**
first meeting with sleeping subject
43–44
had no access to Midwayers after 1955
194
had no access to plates **299**

INDEX 427

had no motivation to write Urantia Papers **127**
had photographic memory **54**
harbored reservations about procedure in 1929 **78**
hoped the question of origins would remain a mystery **81**
informed of meeting and petition ahead of time **139**
interview with Harold Sherman **45**
invited Grimsleys to Chicago **233**
later photos **192**
makes public some admonitions or suggestions regarding publication of The Urantia Book **176**
member of Contact Commission **55**
memorial service statement by Dr. Sprunger **29**
memorizes 52 questions to challenge celestial beings **54**
Midwayers on Declaration of Trust "If that's the best you can come up with it will have to do." **173**
no access to Midwayers after 1955 **121**
no evidence he approved of changes to text **286**
no psychic phenomena associated with Urantia Papers **5**
no supporting documentation that he attempted to get sleeping subject to write **296**
only living Contact Commissioner at time of writing of Histories who had experience since inception of contact **93**
ordained minister **88**
personal integrity & professional competence attacked **295**
photo circa 1914 **47**

photo July, 1944 with Marian Rowley **147**
photo with Christy & sister **164**
pre-education for Papers **92**
probably wrote part of History Two **88**
puzzled about "Moab" **120**
regarded leadership of Forum as most important contribution **39**
relationship with Dr. Sprunger **29**
reproductions of correspondence with Dr. Benjamin Adams **321–329**
served petition from a few Forum members **139**
speculated Midwayers were dubious about authority to reveal Jesus' mission **94**
speculated on materialization technique **94**
stated connection with sleeping subject went dead in 1955 **193**
teaching program **188**
tells Forum about challenge of "electrifying" personality, Dec. 1924 **66**
told Dr. Sprunger Revelators believed Communism dangerous threat to religion of Jesus **165**
told Dr. Sprunger Urantia Papers materialized in written form **119**
tried to write a foreword to Urantia Papers **127**
uses hypnosis on sleeping subject **50–51**
virtually removed from administrative leadership by second printing **194**
warned about psychic phenomena **258**
wrote in letter about handwriting in Jesus Papers **119**

428 INDEX

wrote that mandate to publish forbade
    any alteration of text **194**
Sadler, Leone **189**
Sadlers, Dr. William and Dr. Lena **92**
    agreed no known form of psychic
        methods used to materialize
        Urantia Papers **73**
    as members of Contact Commission
        56
    establish Forum in 1923 **52**
    establish residency at 533 Diversey
        Parkway, 1922 **52**
    first meeting with sleeping subject
        43–49
    read first Papers to Forum, Jan 18,
        1925 **75**
    residences **43–44**
    test handwriting of sleeping subject **69**
    were ordinary people **44–45**
Salem believers **305**
Salvington **114, 239**
Sánchez-Escobar, Dr. Angel **xi, xii, 11**
    on historical inquiry **xi**
Sandburg, Carl **38**
Sanhedrin **157**
sanobim **105, 110**
Santa Monica, CA **281**
Sarmast, Behzad **12**
Satan **239**
Satania **116, 155, 239**
Schaveland, Eric **11, 162, 219, 238, 259**
Schell, Herman **71**
Schlundt, Reverend David **188**
scholars
    need reliable text **214**
School of Meanings and Values **188**
School of the Urantia Brotherhood **130,
188**
Science
    and Urantia Papers **4**

science **98**
scientific beliefs
    in Urantia Papers **89**
scientific discoveries, anticipated could not
    be disclosed **41**
second printing **234**
    dating of **193**
    Dr. Sadler 92 at time of **193**
secondary Circuit Supervisor **153**
Secondary Midwayer **96, 105, 110, 118**
    may have done physical writing of
        Urantia Papers **70, 72**
Secondary Midwayers **71, 102, 111**
    just beyond scope of human vision,
        can manipulate matter **91**
    supervised contacts **91**
Sedona, Arizona **300**
self-acting Adjuster **111**
seraphic guardians **106**
seraphim **96, 105, 110**
Seraphim of Progress **130**
Seres, Florine **190**
service
    as step two of Master's Program **270**
Setting the Record Straight
    Foundation posting **218**
    internet posting
        Urantia Foundation defends 1967
            changes **287**
    Urantia Foundation statement
        regarding changes **201**
Seventy **131, 169, 175, 263, 294**
    becomes Urantia Brotherhood **175**
    forerunner to Brotherhood school **130**
    formed in 1939 **130**
    had 107 students over 17 years **130**
    met Wednesday nights **130**
    read alleged communication in 1951
        regarding publication of
        Book **173**
    read from proofing copies after 1945
        172

INDEX 429

Sherman tempest **135–140**
Sherman, Harold **110, 158, 298, 300, 308**
    accuses Dr. Sadler of corrupting
        Urantia Papers **137**
    advocate of psychic phenomena **137**
    concealed psychic beliefs **137**
    disturbed that psychic phenomena was
        rejected by Urantia Papers **75**
    first visit to Dr. Sadler **135**
    Gardner reported he claimed he could
        make out-of-body trips to
        Jupiter **159**
    interview with Sadlers **45**
    meets with Bedell, other members of
        Forum **137**
    sleeping subject in bed asleep during
        writing process **71**
    tries to establish handwriting as that of
        sleeping subject **74**
    wrote there were 92 Papers in all **136**
Sherman, Martha
    Martin Gardner reported she
        witnessed mind over matter
        feats by Harry Loose **159**
Shermans **81, 139**
    claim to have continued in Forum-
        study group **139**
    did not understand basic tenets of
        Book **136**
    move to Chicago in May of 1942 **136**
    sign oaths of secrecy **135**
Siegel, Morris "Mo" **219, 251, 255, 257**
    built fallout shelter during Grimsley
        crisis **250**
    FOG National Extension
        Representative **249**
    votes to break with Foundation **273**
    warned Urantians to prepare for WW
        III **249**

sleeping subject **5, 6, 22, 44, 46, 54, 87,
107, 185**
    alternate version of first meeting with
        Sadlers **57**
    behavior during deep sleep **49**
    date of death no known **193**
    date of first meeting with Sadlers **43–
46**
    Dr. Sadler first mentions case to
        Forum **66**
    Dr. Sadler uses hypnosis **50**
    examined by Dr. Sadler after first
        contact **49**
    first contact with celestial beings
        through subject **50**
    handwriting tested **69**
    hypnosis used on **50–51**
    moves to be near Sadlers **50**
    never observed writing **70**
    no evidence of writing fatigue **68**
    no subconscious awareness of material
51
    not Edgar Cayce **6**
    only contact involved in entire
        procedure **78**
    probably present at all
        communications until
        connection was broken in
        1955 **80**
    Thought Adjuster of **107**
    why necessary for materialization **80**
    wife of **81**
Snowmass Conference, 1981
    Grimsley speech **241**
Solitary Messenger **110**
Solomon, Meyer **55**
Solonia **108, 109**
Son of God **126**
sources
    how History of Urantia Papers used
        them **9**

Soviet Communism
  collapse of **179**
Spanish-Urantian community **xii**
special agent
  status granted to Myers and Grimsley
    241
spelling
  mistake of spelling of Pantaenus
    explained **119–120**
Spirit of Truth **108**
Spiritual Fellowship Journal **7**
spiritual pride **307**
spiritual renaissance **268**
spiritual unity
  of Urantia Movement **306**
Sprunger, Dr. Meredith **8, 10, 13, 15, 16,
  110, 115, 121, 122, 130, 131, 183, 195,
  222, 243, 263, 264, 268, 269, 271, 277,
  295, 298**
  and Dr. Sadler shared a vision of
    schools **189**
  and Dr. William Sadler **8**
  answered difficult letters to
    Foundation **194**
  discovered book through Jesus Papers
    245
  early photo of **17**
  first meeting with Dr. Sadler **27–36**
  first reads Urantia Book **18**
  introduced Vern Grimsley to Urantia
    Book **233**
  knew three Contact Commissioners **7**
  memorial service statement for Dr.
    Sadler **29**
  Midwayer reaction to Declaration of
    Trust
    "If that's the best you can come up
      with it will have to do."
    173
  on Urantian religion **267–269**
  open about origins **7**
  opposed channeling activities **258**

photo at 1960 picnic **148**
photo in Boulder meeting **261**
rebuked Grimsley "messages" **249**
relationship with Dr. Sadler **29**
researched origins of Urantia Papers **8**
reviews ambiguities associated with
  changes in the text **212–213**
stated that both Dr. Sadler and Christy
  said they were directed to get
  an International Copyright
  180
told by Dr. Sadler & Christy entire
  revelation materialized in
  handwritten form **119**
told by Dr. Sadler Revelators believed
  Communism dangerous
  threat to religion of Jesus **165**
Sprunger, Irene **15, 148**
Stahl, Clara **69, 72**
Strunk, Dr. Jill **11**
student visitors **54**
Study of the Master Universe, A **190**
subconscious mind **30**
Substantive Estate **215, 293**
  all that remains are three 1955 printed
    Books **216**
  destruction of portion **287**
  did not include copyright, marks, or
    name Urantia **237**
  of Declaration of Trust defined **169**
  partially destroyed in 1967 **216**
  portion was destroyed in 1967 without
    knowledge or agreement of
    all Trustees **170**
Summer workshops **188**
sun
  density of **153**
Sunday Study Group **266, 290**
superconscious **90**
  explained in Urantia Papers **39**

INDEX

superconscious mind **30**
superhuman friends
    spent two decades pre-education early
        Contact Commission **92**
Superhuman Planetary Government **130**
superuniverse **90, 105, 106**
superuniverse headquarters **153**
Superuniverse Personalities **114**
Supplementation of planetary knowledge
   108
Supreme Being **90**
T
Table of Contents
    written by Bill Sadler, Jr. **128**
Tavares, Marielle **12**
Teller, Edward **271**
tertiary Circuit Supervisor **153**
Test of a True Teacher (by Emmett Fox)
   304
The Urantia Book **3, 211, 217, 284**
    "only one edition" **202**
    euphoria among Forum when first
        published **187**
    Foundation states changes have not
        been documented **201**
theologians
    postulated Supreme Being **90**
theologic concepts
    of Contact Commission changed **90**
theology **98**
third presentation of Urantia Papers **121**
Thought Adjuster **72, 96, 98, 107, 110,**
   111, 234
    "the age of" **305**
    is Fragment of God **90**
    may have been necessary for
        materialization process **81**
    of sleeping subject **107**
    of sleeping subject used to materialize
        Urantia Papers **102**

Thought Adjuster of the sleeping subject
    probably used in materialization
        process **72**
Thought Adjusters **88, 90, 296**
three concentric azure blue circles
    registered as a trademark by Urantia
        Foundation **237**
Thurston, Angie **12**
Thurston, Claire and Chuck **12**
Thurston, Haley **12**
Thurston, Howard **51**
    consulted with Dr. Sadler about
        sleeping subject. **33**
Thurston, Jesse **12**
Titanic **51, 52**
trance control
    no documentation that sleeping
        subject was under **296**
transcribing
    of manuscript into typewriting **120**
translation **108**
translations
    Book published early to allow **179**
Triennial Delegate Assembly **263, 264**
Trinity government
    material emblem of **239**
Trustee Emeritus
    has no powers **223**
Trustees **235, 280, 287, 292**
    "did not participate in process of
        correcting text of Urantia
        Book" **196**
    "may not wish to expand the written
        record on this matter" **218**
    1999 meeting with Vern Grimsley **254**
    acceptance of responsibility for plates
        170
    all required to be in agreement before
        any portion of Substantive
        Estate was destroyed **170**
    also see Urantia Foundation

432   INDEX

aware of "errors" in plates when
        Foundation was formed **176**
chart of **255**
do not function as cohesive group **223**
given provisional date to act on own
        authority in 1952 **174**
lifetime tenure and self-election
        opposed by Clyde Bedell **136**
met only periodically **208**
primary duties of **169**
provision for **166**
typesetter
        duties of **142**

U

United Brotherhood of Urantia Midwayers
118
United Church of Christ **19**
United Midwayers of Urantia
        intention to defeat Communism **165**
United States **135**
United States Copyright **180**
        can only be acquired for books
                authored by US citizens **180**
        first mentioned by Martin Myers **182**
        not mentioned in either History **180**
        possibly a human idea **180**
United States Copyright Office **182**
Unity not Uniformity
        speech by Myers **235**
Universal Father **4, 101, 239**
Universal Unity **116**
universe Mother Spirit **105**
universe of universes **128**
Universe personalities **89**
University of Kansas **233, 243**
Urantia **xi, 4, 116, 117, 128, 131, 151,
237, 281, 292, 305**
        name of our planet **3**

Urantia - The Great Cult Mystery, book
159
Urantia Book Fellowship **257, 267**
        declares McMullan litigation is a
                "private matter" **262**
        teaching efforts **188**
Urantia Book fundamentalist **213**
Urantia Book Study groups **263**
Urantia Book, The **15, 121, 125, 126, 127,
136, 138, 143, 150, 152, 169, 190, 200,
212, 215, 219, 224, 233, 234, 240, 245,
252, 254, 256, 258, 263, 269, 280, 293**
        1955 printing produced without
                deliberate human intrusion
                275
        1967 printing **209**
        see also Urantia Papers
        accepted by young ministers **19**
        acting Planetary Prince to decide
                publication date (alleged
                message) **175**
        also see Urantia Papers
        at extreme variance with channeling
                activities **301**
        contact broken **302**
        copyright renewed in 1983 **182**
        copyright status **393–394**
        cosmic background of Jesus **126**
        dating of Papers **115–118**
        declared in public domain **259**
        discussion of copyright **180–182**
        distortion of quote in Birth of a Divine
                Revelation **296**
        Dr. Sprunger's first impression was
                negative **16**
        flawed epochal masterpiece **151**
        Forum and Contact Commission
                anticipated publication after
                WW II **165**
        index never published **273**
        mandate to publish **235**

INDEX
433

original text to be preserved inviolate **167**

plates of **166**

preparation for typesetting begins **140**

reception did not parallel psychic phenomena **30**

some trustees told it was entirely reset in 1967 **277**

to be preserved from alteration, modification, revision, or change in any manner or particular **172**

very few purchasers were informed of changes in later printings **212**

written permission required to quote from **237**

Urantia Books

arrival at 533 **181**

Urantia Brotherhood **63, 130, 175, 188, 190, 205, 210, 239, 241, 245, 254, 256, 257, 258, 260, 263, 265, 267, 283**

accepts licensing agreement **237**

becomes "Fellowship" **257**

constitution given approval (alleged message) **175**

Foundation forbids use of "marks" **273**

majority agreed with quiet and gradual presentation of Urantia Book **177**

many leaders bought into Grimsley "messages" **246**

officially begins January 2, 1955 **175**

pressure for Society acceptance of licensing agreement **239**

Urantia Brotherhood Bulletin **209**

Urantia Brotherhood General Council **263, 264, 280**

did not resolve issue of splitting up the book **262**

Urantia Brotherhood General Council Executive Committee **265**

Urantia Brotherhood School **191**

Urantia Brotherhood Societies **237**

Urantia Church **190**

Urantia community **214, 265, 291**

doomsday predictions frightened **249**

Urantia Conferences **264**

Urantia Fellowship conferences **267**

Urantia Foundation **149, 150, 152, 157, 167, 182, 188, 193, 210, 214, 215, 217, 219, 233, 235, 237, 238, 239, 241, 245, 251, 253, 254, 256, 257, 259, 263, 267, 277, 287, 288, 291, 292, 294, 303**

accepted responsibility for and authority over text in 1950 **287**

also see Trustees

and celestial guidance after 1955 **193**

and proprietary activity **278**

and supporters were key sources for this history **288**

assumed full responsibility for original text (plates) **167**

autonomous organization **168**

Bedell protests authoritarianism **240**

breaks with Brotherhood **273**

Carolyn Kendall writes Foundation pledged to reverse changes made after 1982 **196**

copyrighted Myers speech, Unity not Uniformity **180**

creates IUA **258**

culture of **167**

entrusted with publishing the original text **169**

fell into default in 1967 **292**

files suit against Michael Foundation **260**

forbids use of circles or words Urantia or Urantian without written permission **237**

formation of **166**
founded as autonomous entity **276**
given provisional control over
Substantive Estate **169**
given provisional date to act on own
authority in 1952 **174**
given total authority over plates and
other media to reproduce the
original text **169**
Grimsley "messages" **246**
had different organizational structure
than Contact Commission
289
has not published an inviolate version
of the original text since 1955
263
largely on own after 1952 **173**
mission as redefined by Kendalls **196**
moves to copyright name "The Urantia
Book" as trademark **284**
no powers to alter text in any manner
whatsoever **172**
objects of **166**
organized and directed by humans **289**
original mission supplanted by
proprietary activities **292**
permitted to destroy plates provided
only with unanimous
agreement of all Trustees **170**
permitted to transfer plates with
provision that they be
returned to Trustees **170**
policies put original text at risk **215**
policies supported by Grimsley
"messages" **245**
positioned as aggressive central
authority by Myers **235**
powers to control reproduction of text
granted in spirit of protecting
it from change **172**
preserves one text and prints different
versions **214**

publication of Book **144**
published list of corrections in 1994
218
publishes "corrections to the text" in
1994, admits 150 changes
260
responsible to print original text
inviolate **169**
Setting the Record Straight - Website
posting **161**
statement that it has "reason to
believe" that "significant
changes" were made with
"approval from the
revelators" **201**
Trustees sign Declaration of Intent to
Publish The Urantia Book
176
uses alleged 1942 "message" to claim
proprietary rights to word
"Urantia" **283**
was not a successor organization to
Contact Commission **289**
wins reversal in Maaherra litigation
259
withdraws Dr. Sadler's Biblical
studies **264**
Urantia Foundation policy
shifts to legalistic measures **236**
Urantia Foundation policy decisions
influenced by alleged "messages" **280**
Urantia Foundation Trustees **288**
also see Trustees
oath to honor Declaration of Trust **201**
only those sympathetic with
"messages" may have known
about changes **205**
special guidance to end **174**
Urantia Foundation's Declaration of Trust
has been dishonored **220**
Urantia Foundation's proprietary claims
supported by "The Golden Years" **289**

INDEX 435

Urantia International Conference
in Snowmass, 1981 **241**
Urantia Midwayers **118**
Urantia Movement **7, 8, 180, 211, 254,
265, 268, 270, 277, 293, 303**
Bedell warns of threatened schism **240**
Urantia Papers **9, 10, 101, 107, 113, 120,
128, 132, 157, 212, 237, 239, 240, 258,
266, 268, 275, 276, 277, 279, 293, 294,
298, 302, 304, 306, 307**
"channeling" method completely
antithetical to teachings of
301
also Urantia Book, The
all 196 Papers were read to Forum,
revised and amplified **125**
are monotheistic **89**
as epochal revelation **4**
best testimony of own validity **87**
cause paradigm shifts **88**
control of **300**
dangers of "priesthood" **302**
dating of **115–118**
delivered for final readings in 1934 -
1935 **122**
difficulties in putting into English **96–
97**
enter evolutionary mainstream **144**
entire text materialized in handwritten
form **78**
first read to Forum January of 1925 **92**
Forum feared WW II would delay
publication **135**
had not yet begun to appear at time
sleeping subject first
mentioned to Forum **66**
human mind not used to materialize **91**
increased from 76 to 119 during
second reading **114**
integrates three bodies of knowledge **3**
kept in vault and administered by
Contact Commission **142**

length of process to materialize and
convert to book **3**
materialization of **105–111**
everything known can be found in
various parts of the Book
36
message most important thing **74**
name of sleeping subject not to be
disclosed **30**
need for human mind to discern
origins **35**
new concept of universe **89**
no authority on **5**
not channeled **5**
numbered 196 **127**
original manuscript was handwritten
67
original manuscripts disappeared from
safe **77**
photos of various printings **248**
preparation for printing begins **140**
published exactly as received **128**
published with no human input as to
authorship, content or
arrangement **78**
quote on limitations of revelation **4**
reality response of human mind **1**
refute idea Papers were designated
complete in 1934-1935 **116**
refute psychic activities **214**
scientific data **4**
should be evaluated by content **36**
soul of the Revelation **305**
stand on their own content **6**
technique of reception did not parallel
psychic activity **30**
terms "completed and certified" used
in History Two are
misleading **122**
typewritten manuscript of first 57
Papers **78**

INDEX

use of existing human concepts and
written material **97–102**
were delivered, not completed in
1934-1935 **297**
were typed after materialization **68**
written in pencil **119**
Urantia Revelation **140, 157, 187, 220, 279, 302**
early distribution of **177**
Urantia Revelatory Commission
174
replaced by Midwayer Commission in
1951 (alleged
communication) **174**
replaced in early fifties by Midwayer
Commission **201**
Urantia Societies **263**
Urantia Study Groups **267**
Urantia Study Groups and Societies
cannot fulfill functions of religious
institutions **268**
Urantia, the Great Cult Mystery, Book
104, 140
Urantian **152, 156, 237, 256, 269, 278, 279, 292**
Urantian "leaders"
warned of impending danger of WW
III by Grimsley **249**
Urantian believers **307**
Urantian community **xii**
Urantian Foundation **303**
Urantian News **223**
Urantian religion **266**
Urantians **8, 126, 150, 151, 157, 174, 187, 209, 216, 221, 233, 234, 235, 236, 241, 245, 250, 260, 266, 267, 271, 278, 294, 303, 304, 305, 307**
Bedell protests restrictions on **240**
fear of litigation **237**
targets of lawsuits **237**

use concentric circles freely **238**
Uversa **106, 110, 114**
Uversa Corps **114**
Uversa Press **260**

V

values
and political issues **279**
Vargas, Jose Manuel Rodriguez **188**
verbal communications
with Midwayers discussed **78–79**
voice in the Garden **108, 109**

W

Weiss, Jacques **197, 238**
target of alleged "message" **280**
wife of sleeping subject
handwriting tested **69**
Wilkins, Sir Hubert **51, 271**
consulted with Sadler in early days
about Sleeping Subject **33**
sent out Urantia Books **233**
studied Urantia Papers for 20 years at
533 **233**
World Book Encyclopedia **132, 134, 161, 184, 186, 225**
World War I **52**
World War II **52, 132, 165, 167**
World War III **165**
World War III "message" **252**
worship
as step one of Master's program **270**
Wright, Frank Lloyd **42**
written messages
from Midwayers were to be destroyed
79

Y

You are now on your own, alleged final
message **183, 194, 211, 290, 294, 297**
You Live After Death, book **137**
Young, Greg **161**